EAST METRO CENTRAL MINNESOTA
COVERAGE

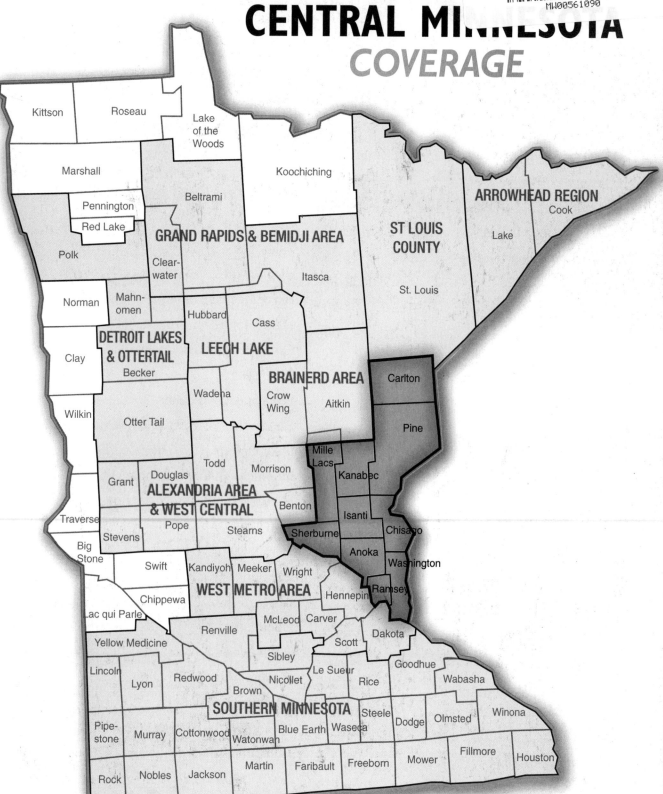

Kittson

Roseau

Lake of the Woods

Koochiching

ARROWHEAD REGION

Cook

Marshall

Pennington

Red Lake

Beltrami

GRAND RAPIDS & BEMIDJI AREA

ST LOUIS COUNTY

Lake

Polk

Clear-water

Itasca

St. Louis

Norman

Mahn-omen

Hubbard

Cass

DETROIT LAKES & OTTERTAIL

LEECH LAKE

Clay

Becker

Wadena

BRAINERD AREA

Carlton

Wilkin

Otter Tail

Crow Wing

Aitkin

Pine

Todd

Morrison

Mille Lacs

Kanabec

Grant

Douglas

ALEXANDRIA AREA & WEST CENTRAL

Benton

Isanti

Chisago

Traverse

Pope

Stearns

Sherburne

Anoka

Washington

Stevens

Big Stone

Swift

Kandiyohi

Meeker

Wright

WEST METRO AREA

Hennepin

Ramsey

Chippewa

Lac qui Parle

McLeod

Carver

Dakota

Yellow Medicine

Renville

Sibley

Scott

Goodhue

Lincoln

Lyon

Redwood

Nicollet

Le Sueur

Rice

Wabasha

Brown

SOUTHERN MINNESOTA

Steele

Dodge

Olmsted

Winona

Pipe-stone

Murray

Cottonwood

Watonwan

Blue Earth

Waseca

Rock

Nobles

Jackson

Martin

Faribault

Freeborn

Mower

Fillmore

Houston

TABLE of CONTENTS

See back cover for alphabetical listing of lakes
MAPS IN THIS GUIDE ARE NOT FOR NAVIGATION

TABLE of CONTENTS

Rivers & Streams

East Metro/Central Minnesota Fishing Map Guide
by Sportsman's Connection

Editor and Publisher *Jim Billig*

Managing Editor *Todd Whitesel, Dave Landahl*

Editorial/Research

　　Chuck Hartley, Kristin Landahl, Steve Meyer, Joel Shangle

Creative & Production Director *Kurt Mazurek*

Page Design/Layout *Shelly Wisniewski, Colleen Kittel*

Cartography *Janet Billig, Linda Hollinday, Hart Graphics,*

　　Mandy Shaw, Jon Wisniewski, Mike Billig

ISBN-13: 978-1-885010-44-5

Sportsman's Connection
Superior, Wisconsin 54880

www.scmaps.com

FOREWORD

Many books have been written about fishing. Most are of the "how-to" variety, focusing on certain species, offering tips regarding the best lures or baits and the best techniques for using them. Few books focus on the fishing waters, offering not just information on how to catch a particular fish species, but on where to catch them.

Where to catch fish in east-central Minnesota is what this book is all about. We've attempted to be as comprehensive as possible, giving readers an in-depth view of the area's best and most notable fishing prospects. Included is information on more than 130 waters of local, regional or state-wide significance.

This, of course, is not a complete picture of the region, or any given body of water. Nor, probably, should it be. Our purpose in publishing this book is to serve the angling public. We've tried, first and foremost, to give our readers information on waters they can use. And we've avoided, we believe, those waters that the public cannot fish.

As we've compiled this book, we've tried to be as accurate as possible in our depiction of each lake, stream or river. Within the limits of the source materials we were able to locate, we believe we have been. We have, in fact, relied not only upon our own expertise, but on the experience and knowledge of many others.

In all cases, we've used the best and most-recent data available. In some instances, however, the available data are several years old and may not accurately reflect the current situation. Readers should bear this in mind before relying solely on the information given for a lake; check the date provided with each table.

Regulations change from year to year. Be sure to consult current state and site-specific regs before fishing any new lake or river.

Readers should also be aware that data tables and management information focus primarily on the sport fishery. We believe this emphasis accurately reflects the interests of our readers. However, maintaining this focus has sometimes meant that data on less-desirable species has been sacrificed in order to present more comprehensive information on game species. The absence of rough fish or other less-desirable species in the information presented, therefore, does not mean these species are not present.

Refer to the "Reader's Guide to Using this Publication" (facing page) for terminology definitions and a map legend that will help you maximize the practical use of this publication.

We've received considerable assistance from a number of public and private agencies, each of which generously and courteously contributed material or knowledge to our work. These people help us develop a better understanding of the region and the resources. Thanks to the U.S. Geological Survey, National Oceanic and Atmospheric Administration and the Minnesota Department of Natural Resources.

Be respectful, please, of the fishery and the land, both public and private. Be especially aware of the growing problem the spread of exotic fish, plants and other aquatic species has on our fisheries, many of which are changing with alarming speed and irreversible consequences. Remove all vegetation from boats and motors, drain live wells and take other precautions before you leave the lake or river. Preserve the recreational opportunities lands, lakes and rivers offer for us all to enjoy.

Special thanks to all agencies, businesses and individuals who contributed to this effort:

Minnesota Department of Natural Resources, Detroit Lakes,   (218) 847-1579

Al Anderson, DNR Assistant Area Manager
Lynn Bergquist, Fisheries GIS
Deserae Hendrickson, Fisheries Manager
Ted Halpern, Fisheries Biologist
Tom Jones, Fisheries Specialist

Timothy Loesch, GIS Operations Supervisor
Kevin E. Peterson, Area Fisheries Supervisor
Don Schreiner, Fisheries Manager
Allen Stevens, Lake and Stream Survey Program Cons.
Maggie Gorsuch, Data Manager - DNR Fish and Wildlife

Frankie's Live Bait & Marine, Brad Dusenka, 10680 South Ave., Chisago City, MN 55013, 651-257-6334
Joe's Sporting Goods, 33 County Road B E, Little Canada, MN, 55117, 651-488-5511
Jimmy's Bait and Tackle, Mike Wren, 806 South Main, Stillwater, MN 55082, 651-430-2554
Larry's Service & Bait/R&B Sports, 314 West Highway 2, Floodwood, MN 55736, 218-476-2225

Marv's Minnows, 25859 2nd St E, Zimmerman, MN 55398, 763-856-4038
Outdoor Advantage, Dianne Bednarek, 1302 Highway 33, Cloquet, MN 55720, 218-879-3185
St. Croix Rods, Dave Lofgren, 856 4th Avenue North, Park Falls, WI, 54552, 715-762-3226

LENGTH TO WEIGHT CONVERSION SCALE

Northern Pike

Inches	24	25	26	27	28	29	30	31	32	33	34	35	36	37	38	39	40	41	42
Pounds	3.9	4.4	5.0	5.6	6.2	7.0	7.7	8.5	9.3	10.2	11.2	12.2	13.3	14.5	15.7	16.9	18.3	19.6	21.2

Walleye

Inches	14	15	16	17	18	19	20	21	22	23	24	25	26	27	28	29
Pounds	1.0	1.2	1.5	1.8	2.2	2.5	3.0	3.4	3.9	4.5	5.1	5.7	6.5	7.2	8.1	9.0

Largemouth Bass

Inches	12	13	14	15	16	17	18	19	20	21	22	23
Pounds	1.0	1.3	1.7	2.1	2.5	3.0	3.6	4.2	5.0	5.7	6.6	7.6

Crappie

Inches	8	9	10	11	12	13	14	15	16	17
Pounds	0.4	0.6	0.8	1.1	1.4	1.8	2.2	2.8	3.4	4.1

Your fishing map guide is a thorough, easy-to-use collection of accurate contour lake maps along with geographic and biologic statistical information to help you locate a lake and enjoy a successful day out on the water of one of Minnesota's excellent fisheries.

The heart of this book is the **contour lake map**. Copyrighted maps are used with permission from the Minnesota Department of Natural Resources and are not intended for navigation. The lakes selected for this guide are confined to those that are accessible to the public.

Each map is accompanied by a **detailed write-up**. In each piece, you'll find fishing tips and hot spots specific to the body of water you're planning to fish.

Lake **stocking records** and **management comments** are provided courtesy of the Minnesota Department of Natural Resources and summarized to reflect management trends and objectives for each fishery represented. Please keep in mind that annual fish stocking aspirations are directly affected by state hatchery production levels and sometimes the numbers available for stocking fluctuate considerably.

Detailed **area road maps** (1:125,000 scale) and **lake access** information is provided to help you plan your route to the lake. If there is more than one access point on a body of water, the GPS coordinates refer to the primary access. To locate a lake on these road maps, simply use the alphabetical lake listing on the back cover. Turn to that page to find the area road map page and coordinates for the lake. As a cross-reference, the area road maps include numbers on or adjacent to featured lakes, which designate the pages of the lake maps and information. Streams and rivers are also referenced in these area road maps.

While every effort is made to create the most accurate maps possible, the process of merging existing DNR maps with the latest GPS information will cause some slight differences to occur. (Especially on larger, more complicated lakes.) Please use the GPS grids provided in this book only as a guideline.

GLOSSARY OF TERMS

Gill net: This is the main piece of equipment used for sampling walleye, northern pike, yellow perch, cisco, whitefish, trout, and salmon. The standard gill net is 6 feet tall by 250 feet long, with 5 different mesh sizes. Gill nets are generally set in off shore areas in water deeper than 9 feet. Nets are fished for a period of 24 hours. Fish are captured by swimming into the net and becoming entangled. Fisheries workers record length and weight data from each fish, determine the sex, look for parasites or disease, and remove several of the fishes scales for determining the fishes age. Most of the fish taken in gill nets are

killed, but only a small portion of the lakes fish population is sampled during an individual survey event. The number of gill nets set during a survey is dependant on the lake acreage.

Trap net: This is the main piece of equipment used for sampling bluegill, crappie, and bullheads. The standard trap net is 4 feet tall by 6 feet wide with a 40 foot lead. Trap nets are generally set perpendicular to shore in water less than 8 feet in depth. Nets are fished for a period of 24 hours. Fish are captured by swimming into the lead and following it towards the trap. Most of the fish collected in trap nets are returned back to the water as soon as the necessary biological data is recorded. The number of trap net sets during a survey is dependant on the lake acreage.

Electrofishing: This is a specialized type of equipment that is most often used for sampling largemouth bass, smallmouth bass, and young of the year walleye. A boat-mounted generator is used to induce electrical current into the water that stuns the fish, allowing fisheries workers to net the fish for placement in live wells. Most of the fish caught by electrofishing recover rapidly and are promptly returned to the water after the necessary biological data is recorded.

CPUE: An acronym representing "Catch Per Unit of Effort," a way of representing the density of a species population. Readings are in fish captured per hour or minute of surveying. The higher the CPUE value, the greater the number of fish present.

PSD: An acronym for "Proportional Stock Density," which is a way of representing the size structure of fish populations. It represents the percentage of "quality-size" fish within a given population. In arriving at this figure, one considers only fish of "stock" length (the size at which members of a given species reach sexual maturity) or greater. Young-of year fish are not included in the calculation. The higher the PSD number, the greater the percentage of "quality" fish within a particular population.

RSD-12 (or -10 or -14, etc.): An acronym for "Relative Stock Density," which is yet another way of representing the size structure of fish populations. This corresponds to the percentage of fish at a given length or larger within a population. Hence, an RSD-14 reading of 25 for largemouth bass indicates that 25 percent of sexually mature bass are at least 14 inches in length. On another measurement scale, the RSD- values could be stated as "preferred," "memorable," or "trophy."

YAR: An acronym for "Young-(to)-Adult Ratio." This refers to the proportion of young-of-year fish in relation to adult or "quality-size" fish within a particular population. For balanced populations, the index should be about 1-to-10. In smaller waters, 1-to-3 is considered a reasonable ratio.

Secchi Disk: Used in measuring water clarity, it is a white-colored, plate-size device submerged on the end of a line until it reaches a point where it's no longer visible; the depth at which this occurs is measured and recorded. In this book, secchi disk readings are given in English measure. Of course, many factors influence water clarity, and secchi disk readings vary according to season, growth of vegetation, weather, location in a lake, even human activity. Hence the readings given are approximations for any lake—snapshots of the water clarity at a given time and in a given location.

LEGEND

Boat Ramp	Fishing Area	Rocks	GPS Grid
Carry Down Access	Boat tie-up	Submerged Culvert	
Access by Navigable Channel	Reservoir Outlet	Submerged Ruins	Red & Green Channel Buoys
Public Fishing Access	Reservoir Inlet	Marsh	
Access Information Marker	Marina	Emergent Vegetation	White Hazard Buoy
Campground	Lilly Pads	Manmade Canal	
Picnic Area	Submergent Vegetation	Marked Fishing Spots	River Mile
Handicap Accessible	Emergent Vegetation	Submerged Rail	Daymarker
Fishing Dock (Pier)	Stumps	Submerged Road	Light & Daymarker
Shore Fishing	Flooded Timber	Bridge	County Road
Fish Attractors		Submerged Riverbed	State Highway
Shipwreck			US Highway
			Interstate

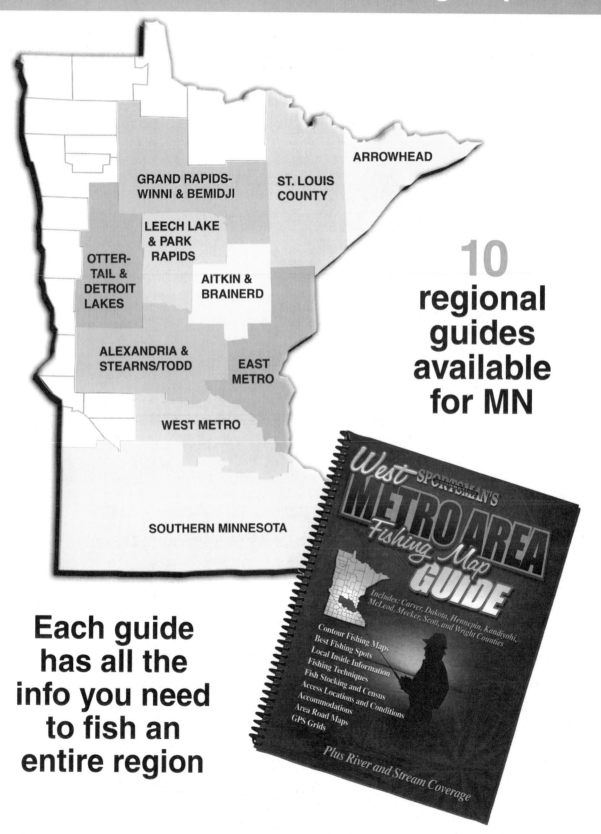

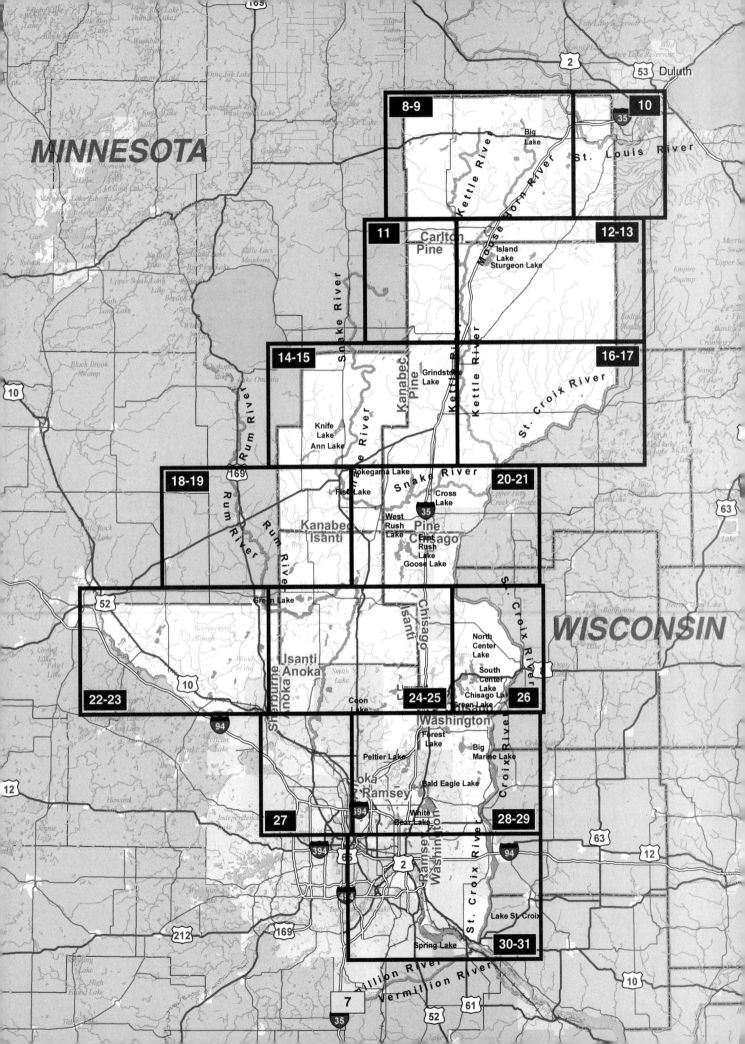

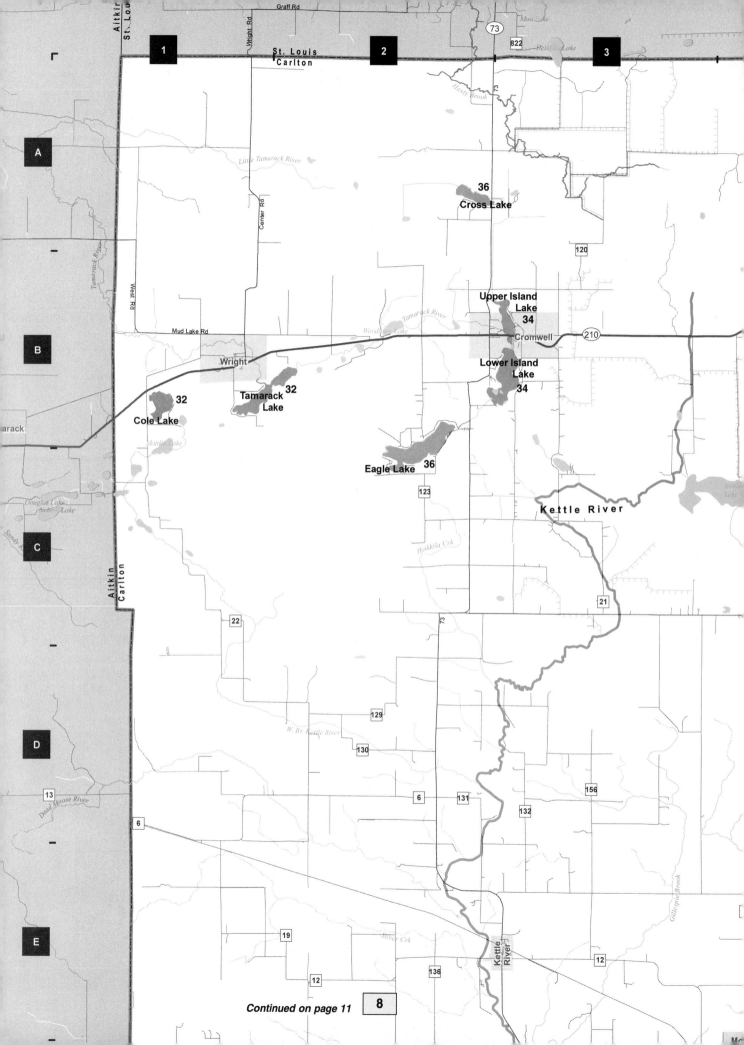

Graff Rd

St. Louis
Carlton

73

822

Mud Lake

Heikkila Lake

Hasty Brook

A

Little Tamarack River

36
Cross Lake

120

Tamarack River

West Rd

Center Rd

Wright Rd

**Upper Island
Lake**
34

Woodpecker Lake

Tamarack River

210

B

Mud Lake Rd

Cromwell

Wright

**Lower Island
Lake**
34

32

**Tamarack
Lake**

32
Cole Lake

Mattson Lake

rack

36
Eagle Lake

123

Kettle Lake

Kettle River

Douglas Lake

Nels Lake

Sandy R

C

Heikkila Crk

21

Aitkin
Carlton

22

73

D

129

W. Br. Kettle River

130

13

6

131

156

Dead Moose River

132

6

E

19

Silver Crk

12

12

Graff Rd

12

136

Kettle River

Continued on page 11   **8**

Mc

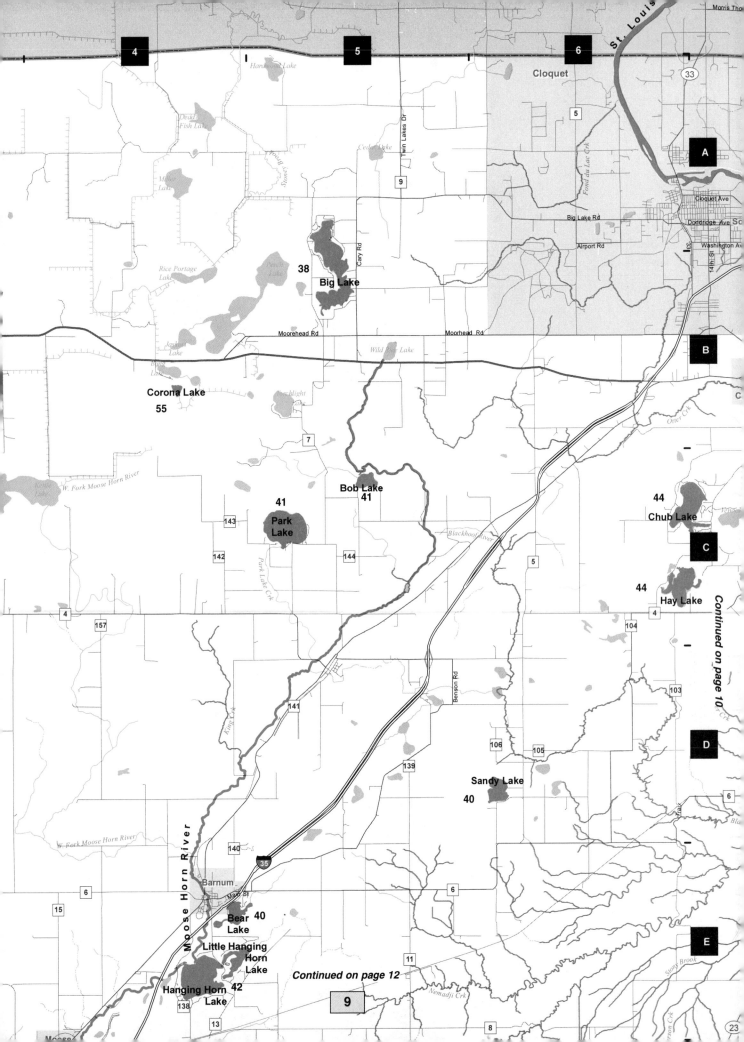

Continued on page 10

Continued on page 12

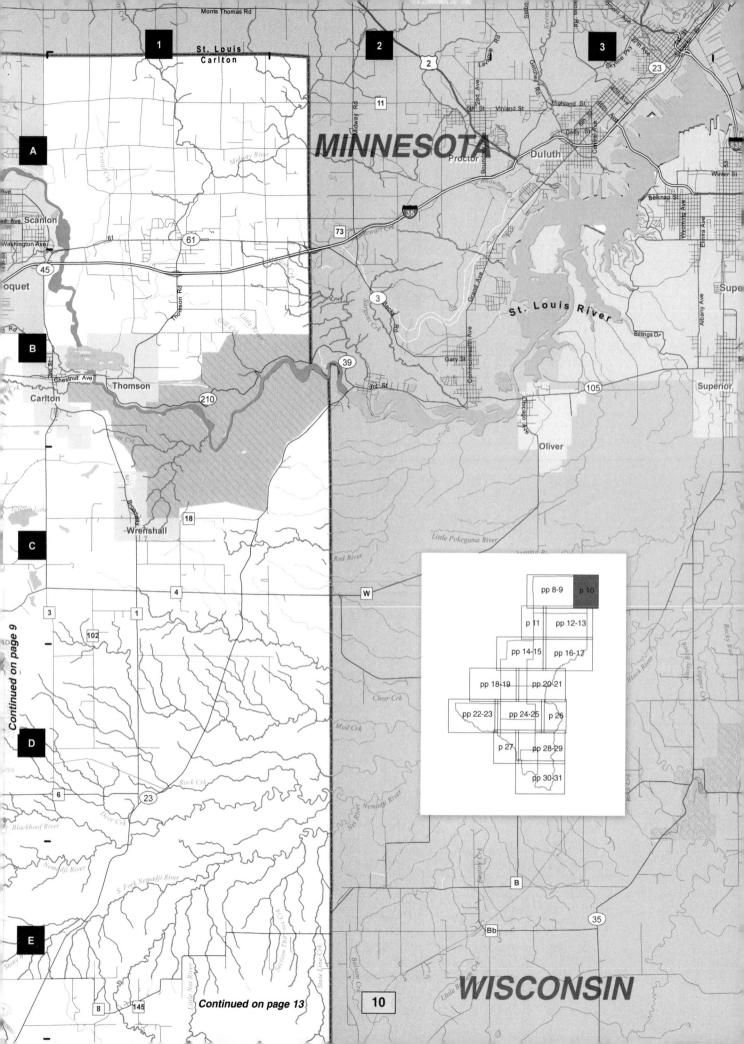

Morris Thomas Rd

St. Louis
Carlton

A

MINNESOTA

11

Proctor

Duluth

5th St   Vinland St   Highland St

Cody

Central Ave

Belknap St

Wyoming Ave   Elmira Ave

53

Winter St

Scanlon

61

61

73

Newart Crk

35

Knowlton Crk

Grand Ave

Albany Ave

Sup

Washington Ave

45

oquet

Thomson Rd

Odd Crk

Little River

3

Bech d Rd

Kingston Crk

Commonwealth Ave

St. Louis River

Billings Dr

B

Chesnut Ave   Thomson

210

39

3rd St

Gary St

Chicago Ave

105

Superior

Carlton

Wrenshall

18

Oliver

C

Continued on page 9

4

3   1

102

Little Pokegama River

Red River

W

Clear Crk

D

6

23

Rock Crk

Deer Crk

Mud Crk

Blackhoof River

Nemadji River

Net River

Nemadji River

Rocky R

Black River

Stony Brook

Copper Crk

S. Fork Nemadji River

B

E

Little Net River

Section Thirty-six Crk

State Line Crk

Bb

35

Eagleport Crk

Little Balsam Crk

Balsam Crk

8   145

Continued on page 13

10

WISCONSIN

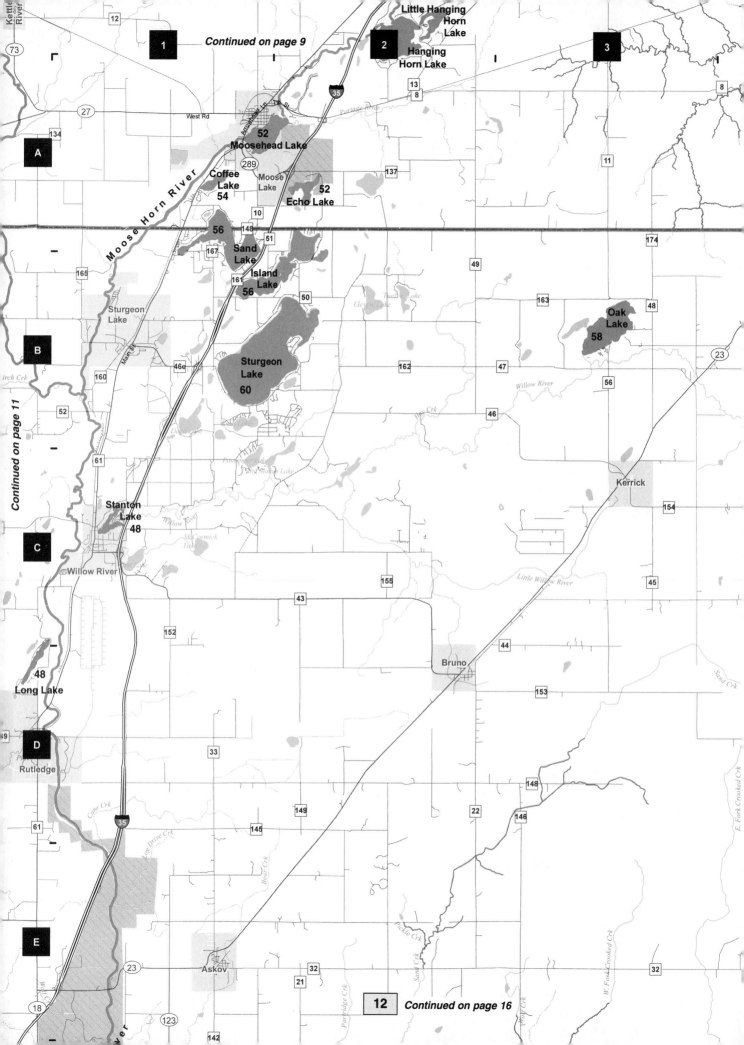

1

Kettle River

73

12

27

134

A

West Rd

Continued on page 9

35

Little Hanging
Horn
Lake

2

Hanging
Horn Lake

13
8

3

8

11

174

Arrowhead Ln — 7th St

Portage River

52
Moosehead Lake

289

137

Coffee
Lake
54

Moose
Lake

52
Echo Lake

Moose Horn River

56

10

148

51

Sand
Lake

167

Island
Lake
56

161

50

49

163

48

Oak
Lake
58

165

Sturgeon
Lake

B

160

46e

162

47

56

Willow River

23

irch Crk

52

Sturgeon
Lake
60

46

61

Kerrick

154

Stanton
Lake
48

Willow River

C

Willow River

McCormick
Lake

155

Little Willow River

45

43

152

44

Bruno

153

48

D

Long Lake

Rutledge

Cone Crk

33

149

145

22

148

146

61

35

E

23

Askov

32

21

Pickle Crk

Sand Crk

E. Fork Crooked Crk

W. Fork Crooked Crk

32

18

123

142

Wolf Crk

Purdue Crk

Continued on page 11

12 Continued on page 16

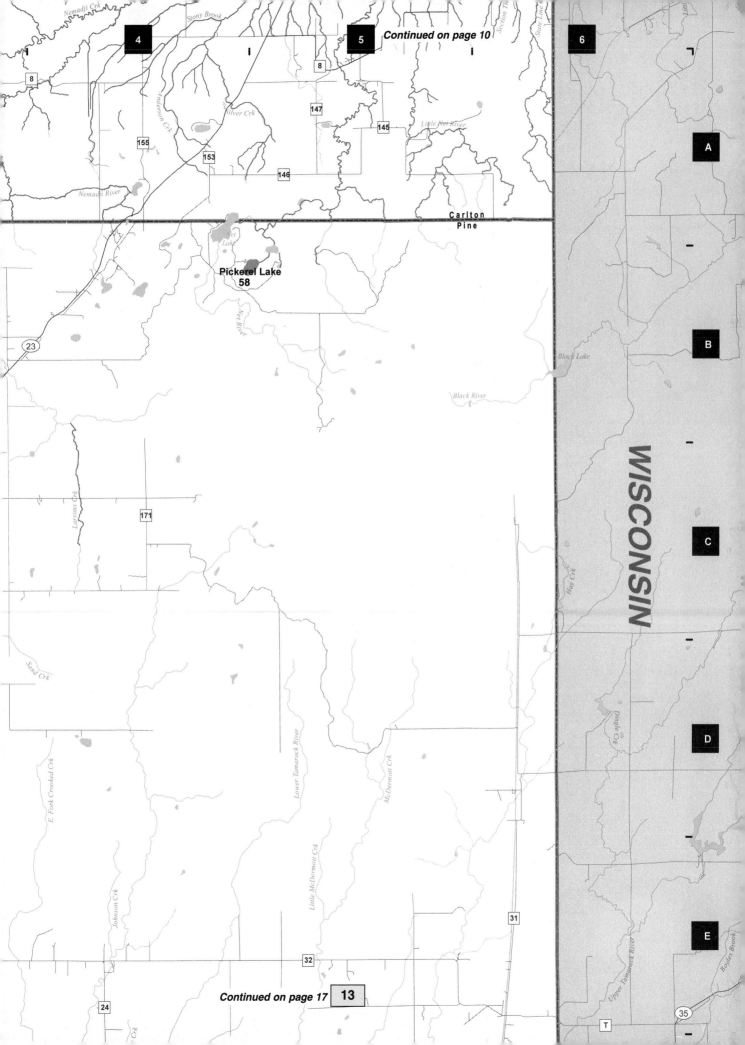

Continued on page 10

4

5

6

8

8

147

155

145

153

146

Pickerel Lake
58

Carlton
Pine

Nemadji Crk

Stony Brook

Section T

State Line

Silver Crk

Little Net River

Anderson Crk

Nemadji River

Net River

Net Lake

23

171

Larsons Crk

Sand Crk

E. Fork Crooked Crk

Johnson Crk

Lower Tamarack River

Little McDermott Crk

McDermott Crk

Black Lake

Black River

Hay Crk

Dingle Crk

Upper Tamarack River

Boyles Brook

WISCONSIN

A

B

C

D

E

31

32

24

T

35

Continued on page 17 **13**

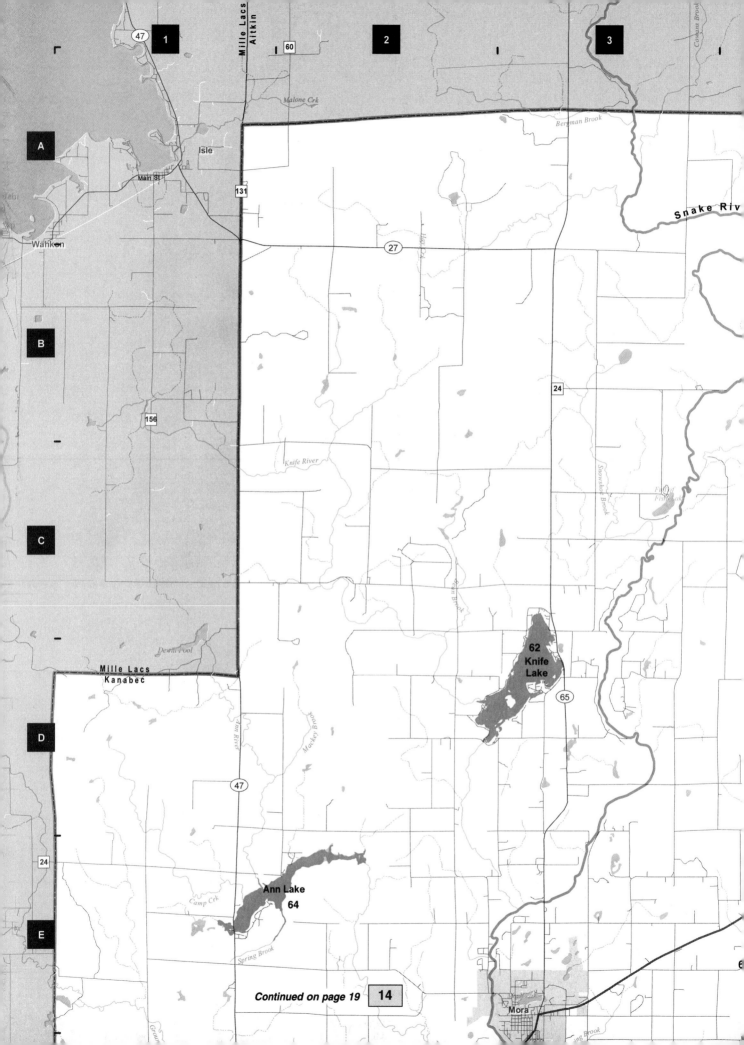

Continued on page 19 14

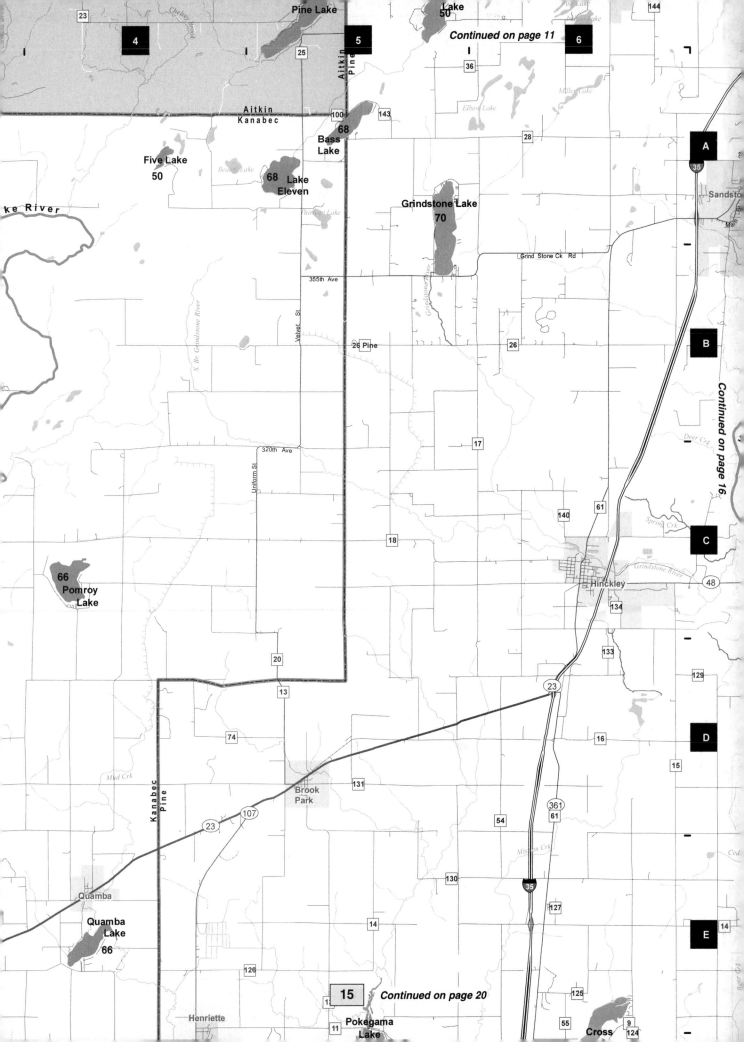

Continued on page 11

4

5

6

Pine Lake

Lake
50

144

36

A

35

Sandsto

Aitkin
Kanabec

100

68
Bass
Lake

143

28

Five Lake
50

68 Lake
Eleven

Grindstone Lake
70

Grind Stone Ck Rd

ke River

355th Ave

B

Velvet St

26 Pine

26

S. Br. Grindstone River

Continued on page 16

320th Ave

17

Uniform St

18

140

61

C

Hinckley

48

Grindstone River

66
Pomroy
Lake

134

20

133

129

13

23

74

16

D

15

Mud Crk

Brook
Park

131

361
61

Kanabec
Pine

23

107

54

130

35

Quamba

127

Quamba
Lake
66

14

E

14

126

15

Continued on page 20

125

Henriette

11

Pokegama
Lake

55

Cross

9
124

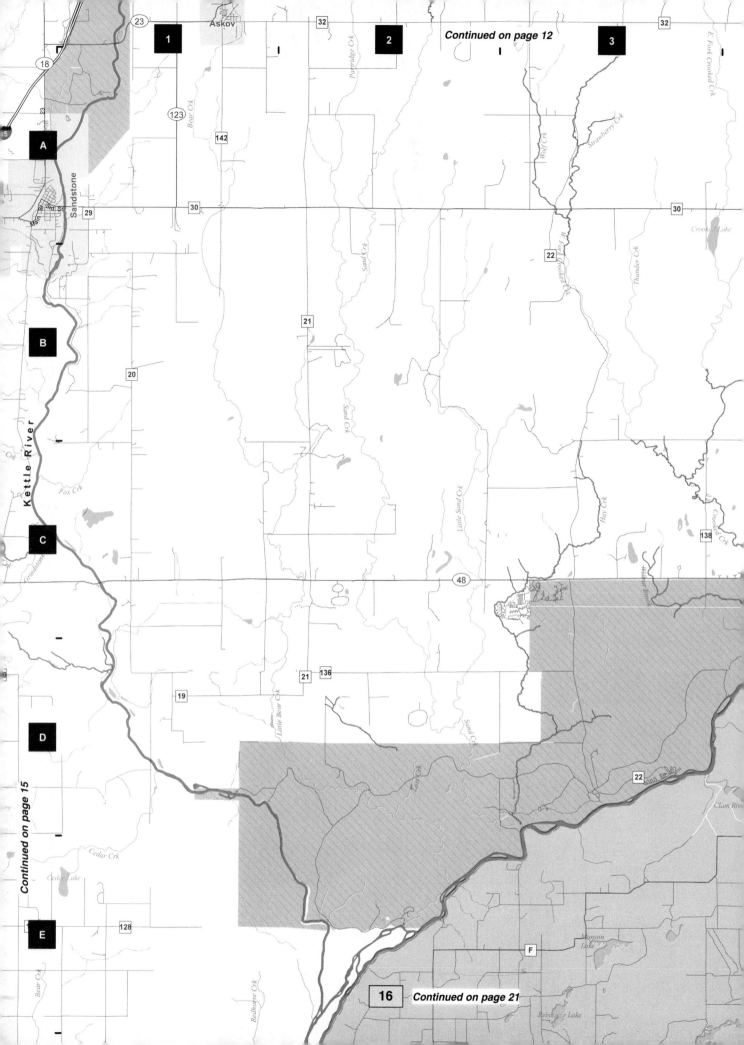

23

ASKOV

32

1

2

Continued on page 12

32

3

18

123

Bear Crk

142

Partridge Crk

Wolf Crk

Strawberry Crk

E. Fork Crooked Crk

5

A

Sandstone

30

30

Crooked Lake

29

Main St

3rd St

Sand Crk

W. Fork Crooked Crk

22

Thunder Crk

21

B

20

Kettle River

Sand Crk

Little Sand Crk

Hay Crk

Crooked Crk

C

Fox Crk

138

Grindstone

48

Crk

Continued on page 15

D

19

21

136

Little Bear Crk

Sand Crk

Bear Crk

22

Clam River

Cedar Crk

Cedar Lake

E

128

F

Monson Lake

Bear Crk

Redhorse Crk

16

Continued on page 21

Reishauer Lake

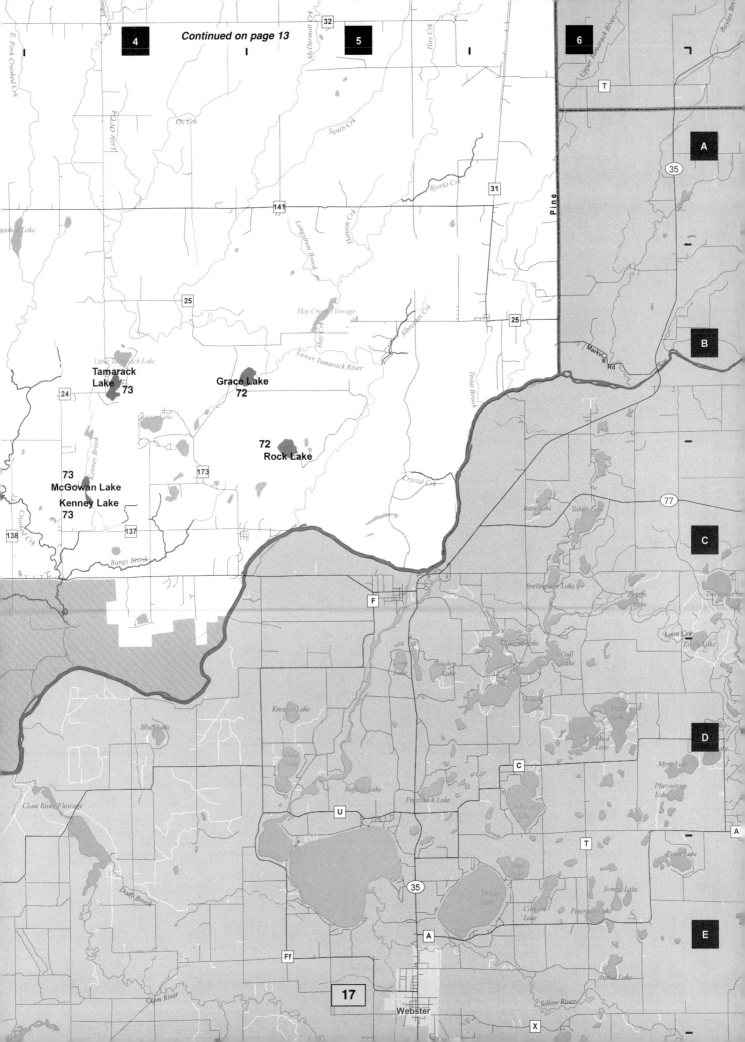

Continued on page 13

4

5

6

A

35

B

Markvile Rd

C

77

D

E

32

McDermott Crk

Hay Crk

Upper Tamarack River

Boyles Br

T

Pine

141

31

Squib Crk

Ox Crk

Little Ox Crk

E. Fork Crooked Crk

ooked Lake

Bjorks Crk

Hunson Crk

Longstream Brook

25

Hay Creek Flowage

Hay Crk

Lower Tamarack River

Albregus Crk

25

24

Little Tamarack Lake

Tamarack Lake 73

Grace Lake 72

Trout Brook

Razor Lake

72 Rock Lake

73

McGowan Lake

Kenney Lake 73

Kenney Brook

173

Crystal Crk

138

Crooked Crk

137

Bangs Brook

Bass Lake

Tabor Lake

Burlingame Lake

Twin ox La

Briggs Lake

Loon Crk
Eden Lake

F

Clam River Flowage

Bluff Lake

Kreitzer Lake

Bear Lake

Long Lake

Breeden Lake

Sand Lake

Gull Lake

Minnow

Flann Lake

Sand Lake

D

Myre Lan

Phernetton Lake

C

Buffalo Lake

Fremstadt Lake

Johnson Lake

T

A

Doty Brook

U

Mud Lake

35

Devils Lake

Conners Lake

Peterson Lake

Point Lake

Tamm Lake

A

Ff

17

Clam River

Yellow River

Webster

Austin Lake

X

E

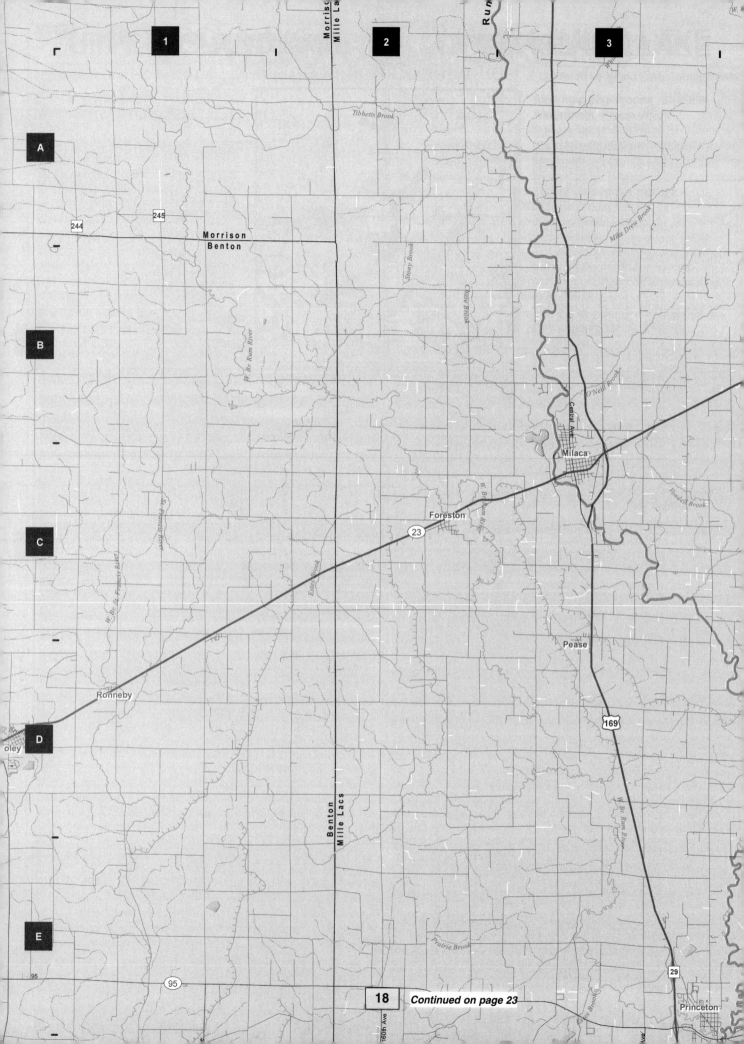

1

2

3

W. Ru

Morris
Mile La

W. R

Tibbetts Brook

A

Mike Drew Brook

244

245

Morrison
Benton

Stony Brook

Chase Brook

W. Br. Rum River

B

O'Neill Brook

Central Ave

Milaca

Randell Brook

W. Br. Rum River

Foreston

23

C

St. Francis River

Estes Brook

W. Br. St. Francis River

Pease

Ronneby

169

D

oley

Benton
Mille Lacs

W. Br. Rum River

E

Prairie Brook

95

29

95

18 *Continued on page 23*

760th Ave

Princeton

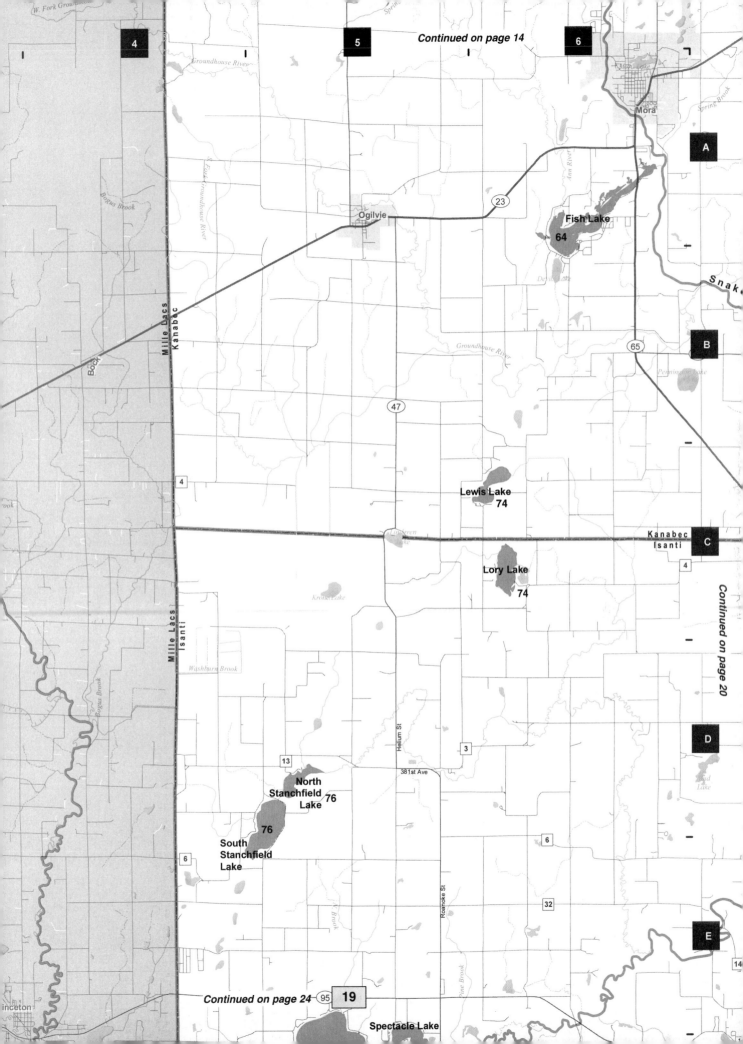

Continued on page 14

4

5

6

A

Mora

Ogilvie

23

Fish Lake

64

B

65

47

Lewis Lake

74

Continued on page 20

Kanabec
Isanti

C

4

Lory Lake

74

Mille Lacs
Kanabec

Mille Lacs
Isanti

Washburn Brook

D

Helium St

381st Ave

3

13

North
Stanchfield
Lake

76

76

South
Stanchfield
Lake

6

6

Roanoke St

32

E

14

Continued on page 24 95 **19**

Spectacle Lake

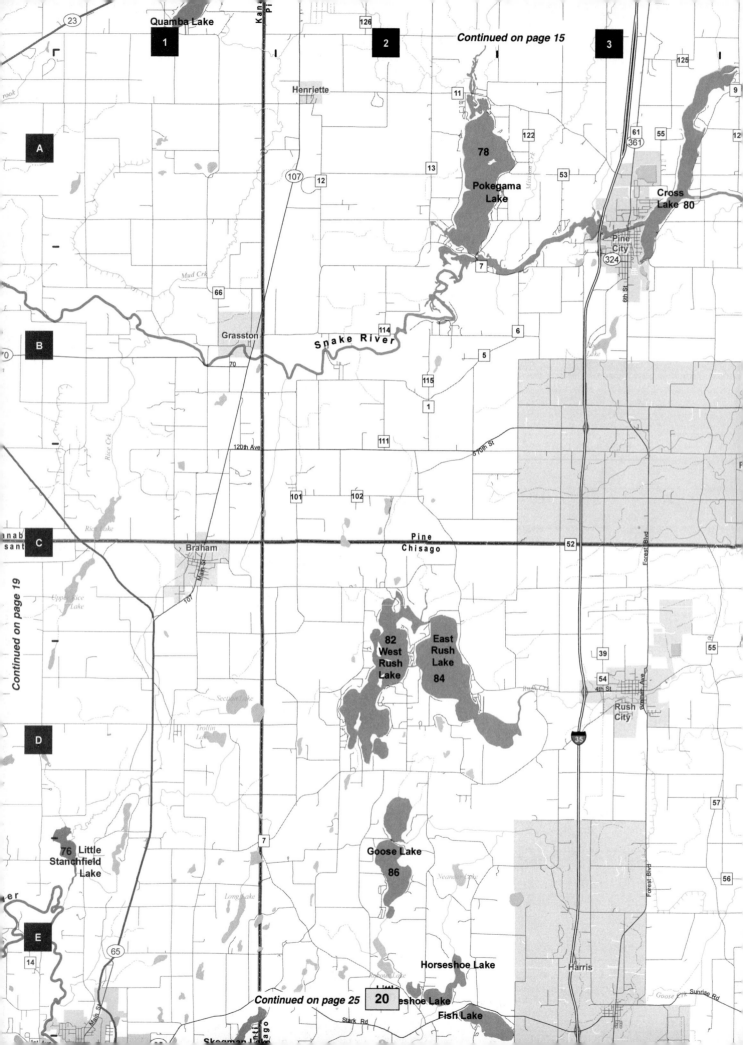

23

Quamba Lake

1

126

2

Continued on page 15

3

125

A

Henriette

11

9

122

61 55

361

12

78

53

13

107 12

Pokegama
Lake

Cross
Lake 80

Pine
City

7

324

Mud Crk

6th St

66

114

Snake River

Grasston

B

6

70

70

5

115

1

120th Ave

111

570th St

101 102

Rice Crk

52

Rice Lake

C

Pine

Braham

Chisago

Forest Blvd

Continued on page 19

Upper Rice
Lake

Section Lake

82
West
Rush
Lake

East
Rush
Lake
84

55

39

54

4th St

Rush
City

Trollin
Lake

D

35

76 Little
Stanchfield
Lake

57

Goose Lake

86

Neanore Lake

56

Long Lake

E

65

Horseshoe Lake

Harris

14

Sunrise Rd

Goose Crk

Continued on page 25

20

seshoe Lake

Fish Lake

Stark Rd

Skogman Lake

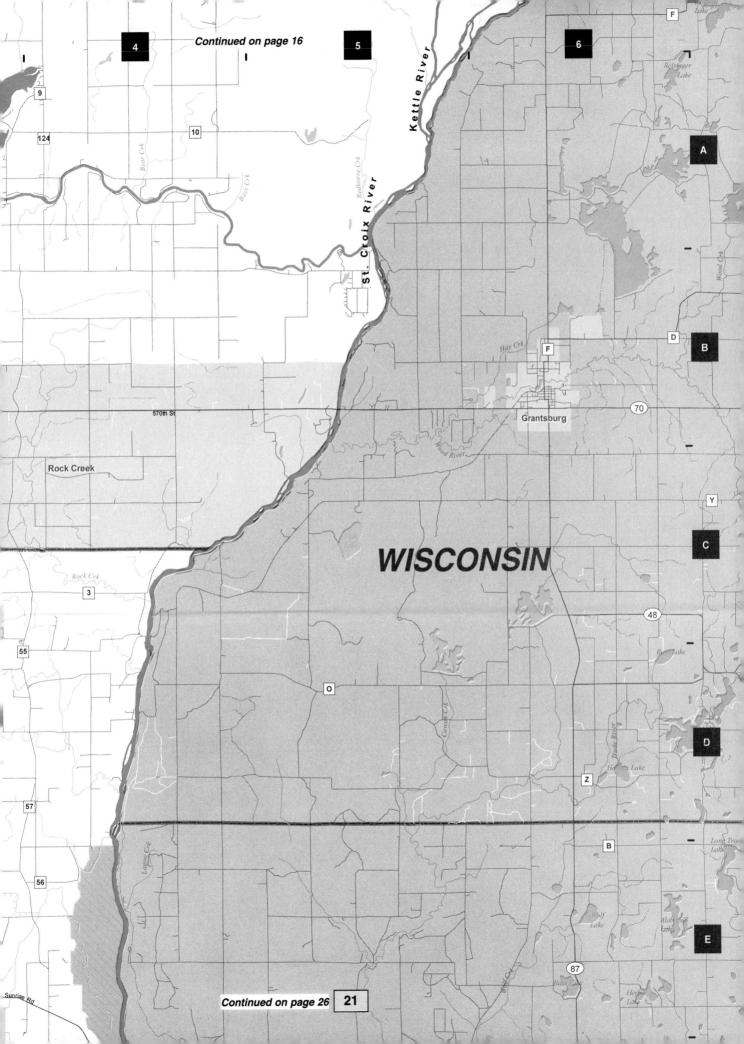

Continued on page 16

4

5

6

F

9

124

10

A

St. Croix River

Kettle River

Redhorse Crk

Bear Crk

Bass Crk

Wood Crk

Retyager Lake

Hay Crk

D

F

B

570th St

Grantsburg

70

Rock Creek

Wood River

Y

Rock Crk

Fish Lake

WISCONSIN

C

3

48

55

Bass Lake

O

Cowan Crk

Trade River

Holmes Lake

D

Z

57

B

Long Trade Lake

56

Lagoo Crk

Wolf Lake

Alaskan Lake

E

87

Bass Lake

Herby Lake

Mill Crk

Sunrise Rd

Continued on page 26 21

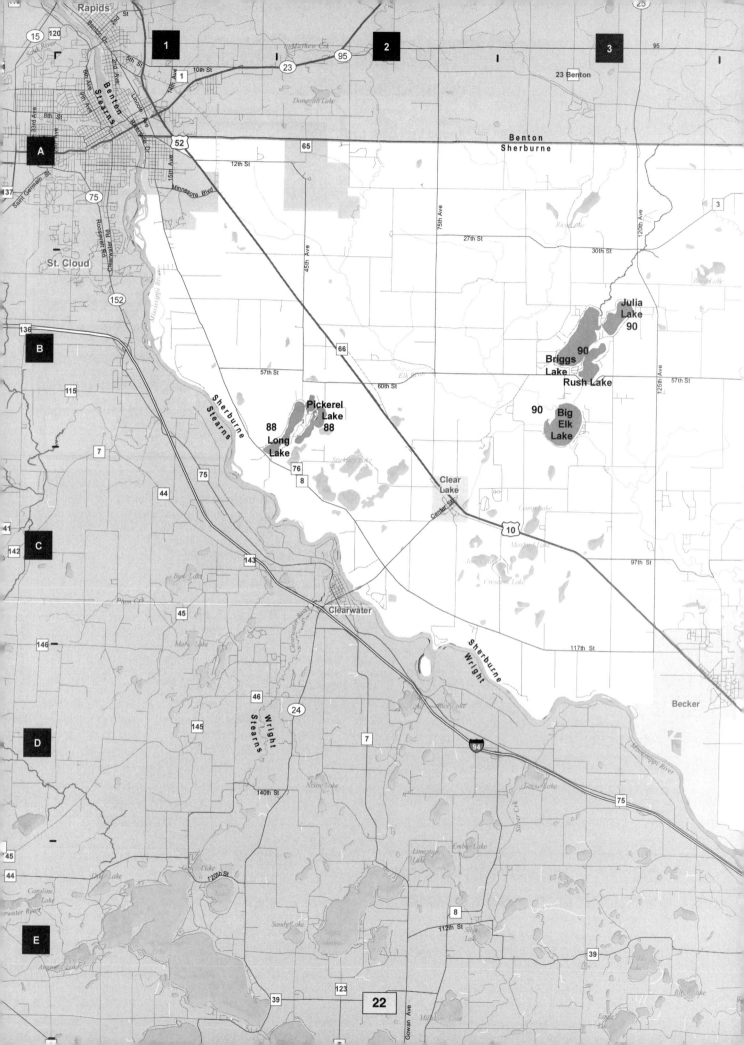

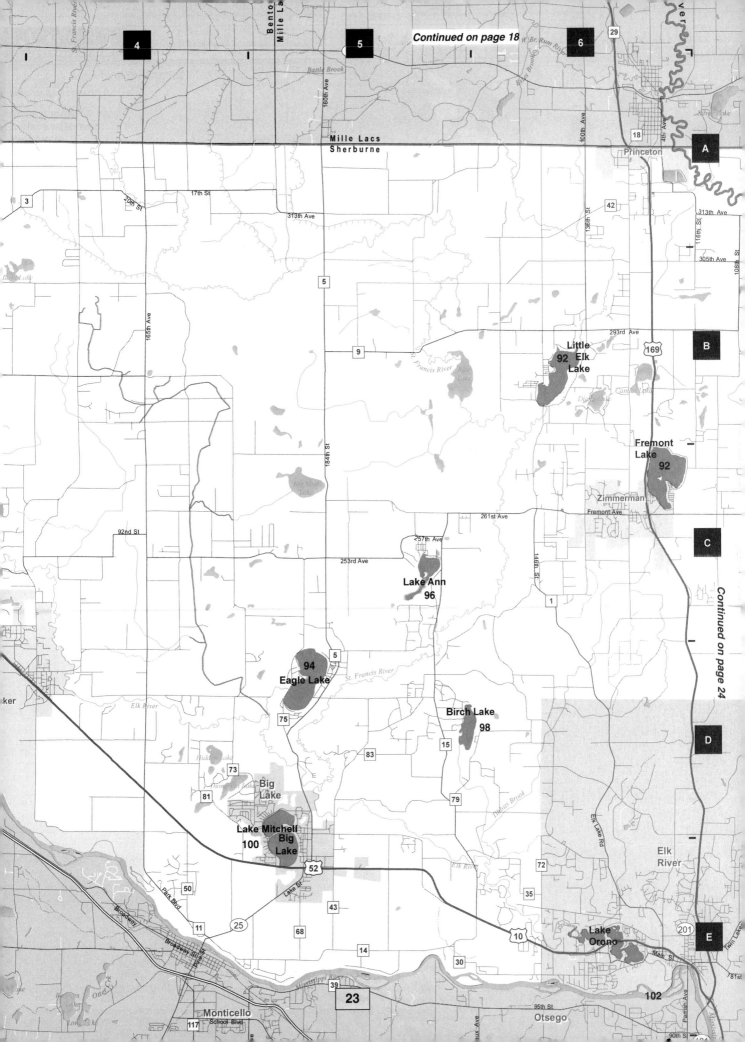

Continued on page 18

4

5

6

29

W. Br. Rum River

Battle Brook

160th Ave

100th Ave

18

4th St

Princeton

A

Mille Lacs
Sherburne

3

17th St

20th St

313th Ave

165th Ave

42

136th St

116th St

313th Ave

305th Ave

108th St

5

9

St. Francis River

Little
Elk
Lake
92

293rd Ave

169

B

184th St

Big Moose Lake

Fremont
Lake
92

Zimmerman

261st Ave

Fremont Ave

92nd St

257th Ave

253rd Ave

Lake Ann
96

146th St

1

C

Continued on page 24

St. Francis River

94
Eagle Lake

75

Birch Lake
98

15

D

83

79

73

Hidden Lake

81

Big
Lake

Elk Lake Rd

Elk
River

Lake Mitchell
Big
Lake
100

52

72

35

Elk River

Park Blvd

50

Lake St

43

201

Lake
Orono

E

Broadway

11

25

68

14

10

30

Main St

81st

Broadway St

Pine St

39

23

Mississippi River

Monticello

School Blvd

117

95th St

Otsego

102

90th St

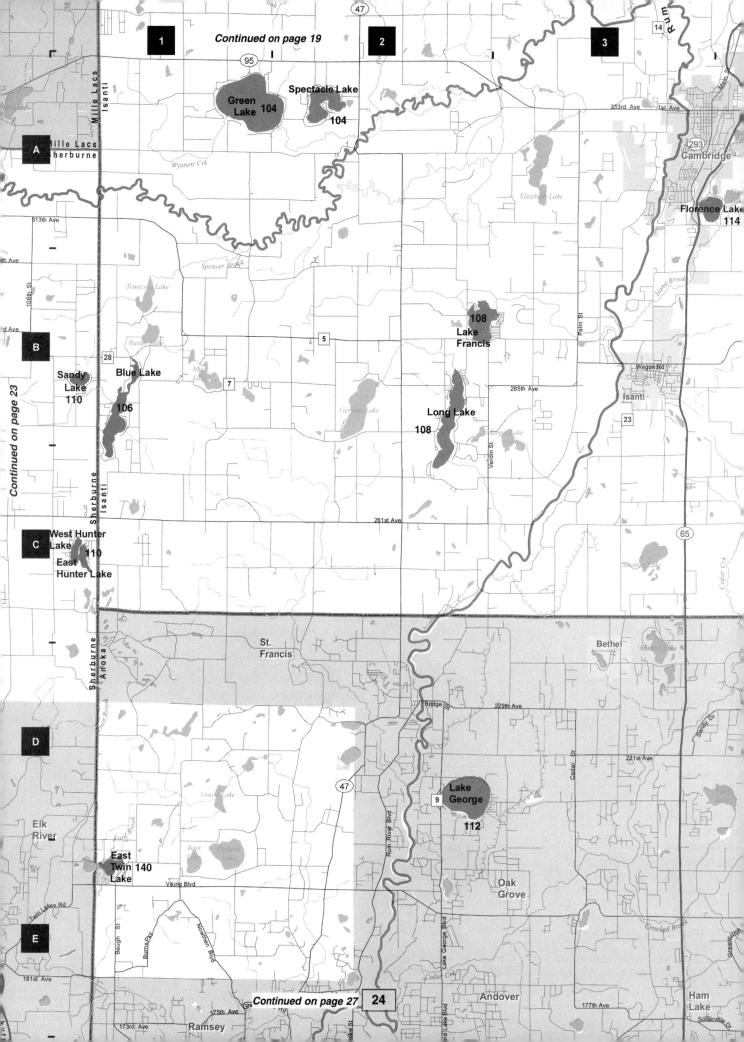

Continued on page 19

1

2

3

47

14

95

Rum

Green Lake 104

Spectacle Lake 104

333rd Ave   1st Ave

A

Mille Lacs
Isanti

Mille Lacs
Sherburne

293

Cambridge

Wyanett Crk

Elizabeth Lake

Florence Lake 114

813th Ave

Spencer Brook

Isanti Brook

th Ave

Tennyson Lake

108
Lake Francis

Palm St

Wagon Rd

Continued on page 23

B

108th St

Baxter Lake

28

Mud Lake

5

Isanti

d Ave

Sandy Lake 110

Blue Lake

7

285th Ave

23

Blue Lake 106

German Lake

Long Lake 108

Verdin St

Marget Lake

261st Ave

65

C

West Hunter Lake 110

East Hunter Lake

Sheaton Lake

Cedar Crk

Sherburne
Isanti

D

Sherburne
Anoka

St.
Francis

Bethel

Minor Lake

Crott Brook

229th Ave

Bridge St

Sandy Dr

Cedar Dr

221st Ave

Goose Lake

47

Mud Lake

Lake George 112

9

Elk
River

Ford Brook

Bass Lake

Pheasant Lake

Oak
Grove

Lake George Blvd

Crooked Brook

Greenbrook

E

East Twin Lake 140

Viking Blvd

Baugh St

Burns Pkwy

Nowthen Blvd

Cedar Crk

181st Ave

Continued on page 27

24

Andover

177th Ave

Ham
Lake

Twin Lakes Rd

173rd Ave

175th Ave

Gre

nd St

Ramsey

Rum River Blvd

Soderville Rd

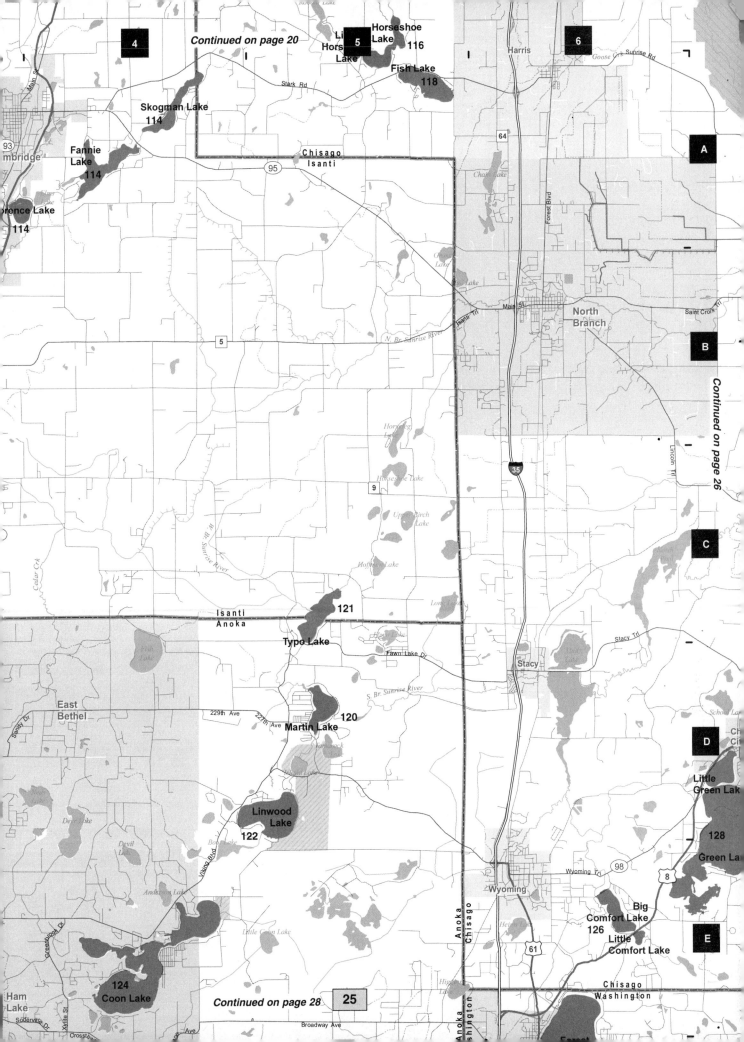

4

Continued on page 20

5

6

Horseshoe Lake 116

Li
Hors
Lake

Harris

Goose Cr Sunrise Rd

Fish Lake 118

Stark Rd

Skogman Lake 114

Chan Lake

64

A

Chisago
Isanti

95

Fannie Lake 114

Forest Blvd

orence Lake 114

Main St

North Branch

Saint Croix Trl

Isanti Trl

B

N. Br. Sunrise River

Continued on page 26

5

Lincoln Trl

Horseleg
L

35

C

9

Horseshoe Lake

W. Br. Sunrise River

Upper Birch
Lake

Long Lake

South

Cedar Crk

Hoffman Lake

121

Stacy Trl

Isanti
Anoka

Abid
Lake

Typo Lake

Fish
Lake

Fawn Lake Dr

Stacy

Schoo La

S. Br. Sunrise River

D

East
Bethel

229th Ave

227th Ave

120

Martin Lake

Ch
Ci

Sandy Dr

Vanstock

Little
Green Lak

Typo Lake

Deer Lake

Linwood
Lake
122

Bob Lake

Viking Blvd

128

Devil
Lake

Green La

Andrews Lake

Wyoming Trl

98

8

Greenbrook Dr

Little Coon Lake

Big
Comfort Lake
126

Wyoming

Heins Lake

61

Little
Comfort Lake

E

124
Coon Lake

Chisago
Washington

Ham
Lake

Continued on page 28

25

Soderville Dr

Xylite St

Crosstown

Anoka
Washington

Broadway Ave

Anoka
Chisago

Higgi
Lake

Forest

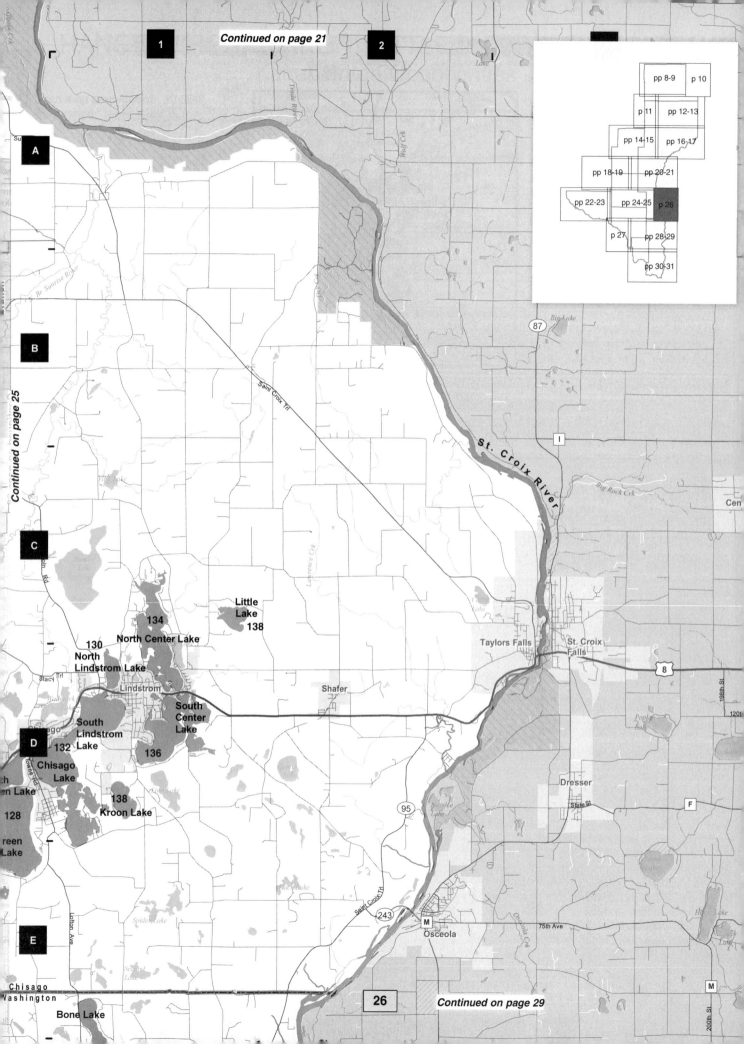

Continued on page 21

1

2

A

B

Continued on page 25

C

D

E

pp 8-9   p 10

p 11   pp 12-13

pp 14-15   pp 16-17

pp 18-19   pp 20-21

pp 22-23   pp 24-25   p 26

p 27   pp 28-29

pp 30-31

87   Big Lake

I

Big Rock Crk

Cen

St. Croix Trl

Trade River

Wolf Crk

St. Croix River

Lawrence Crk

Little Lake
138

134

130
North Center Lake

North Lindstrom Lake

Taylors Falls   St. Croix Falls

8

198th St

Staci Trl   Lindstrom

Shafer

South Center Lake

South Lindstrom Lake

132

136

Chisago Lake

128

Kroon Lake

138

Green Lake

95

Dresser

State St

F

243

M

Osceola   75th Ave

Osceola Crk

Spider Lake

Second Lake

Chisago
Washington

Bone Lake

26

200th St

M

Continued on page 29

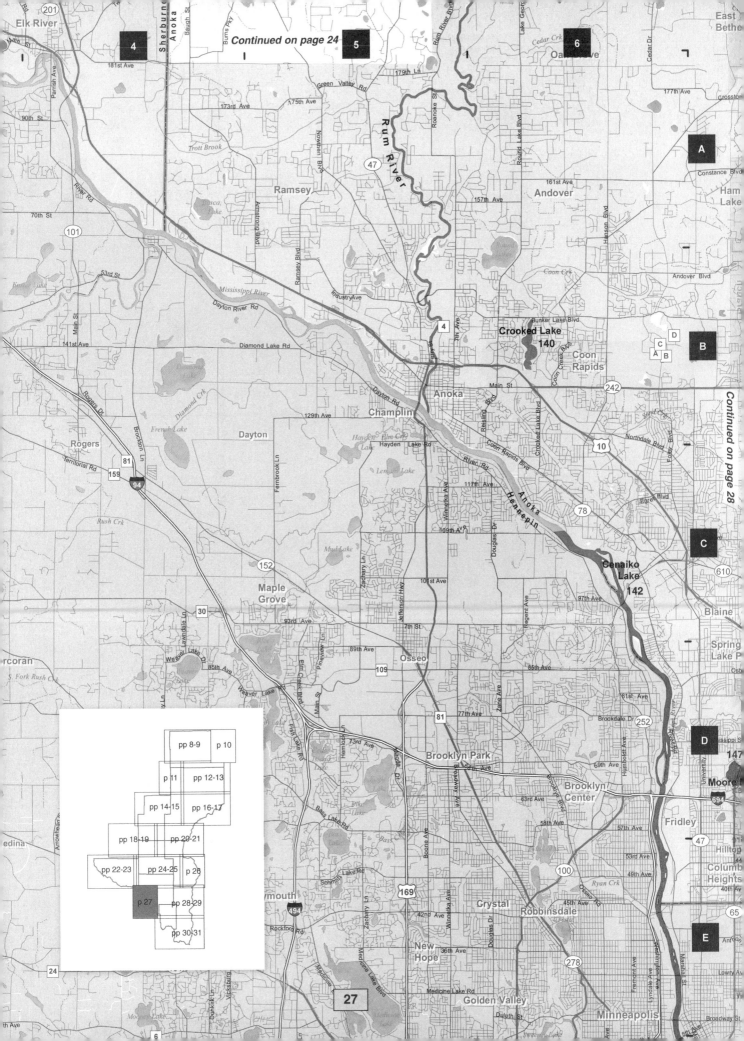

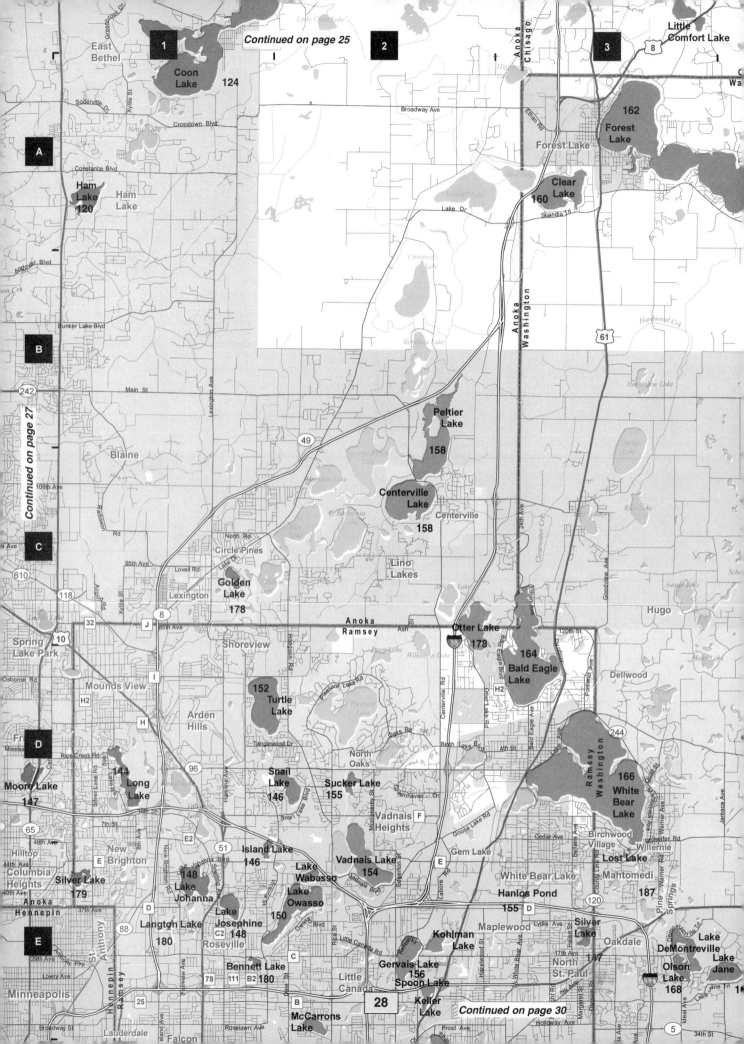

East Bethel

1

Coon Lake 124

Continued on page 25

2

Anoka Chisago

3

Little Comfort Lake

Broadway Ave

Forest Lake 162

Forest Lake

Clear Lake 160

A

Constance Blvd

Ham Lake 120

Ham Lake

Andover Blvd

Lake Dr

Scandia Trl

Crossways Lake

Hardwood Crk

B

242

Main St

Rondeau Lake

Horseshoe Lake

Continued on page 27

109th Ave

Blaine

49

Peltier Lake 158

24th Ave

Clearwater Crk

Goodview Ave

Rice Lake

Bunker Lake Blvd

Radisson Rd

C

95th Ave

Lovell Rd

Circle Pines

North Rd

Lexington

Golden Lake 178

Centerville Lake 158

Centerville

Lino Lakes

Hugo

610

118

8

Lexington

J

85th Ave

Anoka Ramsey

Ash

Otter Lake 178

120th St

Lake

32

Spring Lake Park

10

Shoreview

Hodgson Rd

Deep Lake

Wilkinson Lake

Big Eagle Blvd

Bald Eagle Lake 164

Dellwood

I

Mounds View

H2

Turtle Lake 152

Pleasant Lake Rd

Centerville Rd

H2

Otter Lake Rd

H

Arden Hills

Pleasant Lake

4th St

Ramsey Washington

244

D

Moore Lake 147

Rice Creek Rd

144

Long Lake

96

Tanglewood Dr

North Oaks

Oaks Rd

Birch Lake Blvd

Bald Eagle Ave

166 White Bear Lake

65

7th St

8th Ave

E2

Snail Lake 146

Sucker Lake 155

Greenhaven Dr

Goose Lake Rd

Birchwood Village

Willernie

49th Ave

51

Island Lake 146

Snail Lake Blvd

Vadnais Heights

F

Cedar Ave

Bellaire Ave

Lost Lake

Mahtomedi

Hilltop

44th Ave

New Brighton

148 Lake Johanna

Edgerton St

Vadnais Lake 154

Gem Lake

E

White Bear Lake

120

187

Columbia Heights

E

Silver Lake 179

Lake Wabasso

LaBore Rd

Hanlos Pond 155

D

North St. Paul 147

Silver Lake

Anoka Hennepin

37th Ave

D

Langton Lake 180

New Brighton Rd

Sheldon Ave

Lake Josephine 150

Lake Owasso

Owasso Blvd

Maplewood

Lydia Ave

Oakdale

Lake DeMontreville

29th Ave

88

C2

148

Roseville

C

Little Canada Rd

Little Canada

Kohlman Lake

Hazelwood Rd

17th Ave

White Bear Ave

7th St

Olson Lake 168

Lake Jane

E

Lowry Ave

25

Bennett Lake 180

78

111

B2

Gervais Lake 156 Spoon Lake

North St. Paul

Margaret St

5

Minneapolis

Lauderdale

Falcon

Broadway St

Roselawn Ave

B

McCarrons Lake

28

Keller Lake

Frost Ave

Continued on page 30

Holloway Ave

34th Ave

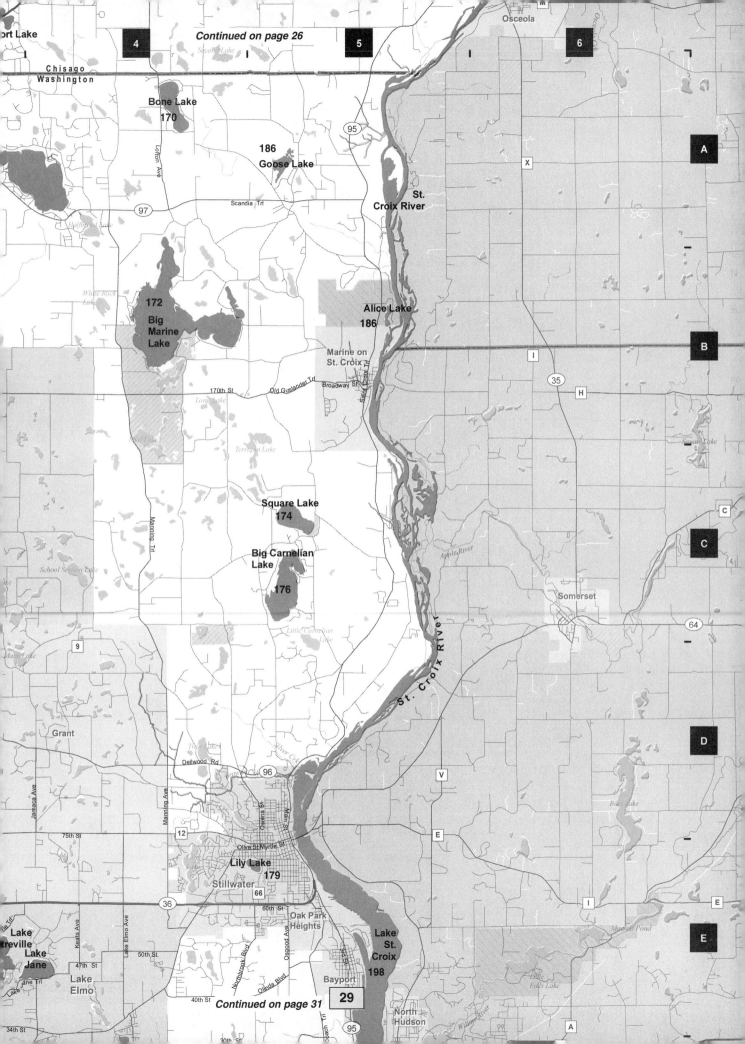

4
Continued on page 26
5
6

Osceola

ort Lake

Chisago
Washington

Bone Lake
170

186
Goose Lake

Scandia Trl

97

White Rock Lake

172
Big
Marine
Lake

St.
Croix River

Alice Lake
186

X

A

Marine on
St. Croix

I

B

35

170th St
Old Guslander Trl
Broadway St

H

Long Lake

Terrapin Lake

Manning Trl

Square Lake
174

Apple River

C

C

Big Carnelian
Lake

Somerset

176

Little Carnelian
Lake

School Section Lake

64

9

St. Croix River

Main Lake

Grant

Twin Lake

Dellwood Rd

96

D

V

Manning Ave

75th St

Silver Cr

Jamaca Ave

12

E

Olive St Myrtle St

Lily Lake
179

Stillwater

66

I

E

36

60th St

Oak Park
Heights

E

Lake
treville
Lake
Jane

Lake Elmo Ave
Keats Ave

50th St

Northbrook Blvd
Osgood Ave

Olinda Blvd

Lake
St.
Croix
198

Lake
Elmo

47th St
Jane Trl

40th St

Bayport

North
Hudson

A

95

34th St
30th St

Continued on page 28

1

2

3

A

B

C

D

E

Langton Lake
88
Roseville
180
Bennett Lake
C2
C
78
111 B2
25
Roselawn Ave
B
147
McCarrons
Lake
49
Falcon
Heights
Lauderdale
52
St. Anthony
St. Anthony Pkw
29th Ave
Silver
Hennepin Ave
Broadway St
65
280
Hennepin
Ramsey
Fairview Ave
Hamline Ave
Lexington Ave
Victoria
Dale St
Rice St
Pier Rd
Prior Ave
Raymond Ave
Como Ave
Energy Park Dr
Transfer Rd
51
Pierce Butler
94
Marshall Ave
University Ave
Summit Ave
Saint Clair Ave
Jefferson Ave
Randolph Ave
Snelling Ave
Cleveland Ave
Saint Paul Ave
Ford Pkw
Minneapolis
Lake St
River Pkwy
46th St
54th St
55
62
63rd St
6th St
28th Ave
Minnehaha Ave
70th St
Post Rd
34th St
Minnehaha Pkw
hfield
36
84th St
86th St
92nd St
Long Meadow
Lake
Hennepin
Dakota
Nicollet Ave
Silver Bell Rd
Old Shakopee Rd
loomington
77
Burnsville
13
urnsville Pky
Kennelly Rd
Palomino Dr
127th
Mcandrews Rd
38
Johnny Cake Ridge Rd
Cedar Ave
Garden
Galaxie Ave
Apple Valley
140th St
144th St
150th St
160th St
11
Lakeville
Como Lake
181
Loeb Lake
181
Crosby
Lake
181
5
Lilydale
Sibley Memorial Hwy
Lexington Pkwy
Dale St
White Bear Ave
Wheelock Pkwy
Larpenteur Ave
Arlington Ave
Como Ave
St. Paul
Lexington Ave
Jackson St
7th St
Robert St
Wabasha St
35
2
Water St
Smith Ave
Annapolis St
George St
Butler Ave
Shepard Rd
Lilydale Rd
Mendota
Heights
Mendota
110
Mendota Heights Rd
Marie Ave
Delaware Ave
Charlton St
Dodd Rd
Sunfish Lake
3
70th St
Upper 55th St
Lone Oak Rd
Yankee Doodle Rd
Eagan
Pilot Knob Rd
Blackhawk Rd
Lexington Ave
Wescott Rd
149
Diffley Rd
Cliff Rd
110th St
117th St
145th St
Rosemount
Coates
Canada
is Lake
Kohlman
Lake
Spoon Lake
Keller Lake
Maplewood
North St. Paul
156
Frost Ave
Holloway Ave
Larpenteur Ave
Lake Phalen
182
Maryland Ave
61
Edgerton St
Parkway Dr
Earl St
Johnson Pkwy
7th St
Mounds Blvd
Burns Ave
Warner Rd
Eva St
Oakdale Ave
19th St
Ramsey
Dakota
West St. Paul
Wentworth Ave
Thompson Ave
South
St. Paul
Southview Blvd
Robert Trl
Mendota Rd
5th St
7th St
Concord St
56
Babcock Trl
Asenia Trl
Barnes Ave
College Trl
Inver Grove Heights
Rich Valley Blvd
Robert Trl
105th St
Blaine Ave
Oakdale
Lake
DeMontreville
Olson Lake
Lake
168
694
17th Ave
34th St
Margaret St
120
Ideal Ave
15th St
Hadley Ave
Granada Ave
Century Ave
Greenway Ave
Stillwater Blvd
Battle Cr
Minnehaha Ave
184
Tanners Lake
Landfall
Battle Creek
Lake
184
Upper Afton Rd
Lower Afton Rd
Highwood Ave
Courtly Rd
Lake Rd
Carver Lake
187
Carver Ave
Sterling St
Woodbu
Century Ave
Valley
Ramsey
Washington
494
10
Newport
65th St
74
22
St. Paul Park
Pullman Ave
80th St
85th St
Courthouse Blvd
Spring Lake
218
Cottage G
Military Rd
Jamaica Ave
Hastings Trl
55
Mississippi River

30

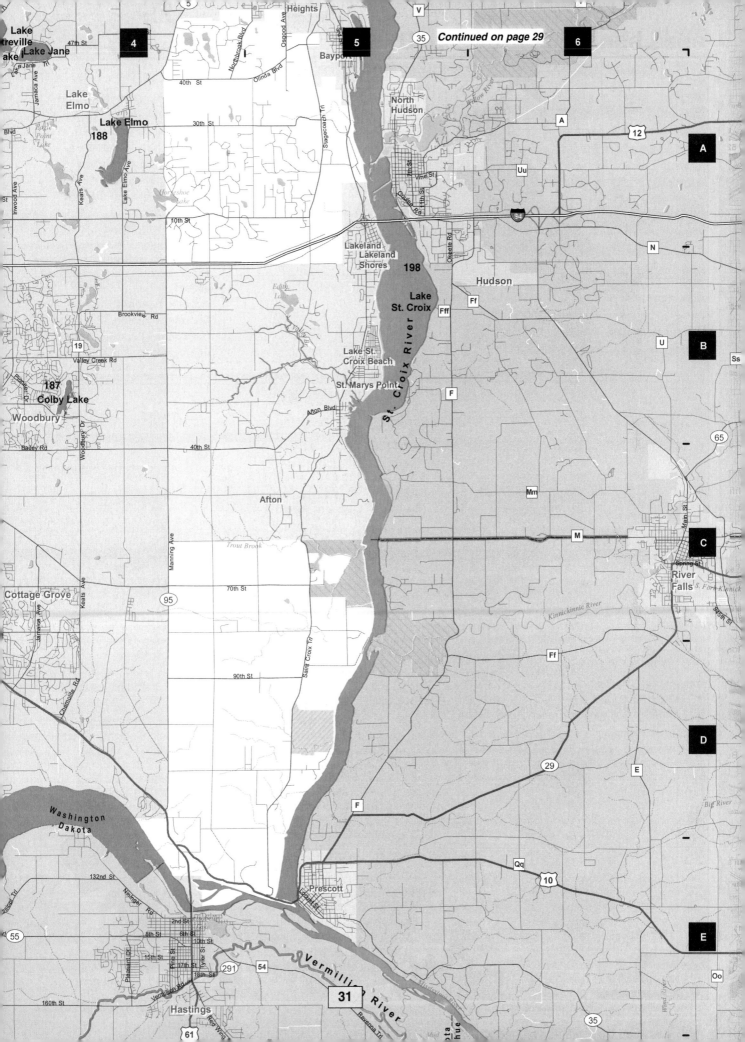

Continued on page 29

COLE LAKE

TAMARACK LAKE

Carlton County

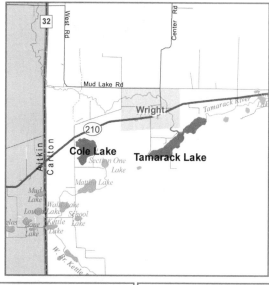

Cole Lake (left column):

Area map page/coord: 8 / B-1
Watershed: Prairie-Willow
Surface area: 154 acres
Shorelength: 3.0 miles
Maximum depth: 24 feet
Mean depth: 11 feet
Secchi disk (water clarity):
7.8 feet (2005)
Water color: Green tint
Accessibility: State-owned public access with gravel ramp on north shore; seven trailer spaces
Accommodations: None
Shoreland zoning: Recreational dev.
Management class: Walleye
Ecological type: Soft-water walleye

Tamarack Lake (right column):

Area map page/coord: 8 / B-1,2
Watershed: Prairie-Willow
Surface area: 235 acres
Shorelength: 4.2 miles
Maximum depth: 48 feet
Mean depth: 8 feet
Secchi disk (water clarity):
6.0 feet (2008)
Water color: Brown
Accessibility: State-owned public access with concrete ramp on west shore of south basin; seven trailer spaces
Accommodations: None
Shoreland zoning: Recreational dev.
Management class: Centrarchid
Ecological type: Centrarchid

COLE LAKE — FISH STOCKING DATA

year	species	size	# released
06	Walleye	Adult	40
08	Walleye	Fry	200,000
10	Walleye	Fry	200,000
12	Walleye	Fry	200,000

NET CATCH DATA — Date: 08/01/05

species	Gill Nets # per net	Gill Nets avg. fish weight (lbs.)	Trap Nets # per net	Trap Nets avg. fish weight (lbs.)
Black Crappie	1.8	0.49	1.1	0.82
Bluegill	0.8	0.25	5.9	0.20
Largemouth Bass	-	-	0.9	2.17
Northern Pike	7.2	2.29	0.6	2.33
Pumpkin. Sunfish	0.5	0.10	0.4	0.13
Walleye	1.5	3.04	0.1	2.20
Yellow Perch	-	-	0.1	0.10

LENGTH OF SELECTED SPECIES SAMPLED FROM ALL GEAR
Number of fish caught for the following length categories (inches):

species	0-5	6-8	9-11	12-14	15-19	20-24	25-29	>30	Total
Black Crappie	2	5	12	2	-	-	-	-	21
Bluegill	17	41	-	-	-	-	-	-	58
Largemouth Bass	1	-	1	3	3	-	-	-	8
Northern Pike	-	-	2	-	14	26	5	1	48
Pumpkin. Sunfish	6	1	-	-	-	-	-	-	7
Walleye	-	-	-	-	7	3	-	-	10
Yellow Perch	1	-	-	-	-	-	-	-	1

TAMARACK LAKE — FISH STOCKING DATA

year	species	size	# released
08	Walleye	Fingerling	5,876
10	Walleye	Fingerling	2,640
12	Walleye	Fingerling	3,378

NET CATCH DATA — Date: 06/19/08

species	Gill Nets # per net	Gill Nets avg. fish weight (lbs.)	Trap Nets # per net	Trap Nets avg. fish weight (lbs.)
Black Crappie	6.4	0.31	13.3	0.18
Bluegill	15.8	0.28	1.0	0.30
Northern Pike	0.6	1.65	5.5	2.53
Pumpkin. Sunfish	2.2	0.27	0.2	0.32
Rock Bass	0.1	0.78	2.3	0.36
Walleye	2.0	1.77	-	-
Yellow Perch	1.3	0.10	-	-

LENGTH OF SELECTED SPECIES SAMPLED FROM ALL GEAR
Number of fish caught for the following length categories (inches):

species	0-5	6-8	9-11	12-14	15-19	20-24	25-29	>30	Total
Black Crappie	40	77	18	-	-	-	-	-	138
Bluegill	19	129	-	-	-	-	-	-	148
Northern Pike	-	-	1	2	14	13	6	2	38
Pumpkin. Sunfish	5	16	-	-	-	-	-	-	21
Rock Bass	1	11	3	-	-	-	-	-	15
Walleye	-	2	2	1	5	2	-	-	12
Yellow Perch	4	4	-	-	-	-	-	-	8

FISHING INFORMATION: Located west of Cromwell, near the town of Wright at the far western edge of Carlton County, these two lakes have been stocked regularly with walleyes by the DNR.

Cole Lake gives up some very nice walleyes, according to local reports. Try live bait rigs to fool a few. A split shot, Lindy or Mojo rigged leech or crawler will tempt a few fish from the weeds. A jig-and-minnow combo is best later in fall when the weather cools. Crappies and panfish provide pretty steady action, with many running in the 1/2-pound range. Small minnows floated under a bobber will do the trick for crappies, while a chunk of nightcrawler, wax worm or small leech will take a variety of panfish. Habitat is ideal for largemouth bass, and anglers report doing well. The lake isn't loaded with giants, according to Dianne Bednarek at Outdoor Advantage, 1302 Highway 33, Cloquet, MN, 218-879-3185, but there are decent numbers of fish available. Try a popper for a little topwater action early in the day during summer. Fish holes or pockets in weeds with jig-and-pigs or Texas-rigged plastics. Stick with dark colors when choosing a jig or plastic bait. Black, green pumpkin, brown or watermelon are good choices. Some decent northern pike action occurs, too. Pike up to 30 inches long have been reported. Flashy lures or large minnows are best for attracting pike.

There is an access off State Highway 210 on the north side of the lake.

Tamarack Lake gives up pretty good numbers of walleyes, up to 3 pounds, along with the more common "eaters". Anglers seem to do best for them around the small islands in the lower basin during summer months. Walleyes have been stocked in this lake by the DNR in the fall of even-numbered years since 1990. According to DNR statistics, walleye abundance on Tamarack is typical compared to other similar Minnesota lakes. The mean length for walleyes was 15.4 inches. Bluegills, which run about 1/2 pound, hang around weedlines during spring. The size and abundance of bluegills on this lake is good, according to DNR statistics. Crappie angling is best during winter months, when 1/2- to 3/4-pounders are caught in both of the lake's lobes. Try small teardrop jigs tipped with a wax worm or small minnow. Some bigger pike are hooked and released by locals interested in seeing a trophy fishery develop. Most of the northern pike are on the smaller side with the average length, according to the DNR, being 21.7 inches long. Try for pike in shallows both early and late in the day. Cast spinnerbaits, spoons or jerkbaits to hook active fish. If fishing action slows, switch to live bait such as large shiner minnows or suckers.

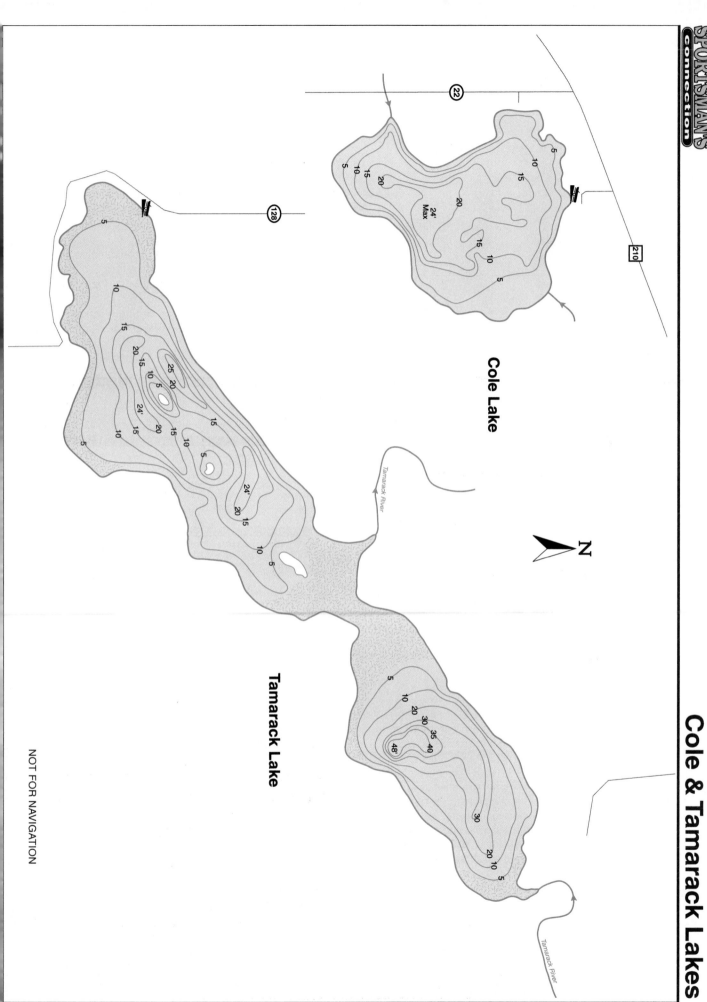

Cole Lake

Tamarack Lake

N

Cole & Tamarack Lakes

NOT FOR NAVIGATION

UPPER ISLAND LAKE   LOWER ISLAND LAKE
Carlton County

Area map page/coord: 8 / B-2,3
Watershed: Prairie-Willow
Surface area: 114 acres
Shorelength: 6.8 miles (upper & lower)
Maximum depth: 25 feet
Mean depth: NA
Secchi disk (water clarity):
9.5 feet (2010)
Water color: Brown stain
Accessibility: State-owned public access with gravel ramp on east shore of lower lake; six trailer spaces
Accommodations: Park, picnicking, restroom
Shoreland zoning: General dev.
Management class: Walleye-centrarchid
Ecological type: Walleye

Bordered by Island Lake County Park

Area map page/coord: 8 / B-2,3
Watershed: Prairie-Willow
Surface area: 320 acres
Shorelength: 6.8 miles (upper & lower)
Maximum depth: 22 feet
Mean depth: NA
Secchi disk (water clarity):
6.0 feet (2007)
Water color: Brown stain
Accessibility: State-owned public access with gravel ramp on east shore of lower lake; six trailer spaces
Accommodations: Park, picnicking, restroom
Shoreland zoning: General dev.
Management class: Walleye-centrarchid
Ecological type: Centrarchid

FISH STOCKING DATA

year	species	size	# released
08	Walleye	Fry	87,000
10	Walleye	Fry	87,000
12	Walleye	Fry	87,000

NET CATCH DATA

Date: 07/26/2010

	Gill Nets		Trap Nets	
species	# per net	avg. fish weight (lbs.)	# per net	avg. fish weight (lbs.)
Black Crappie	5.5	0.23	1.6	0.25
Bluegill	0.3	0.25	10.4	0.18
Largemouth Bass	0.2	1.63	0.2	0.75
Northern Pike	2.7	2.30	0.7	2.34
Walleye	0.3	2.87	-	-

LENGTH OF SELECTED SPECIES SAMPLED FROM ALL GEAR

Number of fish caught for the following length categories (inches):

species	0-5	6-8	9-11	12-14	15-19	20-24	25-29	>30	Total
Black Bullhead	-	-	-	1	-	-	-	-	1
Black Crappie	6	37	3	-	-	-	-	-	47
Bluegill	56	39	-	-	-	-	-	-	96
Bowfin (Dogfish)	-	-	-	-	1	5	2	-	8
Brown Bullhead	-	-	12	5	-	-	-	-	17
Largemouth Bass	1	-	-	2	-	-	-	-	3
Northern Pike	-	-	1	-	4	13	3	1	22
Pumpkin. Sunfish	3	4	-	-	-	-	-	-	7
Rock Bass	1	2	-	-	-	-	-	-	3
Walleye	-	-	-	-	1	1	-	-	2
White Sucker	-	-	-	-	3	-	-	-	3
Yellow Bullhead	-	-	28	4	-	-	-	-	32
Yellow Perch	1	1	-	-	-	-	-	-	2

FISH STOCKING DATA

year	species	size	# released
08	Walleye	Fry	420,000
10	Walleye	Fry	420,000
12	Walleye	Fry	420,000

NET CATCH DATA

Date: 07/23/2007

	Gill Nets		Trap Nets	
species	# per net	avg. fish weight (lbs.)	# per net	avg. fish weight (lbs.)
Black Crappie	2.8	0.20	0.4	0.25
Bluegill	3.0	0.23	16.0	0.30
Largemouth Bass	0.3	1.23	0.2	0.23
Northern Pike	7.0	2.24	0.6	1.92
Walleye	4.8	2.04	-	-

LENGTH OF SELECTED SPECIES SAMPLED FROM ALL GEAR

Number of fish caught for the following length categories (inches):

species	0-5	6-8	9-11	12-14	15-19	20-24	25-29	>30	Total
Black Bullhead	-	-	-	6	1	-	-	-	7
Black Crappie	15	2	3	1	-	-	-	-	21
Bluegill	32	129	1	-	-	-	-	-	162
Brown Bullhead	-	-	1	8	-	-	-	-	9
Largemouth Bass	-	2	1	-	1	-	-	-	4
Northern Pike	-	-	-	1	20	17	8	1	47
Pumpkin. Sunfish	1	24	-	-	-	-	-	-	25
Rock Bass	-	2	-	-	-	-	-	-	2
Walleye	-	-	-	2	21	6	-	-	29
Yellow Bullhead	-	-	51	28	-	-	-	-	79
Yellow Perch	4	2	1	-	-	-	-	-	7

FISHING INFORMATION: Located in the town of Cromwell, the Island Lakes, Upper and Lower, are being managed as walleye and largemouth bass fisheries with secondary management species being bluegills and black crappies. The DNR has been stocking walleye fry for several years, and angling for this species is reportedly "pretty good," according to lakeshore property owners. Many fish in the 2- to 3-pound class are being caught, along with the occasional wall-hanger. Nice panfish, both bluegills and crappies, are found in the lake's weedbeds. You'll find 10-inch crappies and 8-inch bluegills out there for the taking; normal panfish techniques do well. Largemouth bass anglers do quite well here, too, and local anglers report getting good action in the 2- to 3-pound range. Panfish are hit hardest by ice anglers; jigs and wax worms or jig-and-minnow combos work well. The ample northern pike population includes some big ones, but hammer handles are the rule. Both lakes' shorelines have been substantially developed.

Upper Island Lake covers 114 acres with a maximum depth of 25 feet. During the most recent DNR survey, walleyes sampled were less abundant compared to similar Minnesota lakes. However,

lake property owners report that walleye fishing is good. The mean length for walleyes on Upper Island was 17.3 inches, which is considered large. The mean length for largemouth bass on the lake was 12.3 inches and they're considered fast growers here. Black crappies are considered abundant compared to similar lakes. The mean length is also large at 8.4 inches. The bluegill population is considered average. They are considered fast growers and have a mean length of 7.2 inches. Northern pike abundance is average and they tend to be small.

Lower Island Lake is the larger of the two lakes at 320 acres. Like Upper Island Lake, Lower Island's walleyes have a mean length of 17.2 inches, which makes for a large average, according to the latest DNR survey. Largemouth bass are fast growers on this lake with a mean size of 13.8 inches. Bluegill abundance is average and black crappies are below average in abundance. Northern pike abundance is average and the size is small like Upper Island. The yellow perch population is average, but brown and yellow bullhead populations were reported as being above average.

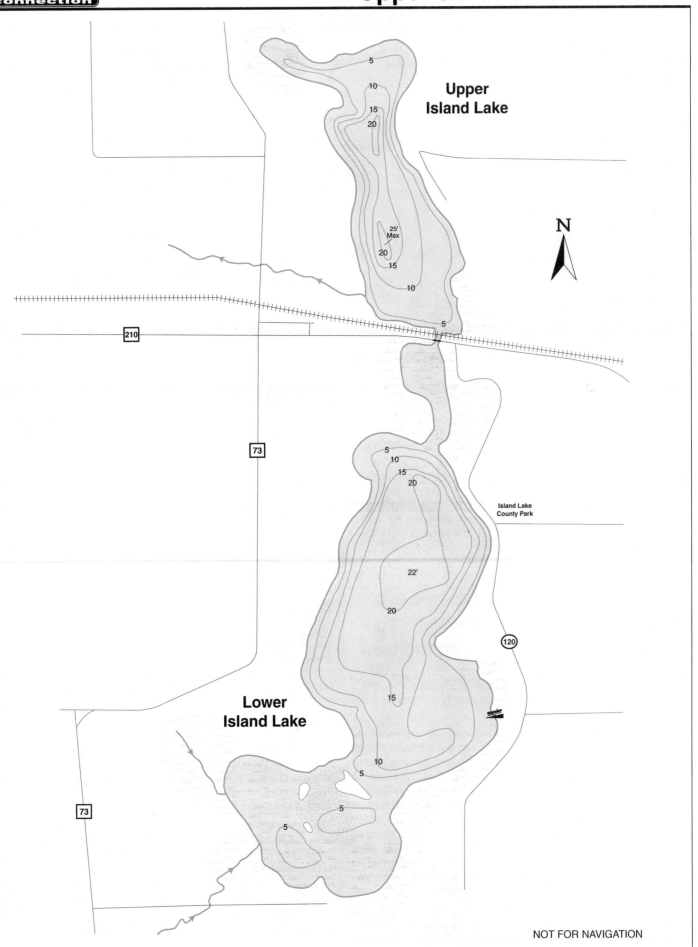

SPORTSMAN'S
connection

Upper
Island Lake

N

25'
Max

Lower
Island Lake

Island Lake
County Park

210

73

73

120

NOT FOR NAVIGATION

EAGLE LAKE

Carlton County

CROSS LAKE

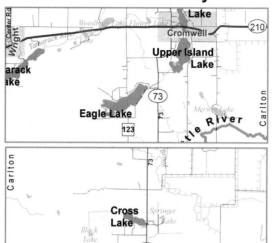

Area map page/coord: 8 / B,C-2
Watershed: Prairie-Willow
Surface area: 389 acres
Shorelength: 5.1 miles
Maximum depth: 35 feet
Mean depth: 23 feet
Secchi disk (water clarity):
9.5 feet (2008)
Water color: NA
Accessibility: State-owned public access with concrete ramp on northeast side of lake
Accommodations: Restroom
Shoreland zoning: Recreational dev.
Management class: Walleye-centrarchid
Ecological type: Centrarchid-walleye

Area map page/coord: 8 / A-2,3
Watershed: Prairie-Willow
Surface area: 104 acres
Shorelength: 2.3 miles
Maximum depth: 23 feet
Mean depth: 8 feet
Secchi disk (water clarity):
3.3 feet (2009)
Water color: Brown
Accessibility: State-owned right-of-way access with gravel ramp on east shore off Hwy. 73
Accommodations: None
Shoreland zoning: Natural envt.
Management class: Centrarchid
Ecological type: Centrarchid

NO RECORD OF STOCKING SINCE 1989

NET CATCH DATA

Date: 08/04/2008	Gill Nets		Trap Nets	
		avg. fish		avg. fish
species	# per net	weight (lbs.)	# per net	weight (lbs.)
Black Crappie	-	-	0.2	0.58
Bluegill	1.1	0.37	5.3	0.12
Northern Pike	4.0	3.45	0.9	2.67
Pumpkin. Sunfish	-	-	1.2	0.11
Rock Bass	1.0	0.38	1.4	0.26
Walleye	9.9	1.03	0.4	1.17
Yellow Perch	36.7	0.19	7.0	0.13

LENGTH OF SELECTED SPECIES SAMPLED FROM ALL GEAR
Number of fish caught for the following length categories (inches):

species	0-5	6-8	9-11	12-14	15-19	20-24	25-29	>30	Total
Black Crappie	-	1	1	-	-	-	-	-	2
Bluegill	38	18	2	-	-	-	-	-	58
Brown Bullhead	-	-	5	3	-	-	-	-	8
Northern Pike	-	-	-	-	3	28	11	2	44
Pumpkin. Sunfish	11	-	-	-	-	-	-	-	11
Rock Bass	10	11	1	-	-	-	-	-	22
Walleye	-	16	31	22	14	10	-	-	93
Yellow Bullhead	-	-	3	1	-	-	-	-	4
Yellow Perch	150	178	61	-	-	-	-	-	393

FISH STOCKING DATA

year	species	size	# released
01	Walleye	Fingerling	3,000
03	Walleye	Fingerling	4,086

NET CATCH DATA

Date: 07/27/2009	Gill Nets		Trap Nets	
		avg. fish		avg. fish
species	# per net	weight (lbs.)	# per net	weight (lbs.)
Black Crappie	1.8	0.09	1.1	0.25
Bluegill	0.8	0.06	19.0	0.07
Northern Pike	1.5	3.02	0.7	3.38
Pumpkin. Sunfish	0.2	0.13	1.6	0.07
Walleye	0.5	2.64	0.3	3.56
Yellow Perch	-	-	0.1	0.07

LENGTH OF SELECTED SPECIES SAMPLED FROM ALL GEAR
Number of fish caught for the following length categories (inches):

species	0-5	6-8	9-11	12-14	15-19	20-24	25-29	>30	Total
Black Crappie	11	7	3	-	-	-	-	-	21
Bluegill	164	12	-	-	-	-	-	-	176
Bowfin (Dogfish)	-	-	-	-	-	7	-	-	7
Northern Pike	-	-	-	-	1	8	6	-	15
Pumpkin. sunfish	15	-	-	-	-	-	-	-	15
Walleye	-	-	-	-	3	3	-	-	6
White Sucker	-	-	-	-	1	-	-	-	1
Yellow Bullhead	-	4	16	8	-	-	-	-	28
Yellow Perch	1	-	-	-	-	-	-	-	1

FISHING INFORMATION: Eagle Lake is a 389-acre lake with a maximum depth of 35 feet. The water is clear to 9.5 feet and it is loaded with lots of different species of fish.

Walleyes and yellow perch are the primary management species, according to a 2008 DNR survey. Even though the DNR no longer stocks the lake, the walleye population is thriving and is naturally reproducing. The mean walleye length of 13 inches is average among Duluth area lakes. Walleyes are above average in abundance. Yellow perch populations are thriving, with abundance being well above average. Perch have an average length of 7.2 inches, so it is easy to see why the walleye population is doing so well, since perch make up a large portion of their diet. Try using a slip bobber and bait over the submerged humps early or late in the day during the summer months. You can also troll these same areas, along with the various drop-offs, with crankbaits and spinner rigs to hook a few walleyes.

There are also decent numbers of northern pike in the lake, and the average 4-year-olds are 24.3 inches long. Bluegills are not as abundant as in other lakes, but they have a faster-than-average growth rate here. Crappies are decent, as well, with sizes falling in the average range. Eagle Lake receives a fair amount of fishing pressure in summer, but seems to hold up well.

Cross Lake is less than one-third the size of Eagle Lake, at 104 acres. Walleye fingerlings, fry and even some adults have been stocked to varying degrees over the years since 1993. However, the lake has not been stocked since 2003, when 4,086 fingerlings were introduced.

Bluegills and black crappies are the secondary species on this lake. Crappie abundance and length are average and show a slow growth rate. Bluegills are considered average in abundance, but are smaller than the norm.

Northern pike also inhabit this lake in low numbers. Size is pretty decent, though. If you catch a northern, you're likely to tie into a 23-plus incher; the average size according to the most recent DNR survey. Toss a spinnerbait, spoon or try a large minnow fished under a bobber.

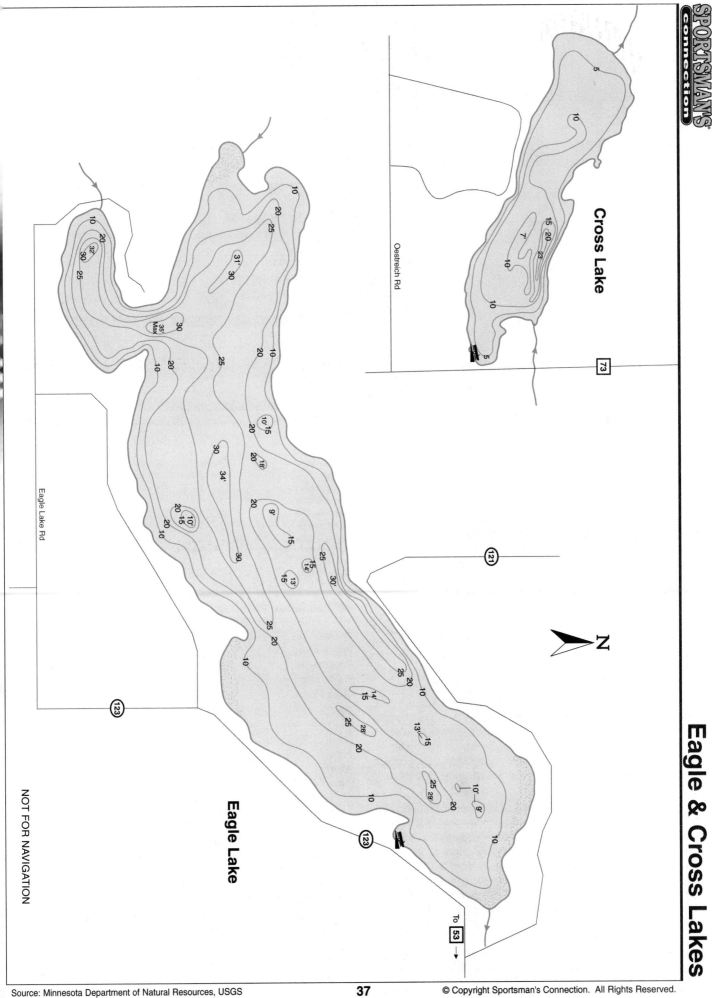

Eagle & Cross Lakes

Cross Lake

Eagle Lake

N

NOT FOR NAVIGATION

Oestreich Rd

Eagle Lake Rd

73

121

123

123

To 53

35' Max

34'

31'

Source: Minnesota Department of Natural Resources, USGS

BIG LAKE
Carlton County

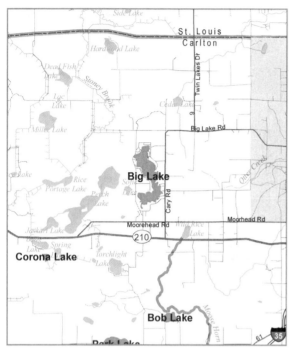

Area map pg / coord: 9 / A,B-5
Watershed: St. Louis
Secchi disk (water clarity): 12.8 ft. (2008)
Water color: Green tint

Surface area: 529 acres
Shorelength: 7.7 miles
Maximum depth: 25 feet
Mean depth: 8 feet

Accessibility: State-owned public access on northwest shore
Boat ramp: Concrete
Parking: Twenty trailer spaces
Accommodations: Dock, restroom

Shoreland zoning classification: Recreational development
Management class: Centrarchid
Ecological type: Centrarchid

FISH STOCKING DATA

year	species	size	# released
04	Walleye	Fingerling	31,904
09	Walleye	Fry	440,000
10	Walleye	Fry	440,000

NET CATCH DATA

Date: 07/28/2008

	Gill Nets		Trap Nets	
species	# per net	avg. fish weight (lbs.)	# per net	avg. fish weight (lbs.)
Black Bullhead	1.4	0.90	0.6	0.80
Black Crappie	3.0	0.25	3.4	0.11
Bluegill	2.6	0.08	22.0	0.09
Brown Bullhead	2.7	1.13	0.4	1.21
Golden Shiner	-	-	0.1	0.09
Green Sunfish	0.2	0.21	2.9	0.18
Largemouth Bass	1.6	1.45	-	-
Northern Pike	16.3	2.42	1.6	2.73
Pumpkin. Sunfish	1.4	0.05	3.1	0.10
Walleye	0.9	3.56	-	-
Yellow Perch	6.2	0.16	0.7	0.08

LENGTH OF SELECTED SPECIES SAMPLED FROM ALL GEAR

Number of fish caught for the following length categories (inches):

species	0-5	6-8	9-11	12-14	15-19	20-24	25-29	>30	Total
Black Bullhead	-	1	10	7	-	-	-	-	18
Black Crappie	26	25	6	-	-	-	-	-	58
Bluegill	195	25	-	-	-	-	-	-	221
Brown Bullhead	-	-	7	21	-	-	-	-	28
Green Sunfish	12	16	-	-	-	-	-	-	28
Largemouth Bass	-	-	2	9	3	-	-	-	14
Northern Pike	-	-	1	7	39	78	32	2	161
Pumpkin. Sunfish	33	7	-	-	-	-	-	-	40
Walleye	-	-	-	-	2	5	1	-	8
Yellow Perch	5	53	1	-	-	-	-	-	59

FISHING INFORMATION: Big Lake is a 529-acre impoundment located one mile north of Sawyer, MN. According to the DNR's 2008 survey, walleyes and largemouth bass are the primary management species, while black crappies and bluegills are secondary. The walleyes average 22.6 inches and have a fast growth rate. Largemouth bass average 12.6 inches with a slower-than-normal growth rate indicated. Black crappies and bluegills were average in abundance and also showed slow growth rates. Northern pike had numbers well above average. Walleye fingerlings were stocked for 9 years from 1989-2004, the lake only being stocked in years with surplus walleye production. Now it's primarily fry that are stocked.

Big Lake is best known as a northern pike, bass and panfish lake that is a consistent producer of smaller crappies and some big largemouth bass. While most of the sunfish are small, you can catch some pretty decent ones. Fish shorelines in early summer for good crappie action.

Northern pike can be found throughout the lake. Some 12- to 14-pound fish are taken during winter, along with the occasional 20-pounder. During the summer and fall, look for pike to hold in the shallows early and late in the day. Work a spinnerbait just under the surface or try a buzzbait over the flats where submerged vegetation is present. Of course, a large minnow fished under a bobber is always an option, especially when the fishing is slow.

Largemouth bass fishing is quite good with some 5-pound-plus fish being taken each year. The docks along the gently sloping east shore of the lake's northern lobe are reliable producers on summer evenings, as is the little heavily weeded bay opposite the public landing. Bass fishing doesn't get a lot of attention, but those who hit it do pretty well. Most of the cover in the lake consists of weed beds which is home to most of the bass. If the weeds aren't producing well for you, switch to the boat docks. Flip a jig-and-pig, tube or plastic worm into shaded areas. If you're after a big fish, try working a swim bait under a dock. If you're an early riser, try working a large surface lure right along the edges of the docks at sunrise. If a bass is present, you may not need your morning cup of coffee.

There are a few walleyes taken out of the lake, but this lake is not generally known as a good walleye producer. Even so, you can do fairly well trolling Rapalas through the narrows separating the lake's northern and southern arms. Try a slip bobber with a leech or night crawler or troll with crankbaits both early and late in the day. The sandbar which runs down the northern lobe of the lake is good for walleyes. The deeper side of the bar is better during the day.

During summer, the lake gets a lot of pleasure boat traffic, so fishing during early morning hours is your best bet. The public access has a concrete launch and plenty of parking.

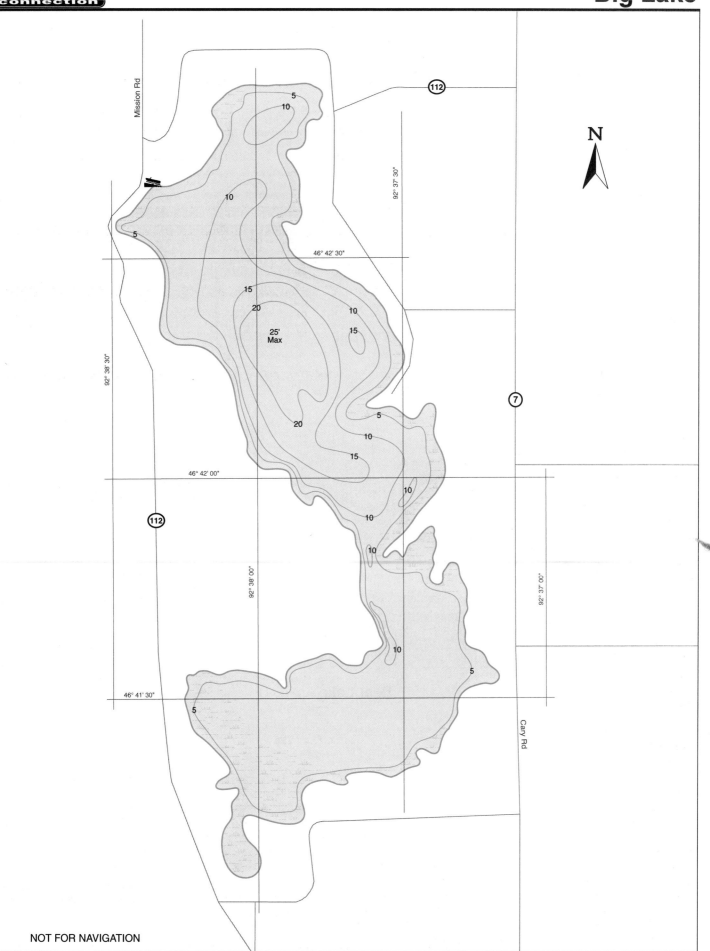

NOT FOR NAVIGATION

Source: Minnesota Department of Natural Resources, USGS

Sandy & Bear Lakes

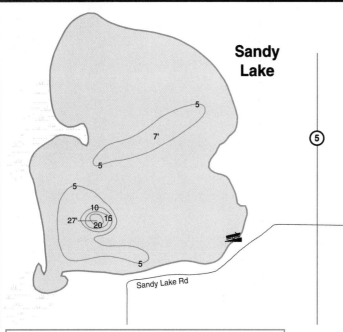

Sandy Lake

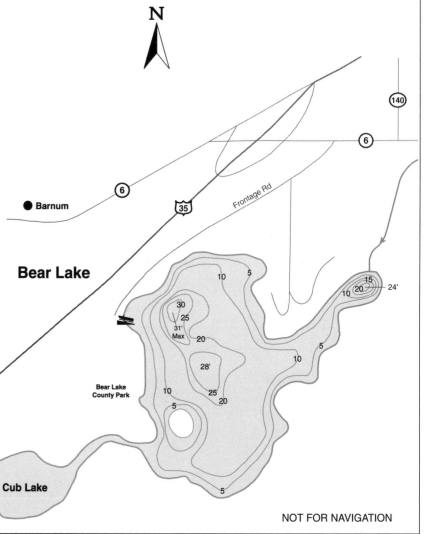

Sandy (Sand) Lake, Carlton County
Bordered by Sandy Lake County Park

Map pg/coord: 9 / D-6
Watershed: Beartrap-Nemadji
Mgmt. classification: Centrarchid

Surface area: 128 acres
Shorelength: 2.1 miles
Max depth: 27 feet
Mean depth: 3 feet
Water clarity: 4.5 ft. (2009)

Accessibility: County-owned public access with gravel ramp on southeast shore in park; six vehicle spaces, two trailer spaces
Accommodations: Park, picnicking, restroom

NO RECORD OF STOCKING

LENGTH OF SELECTED SPECIES SAMPLED FROM ALL GEAR
Survey Date: 07/13/2009   **Survey method:** gill net, trap net
Number of fish caught for the following length categories (inches):

species	0-5	6-8	9-11	12-14	15-19	20-24	25-29	>30	Total
Black Bullhead	-	-	8	-	-	-	-	-	8
Black Crappie	8	16	1	1	-	-	-	-	26
Bluegill	66	1	-	-	-	-	-	-	67
Golden Shiner	24	12	-	-	-	-	-	-	36
Northern Pike	-	-	-	1	6	-	13	10	30
Pumpkin. Sunfish	118	-	-	-	-	-	-	-	118
White Sucker	-	-	-	-	7	-	-	-	7
Yellow Bullhead	4	104	28	-	-	-	-	-	136
Yellow Perch	225	143	-	-	-	-	-	-	371

Bear Lake, Carlton County
Bordered by Bear Lake County Park

Map pg/coord: 9 / E-4,5
Watershed: Kettle
Mgmt. classification: Centrarchid

Surface area: 100 acres
Shorelength: 2.1 miles
Max depth: 31 feet
Mean depth: 11 feet
Water clarity: 6.1 ft. (2007)

Accessibility: County-owned public access with concrete ramp on west shore in park; six trailer spaces
Accommodations: Park, dock, camping, picnicking, restroom

FISH STOCKING DATA

year	species	size	# released
08	Walleye	Fingerling	2,338
10	Walleye	Fingerling	1,319
12	Walleye	Fingerling	1,689

LENGTH OF SELECTED SPECIES SAMPLED FROM ALL GEAR
Survey Date: 08/14/2007   **Survey method:** gill net, trap net
Number of fish caught for the following length categories (inches):

species	0-5	6-8	9-11	12-14	15-19	20-24	25-29	>30	Total
Black Bullhead	-	-	19	16	-	-	-	-	35
Black Crappie	40	63	4	-	-	-	-	-	109
Bluegill	69	173	-	-	-	-	-	-	247
Largemouth Bass	-	-	1	-	2	-	-	-	3
Northern Pike	-	-	1	2	11	8	2	-	26
Pumpkin. Sunfish	21	60	-	-	-	-	-	-	81
Walleye	-	-	-	2	1	-	1	-	4
White Sucker	-	-	-	8	12	2	-	-	22
Yellow Bullhead	-	-	2	5	-	-	-	-	7

Bear Lake

NOT FOR NAVIGATION

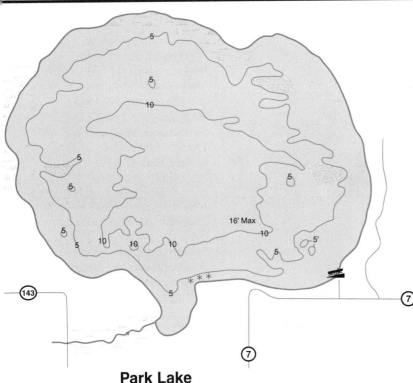

Park Lake

Park Lake, Carlton County

Map pg/coord: 9 / C-5
Watershed: Kettle
Mgmt. classification:
Centrarchid

Surface area: 376 acres
Shorelength: NA
Max depth: 16 feet
Mean depth: 6 feet
Water clarity: 9.25 ft. (2004)

Accessibility: County-owned public access with gravel ramp on southeast shore
Accommodations: None

FISH STOCKING DATA

year	species	size	# released
06	Walleye	Adult	40
08	Walleye	Fingerling	12,552
10	Walleye	Fingerling	5,627
12	Walleye	Fingerling	7,216

LENGTH OF SELECTED SPECIES SAMPLED FROM ALL GEAR
Survey Date: 08/02/2004 **Survey method:** gill net, trap net
Number of fish caught for the following length categories (inches):

species	0-5	6-8	9-11	12-14	15-19	20-24	25-29	>30	Total
Black Bullhead	-	1	46	5	-	-	-	-	52
Black Crappie	9	10	10	-	-	-	-	-	29
Bluegill	85	61	1	-	-	-	-	-	147
Brown Bullhead	-	13	39	4	-	-	-	-	56
Largemouth Bass	-	1	1	3	4	2	-	-	11
Northern Pike	-	-	1	29	67	23	9	1	130
Pumpkin. Sunfish	82	65	-	-	-	-	-	-	147
Rock Bass	-	1	-	-	-	-	-	-	1
Walleye	-	-	-	-	2	7	-	1	10
Yellow Perch	4	23	19	-	-	-	-	-	46

N

Bob Lake, Carlton County

Map pg/coord: 9 / B,C-5
Watershed: Kettle
Mgmt. classification:
Centrarchid-walleye

Surface area: 74 acres
Shorelength: 1.6 miles
Max depth: 30 feet
Mean depth: 14 feet
Water clarity: 8.2 ft. (2003)

Accessibility: Township-owned public access with earthen ramp on southwest shore
Accommodations: None

FISH STOCKING DATA

year	species	size	# released
06	Walleye	Fingerling	480
06	Walleye	Adult	17

LENGTH OF SELECTED SPECIES SAMPLED FROM ALL GEAR
Survey Date: 08/11/2003 **Survey method:** gill net, trap net
Number of fish caught for the following length categories (inches):

species	0-5	6-8	9-11	12-14	15-19	20-24	25-29	>30	Total
Black Crappie	7	4	5	-	-	-	-	-	16
Bluegill	29	27	-	-	-	-	-	-	56
Largemouth Bass	1	-	-	1	1	-	-	-	3
Northern Pike	-	-	-	3	11	5	1	2	22
Pumpkin. Sunfish	8	-	-	-	-	-	-	-	8
Walleye	-	-	-	-	1	2	-	-	3
Yellow Bullhead	-	-	3	1	-	-	-	-	4
Yellow Perch	1	1	-	-	-	-	-	-	2

Bob Lake

NOT FOR NAVIGATION

HANGING HORN LAKE   LITTLE HANGING HORN LAKE
Carlton County

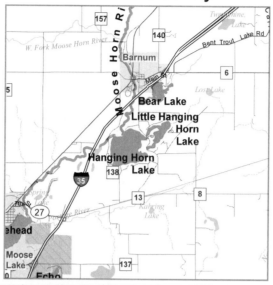

Area map page/coord: 9 / E-4
Watershed: Kettle River
Surface area: 409 acres
Shorelength: 3.8 miles
Maximum depth: 80 feet
Mean depth: 35 feet
Secchi disk (water clarity):
5.5 ft. (2010)
Accessibility: City-owned public access with concrete ramp on Moose Horn River (six trailer spaces); carry-down access off Cty. Road 13 at culvert between Hanging Horn and Little Hanging Horn lakes
Accommodations: Fishing pier, camping, picnicking, restroom
Shoreland zoning: Recreational dev.
Management class: Centrarchid
Ecological type: Centrarchid

Area map page/coord: 9 / E-4
Watershed: Kettle River
Surface area: 117 acres
Shorelength: 3.1 miles
Maximum depth: 70 feet
Mean depth: 17 feet
Secchi disk (water clarity):
13.1 ft. (2000)
Water color: Clear
Accessibility: Township-owned public access with gravel ramp on north shore; carry-down access off Cty. Road 13 at culvert between Hanging Horn and Little Hanging Horn lakes
Accommodations: Resort
Shoreland zoning: Recreational dev.
Management class: Centrarchid
Ecological type: Centrarchid

FISH STOCKING DATA

year	species	size	# released
07	Lake Trout	Yearling	4,123
09	Lake Trout	Yearling	4,082
10	Lake Trout	Yearling	4,175
11	Lake Trout	Yearling	4,682

NET CATCH DATA
Date: 07/12/2010

	Gill Nets		Trap Nets	
species	# per net	avg. fish weight (lbs.)	# per net	avg. fish weight (lbs.)
Black Crappie	-	-	3.6	0.40
Bluegill	-	-	19.3	0.13
Lake Trout	0.1	0.13	-	-
Northern Pike	0.9	3.89	0.8	1.44
Rock Bass	-	-	0.8	0.16
Smallmouth Bass	0.1	1.37	-	-
Walleye	0.5	2.87	0.4	3.05
Yellow Perch	0.1	0.09	0.3	0.16

LENGTH OF SELECTED SPECIES SAMPLED FROM ALL GEAR
Number of fish caught for the following length categories (inches):

species	0-5	6-8	9-11	12-14	15-19	20-24	25-29	>30	Total
Black Crappie	-	15	17	-	-	-	-	-	32
Bluegill	132	42	-	-	-	-	-	-	174
Burbot	-	-	-	1	-	1	-	-	2
Lake Trout	-	2	-	-	-	-	-	-	2
Northern Pike	-	-	-	2	4	8	6	1	21
Pumpkin. Sunfish	3	-	-	-	-	-	-	-	3
Rock Bass	6	1	-	-	-	-	-	-	7
Smallmouth Bass	-	-	-	1	-	-	-	-	1
Tullibee (Cisco)	-	211	480	16	-	-	-	-	707
Walleye	-	3	-	-	1	6	2	-	12
White Sucker	-	-	1	15	15	-	-	-	31
Yellow Bullhead	-	-	1	3	-	-	-	-	4
Yellow Perch	2	2	-	-	-	-	-	-	4

FISH STOCKING DATA

year	species	size	# released
01	Walleye	Fingerling	2,040

NET CATCH DATA
Date: 08/14/2000

	Gill Nets		Trap Nets	
species	# per net	avg. fish weight (lbs.)	# per net	avg. fish weight (lbs.)
Black Crappie	0.2	0.12	1.8	0.18
Bluegill	1.3	0.15	6.3	0.11
Green Sunfish	-	-	0.2	0.12
Largemouth Bass	0.5	0.27	0.1	0.81
Northern Pike	6.3	1.77	0.3	1.10
Pumpkin. Sunfish	0.2	0.28	1.2	0.11
Rock Bass	0.2	0.41	0.1	0.09
Tullibee (Cisco)	0.2	0.33	-	-
Walleye	0.5	1.04	-	-
White Sucker	2.0	1.07	0.2	0.79
Yellow Perch	-	-	0.2	0.07

LENGTH OF SELECTED SPECIES SAMPLED FROM ALL GEAR
Number of fish caught for the following length categories (inches):

species	0-5	6-8	9-11	12-14	15-19	20-24	25-29	>30	Total
Black Crappie	6	9	2	-	-	-	-	-	17
Bluegill	52	13	-	-	-	-	-	-	65
Green Sunfish	2	-	-	-	-	-	-	-	2
Largemouth Bass	1	2	1	-	-	-	-	-	4
Northern Pike	-	-	-	2	28	5	4	-	39
Pumpkin. Sunfish	11	1	-	-	-	-	-	-	12
Rock Bass	1	1	-	-	-	-	-	-	2
Tullibee (Cisco)	-	-	1	-	-	-	-	-	1
Walleye	-	-	-	2	1	-	-	-	3
Yellow Bullhead	-	-	5	-	-	-	-	-	5
Yellow Perch	2	-	-	-	-	-	-	-	2

FISHING INFORMATION: Hanging Horn Lake is a fairly deep and clear lake that has some large northern pike in it. Some fish in the 20- to 25-pound range are taken in the winter where the river flows into the lake.

Crappies caught in Hanging Horn seem to run in two size classes. The hand-size examples are numerous; 1- to 2-pound slabs are less so, but still available. Crappie fishing overall is pretty good. There are also some nice largemouth bass to be found, but not many anglers fish for them. This lake is full of structure, including many reefs and sunken islands.

The bluegill population is average compared to other Minnesota lakes of similar size. The size of the bluegills has been good with solid growth rates according to the DNR's latest survey.

Despite this abundance of habitat, walleye fishing is hit-and-miss according to local anglers. You'll find a fishing pier on the lake's northeast side.

Little Hanging Horn, connected to Hanging Horn, is a good all-around fishery, containing walleyes, northern pike, largemouth bass and crappies.

Anglers catch walleyes off the main point on the east side of the lake. Largemouth bass don't receive much attention, but those who do fish them get some nice ones. Try soft plastics fished in and around the weeds. Crappies are available in decent numbers, as are bluegills. Small minnows work well for hooking crappies. Fish a small leech or piece of crawler to hook a bluegill. Little Hanging Horn is crystal clear, which means fishing in low-light conditions, early morning, late evening, at night, or on overcast days will tend to produce the most fish for you.

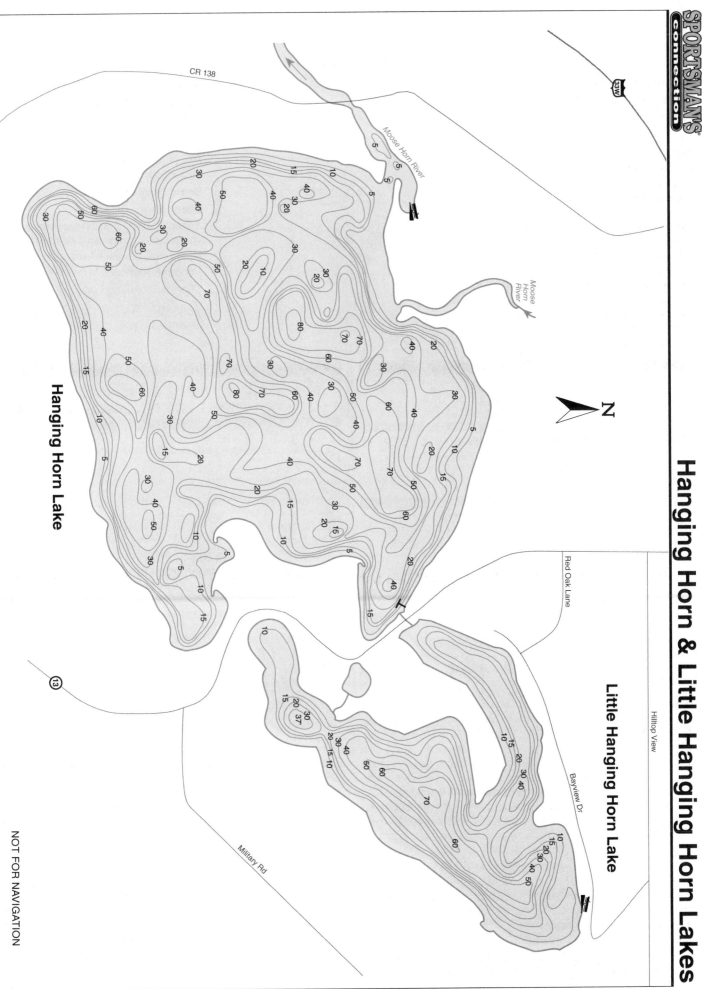

Hanging Horn Lake

Little Hanging Horn Lake

N

CR 138

Moose Horn River

Moose Horn River

33W

Red Oak Lane

Hilltop View

Bayview Dr

Military Rd

13

NOT FOR NAVIGATION

CHUB LAKE

Bordered by Chub Lake County Park

Area map page/coord: 9 / C-6
Watershed: Beartrap-Nemadji
Surface area: 313 acres
Shorelength: 3.7 miles
Maximum depth: 28 feet
Mean depth: 15 feet
Secchi disk (water clarity):
4.8 ft. (2009)
Water color: Greenish
Accessibility: State-owned public access with concrete ramp on north shore in park; eight trailer spaces
Accommodations: Park, dock, picnicking, restrooms
Shoreland zoning: Recreational dev.
Management class: Centrarchid
Ecological type: Centrarchid

Carlton County

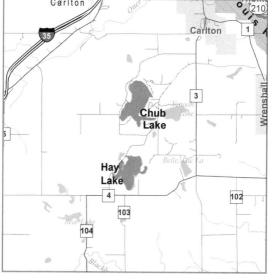

HAY LAKE

Area map page/coord: 9 / C-6
Watershed: Beartrap-Nemadji
Surface area: 215 acres
Shorelength: 5.1 miles
Maximum depth: 16 feet
Mean depth: 5 feet
Secchi disk (water clarity): 6.5 (2011)
Water color: Brown
Accessibility: County-owned public access with earthen ramp on south shore; twelve trailer spaces
Accommodations: None
Shoreland zoning: Natural envt.
Management class: Centrarchid
Ecological type: Centrarchid

FISH STOCKING DATA

year	species	size	# released
08	Walleye	Fingerling	11,264
10	Walleye	Fingerling	5,066
12	Walleye	Fingerling	6,427

NET CATCH DATA

Date: 08/31/2009

	Gill Nets		Trap Nets	
species	# per net	avg. fish weight (lbs.)	# per net	avg. fish weight (lbs.)
Black Crappie	7.8	0.21	5.0	0.22
Bluegill	1.5	0.19	9.3	0.09
Walleye	9.2	2.73	0.2	3.46

LENGTH OF SELECTED SPECIES SAMPLED FROM ALL GEAR

Number of fish caught for the following length categories (inches):

species	0-5	6-8	9-11	12-14	15-19	20-24	25-29	>30	Total
Black Bullhead	-	-	8	1	-	-	-	-	9
Black Crappie	38	47	6	-	-	-	-	-	92
Bluegill	73	20	-	-	-	-	-	-	93
Brown Bullhead	-	-	1	11	1	-	-	-	13
Golden Shiner	9	1	-	-	-	-	-	-	10
Largemouth Bass	4	6	2	3	3	-	-	-	18
Northern Pike	-	-	-	1	32	54	12	3	103
Pumpkin. Sunfish	43	9	-	-	-	-	-	-	53
Rock Bass	14	20	3	-	-	-	-	-	37
Walleye	-	-	2	-	24	31	-	-	57
White Sucker	-	-	-	3	12	-	-	-	15
Yellow Perch	1	11	-	-	-	-	-	-	12

FISH STOCKING DATA

year	species	size	# released
07	Walleye	Fry	215,000
11	Walleye	Fry	214,000

NET CATCH DATA

Date: 06/27/2011

	Gill Nets		Trap Nets	
species	# per net	avg. fish weight (lbs.)	# per net	avg. fish weight (lbs.)
Black Crappie	0.3	0.50	3.8	0.83
Bluegill	-	-	3.2	0.81
Brown Bullhead	0.2	1.81	0.9	1.78
Golden Shiner	-	-	0.1	0.04
Northern Pike	7.3	1.70	1.5	2.16
Pumpkin. Sunfish	-	-	1.1	0.57
Walleye	0.7	1.67	1.1	2.69
White Sucker	3.2	2.67	5.6	3.84
Yellow Perch	4.5	0.13	0.1	0.51

LENGTH OF SELECTED SPECIES SAMPLED FROM ALL GEAR

Number of fish caught for the following length categories (inches):

species	0-5	6-8	9-11	12-14	15-19	20-24	25-29	>30	Total
Black Crappie	1	9	26	12	-	-	-	-	48
Bluegill	3	11	24	-	-	-	-	-	38
Brown Bullhead	-	-	1	11	-	-	-	-	12
Golden Shiner	1	-	-	-	-	-	-	-	1
Northern Pike	-	-	-	4	39	11	6	2	62
Pumpkin Sunfish	1	10	2	-	-	-	-	-	13
Walleye	-	-	-	1	4	-	-	-	5
White Sucker	-	-	1	2	28	55	-	-	86
Yellow Perch	3	24	1	-	-	-	-	-	28

FISHING INFORMATION: Chub Lake is a good all-around fishery that consistently produces bluegills, crappies, largemouth bass, northern pike and walleyes. DNR stocking efforts seem to be bearing fruit, as many 1-1/2- to 2-pound walleyes are taken, along with quite a few larger ones. In fact, Chub is one of the better walleye lakes in the area. Largemouth anglers also fare well on Chub, with many fish in the 2- to 5-pound range being caught and released. In order to protect spawning bass, fishing and boating in the southeast bay is prohibited from the general opener of the fishing season until June 30. Northern pike fishing can be good with the majority of pike in the DNR survey measuring longer than 20 inches. There have been reports of pike weighing in excess of 20 pounds. The average Chub Lake northern is closer to 3 pounds. Bluegills and crappies are fished year-round. They tend to run small, but they're plentiful, and finding and catching them is not a problem. Dianne Bednarek at Outdoor Advantage, 1302 Highway 33, Cloquet, MN, 218-879-3185, says the crappie fishing can be good. The public access has a beautiful swimming beach and picnic grounds, even a ball field to keep you occupied when the fishing goes south. You can get swimmers' itch in August on this lake, though.

Hay Lake is a small, dark lake subject to occasional winterkill. The mean length of the walleyes captured during the 2011 DNR survey was 16.5 inches long. There are also some decent crappies and northerns present. Crappies are fished year around, with the best fishing occurring in early May along the muddy-bottomed west shore, near the culvert. Finding crappies becomes more difficult in summer, as they tend to head toward deeper water. Try locating schools with your depth finder during this period. One of the best weapons in a crappie angler's arsenal is a slip bobber. Since crappies move around a bit, this simple tool will allow you to quickly change depths until you zero in on their location. Try a small minnow or leech for bait. Northerns are fished throughout the season on Hay Lake. The average is an 18-incher, but some nice fish are occasionally taken along edges of weed beds. Bednarek says the water can get low on Hay Lake, so call or stop by Outdoor Advantage for current conditions.

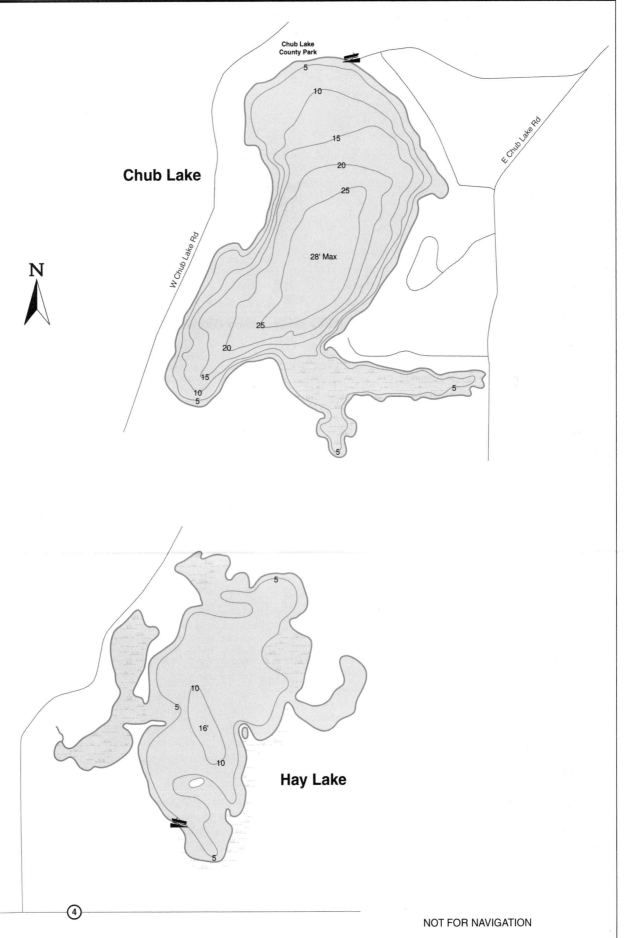

N

Chub Lake County Park

Chub Lake

W Chub Lake Rd

E Chub Lake Rd

5
10
15
20
25
28' Max
25
20
15
10
5
5
5

Hay Lake

5
10
5
16'
10
5

④

Source: Minnesota Department of Natural Resources, USGS

NORTH BIG PINE LAKE   SOUTH BIG PINE LAKE
Pine / Aitkin Counties

Area map page/coord: 11 / E-5
Watershed: Kettle
Surface area: 399 acres
Shorelength: 5.4 miles
Maximum depth: 22 feet
Mean depth: 15 feet
Secchi disk (water clarity):
4.8 ft. (2009) / Green
Accessibility: MNDOT-owned public access with earthen ramp in wayside rest area on north shore; access via navigable channel from South Big Pine
Accommodations: Picnicking, restroom
Shoreland zoning: Recreational dev.
Management class: Walleye-centrarchid
Ecological type: Centrarchid

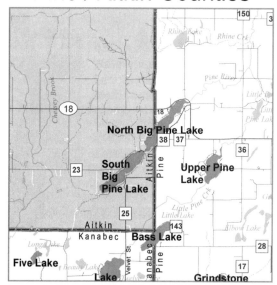

Area map page/coord: 11 / E-5
Watershed: Kettle
Surface area: 378 acres
Shorelength: 4.8 miles
Maximum depth: 28 feet
Mean depth: 15 feet
Secchi disk (water clarity): 6.9 feet (2009)
Water color: Green tint
Accessibility: State-owned public access with concrete ramp on north shore; eight trailer spaces
Accommodations: Dock, restroom
Shoreland zoning: Recreational dev.
Management class: Walleye-centrarchid
Ecological type: Centrarchid-walleye

FISH STOCKING DATA

year	species	size	# released
10	Walleye	Fingerling	6,242
11	Walleye	Fry	600,000
11	Walleye	Fingerling	6,396
12	Walleye	Fingerling	16,800

NET CATCH DATA

Date: 08/10/2009

species	Gill Nets # per net	avg. fish weight (lbs.)	Trap Nets # per net	avg. fish weight (lbs.)
Black Crappie	0.8	0.31	7.9	0.26
Bluegill	3.7	0.23	12.1	0.14
Northern Pike	4.7	5.75	0.1	3.09
Pumpkin. Sunfish	-	-	0.4	0.16
Yellow Perch	31.0	0.14	1.3	0.13

LENGTH OF SELECTED SPECIES SAMPLED FROM ALL GEAR

Number of fish caught for the following length categories (inches):

species	0-5	6-8	9-11	12-14	15-19	20-24	25-29	>30	Total
Black Bullhead	-	1	-	-	-	-	-	-	1
Black Crappie	11	53	6	-	-	-	-	-	70
Bluegill	66	62	-	-	-	-	-	-	130
Northern Pike	-	-	-	-	-	9	18	16	43
Pumpkin. Sunfish	2	1	-	-	-	-	-	-	3
White Sucker	-	-	1	-	21	2	-	-	26
Yellow Perch	25	260	-	-	-	-	-	-	289

FISH STOCKING DATA

year	species	size	# released
10	Walleye	Fry	800,000
10	Walleye	Fingerling	3,736
11	Walleye	Fry	600,000
11	Walleye	Fingerling	4,500
12	Walleye	Fry	197,351
12	Walleye	Fingerling	1,064
12	Walleye	Yearling	628

NET CATCH DATA

Date: 08/03/2009

species	Gill Nets # per net	avg. fish weight (lbs.)	Trap Nets # per net	avg. fish weight (lbs.)
Black Crappie	1.0	0.30	6.2	0.30
Bluegill	1.4	0.21	11.6	0.14
Northern Pike	2.2	5.63	0.2	4.32
Rock Bass	-	-	0.2	0.04
Walleye	1.6	2.54	0.2	0.28
White Sucker	1.8	1.32	0.3	2.76
Yellow Perch	27.7	0.14	1.3	0.14

LENGTH OF SELECTED SPECIES SAMPLED FROM ALL GEAR

Number of fish caught for the following length categories (inches):

species	0-5	6-8	9-11	12-14	15-19	20-24	25-29	>30	Total
Black Crappie	2	57	6	-	-	-	-	-	65
Bluegill	64	53	-	-	-	-	-	-	117
Northern Pike	-	-	-	-	1	5	8	8	22
Pumpkin. Sunfish	3	5	-	-	-	-	-	-	8
Rock Bass	2	-	-	-	-	-	-	-	2
Walleye	-	2	5	-	3	3	3	-	16
White Sucker	-	-	6	4	9	-	-	-	19
Yellow Perch	17	237	-	-	-	-	-	-	261

FISHING INFORMATION: Many people call these connected lakes Pine and Big Pine, while others consider the two as one lake: South Big Pine and North Big Pine. Whatever you call them, these lakes are two of the most popular in the area. The lakes are connected by a channel, which is navigable. Both boats and fish can move between the lakes easily. South Big Pine Lake has an area of 378 acres and a maximum depth of 28 feet. North Big Pine Lake is 399 acres with a maximum depth of 22 feet. The water is abundant with fish, although some of them tend to be on the smaller side, and receives a moderate amount of fishing pressure. Algae blooms are not uncommon here.

Both lakes are stocked with walleye fingerlings and fry regularly, and they do well in both basins. Walleye numbers decreased since the mid-90s, but the size structure increased. More than half of the recorded catch exceeded 15 inches. There are some excellent points with bars near mid-lake in South Big Pine that provide the sort of early season feeding areas favored by marble eyes. North Big Pine can be fished for walleyes along steep breaks off its northwest shore. The narrows between the lakes are also productive, though it's a better place to catch northerns.

Northern pike numbers are normal for this lake type. The 2009 DNR survey found quality-sized northerns, with most fish measuring over 24 inches and several over 30 inches. Northerns will move through the shallows under the bridge near the public access area looking for baitfish. Anglers like to troll or still-fish there with live bait under a bobber. There is also good northern pike fishing at weedbeds along the shores, especially near emergent vegetation.

Largemouth bass numbers are good, with numbers of fish measuring 15 inches or better present. The north end of the north basin, which is heavy with vegetation, is a good spot for early season panfish and bass. The water gets somewhat cloudy with algae blooms, so you may want to use brightly-colored lures in weedbeds as the season advances.

Yellow perch numbers have declined, but still are a main forage species. Bluegills and crappies are abundant, but fairly small in size.

North & South Big Pine Lakes

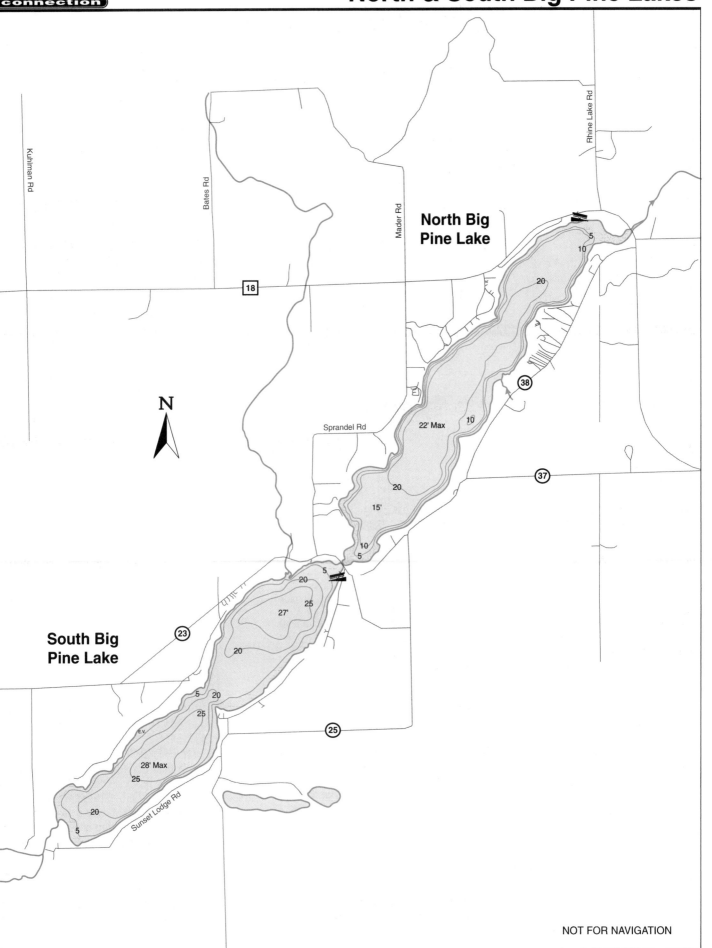

Kuhlman Rd

Bates Rd

Mader Rd

Rhine Lake Rd

North Big Pine Lake

18

N

Sprandel Rd

22' Max

38

37

15'

20

10

5

20

25

27'

20

South Big Pine Lake

23

5

20

25

25

E.V.

28' Max

25

20

5

Sunset Lodge Rd

25

NOT FOR NAVIGATION

Source: Minnesota Department of Natural Resources, USGS

STANTON (ZALESKY) LAKE   LONG LAKE
Pine County

Bordered by General C.C. Andrews State Forest

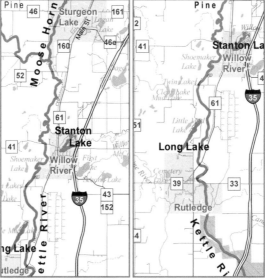

Area map page/coord: 12 / C-1

Watershed: Kettle

Surface area: 87 acres

Shorelength: NA

Maximum depth: 12 feet

Mean depth: NA

Secchi disk (water clarity): 3.3 feet (2007)

Water color: NA

Accessibility: State-owned public access with concrete ramp on northeast shore in state forest campground

Accommodations: None

Shoreland zoning: Natural envt.

Management class: Centrarchid

Ecological type: Centrarchid

Area map page/coord: 12 / C,D-1

Watershed: Kettle

Surface area: 77 acres

Shorelength: NA

Maximum depth: 24 feet

Mean depth: NA

Secchi disk (water clarity): 8.8 feet (2008)

Water color: Clear

Accessibility: State-owned public access with concrete ramp on northeast shore; two trailer spaces

Accommodations: Resort, camping

Shoreland zoning: Recreational dev.

Management class: Centrarchid

Ecological type: Centrarchid

FISH STOCKING DATA

year	species	size	# released
07	Walleye	Fry	210,000
09	Walleye	Fry	160,000
11	Walleye	Fry	160,000
12	Walleye	Fry	160,000

NET CATCH DATA

Date: 06/27/2007

	Gill Nets		Trap Nets	
species	# per net	avg. fish weight (lbs.)	# per net	avg. fish weight (lbs.)
Black Crappie	-		0.6	0.37
Bluegill	1.7	0.16	7.4	0.12
Golden Redhorse	0.7	2.32	0.1	1.26
Northern Pike	1.7	3.50	0.6	3.43
Pumpkin. Sunfish	-		0.4	0.18
Walleye	0.7	0.45	0.1	1.23
White Sucker	1.0	1.42	0.6	2.05
Yellow Perch	1.7	0.08	0.4	0.10

LENGTH OF SELECTED SPECIES SAMPLED FROM ALL GEAR

Number of fish caught for the following length categories (inches):

species	0-5	6-8	9-11	12-14	15-19	20-24	25-29	>30	Total
Black Crappie	-	2	2	-	-	-	-	-	4
Bluegill	43	14	-	-	-	-	-	-	57
Golden Redhorse	-	-	-	1	2	-	-	-	3
Largemouth Bass	-	-	-	1	1	-	-	-	2
Northern Pike	-	-	-	-	2	3	2	1	9
Pumpkin. Sunfish	1	2	-	-	-	-	-	-	3
Walleye	-	1	-	1	1	-	-	-	3
White Sucker	-	-	1	2	4	-	-	-	7
Yellow Perch	6	2	-	-	-	-	-	-	8

FISH STOCKING DATA

year	species	size	# released
07	Walleye	Fingerling	1,387
09	Walleye	Fingerling	720

NET CATCH DATA

Date: 07/28/2008

	Gill Nets		Trap Nets	
species	# per net	avg. fish weight (lbs.)	# per net	avg. fish weight (lbs.)
Black Crappie	0.3	0.24	0.5	0.15
Bluegill	8.3	0.14	9.4	0.13
Brown Bullhead	0.3	.88	3.5	0.75
Green Sunfish	-	-	0.1	0.03
Hybrid Sunfish	-	-	1.0	.28
Northern Pike	2.7	3.02	0.3	1.38
Pumpkin. Sunfish	-	-	2.3	0.17
White Sucker	0.7	2.57	-	-

LENGTH OF SELECTED SPECIES SAMPLED FROM ALL GEAR

Number of fish caught for the following length categories (inches):

species	0-5	6-8	9-11	12-14	15-19	20-24	25-29	>30	Total
Black Crappie	1	4	-	-	-	-	-	-	5
Bluegill	44	56	-	-	-	-	-	-	100
Brown Bullhead	0	4	18	5	-	-	-	-	29
Green Sunfish	1	-	-	-	-	-	-	-	1
Hybrid Sunfish	2	6	-	-	-	-	-	-	8
Northern Pike	-	-	-	-	3	5	1	1	10
Pumpkin. Sunfish	12	6	-	-	-	-	-	-	18
White Sucker	0	0	0	1	1	0	0	0	2

FISHING INFORMATION: Overshadowed by the bigger, more popular lakes like Sturgeon, Island and Sand to its north, little **Stanton Lake** near the town of Willow River, is largely ignored by all but a few locals and visitors to the small campground located on the lake's southeast lobe. Willow River flows in and out of the lake, and this helps to sustain oxygen levels and prevent winterkill. In this shallow, 87-acre body of water, some decent bluegills and crappies are caught around the numerous weedbeds. There are also fishable populations of northern pike and walleyes, although their numbers are on the decline in recent years.

Walleye fry have been stocked in an attempt to bolster numbers. Northern pike, crappies and yellow perch numbers were below average for the lake class. Bluegills are in the normal range.

Largemouth bass hold the bragging rights on this lake. Bass search for cover from the summer heat, so look for them in weedbeds and in other shady areas on the lake.

Public access with a concrete boat ramp is located in the state forest campground and can be reached from the town of Willow River.

Long Lake, north of Rutledge, is a 77-acre lake with an abundance of aquatic plants, which grow down to 10 feet deep. This is a small, fairly heavily developed lake that sustains a bass, panfish, and northern pike fishery. Crappies receive much of the attention from residents and locals, with some in the 1/2-pound range being caught. The 2008 DNR survey showed that crappies, bass, pike, bluegills and yellow perch were all within the normal range for abundance and that they were reproducing well.

Long Lake's state-owned access with concrete boat ramp is located on the northeast end. The access was constructed in 1996, courtesy of Moose Lake Trail & Waterways.

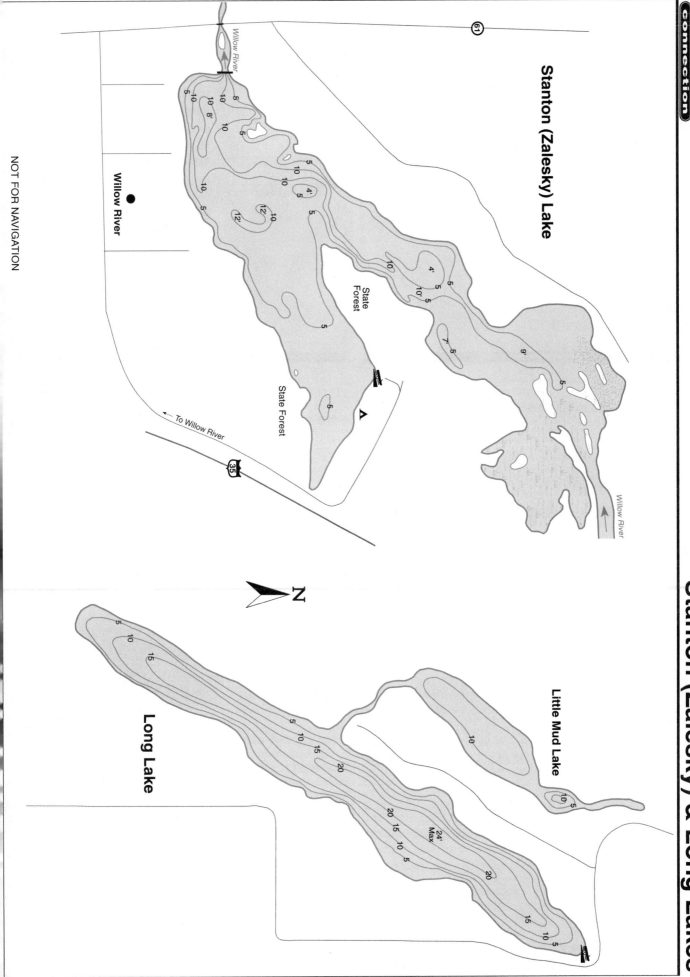

Stanton (Zalesky) Lake

Willow River

Willow River

61

NOT FOR NAVIGATION

Willow River

State
Forest

State Forest

← To Willow River

35

N

Little Mud Lake

10

5

5

10

10

5

Long Lake

5
10
15

5
10
15
20

20
15
24'
Max
10
5

20

15
10
5

5
10

Stanton (Zalesky) & Long Lakes

FIVE (BLAND) LAKE   UPPER PINE LAKE

Bordered by Lake Five Wildlife Mgmt. Area **Kanabec / Pine Counties**

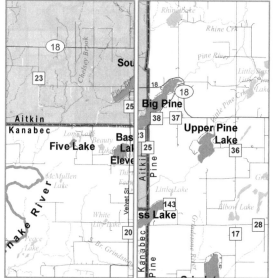

Area map page/coord: 15 / A-4
Watershed: Kettle
Surface area: 51 acres
Shorelength: NA
Maximum depth: 32 feet
Mean depth: NA
Secchi disk (water clarity): 9.5 feet (2011)
Water color: Clear
Accessibility: State-owned public access with earthen ramp on southeast shore
Accommodations: None
Shoreland zoning: Natural envt.
Management class: Centrarchid
Ecological type: Centrarchid

Area map page/coord: 11 / E-5
Watershed: Kettle
Surface area: 233 acres
Shorelength: 3.3 miles
Maximum depth: 15 feet
Mean depth: 9 feet
Secchi disk (water clarity): 4.0 feet (2008)
Water color: NA
Accessibility: State-owned public access with concrete ramp on north shore; fifteen trailer spaces
Accommodations: Dock
Shoreland zoning: Recreational dev.
Management class: Centrarchid
Ecological type: Centrarchid

FISH STOCKING DATA

year	species	size	# released
07	Walleye	Fingerling	1,085
09	Walleye	Fingerling	315

NET CATCH DATA

Date: 06/15/2011

	Gill Nets		Trap Nets	
species	# per net	avg. fish weight (lbs.)	# per net	avg. fish weight (lbs.)
Black Crappie	-	-	1.4	0.33
Bluegill	0.3	0.24	41.6	0.14
Largemouth Bass	0.7	2.78	0.1	0.09
Northern Pike	4.3	2.48	0.2	1.61
Yellow Perch	3.7	0.11	0.9	0.13

LENGTH OF SELECTED SPECIES SAMPLED FROM ALL GEAR

Number of fish caught for the following length categories (inches):

species	0-5	6-8	9-11	12-14	15-19	20-24	25-29	>30	Total
Black Crappie	1	9	1	1	-	-	-	-	12
Bluegill	239	130	1	-	-	-	-	-	375
Largemouth Bass	-	1	-	-	2	-	-	-	3
Northern Pike	-	-	-	1	-	11	3	-	15
Yellow Perch	2	16	-	-	-	-	-	-	18

FISH STOCKING DATA

year	species	size	# released
10	Walleye	Fry	250,000
11	Walleye	Fry	250,000
12	Walleye	Fry	300,000

NET CATCH DATA

Date: 07/14/2008

	Gill Nets		Trap Nets	
species	# per net	avg. fish weight (lbs.)	# per net	avg. fish weight (lbs.)
Black Bullhead	0.3	0.64	0.2	0.39
Black Crappie	2.0	0.12	3.78	0.25
Bluegill	-	-	15.3	0.19
Brown Bullhead	0.3	0.56	4.3	0.70
Largemouth Bass	-	-	0.1	0.18
Northern Pike	1.3	1.30	4.2	1.43
Pumpkinseed	0.2	0.02	5.9	0.27
Walleye	0.2	3.75	-	-
White Sucker	2.0	1.70	0.3	2.34
Yellow Perch	-	-	0.2	0.07

LENGTH OF SELECTED SPECIES SAMPLED FROM ALL GEAR

Number of fish caught for the following length categories (inches):

species	0-5	6-8	9-11	12-14	15-19	20-24	25-29	>30	Total
Black Bullhead	-	1	3	-	-	-	-	-	4
Black Crappie	6	32	8	-	-	-	-	-	46
Bluegill	62	76	-	-	-	-	-	-	138
Brown Bullhead	-	3	37	1	-	-	-	-	41
Largemouth Bass	-	1	-	-	-	-	-	-	1
Northern Pike	-	-	2	4	18	11	1	-	37
Pumpkin. Sunfish	21	29	-	-	-	-	-	-	54
Walleye	-	-	-	-	1	-	-	-	1
White Sucker	-	-	2	5	6	-	-	-	15
Yellow Perch	1	1	-	-	-	-	-	-	2

FISHING INFORMATION: Lake Five, also known as Bland Lake, is a good bass lake. There are pretty good numbers of 2- and 3-pound fish, along with some larger fish available. The average bass, according to DNR sampling, is 12.6 inches long weighing 1.2 pounds. Spinnerbaits, soft plastics and jerkbaits are favorite lures among those who regularly fish Lake Five. Northern pike are also fairly abundant with normal sampling numbers. The average pike on Lake Five weighs 3.1 pounds.

Bluegills are very plentiful and can be found almost anywhere near vegetation. They're not giants, ranging from 3.1- to 7.3-inches long. Their abundance makes this lake a good choice when taking the kids fishing. In fact, this is a good all-around lake to get a little relaxation, with little development and limited fishing pressure. Lake Five can be accessed from its south shore.

Upper Pine Lake is regarded as a good largemouth bass fishery by local anglers. The most recent DNR survey showed the average bass to be 12 inches long and weigh a pound. Bass weighing in excess of 5 pounds are occasionally caught. Weedbeds are where you want to fish for them. The east shoreline has a well-defined, heavy weedline that holds some good largemouths. Spinnerbaits take their share of fish there. Of course, Texas-rigged soft plastics will be your best option under a variety of conditions. Stick with classics like a tube, lizard or worm. Don't forget to bring along a good supply of Senkos, too.

Northern pike also roam the lake and range from the common hammer-handle size up to 12 pounds. The last DNR gill net survey showed pike to average 2.06 pounds. Spear fishermen take their share of larger northern pike.

Walleyes aren't monsters here, but you can catch them. Most of the walleyes will measure between 12 and 19 inches long. Drift a leech or nightcrawler under a slip bobber along deeper weed edges during early morning and evening to find walleyes in summer months.

Bluegill and black crappie numbers aren't high, but their size is acceptable, according to the DNR. The majority of the bluegill and crappies sampled measured between 6 and 8 inches long. Stick with minnows to catch the most crappies. Try pieces of nightcrawler, small leeches or wax worms to catch bluegills. Upper Pine's public access is on the north shore.

Five (Bland) & Upper Pine Lakes

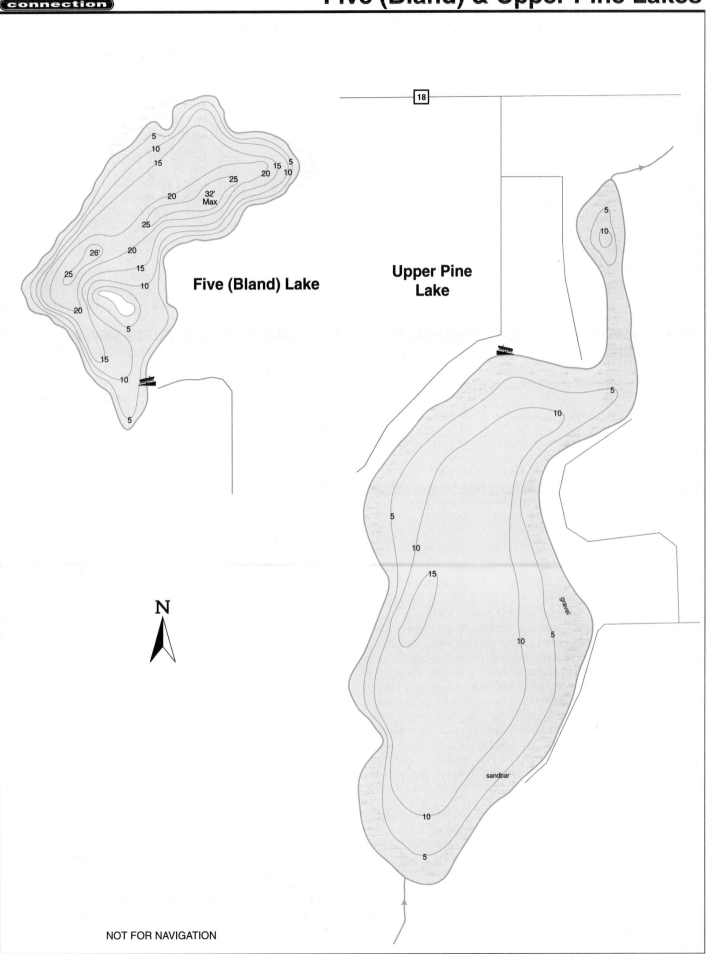

Five (Bland) Lake

5
10
15
20
25
15
5
10
32'
Max
20
25
26'
20
25
15
10
5
20
15
10
5

Upper Pine Lake

18

5
10
5
10
5
15
5
gravel
10
5
10
sandbar
10
5

N

NOT FOR NAVIGATION

Source: Minnesota Department of Natural Resources, USGS

MOOSEHEAD LAKE

Bordered by Moose Lake State Park

Area map page/coord: 12 / A-1,2

Watershed: Kettle

Surface area: 279 acres

Shorelength: 1.2 miles

Maximum depth: 18 feet

Mean depth: 12 feet

Secchi disk (water clarity): 3.1 feet (2006)

Water color: Brownish

Accessibility: City-owned public access with concrete ramp on west shore in park; seven trailer spaces

Accommodations: Fishing pier, dock

Shoreland zoning: General dev.

Management class: Centrarchid

Ecological type: Centrarchid

Carlton County

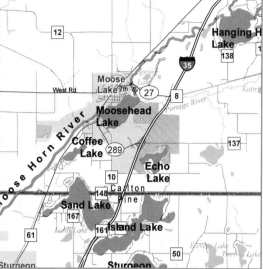

ECHO LAKE

Bordered by Moose Lake State Park

Area map page/coord: 12 / A-2

Watershed: Kettle

Surface area: 104 acres

Shorelength: 2.7 miles

Maximum depth: 47 feet

Mean depth: 20 feet

Secchi disk (water clarity): 10 feet (2011)

Water color: Clear

Accessibility: State-owned public access with concrete ramp on northeast bay in state park; fifteen trailer spaces

Accommodations: Park, dock, restroom

Shoreland zoning: Natural envt.

Management class: Centrarchid

Ecological type: Centrarchid

NO RECORD OF STOCKING

NET CATCH DATA

Date: 06/12/2006

species	Gill Nets # per net	avg. fish weight (lbs.)	Trap Nets # per net	avg. fish weight (lbs.)
Black Crappie	1.0	0.50	1.7	0.56
Bluegill	-	-	5.1	0.32
Northern Pike	9.0	1.19	0.8	1.18
Pumpkin. Sunfish	0.3	0.21	0.3	0.23
Rock Bass	0.3	0.07	0.6	0.19
Walleye	3.3	1.02	-	-
Yellow Bullhead	-	-	0.2	0.69
Yellow Perch	7.0	0.15	0.1	0.13

LENGTH OF SELECTED SPECIES SAMPLED FROM ALL GEAR

Number of fish caught for the following length categories (inches):

species	0-5	6-8	9-11	12-14	15-19	20-24	25-29	>30	Total
Black Crappie	3	-	23	-	-	-	-	-	26
Bluegill	12	48	1	-	-	-	-	-	61
Northern Pike	-	-	3	11	36	13	-	-	63
Pumpkin. Sunfish	3	3	-	-	-	-	-	-	6
Rock Bass	7	2	-	-	-	-	-	-	9
Walleye	-	2	-	12	5	1	-	-	20
Yellow Bullhead	-	1	1	-	-	-	-	-	2
Yellow Perch	9	34	-	-	-	-	-	-	43

NO RECORD OF STOCKING

NET CATCH DATA

Date: 08/22/2011

species	Gill Nets # per net	avg. fish weight (lbs.)	Trap Nets # per net	avg. fish weight (lbs.)
Black Crappie	0.5	0.28	1.0	0.23
Bluegill	5.0	0.19	3.7	0.13
Golden Shiner	-	-	0.2	0.09
Largemouth Bass	0.2	1.63	0.1	0.99
Northern Pike	5.5	2.03	0.3	2.05
Pumpkin. Sunfish	-	-	0.3	0.03
Yellow Bullhead	0.2	1.37	-	-

LENGTH OF SELECTED SPECIES SAMPLED FROM ALL GEAR

Number of fish caught for the following length categories (inches):

species	0-5	6-8	9-11	12-14	15-19	20-24	25-29	>30	Total
Black Crappie	4	5	3	-	-	-	-	-	12
Bluegill	40	23	-	-	-	-	-	-	63
Golden Shiner	-	1	-	-	-	-	-	-	1
Largemouth Bass	-	-	2	-	-	-	-	-	2
Northern Pike	-	-	-	-	14	19	3	-	36
Pumpkin. Sunfish	3	-	-	-	-	-	-	-	3
Yellow Perch	-	-	-	1	-	-	-	-	1

FISHING INFORMATION: Moosehead Lake is part of the Kettle River flowage, which provides a diverse fishery. Walleyes are primarily migratory, although some live and evidently reproduce in the lake. Local anglers say walleyes in this lake are excellent in both numbers and size, with some real lunkers being caught on occasion. Anglers have good success by jigging or Lindy-rigging a fathead minnow in the current around the inlet, especially in spring and fall. Walleyes are also taken at the fishing pier on the southwest shore, primarily in late evening. Try trolling small spinner rigs above weeds. Place a whole or half crawler on your spinner rig and cover water until you find an active walleye or two. You can then continue to troll or set up shop with a slip bobber and jumbo leech or crawler. Crappies are nice-sized, but tough to find. Try a fathead minnow fished with little or no weight early in the year or under a slip bobber on outside weedlines during summer. Lots of small to medium-size bluegills are also caught. Bluegill anglers will catch fish using a bobber and a chunk of crawler. Largemouth bass are fairly common. Soft plastics will catch plenty of bass here. Since the lake is shallow with a maximum depth of only 18 feet, you'll need to focus your efforts in the shallows and on shallow-water presentations. Lots of bass will hold in thick weeds. You can either fish right in dense weeds with a pegged Texas-rigged soft plastic or you can try outside weed edges where you can find sparse clumps of weeds closer to

drop-offs. Fish the outside area with spinnerbaits, topwater lures or a plastic worm. If weeds aren't too thick when you're out, try fishing deep on occasion with a crankbait like a Fat-Free Shad or a Rapala DT 16. Occasionally, a big sturgeon is hooked.

Echo Lake provides anglers with pretty solid action for largemouth bass. Word is that this lake has good numbers of 1- to 2-pound largemouths, along with a few in the 5-pound range. During the most recent DNR survey, the bass population appeared to be average to above average with a mean length of 12.9 inches. Like most natural lakes, soft-plastic lures rule here. Green pumpkin, black, watermelon or any similarly colored tube, worm, lizard or creature bait can attract attention from bass. Fish various weedy coves to find bass early. Move to outside weed edges as the weather heats up during summer. In early fall, cast shoreline cover with a buzzbait both early and late in the day. Dianne Bednarek at Outdoor Advantage, 1302 Highway 33, Cloquet, MN, 218-879-3185, reports lots of anglers head to Echo in search of panfish, especially in spring and winter. Bluegill abundance was below average for lakes in the area, but the mean length was average at 5.8 inches long. Both crappies and yellow perch abundance were below average for lakes in the area. Fish for bluegills around weeds with crawler chunks. Try for crappies on outside weed edges using small minnows or leeches. Northerns are fairly abundant with a few even approaching 30 inches, with the mean length being 21.7 inches long. Cast spinnerbaits, spoons, or jerkbaits to attract some attention.

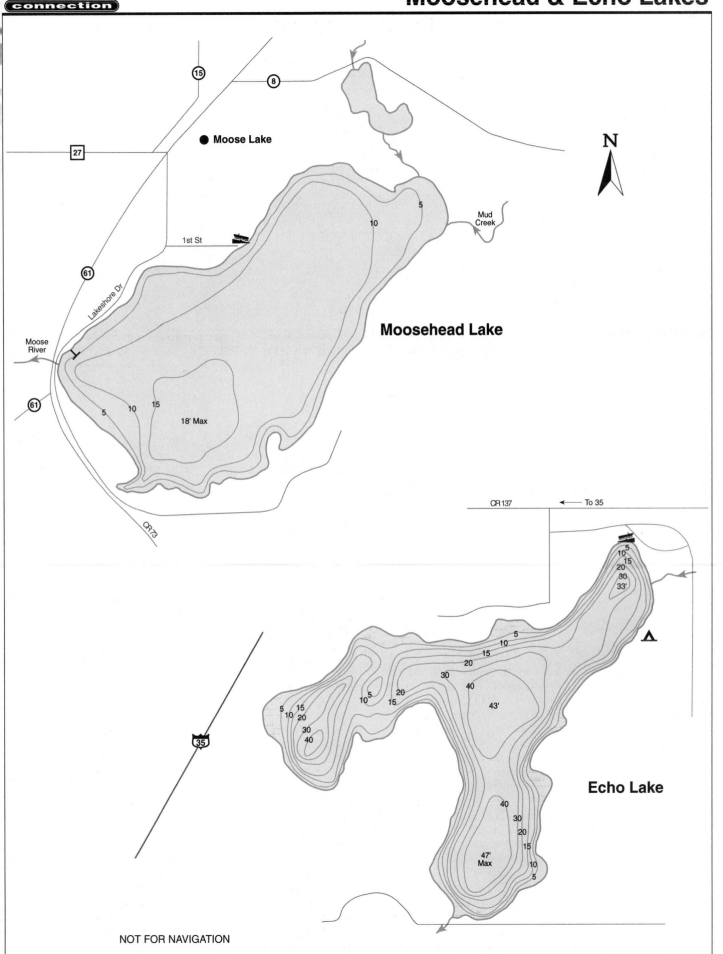

Moosehead Lake

Moose Lake

Mud Creek

1st St

Lakeshore Dr

Moose River

CR 73

5
10
15
18' Max

Echo Lake

CR 137   To 35

5
10
15
20
30
33'

5
10
15
20
30
40

5
10
15
20
43'

5
10
15
20
30
40

40
30
20
15
10
5
47' Max

NOT FOR NAVIGATION

Coffee Lake

Carlton County

Map page / coord: 12 A-1

Nearest town: Moose Lake
Surface water area: 68 acres
Max depth: 53 feet
Secchi disc: 11.0 feet (1992)
Accessibility: Carry-down access from Hwy. 61 to north-west shore near outlet
Accommodations: None

NO RECORD OF STOCKING

LENGTH OF SELECTED SPECIES SAMPLED FROM ALL GEAR
Survey Date: 08/13/1992   **Survey method:** gill net, trap net
Number of fish caught for the following length categories (inches):

species	0-5	6-8	9-11	12-14	15-19	20-24	25-29	>30	Total
Black Bullhead	-	5	13	-	-	-	-	-	18
Black Crappie	-	2	11	-	-	-	-	-	13
Bluegill	51	76	-	-	-	-	-	-	127
Brown Bullhead	-	-	1	-	-	-	-	-	1
Largemouth Bass	-	2	1	-	-	-	-	-	3
Northern Pike	-	-	1	4	14	2	3	-	24
Pumpkin. Sunfish	6	2	-	-	-	-	-	-	8
Rock Bass	1	2	-	-	-	-	-	-	3
Yellow Bullhead	-	11	14	-	-	-	-	-	25
Yellow Perch	-	1	-	-	-	-	-	-	1

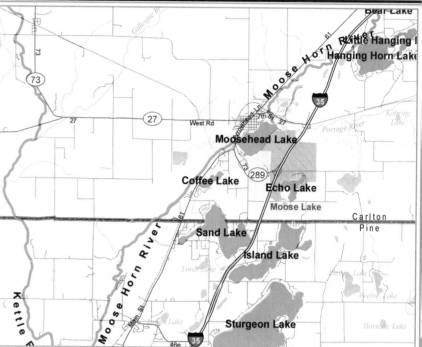

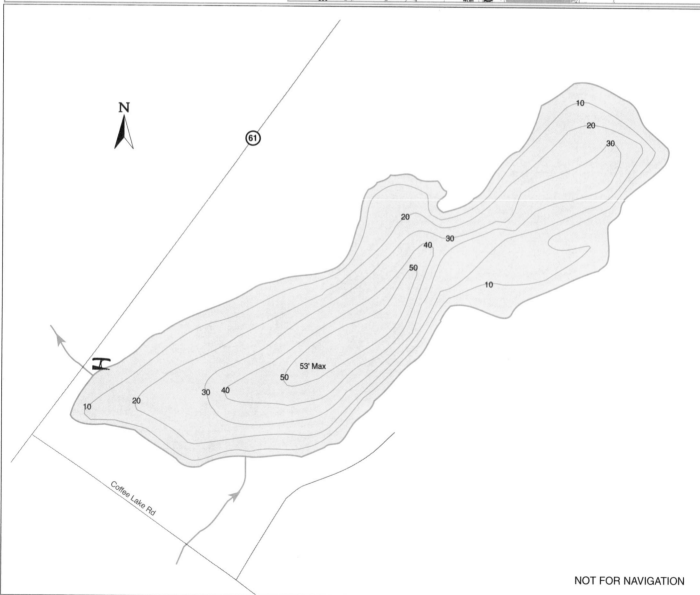

NOT FOR NAVIGATION

Source: Minnesota Department of Natural Resources, USGS

Corona Lake

Carlton County

Map page / coord: 9 / B-4

Nearest town: Carlton
Surface water area: 27 acres
Max depth: 30 feet
Secchi disc: 8.0 feet (2007)
Accessibility: Carry-down access to north side of lake
Accommodations: None

FISH STOCKING DATA

year	species	size	# released
07	Rainbow Trout	Yearling	2,496
08	Rainbow Trout	Yearling	2,500
09	Rainbow Trout	Yearling	2,749
10	Rainbow Trout	Yearling	1,876
11	Rainbow Trout	Yearling	2,524
12	Rainbow Trout	Yearling	2,500

LENGTH OF SELECTED SPECIES SAMPLED FROM ALL GEAR

Survey Date: 10/09/2007   **Survey method:** gill net, trap net

Number of fish caught for the following length categories (inches):

species	0-5	6-8	9-11	12-14	15-19	20-24	25-29	>30	Total
Brown Bullhead	33	66	3	1	-	-	-	-	110
Golden Shiner	3	-	-	-	-	-	-	-	3
Rainbow Trout	-	9	33	2	-	-	-	-	44

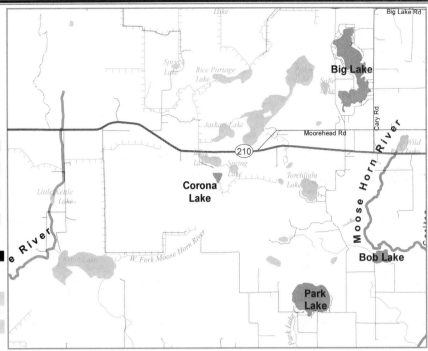

Fishing Information: Corona Lake is accesible by a .2-mile-long footpath located at the end of Long Lake Road. Managed as a put-and-take rainbow trout fishery, Corona is stocked annually with yearling rainbow trout averaging 7 to 9 inches. The lake also contains low numbers of golden shiners and a large quantity of brown bullheads.

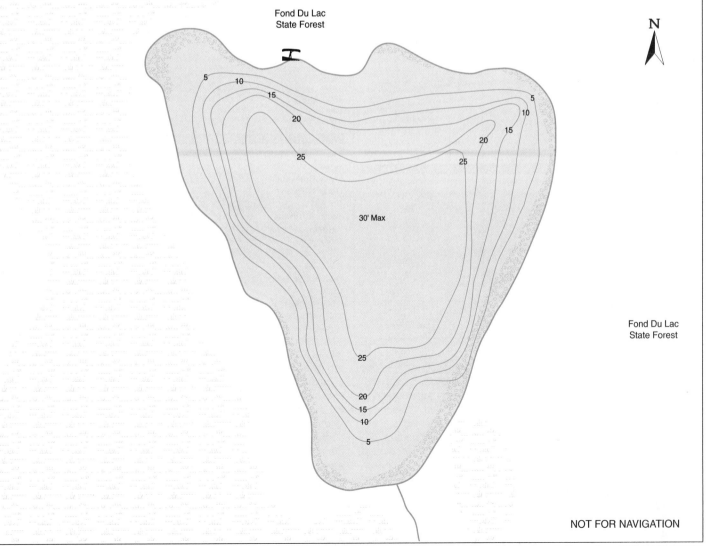

NOT FOR NAVIGATION

SAND LAKE
ISLAND LAKE
Pine County

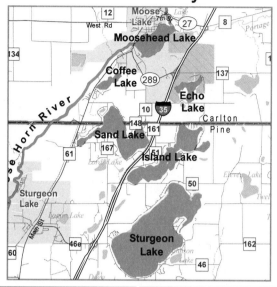

Area map page/coord: 12 / A,B-1,2
Watershed: Kettle
Surface area: 516 acres
Shorelength: 6.9 miles
Maximum depth: 47 feet
Mean depth: 18 feet
Secchi disk (water clarity): 9.7 feet (2007)
Water color: Clear
Accessibility: State-owned public access with concrete ramp on northwest shore; eight trailer spaces
Accommodations: Dock, resort, restroom
Shoreland zoning: Recreational dev.
Management class: Walleye-centrarchid
Ecological type: Centrarchid-walleye

Area map page/coord: 12 / A,B-1,2
Watershed: Kettle
Surface area: 536 acres
Shorelength: 6.3 miles
Maximum depth: 42 feet
Mean depth: 15 feet
Secchi disk (water clarity): 6.0 feet (2009)
Water color: Clear
Accessibility: State-owned public access with concrete ramp on north shore; fifteen trailer spaces
Accommodations: Dock, restroom
Shoreland zoning: Recreational development
Management class: Walleye-centrarchid
Ecological type: Centrarchid-walleye

FISH STOCKING DATA

year	species	size	# released
09	Walleye	Fingerling	5,601
10	Walleye	Fingerling	1,620
11	Walleye	Fingerling	4,325
12	Walleye	Fingerling	1,680
12	Walleye	Yearling	580

NET CATCH DATA
Date: 07/23/2007

	Gill Nets		Trap Nets	
species	# per net	avg. fish weight (lbs.)	# per net	avg. fish weight (lbs.)
Black Crappie	0.7	0.31	0.8	0.33
Bluegill	13.6	0.20	11.4	0.17
Brown Bullhead	0.6	0.65	1.3	0.64
Hybrid Sunfish	-	-	0.3	0.22
Largemouth Bass	1.3	0.54	1.1	1.00
Northern Pike	11.4	2.06	1.6	0.95
Pumpkin. Sunfish	0.7	0.24	3.0	0.23
Rock Bass	0.1	0.17	0.4	0.10
Walleye	1.0	2.79	-	-
Yellow Bullhead	2.9	0.65	1.6	0.54
Yellow Perch	-	-	0.1	0.09

LENGTH OF SELECTED SPECIES SAMPLED FROM ALL GEAR
Number of fish caught for the following length categories (inches):

species	0-5	6-8	9-11	12-14	15-19	20-24	25-29	>30	Total
Black Crappie	2	8	2	-	-	-	-	-	12
Bluegill	89	117	-	-	-	-	-	-	213
Brown Bullhead	-	-	13	2	-	-	-	-	15
Hybrid Sunfish	1	1	-	-	-	-	-	-	2
Largemouth Bass	1	10	6	2	2	-	-	-	21
Northern Pike	-	-	3	11	42	47	11	2	116
Pumpkin. Sunfish	9	21	-	-	-	-	-	-	30
Rock Bass	3	1	-	-	-	-	-	-	4
Walleye	-	-	-	1	4	4	-	-	9
Yellow Bullhead	1	4	33	1	-	-	-	-	39
Yellow Perch	1	-	-	-	-	-	-	-	1

FISH STOCKING DATA

year	species	size	# released
10	Walleye	Fingerling	6,015
11	Muskellunge	Fingerling	400
11	Walleye	Fingerling	4,756
12	Muskellunge	Fingerling	400
12	Walleye	Fingerling	11,872

NET CATCH DATA
Date: 07/27/2009

	Gill Nets		Trap Nets	
species	# per net	avg. fish weight (lbs.)	# per net	avg. fish weight (lbs.)
Black Crappie	0.2	0.38	0.9	0.31
Bluegill	16.0	0.17	24.2	0.10
Largemouth Bass	0.6	0.61	0.7	0.15
Muskellunge	0.1	26.50	-	-
Northern Pike	5.1	3.23	0.8	0.99
Rock Bass	-	-	1.1	0.17
Walleye	2.2	2.28	0.1	0.13
Yellow Perch	25.7	0.18	0.7	0.13

LENGTH OF SELECTED SPECIES SAMPLED FROM ALL GEAR
Number of fish caught for the following length categories (inches):

species	0-5	6-8	9-11	12-14	15-19	20-24	25-29	>30	Total
Black Bullhead	-	2	-	-	-	-	-	-	2
Black Crappie	1	6	3	-	-	-	-	-	10
Bluegill	237	118	-	-	-	-	-	-	362
Brown Bullhead	-	8	9	-	-	-	-	-	17
Largemouth Bass	2	5	3	-	-	-	-	-	11
Muskellunge	-	-	-	-	-	-	-	1	1
Northern Pike	-	-	1	1	19	18	8	6	53
Pumpkin. Sunfish	37	2	-	-	-	-	-	-	41
Rock Bass	4	6	-	-	-	-	-	-	10
Walleye	-	1	5	4	6	2	3	-	21
White Sucker	-	-	1	-	-	1	-	-	2
Yellow Bullhead	-	-	2	-	-	-	-	-	2
Yellow Perch	30	194	4	-	-	-	-	-	237

FISHING INFORMATION: Sand and Island Lakes, located south of Moose Lake, are passed by thousands of motorists daily along Interstate 35. **Sand Lake** is regarded as one of the better largemouth bass lakes in the area. Locals say 2- and 3-pounders are fairly common, and some 6-pound-plus trophies are also hooked. Jig-and-pig combos are great for taking the biggest bass. Crappie fishing is good, too, especially on spring evenings, when 1/2- to 1-pounders are caught. Walleye action can be tough. Try the sunken island located in the east bay and the points just northwest of there for them. Northern pike are fairly plentiful and of quality size. Try the weed edges. Island Lake has a large quantity of panfish according to a 2007 DNR survey, but they are smaller than average. This might be a good lake for teaching panfish techniques to the young 'uns, but not the best for filling your frying pan.

Island Lake holds walleyes, nice muskies, largemouth bass, northern pike, crappies and sunfish. Each of these species gets its share of attention; this helps keep everybody happy and fish populations stable. Walleyes can be found around shoreline drop-offs and near the sunken island in the southeast section of the lake. Average size is about a pound. Muskies up to 50 inches or more coexist with northerns here, and both species have reached trophy size. Work the weedbeds, especially the one which parallels County Road 51, with large bucktails and jerkbaits in chartreuse or black, and you may get not only a muskie, but a "bonus" northern pike. Largemouth bass, crappies and sunfish are all present in good numbers and quality size. Use soft plastics for bass during warm weather. Crappies and other sunfish will take small leeches or wax worms. Crappies are also quite fond of small minnows.

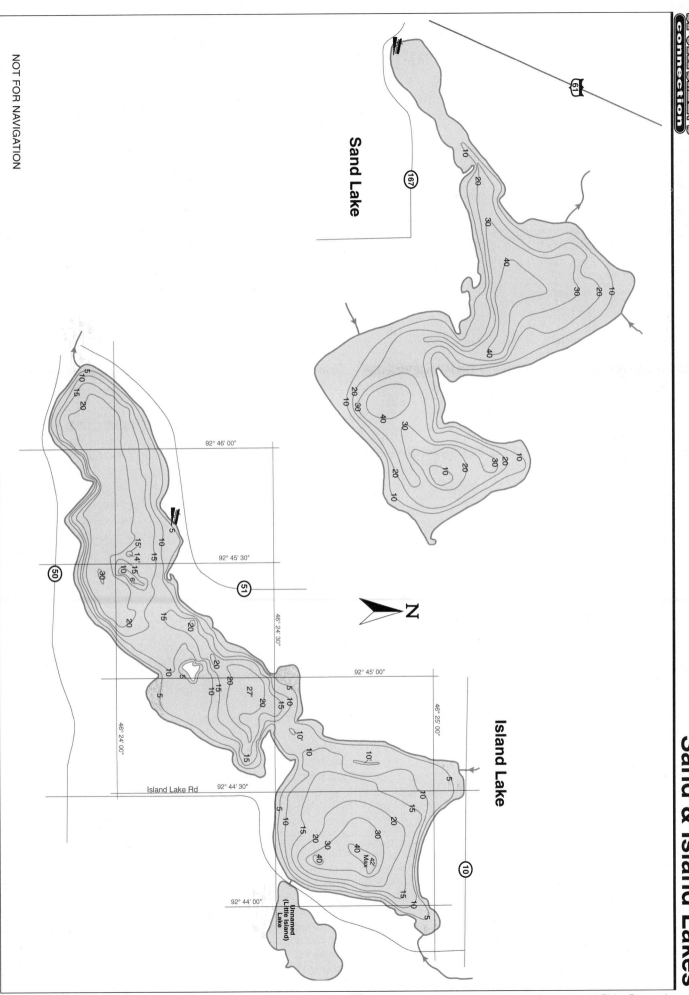

Sand & Island Lakes

Sand Lake

Island Lake

Unnamed
(Little Island)
Lake

N

NOT FOR NAVIGATION

OAK LAKE

Pine County

PICKEREL LAKE

Located in Nemadji State Forest

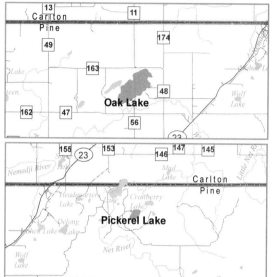

Area map page/coord: 12 / B-3
Watershed: Kettle
Surface area: 456 acres
Shorelength: 3.7 miles
Maximum depth: 20 feet
Mean depth: 8 feet
Secchi disk (water clarity): 5.6 feet
Water color: Green
Accessibility: State-owned public access with concrete ramp on south shore; twelve trailer spaces
Accommodations: Dock, camping, picnicking, restroom
Shoreland zoning: Recreational dev.
Management class: Walleye-centrarchid
Ecological type: Centrarchid

Area map page/coord: 13 / A,B-4,5
Watershed: Beartrap-Nemadji
Surface area: 59 acres
Shorelength: NA
Maximum depth: 8 feet
Mean depth: NA
Secchi disk (water clarity): 5.36 feet (2009)
Water color: Brown tint
Accessibility: State-owned public access on west shore in campground; eight trailer spaces
Accommodations: Dock, camping, picnicking, toilet
Shoreland zoning: Natural envt.
Management class: Centrarchid
Ecological type: Centrarchid

FISH STOCKING DATA

year	species	size	# released
07	Walleye	Adult	135
09	Walleye	Fingerling	6,480
10	Walleye	Fingerling	225
11	Walleye	Fingerling	3,219
12	Walleye	Fingerling	676

NET CATCH DATA

Date: 08/10/2010

species	Gill Nets # per net	Gill Nets avg. fish weight (lbs.)	Trap Nets # per net	Trap Nets avg. fish weight (lbs.)
Black Crappie	6.3	0.28	6.6	0.29
Bluegill	10.0	0.23	13.7	0.19
Hybrid Sunfish	0.1	0.21	0.1	0.17
Largemouth Bass	0.3	0.55	0.1	3.31
Northern Pike	3.9	3.99	0.6	1.39
Pumpkin. Sunfish	0.7	0.22	0.7	0.21
Walleye	2.7	2.44	0.1	3.64
Yellow Perch	9.9	0.12	1.2	0.20

LENGTH OF SELECTED SPECIES SAMPLED FROM ALL GEAR

Number of fish caught for the following length categories (inches):

species	0-5	6-8	9-11	12-14	15-19	20-24	25-29	>30	Total
Black Bullhead	-	-	27	11	-	-	-	-	38
Black Crappie	1	108	7	-	-	-	-	-	116
Bluegill	85	127	1	-	-	-	-	-	213
Hybrid Sunfish	1	1	-	-	-	-	-	-	2
Largemouth Bass	1	-	2	-	1	-	-	-	4
Northern Pike	-	-	-	1	9	12	10	8	40
Pumpkin. Sunfish	3	9	-	-	-	-	-	-	12
Walleye	-	7	4	-	1	11	1	1	25
White Sucker	-	-	-	13	17	1	-	-	31
Yellow Bullhead	-	-	19	2	-	-	-	-	21
Yellow Perch	14	85	1	-	-	-	-	-	100

FISH STOCKING DATA

year	species	size	# released
07	Walleye	Fry	100,000
09	Walleye	Fry	100,000

NET CATCH DATA

Date: 07/20/2009

species	Gill Nets # per net	Gill Nets avg. fish weight (lbs.)	Trap Nets # per net	Trap Nets avg. fish weight (lbs.)
Black Crappie	-	-	1.3	0.27
Bluegill	-	-	4.8	0.11
Northern Pike	1.5	3.00	0.1	1.09

LENGTH OF SELECTED SPECIES SAMPLED FROM ALL GEAR

Number of fish caught for the following length categories (inches):

species	0-5	6-8	9-11	12-14	15-19	20-24	25-29	>30	Total
Black Crappie	3	5	4	-	-	-	-	-	12
Bluegill	29	14	-	-	-	-	-	-	43
Northern Pike	-	-	-	-	1	3	-	-	4
Pumpkin. Sunfish	5	14	-	-	-	-	-	-	19
Yellow Perch	-	2	-	-	-	-	-	-	2

FISHING INFORMATION: Oak Lake is a 456-acre lake located near the town of Duquette. Oak Lake is a little more isolated than many other lakes in this area, and it doesn't get lots of fishing pressure as a result. The DNR has been stocking walleyes - fingerlings, yearlings and adults - since 1997 and that's helped provide a pretty good population of marble eyes. According to the 2010 DNR survey, there was a high walleye catch rate for lakes in this class and statistics exceeded the long-range management goal. All that means anglers will find walleyes averaging 18 inches and better than 2 pounds. Early season seems to be the best time to cash in on walleyes. Try the areas near the bars on the east shore, the reef and 9-foot hole nearby, and around the islands. The shoreline along the west side also produces.

Crappie fishing can also be good on Oak, with good numbers of 1/2-pounders and some 1-pound slabs being present. Locals regularly winter-spear northern pike, according to patrons of a local bait shop. There have been reports of some 20- to 25-pound pike being taken this way. Largemouth bass go largely unnoticed by most anglers, but some trophies have been seen swimming below spear anglers' holes. Cast topwater lures along shoreline cover early and late in day during summer months. Work a jig or a plastic worm on points or near the channel connecting Oak to Little Oak Lake. Stick with darker colors like black, green pumpkin or watermelon.

Pickerel Lake is tiny at 59 acres, and its deepest spots are only 8 feet, but it sustains a pretty good population of sunfish, crappies, northern pike and largemouth bass. Shore-fishing is popular, with the presence of a small campground in the surrounding Nemadji State Forest. The fishing pressure is rather light here, and the lake is primarily fished by campers. Along with northern pike, largemouth bass are abundant, making this a fun place to wet a line. Crappies average 7 to 8 inches. Bluegills tend to be smaller, around 5.3 inches, but are plentiful, which means there's a good chance you'll smell those on the grills in the campground. Public access is available at the campground on the lake's west side.

Oak & Pickerel Lakes

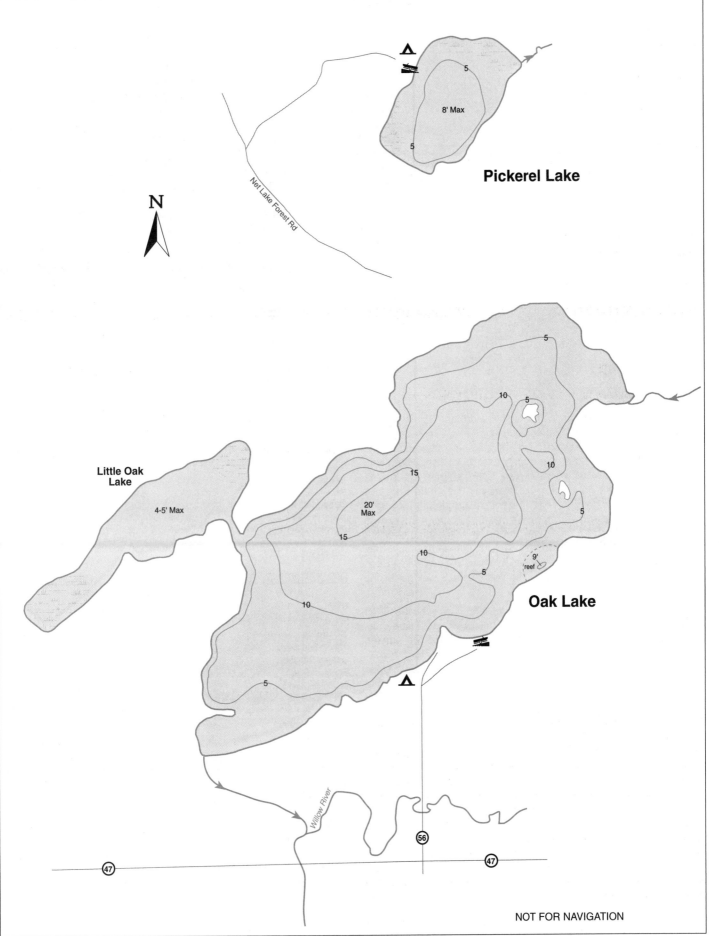

Pickerel Lake

8' Max

5

5

Net Lake Forest Rd

N

Little Oak Lake

4-5' Max

20' Max

15

15

10

10

5

5

5

10

10

5

9' reef

5

Oak Lake

5

Willow River

56

47

47

STURGEON LAKE
Pine County

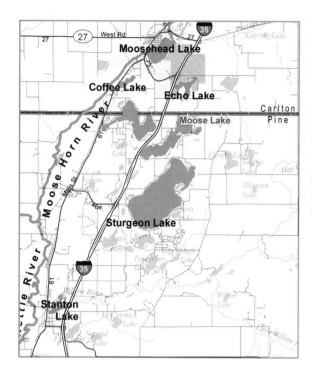

Area map pg / coord: 12 / B-1,2
Watershed: Kettle
Secchi disk: 12.1 feet (2011)
Water color: Clear

Surface area: 1,706 acres
Shorelength: 8.0 miles
Maximum depth: 40 feet
Mean depth: 22 feet

Accessibility: State-owned public access on north shore
Boat ramp: Concrete
Parking: Twenty trailer spaces
Accommodations: Dock, resort, camping, picnicking, restroom

Shoreland zoning classification: Recreational development
Management class: Walleye-centrarchid
Ecological type: Centrarchid-walleye

FISH STOCKING DATA

year	species	size	# released
07	Walleye	Fingerling	4,319
07	Walleye	Yearling	839
07	Walleye	Adult	740
07	Yellow Perch	Adult	11,100
08	Yellow Perch	Adult	1,385
09	Walleye	Fingerling	10,782
10	Walleye	Fingerling	4,103
11	Walleye	Fingerling	15,597
12	Walleye	Fingerling	13,270

NET CATCH DATA

Date: 04/11/2011

	Gill Nets		Trap Nets	
species	# per net	avg. fish weight (lbs.)	# per net	avg. fish weight (lbs.)
Black Crappie	4.7	0.39	1.9	0.30
Bluegill	9.1	0.08	7.3	0.14
Hybrid Sunfish	4.0	0.33	0.1	0.18
Largemouth Bass	3.3	1.27	-	-
Northern Pike	11.0	1.43	1.7	1.21
Pumpkin. Sunfish	6.4	0.15	0.6	0.12
Walleye	3.8	1.81	0.1	5.95
Yellow Perch	1.2	0.17	-	-

LENGTH OF SELECTED SPECIES SAMPLED FROM ALL GEAR
Number of fish caught for the following length categories (inches):

species	0-5	6-8	9-11	12-14	15-19	20-24	25-29	>30	Total
Black Crappie	3	47	26	3	-	-	-	-	79
Bluegill	141	51	-	-	-	-	-	-	192
Hybrid Sunfish	11	37	1	-	-	-	-	-	49
Largemouth Bass	-	6	9	17	7	-	-	-	49
Northern Pike	-	-	3	36	68	31	6	4	152
Pumpkin. Sunfish	52	26	1	-	-	-	-	-	84
Rock Bass	5	18	16	-	-	-	-	-	39
Walleye	-	-	3	17	15	8	3	-	46
Yellow Bullhead	-	28	68	14	-	-	-	-	110
Yellow Perch	3	9	-	-	-	-	-	-	12

FISHING INFORMATION: Located in northern Pine County, around 45 miles south of Duluth, Sturgeon Lake is home to a lot of people who have built year-round houses on its shores. Despite the development, however, it is home to a lot of fish. There are, for example, lots of small northern pike. DNR fisheries experts are optimistic about the fishing for this species. They note that pike growth is close to average, and the population should include a high proportion of quality-sized fish in years to come, if the growth trend continues. Fish for northerns around weedlines and over the sunken islands off the southwest shore. Cast spinnerbaits, spoons, and crankbaits or float a big sucker minnow to hook pike. Even small fish will whack a big offering, so you might as well go for the big fish with big baits.

Walleyes are stocked frequently by the DNR. During the last DNR survey, the average walleye on Sturgeon Lake weighed 2.5 pounds. Check the weedlines off the southeastern shore and the sunken island where the northern pike congregate; fish deeper for the wall-eyes. Use jig-and-bait combinations or troll with a crankbait. Don't forget to work the rock pile right next to the 40-foot hole, the one right off the big hill at the lake's northern end. Try a slip-bobber rig and jumbo leech fished over the sunken humps. This method works best during low-light conditions or on breezy and cloudy days.

Yellow perch hold in the same areas walleyes live - along the deeper weedlines. The yellow perch ranged in size from 6 inches to 8 inches in the last DNR survey. Favorite perch offerings include small leeches, crawlers, minnows; just about all the same baits that work for walleyes, except slightly smaller.

Largemouth bass are very numerous and will be lurking in shallows along the lake edges. The areas around the YMCA camp and the northwestern and northeastern corners of the lake are known hot spots for bass. The average bass weighs just over a pound, with some fish measuring as long as 20 inches available. Fish a floating worm, Senko or jig-and-pig combo in weeds or under a dock to hook a few bass. Don't forget about flinging a few topwater plugs along the shoreline cover early and late in the day. This is especially productive during warm weather months. Poppers are good, as are walking baits like a Zara Spook or Sammy.

Sturgeon Lake is also known for good crappies and bluegills. Crappies are about average in numbers and size. The last DNR survey showed crappies ranging from 5.4 to 11 inches in length, with a mean length of 7.7 inches. A slip-bobber rig baited with a minnow or leech is a consistent producer of crappies. Fish deeper weed edges to find the slabs. Bluegill numbers are normal according to the latest DNR survey, but they tend to run small. Only 10 percent of bluegills exceeded 7 inches in length. Target shallow water, particularly at the lake's southern end. Small worms, leeches or pieces of crawler will catch them.

Sturgeon Lake

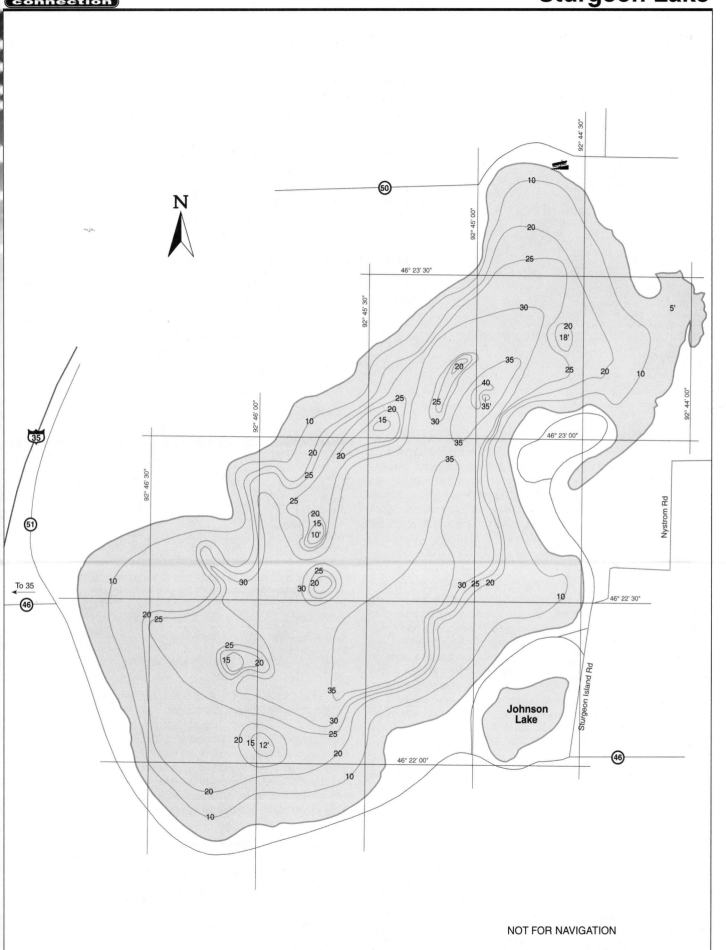

NOT FOR NAVIGATION

KNIFE LAKE
Kanabec County

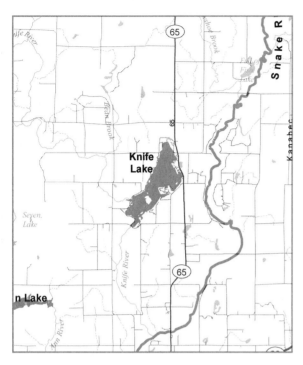

Area map pg / coord: 14 / D-3
Watershed: Snake
Secchi disk: 3.5 feet (2011)
Water color: Brown-green

Surface area: 1,259 acres
Shorelength: 11.1 miles
Maximum depth: 15 feet
Mean depth: 4 feet

Accessibility: 1) State-owned public access on south shore; 2) MNDOT-owned public access on east shore in wayside rest area
Boat ramp: 1) Concrete; 2) Concrete
Parking: 1) Eight trailer spaces; 2) Fifteen trailer spaces
Accommodations: Fishing pier, dock, wayside rest area, restrooms

Shoreland zoning classification: Recreational development
Management class: Walleye-centrarchid
Ecological type: Centrarchid-walleye

FISH STOCKING DATA

year	species	size	# released
10	Walleye	Fry	1,500,000
11	Walleye	Fry	1,475,000
11	Walleye	Fingerling	19,614
11	Walleye	Yearling	39
12	Walleye	Fingerling	17,347

NET CATCH DATA

Date: 04/19/2011	Gill Nets		Trap Nets	
species	# per net	avg. fish weight (lbs.)	# per net	avg. fish weight (lbs.)
Black Crappie	15.9	0.17	-	-
Bluegill	3.0	0.24	-	-
Northern Pike	2.8	5.18	-	-
Short. Redhorse	2.0	2.42	-	-
Walleye	2.4	1.61	-	-
Yellow Perch	23.2	0.18	-	-

LENGTH OF SELECTED SPECIES SAMPLED FROM ALL GEAR
Number of fish caught for the following length categories (inches):

species	0-5	6-8	9-11	12-14	15-19	20-24	25-29	>30	Total
Black Crappie	105	65	9	1	-	-	-	-	191
Bluegill	16	16	2	-	-	-	-	-	34
Northern Pike	-	-	-	-	1	10	11	11	33
Short. Redhorse	-	-	5	2	14	1	-	-	24
Walleye	-	-	1	10	15	3	-	-	29
Yellow Perch	49	215	7	-	-	-	-	-	278

FISHING INFORMATION: Located off Highway 65, roughly seven miles north of Mora, this lake is long at 1,259 acres and shallow, at a mere 15 feet deep. The water clarity is 3.5 feet. It is home to pretty fair numbers of walleyes, as well as decent northern pike and the usual supplies of "eating-size" panfish. Gamefish are not as plentiful as in years past, but there are still quality fish in good abundance here. Fishing pressure can be high at times, especially when the walleye season opens.

In the fall of 2001, the DNR instituted a protected slot limit between 18 and 24 inches for walleyes. The DNR's 2006 survey showed a catch rate improvement over the 2001 survey, however the species still fell short of the long-range management goals on the lake. In general, walleye numbers are now lower than what they used to be, but the size structure is a little bigger, which isn't a bad thing. Regular stocking should hopefully increase numbers as well. Look for walleyes off the sandbar straight out from the public access; in summer, they should be holding where the bottom slopes to the lake's deepest reaches. A jig-and-minnow combo works in this area, as does a split shot or small Lindy rig and bait. The downstream side of the big island is another place for some action. Don't pass up on floating a slip bobber with a jumbo leech or a nightcrawler over the various rockpiles or submerged humps, especially on windy days during summer.

Northern pike were stocked on this lake years ago, Although their numbers are shy of the DNR's management goal, there are some fish of quality size, with a number of fish exceeding 30 inches. Knife Lake's pike population averages 2.2 pounds and 22.5 inches. Northerns can be found in the area close to the dam, at inlets on the western side and around submerged stumps near the Knife River inlet. Cast spinnerbaits, inline spinners or jerkbaits to attract active pike. Use bright colors like white, chartreuse, silver or gold in these stained, low-visibility waters. Try floating a minnow around the weed edges, too, and you should be able to hook a few gators. There is a 24-to 36-inch protected slot limit for northern pike.

Crappie numbers and size are average, although you will get the occasional slab topping the 12-inch mark. There are lots of small bluegills to keep the kids happy. Bluegills, like most species in Knife Lake, have followed the trend of a decreased population but an increase in average size in recent years. Fish a small minnow off the rocks and bar near the public access for crappies; bluegills will be found in the shallows along any weedline. Bluegills will aggressively take pieces of crawler or small leeches, especially late in spring or early in summer when they're often still in the shallows or on spawning beds.

Yellow perch numbers decreased, although there are still plenty of these bait-stealers around. Most fish are on the small side.

The public access site off Highway 65, located on the east side of the lake, has a concrete ramp and picnic park. On the south end of the lake you'll find another concrete ramp, along with a fishing pier right off Highway 19.

Knife Lake

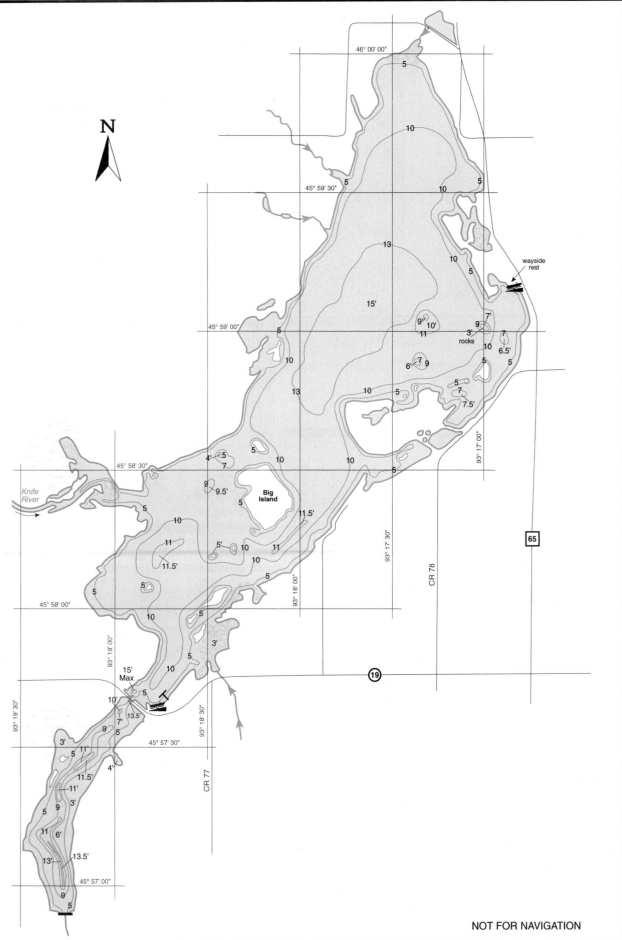

NOT FOR NAVIGATION

Source: Minnesota Department of Natural Resources, USGS

ANN LAKE

Bordered by Ann Lake Wildlife Mgmt. Area

Area map page/coord: 14 / E-1,2
Watershed: Snake
Surface area: 654 acres
Shorelength: 4.7 miles
Maximum depth: 17 feet
Mean depth: NA
Secchi disk (water clarity): 3.9 feet (2010)
Water color: Brown
Accessibility: State-owned public access with concrete ramp on southeast corner; ten trailer spaces
Accommodations: Dock, resort, boat rental, restroom
Shoreland zoning: Recreational dev.
Management class: Walleye-centrarchid
Ecological type: Centrarchid-walleye

FISH LAKE

Area map page/coord: 19 / A-6
Watershed: Snake
Surface area: 503 acres
Shorelength: 8.0 miles
Maximum depth: 8 feet
Mean depth: 5 feet
Secchi disk (water clarity): 1.0 feet (2007)
Water color: Green-brown
Accessibility: State-owned public access with concrete ramp on south shore; fifteen trailer spaces; carry-down access from rest area on north shore
Accommodations: Dock, restroom
Shoreland zoning: Recreational dev.
Management class: Centrarchid
Ecological type: Centrarchid

Kanabec County

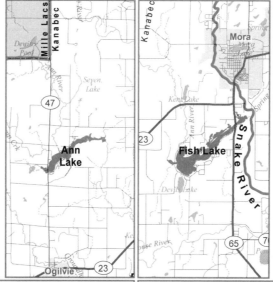

ANN LAKE

FISH STOCKING DATA

year	species	size	# released
08	Walleye	Fingerling	2,340
08	Walleye	Yearling	234
09	Walleye	Fingerling	3,530
10	Walleye	Fingerling	27,600
11	Walleye	Fingerling	6,810
12	Walleye	Fingerling	1,910
12	Walleye	Yearling	598

NET CATCH DATA

Date: 06/21/2010

species	Gill Nets # per net	Gill Nets avg. fish weight (lbs.)	Trap Nets # per net	Trap Nets avg. fish weight (lbs.)
Black Bullhead	-	-	0.4	1.10
Black Crappie	5.3	0.26	3.3	0.27
Bluegill	0.3	0.43	8.0	0.36
Bowfin (Dogfish)	0.2	3.80	0.7	5.20
Brown Bullhead	0.2	0.88	0.9	1.03
Northern Pike	2.0	3.71	0.1	1.43
Pumpkin. Sunfish	-	-	0.3	0.27
Walleye	1.6	1.01	0.6	1.99
White Sucker	2.4	2.63	0.3	2.07
Yellow Perch	21.9	0.17	0.6	0.12

LENGTH OF SELECTED SPECIES SAMPLED FROM ALL GEAR

Number of fish caught for the following length categories (inches):

species	0-5	6-8	9-11	12-14	15-19	20-24	25-29	>30	Total
Black Bullhead	-	-	1	2	-	-	-	-	3
Black Crappie	17	41	12	-	-	-	-	-	71
Bluegill	5	49	1	-	-	-	-	-	59
Bowfin (Dogfish)	-	-	-	-	-	5	2	-	7
Brown Bullhead	-	-	3	5	-	-	-	-	8
Northern Pike	-	-	-	-	2	9	6	2	19
Pumpkin. Sunfish	-	2	-	-	-	-	-	-	2
Walleye	-	1	6	3	4	4	-	-	18
White Sucker	-	-	-	3	17	-	-	-	23
Yellow Perch	52	131	10	-	-	-	-	-	201

FISH LAKE

FISH STOCKING DATA

year	species	size	# released
09	Walleye	Fingerling	4,248
10	Walleye	Fingerling	9,384
11	Walleye	Fingerling	5,171
12	Walleye	Fingerling	2,189
12	Walleye	Yearling	733

NET CATCH DATA

Date: 07/09/2007

species	Gill Nets # per net	Gill Nets avg. fish weight (lbs.)	Trap Nets # per net	Trap Nets avg. fish weight (lbs.)
Black Crappie	48.5	0.33	10.1	0.34
Bluegill	3.8	0.29	14.4	0.25
Channel Catfish	1.3	4.18	-	-
Largemouth Bass	0.2	3.75	0.3	3.86
Northern Pike	6.7	2.75	1.4	2.22
Pumpkin. Sunfish	-	-	0.3	0.16
Walleye	2.3	1.80	2.7	2.86
Yellow Perch	2.5	0.23	0.	0.04

LENGTH OF SELECTED SPECIES SAMPLED FROM ALL GEAR

Number of fish caught for the following length categories (inches):

species	0-5	6-8	9-11	12-14	15-19	20-24	25-29	>30	Total
Black Crappie	23	302	57	-	-	-	-	-	382
Bluegill	67	85	1	-	-	-	-	-	153
Channel Catfish	-	-	-	-	-	7	1	-	8
Common Carp	-	-	-	-	1	2	24	8	38
Largemouth Bass	-	-	-	-	4	-	-	-	4
Northern Pike	-	-	-	-	5	37	10	1	53
Pumpkin. Sunfish	2	1	-	-	-	-	-	-	3
Walleye	-	1	5	2	14	12	4	-	38
White Sucker	-	1	1	16	68	3	-	-	89
Yellow Bullhead	-	2	12	46	-	-	-	-	60
Yellow Perch	2	13	1	-	-	-	-	-	16

Northerns grow large here, so be prepared to land a big one. There is a lot of nice structure for largemouth bass on Ann Lake, like boulders, rubble, submerged vegetation, and flooded brush. Fish any of it with a spinnerbait or crankbait, or drop a surface lure into weeds in evenings. Ann Lake has two public accesses, both at the southwest end, just off County Highway 47.

FISHING INFORMATION: Ann Lake is a relatively shallow lake filled with good structure. This long, skinny body of water north of Ogilvie has a strong bluegill population. This species has undergone a pretty hefty expansion in recent years, from scarce to well above median numbers for the lake class. Try fishing shoreline shallows virtually anywhere in the western two-thirds of this lake; worm chunks suspended below a bobber will get you a meal fairly fast. Despite regular stocking, walleyes are scarce and hard to catch. Work a jig-and-minnow combo along drop-offs at the mouth of the Ann River and breaks off the south shore, where water deepens rapidly. Like bluegills, northern pike can be found in the shallows. Try areas of flooded brush, particularly the one at Spring Brook inlet.

Fish Lake was created with the damming of the Ann River. Walleyes are stocked regularly by the DNR and have firmly established themselves. Their numbers are about normal for lakes of this type and the population contains a fair number of fish 15 inches and larger. Work a jig-and-minnow combo along breaks off the public access. The bottom drops off gradually to the lake's maximum depth of 8 feet, where you'll find walleyes during daylight. Deeper areas toward mid-channel also yield some fish. The northern pike population is about normal, too, and there are some nice fish present. Work off the Tosher Creek and Ann River inlets with a spoon or crankbait and shallows near the dam.

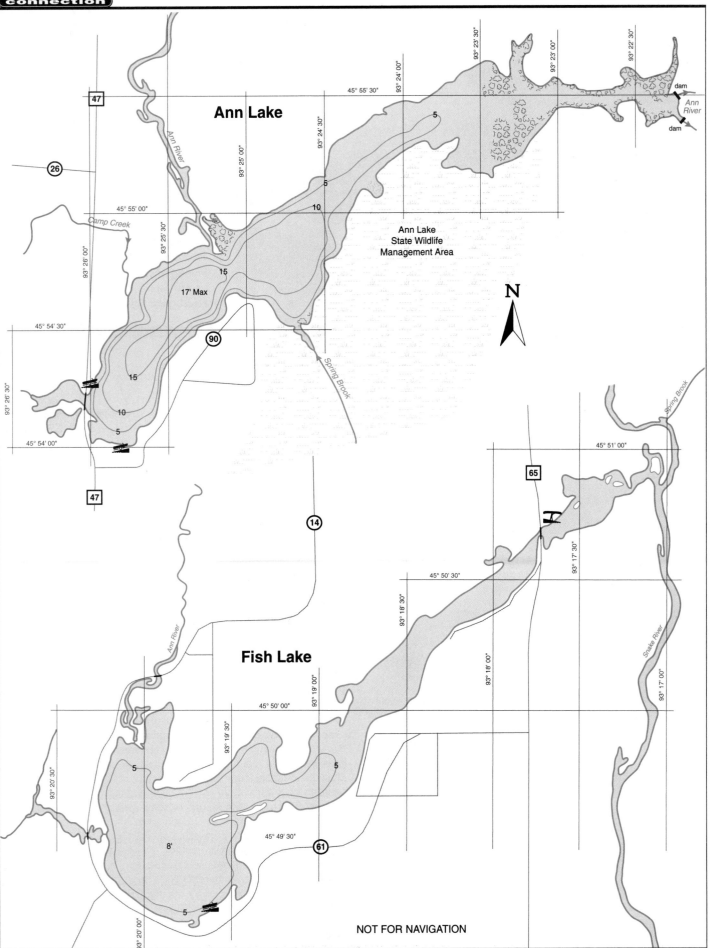

Ann Lake

Ann River

dam

Ann River

dam

Camp Creek

Ann Lake
State Wildlife
Management Area

17' Max

15

15

10

5

N

Spring Brook

Spring Brook

Snake River

Ann River

Fish Lake

8'

5

5

5

5

NOT FOR NAVIGATION

POMROY LAKE   QUAMBA (MUD) LAKE
Kanabec County

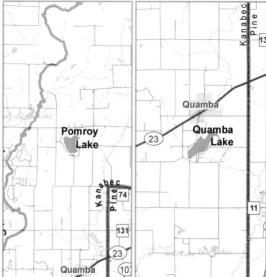

Area map page/coord: 15 / C-4

Watershed: Snake

Surface area: 412 acres

Shorelength: 3.2 miles

Maximum depth: 11 feet

Mean depth: 3 feet

Secchi disk (water clarity): 4.2 feet (2010)

Water color: NA

Accessibility: State-owned public access with concrete ramp on east shore; twelve trailer spaces

Accommodations: Dock

Shoreland zoning: Recreational dev.

Management class: Centrarchid

Ecological type: Centrarchid

Area map page/coord: 15 / E-4

Watershed: Snake

Surface area: 226 acres

Shorelength: 3.1 miles

Maximum depth: 11 feet

Mean depth: 7 feet

Secchi disk (water clarity): 3.9 feet (2010)

Water color: Green-brown

Accessibility: State-owned public access with concrete ramp on south shore; ten trailer spaces

Accommodations: Dock

Shoreland zoning: Recreational dev.

Management class: Walleye-centrarchid

Ecological type: Centrarchid

FISH STOCKING DATA

year	species	size	# released
07	Walleye	Fry	400,000
09	Walleye	Fry	400,000
10	Walleye	Fry	250,000
11	Walleye	Fry	400,000

NET CATCH DATA

Date: 09/06/2010

species	Gill Nets # per net	Gill Nets avg. fish weight (lbs.)	Trap Nets # per net	Trap Nets avg. fish weight (lbs.)
Black Crappie	3.2	0.31	2.1	0.30
Bluegill	5.7	0.32	6.4	0.25
Largemouth Bass	1.0	1.09	-	-
Northern Pike	4.0	2.02	0.1	0.87
Pumpkin. Sunfish	3.5	0.21	1.4	0.29
Walleye	1.2	3.38	-	-
Yellow Perch	17.5	0.12	0.1	0.07

LENGTH OF SELECTED SPECIES SAMPLED FROM ALL GEAR

Number of fish caught for the following length categories (inches):

species	0-5	6-8	9-11	12-14	15-19	20-24	25-29	>30	Total
Black Bullhead	-	1	37	8	-	-	-	-	46
Black Crappie	11	13	7	3	-	-	-	-	34
Bluegill	6	73	-	-	-	-	-	-	79
Brown Bullhead	-	-	11	7	-	-	-	-	18
Largemouth Bass	-	2	1	1	2	-	-	-	6
Northern Pike	-	-	-	1	11	6	5	2	25
Pumpkin. Sunfish	9	22	-	-	-	-	-	-	31
Walleye	-	-	-	-	-	7	-	-	7
Yellow Bullhead	-	-	2	-	-	-	-	-	2
Yellow Perch	34	69	-	-	-	-	-	-	106

FISH STOCKING DATA

year	species	size	# released
07	Walleye	Fry	557,000
08	Walleye	Fry	505,000
09	Walleye	Fry	400,000
11	Walleye	Fry	400,000
12	Walleye	Fry	400,000

NET CATCH DATA

Date: 07/06/2010

species	Gill Nets # per net	Gill Nets avg. fish weight (lbs.)	Trap Nets # per net	Trap Nets avg. fish weight (lbs.)
Black Crappie	13.3	0.21	2.8	0.48
Bluegill	0.5	0.30	4.5	0.27
Brown Bullhead	-	-	1.6	1.15
Common Carp	-	-	0.1	15.23
Northern Pike	6.0	2.71	1.9	2.66
Pumpkin. Sunfish	-	-	1.8	0.18
Walleye	1.8	3.78	-	-
White Sucker	7.8	2.34	0.5	2.42
Yellow Perch	6.5	0.13	0.3	0.05

LENGTH OF SELECTED SPECIES SAMPLED FROM ALL GEAR

Number of fish caught for the following length categories (inches):

species	0-5	6-8	9-11	12-14	15-19	20-24	25-29	>30	Total
Black Bullhead	-	-	-	-	1	-	-	-	1
Black Crappie	28	26	18	1	-	-	-	-	75
Bluegill	15	22	1	-	-	-	-	-	38
Brown Bullhead	-	-	2	11	-	-	-	-	13
Northern Pike	-	-	-	2	11	18	2	6	39
Pumpkin. Sunfish	8	6	-	-	-	-	-	-	14
Walleye	-	-	-	1	2	2	2	-	7
White Sucker	-	-	2	4	25	2	-	-	35
Yellow Perch	15	10	-	-	-	-	-	-	28

FISHING INFORMATION: Pomroy Lake, located northeast of Knife Lake, is shallow at only 11 feet max, and it does experience winterkill during severe winters. Fishing is popular for crappies and sunfish; anglers use glow jigs tipped with wax worms or small minnows. Depending upon current conditions, 1/2-pound panfish are not uncommon. You'll most likely have to sort some little ones to get to the more desirable specimens. Largemouth bass are also present and you may find the action worthwhile. Without much in the way of structure or depth variations, gamefish utilize the weeds in Pomroy. It's a good idea to cover a lot of water, trolling various artificials, as well as live bait, in and around weedbeds, bulrushes and other vegetation throughout the lake. Once again, you'll want to check locally on conditions; sometimes the fishing's quite good and then again, sometimes it truly isn't.

Quamba Lake, also referred to as Mud Lake, has a history of producing some nice northern pike, largemouth bass, walleyes and panfish. Shallow, with a median depth of only 7 feet, Quamba avoids winterkill most years because of inflowing water from Mud Creek and because it has several springs along its shoreline. While many anglers concentrate on the plump crappies and bluegills found near weedbeds, bass anglers also cash in on some good action. Most serious bass anglers release their fish, so their numbers seem to hold up; natural reproduction appears to be good for this species. There are also reports of some northern pike approaching 20 pounds being caught in Quamba. While boating a pike this big is rare, there is a good population of bigger ones in the lake, along with the inevitable hammer-handles. Walleye fishing in a structureless lake like this can be a head-scratcher. However, keep in mind that the structure fish adhere to in this type of lake is weeds. Work edges with live-bait rigs, or try trolling a Rapala along the outside edge of weedlines for a few walleyes. As is true with most species in Quamba, the average size of most fish is pretty respectable in most years.

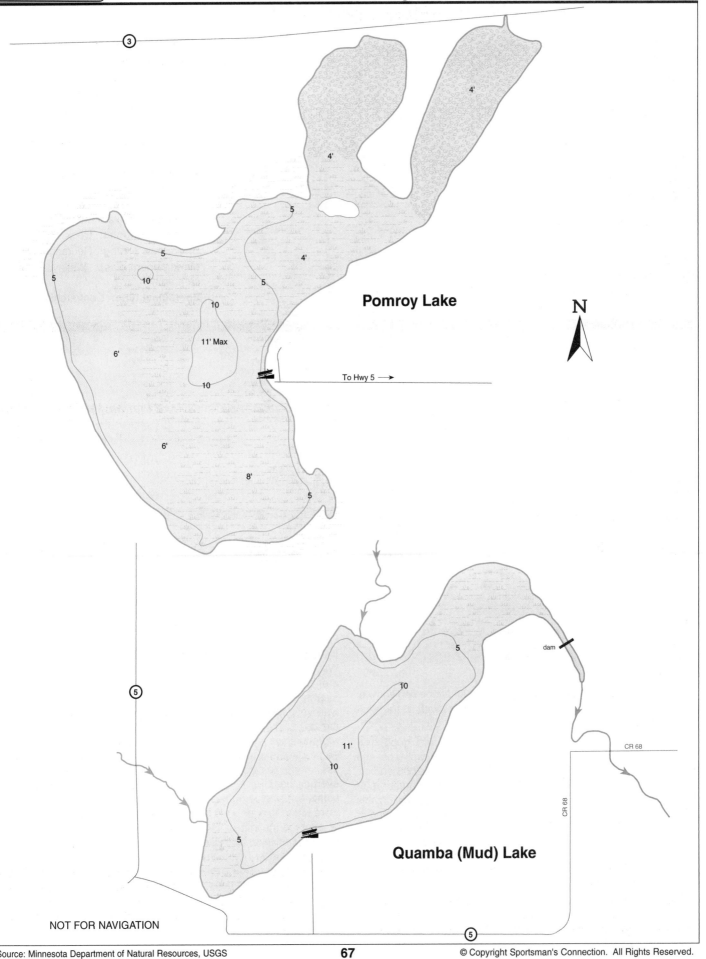

Pomroy Lake

N

To Hwy 5 →

11' Max

Quamba (Mud) Lake

dam

CR 68

NOT FOR NAVIGATION

Source: Minnesota Department of Natural Resources, USGS

LAKE ELEVEN

BASS LAKE

Kanabec / Pine Counties

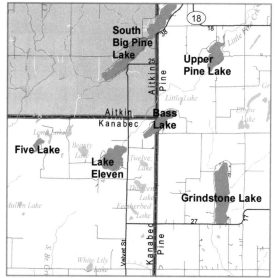

Area map page/coord: 15 / A-4,5
Watershed: Kettle
Surface area: 314 acres
Shorelength: 3.0 miles
Maximum depth: 13 feet
Mean depth: 7 feet
Secchi disk (water clarity): 2.0 feet (2008)
Water color: Green
Accessibility: State-owned public access with concrete ramp on south shore; six trailer spaces
Accommodations: Dock, restroom
Shoreland zoning: Recreational dev.
Management class: Walleye-centrarchid
Ecological type: Centrarchid

Area map page/coord: 15 / A-5
Watershed: Kettle
Surface area: 224 acres
Shorelength: 3.3 miles
Maximum depth: 24 feet
Mean depth: 12 feet
Secchi disk (water clarity): 6.3 feet (2011)
Water color: Clear
Accessibility: State-owned public access with concrete ramp on north shore; eight trailer spaces
Accommodations: Dock, restroom
Shoreland zoning: Recreational dev.
Management class: Walleye-centrarchid
Ecological type: Centrarchid

FISH STOCKING DATA

year	species	size	# released
08	Walleye	Fingerling	13,630
10	Walleye	Fingerling	6,900
11	Walleye	Fingerling	3,711

NET CATCH DATA

Date: 07/07/2008

	Gill Nets		Trap Nets	
species	# per net	avg. fish weight (lbs.)	# per net	avg. fish weight (lbs.)
Black Crappie	17.8	0.17	12.0	0.27
Bluegill	5.5	0.26	29.0	0.23
Brown Bullhead	-	-	0.7	0.95
Largemouth Bass	-	-	0.1	2.54
Northern Pike	9.3	2.95	0.4	1.98
Pumpkin. Sunfish	0.8	0.21	2.3	0.25
Walleye	1.7	2.44	0.2	4.35
Yellow Perch	4.2	0.13	-	-

LENGTH OF SELECTED SPECIES SAMPLED FROM ALL GEAR

Number of fish caught for the following length categories (inches):

species	0-5	6-8	9-11	12-14	15-19	20-24	25-29	>30	Total
Black Bullhead	1	1	-	2	-	-	-	-	4
Black Crappie	12	172	18	-	-	-	-	-	215
Bluegill	75	210	1	-	-	-	-	-	294
Brown Bullhead	-	-	3	3	-	-	-	-	6
Largemouth Bass	-	-	-	-	1	-	-	-	1
Northern Pike	-	-	-	-	14	30	13	3	60
Pumpkin. Sunfish	11	15	-	-	-	-	-	-	26
Walleye	-	-	1	3	1	6	1	-	12
Yellow Bullhead	-	9	7	3	-	-	-	-	19
Yellow Perch	5	20	-	-	-	-	-	-	25

FISH STOCKING DATA

year	species	size	# released
08	Walleye	Fingerling	1,764
09	Walleye	Fingerling	2,772
09	Walleye	Yearling	1,533
10	Walleye	Fingerling	1,332
11	Walleye	Fingerling	3,020

NET CATCH DATA

Date: 08/29/2011

	Gill Nets		Trap Nets	
species	# per net	avg. fish weight (lbs.)	# per net	avg. fish weight (lbs.)
Black Crappie	1.7	0.18	4.6	0.33
Bluegill	0.8	0.06	3.5	0.14
Largemouth Bass	0.8	0.97	-	-
Northern Pike	6.3	1.04	1.0	1.31
Walleye	0.2	4.41	0.1	1.41

LENGTH OF SELECTED SPECIES SAMPLED FROM ALL GEAR

Number of fish caught for the following length categories (inches):

species	0-5	6-8	9-11	12-14	15-19	20-24	25-29	>30	Total
Black Crappie	2	34	10	1	-	-	-	-	47
Bluegill	23	9	-	-	-	-	-	-	32
Brown Bullhead	2	57	51	-	-	-	-	-	110
Hybrid Sunfish	2	11	-	-	-	-	-	-	13
Largemouth Bass	-	1	1	3	-	-	-	-	5
Northern Pike	-	-	-	5	33	8	-	-	46
Pumpkin. Sunfish	-	1	-	-	-	-	-	-	1
Walleye	-	-	-	-	1	1	-	-	2

FISHING INFORMATION: Located west of Sandstone on Highway 28, these two smaller lakes offer decent fishing much of the year and a minimum of fishing pressure.

Lake Eleven boasts 314 acres of fishing fun, with good oxygen levels year-round. It offers decent numbers of walleyes and bass averaging just over 14 inches. According to the 2008 survey, northerns average 23.3 inches. You'll encounter good numbers of black crappies and bluegills, both of which are abundant on this lake, to provide a good day's fishing. Thread live bait on the end of your hook, leeches and worms in particular, and watch them feast on your offering. Largemouth bass are more abundant in Eleven than in most neighboring lakes. Heavily weeded and somewhat dark with algae bloom, the lake has plenty of bass and panfish hiding in weeds. Anglers using minnow-tipped jigs do well here. Also try a Texas-rigged tube, lizard or plastic worm. Dark colors like green pumpkin or black work well. Public access is available at the south end of the lake.

Bass Lake is a 224-acre lake with a maximum depth of 24 feet. It's a good producer of northern pike, largemouth bass and panfish. Walleyes are stocked annually, but according to the DNR, there aren't a lot of them to be caught. The walleye population is below average compared to other Minnesota lakes of similar type. The walleye population has fluctuated throughout the years, depending on stocking success, harvest levels, and success of natural reproduction. The northern population is very good, and individuals generally average about 20 inches. The bass population is on the rise, which indicates that reproduction is successful on this lake. The average bass is 13.7 inches. The bluegill population has dropped some, but black crappies are in the normal range. Brown bullheads were found to average 8 inches. Pumpkinseed sunfish were caught in average quantites and averaged 5.4 inches. Only one white sucker was sampled. Historically that species has been sampled in low numbers. This is a shallow lake, so you'll want to fish either inside or just outside weedbeds most of the time. The state-owned public access has parking for eight vehicles with trailers. It is located on the northwest side of the lake.

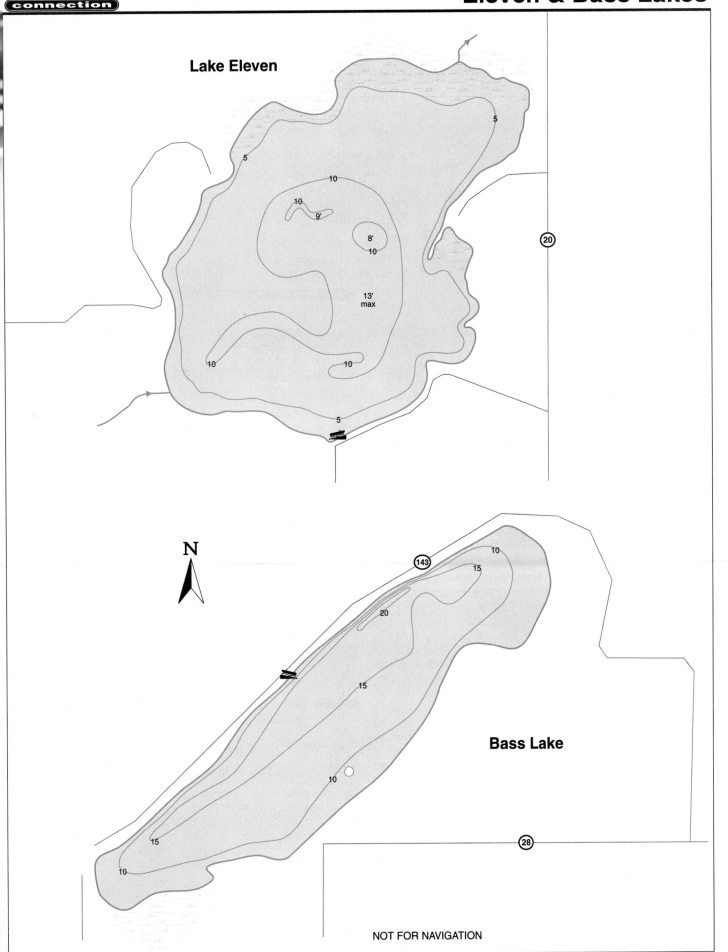

Lake Eleven

5

5

10

10

9'

8'
10

13'
max

10

10

5

N

20

143

10

15

20

15

Bass Lake

10

15

10

28

NOT FOR NAVIGATION

GRINDSTONE LAKE
Pine County

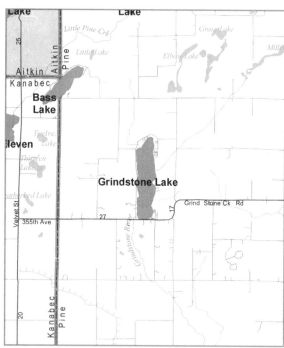

Area map pg / coord: 15 / A-5,6
Watershed: Kettle
Secchi disk: 12.9 feet (2007)
Water color: Brown tint

Surface area: 528 acres
Shorelength: 4.8 miles
Maximum depth: 153 feet
Mean depth: NA

Accessibility: State-owned public access on north shore; access at times is limited to smaller boats due to siltation
Boat ramp: Concrete
Parking: Fifteen trailer spaces
Accommodations: None

Shoreland zoning classification: Recreational development
Management class: Lake Trout
Ecological type: Trout

FISH STOCKING DATA

year	species	size	# released
07	Lake Trout	Yearling	5,385
07	Rainbow Trout	Yearling	7,700
08	Rainbow Trout	Yearling	3,000
09	Brown Trout	Adult	2,500
09	Rainbow Trout	Yearling	7,838
10	Brown Trout	Yearling	2,000
10	Lake Trout	Adult	433
10	Rainbow Trout	Yearling	8,166
11	Brown Trout	Yearling	2,500
11	Lake Trout	Yearling	5,960
11	Rainbow Trout	Yealing	8,999
12	Brown Trout	Yearling	2,500
12	Rainbow Trout	Yealing	9,000

NET CATCH DATA

Date: 08/06/2007

species	Gill Nets # per net	Gill Nets avg. fish weight (lbs.)	Trap Nets # per net	Trap Nets avg. fish weight (lbs.)
Black Crappie	-	-	2.8	0.26
Bluegill	0.2	0.27	5.4	0.13
Lake Trout	3.1	1.19	-	-
Northern Pike	1.5	3.42	0.3	0.68
Pumpkin. Sunfish	-	-	0.1	0.04
Rainbow Smelt	4.3	0.11	-	-
Rainbow Trout	0.4	1.08	-	-
Rock Bass	0.6	0.20	2.0	0.18
Smallmouth Bass	0.4	1.24	-	-
White Sucker	0.2	2.17	0.2	1.87
Yellow Perch	0.2	0.12	-	-

LENGTH OF SELECTED SPECIES SAMPLED FROM ALL GEAR

Number of fish caught for the following length categories (inches):

species	0-5	6-8	9-11	12-14	15-19	20-24	25-29	>30	Total
Black Crappie	4	20	1	-	-	-	-	-	25
Bluegill	32	20	-	-	-	-	-	-	53
Lake Trout	-	15	13	29	13	3	1	1	75
Northern Pike	-	-	1	2	8	17	7	3	38
Pumpkin. Sunfish	1	-	-	-	-	-	-	-	1
Rainbow Trout	-	-	-	9	-	1	-	-	10
Rock Bass	15	13	-	-	-	-	-	-	28
Smallmouth Bass	-	4	2	2	2	-	-	-	10
White Sucker	-	-	-	2	4	1	-	-	7
Yellow Perch	-	4	-	-	-	-	-	-	4

FISHING INFORMATION: Surprisingly deep at 150-plus feet, Grindstone Lake is one of the most unusual inland lakes in the state. This 528-acre lake is home to a large number of gamefish, both cold-water and warm-water varieties, and boasts its own smelt run. While no one knows how smelt were first introduced into the lake, according to the DNR, the population has become well estabalished. Once designated an experimental lake with year-around fishing, Grindstone is now subject to regular regulations (check current regulations for specifics). Brown trout and rainbow trout, which are stocked annually, receive most of the attention.

The depths can be pretty intimidating for the average angler, and the fact that oxygen runs down below 100 feet doesn't make locating the fish any easier. There are, however, some patterns that anglers who fish the lake regularly follow. Brown trout can often be found around the 25- to 40-foot depth range, and basic panfish techniques usually work well. Use a light line and small hooks tipped with wax worms, small red worms or crappie minnows. The water is usually very clear, with secchi disk readings near 13 feet, so 6-pound line or lighter and number 8 and smaller hooks are recommended. Rainbow trout are usually found in the upper reaches. During summer, after the mayflies have hatched, is a good time to try for them; rainbows will rise to the surface where you can hook them by throwing a mayfly-imitating bait, small worm or salmon egg on top of the water with no weight. Lake trout are tougher to locate because they're usually found in very deep water. Experienced anglers will graph schools and either vertical-jig with 2- and 3-ounce jigs tipped with smelt, or troll spoons and crankbaits under downriggers, often in depths of 100 feet or more. Big northern pike are sometimes caught using similar methods. In fact, one approach to fishing Grindstone is simply to troll around the lake, varying bait depth, until you catch something. Actually, trolling can be the most productive technique overall in trout lakes. Trolling small stickbaits like Dave's Ka-Boom Shiners or original Rapalas, or a small trolling spoon off planer boards can really up your catch at times. Most anglers aren't using this gear, but give it a shot and vary your depths accordingly. Electronics can be a big help. Use your depth finder to locate fish.

Don't waste a lot of time trolling in water where you're not marking fish. Ice fishing for trout is also popular. Some anglers also target Grindstone's smelt, which tend to run bigger than their nearby Lake Superior counterparts. A good concrete ramp is provided at the public access on the northwest shore.

Grindstone Lake

NOT FOR NAVIGATION

N

93° 00' 30"

46° 08' 00"

93° 00' 00"

46° 07' 30"

46° 07' 00"

46° 06' 30"

20
40
60
80
100
120
110
110
146'
140
34'
40
40
36'
20
40
60
80
100
110
100
110
130
140
142'
120
110
100
90'
80
70
60
80
100
110
50 42'
40
20
20
30
40
110
100
80
60
40
20
70
141'
120
130
120
140
61'
110
70
100
20
40
60
80
153' Max
140
120
110
100
93'
102'
110
110
100
80
60
40
20
33'
50

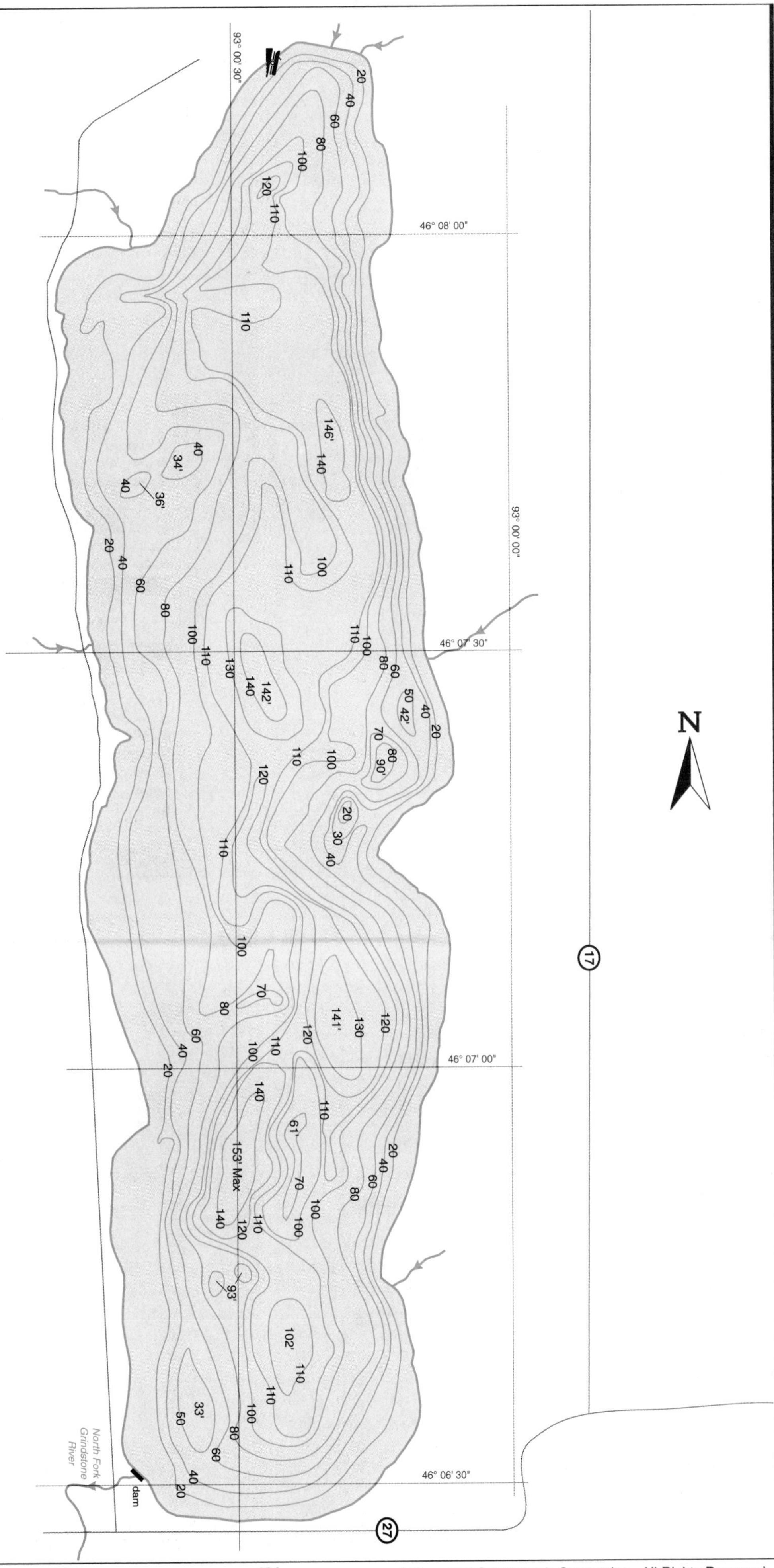

North Fork
Grindstone
River

dam

17

27

Source: Minnesota Department of Natural Resources, USGS

71

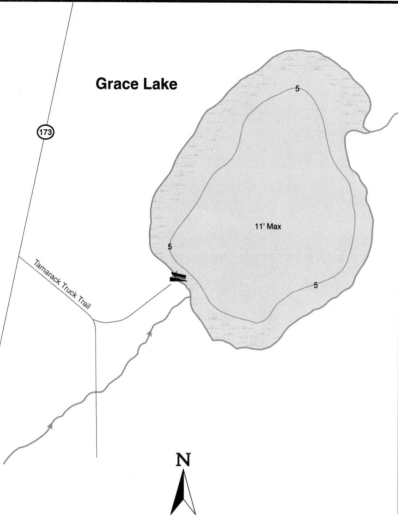

Grace Lake

173

Tamarack Truck Trail

11' Max

5

5

5

5

N

Grace Lake, Pine County

Map pg/coord: 17 / B-4,5
Watershed: Upper St. Croix
Mgmt. classification: Centrarchid
Surface area: 80 acres
Shorelength: NA
Max depth: 11 feet
Water clarity: 2.9 feet (2008)

Accessibility: State-owned public access with gravel ramp on southwest shore; three trailer spaces
Accommodations: None

FISH STOCKING DATA			
year	species	size	# released
07	Walleye	Fry	100,000

LENGTH OF SELECTED SPECIES SAMPLED FROM ALL GEAR
Survey Date: 07/21/2008   Survey method: gill net, trap net
Number of fish caught for the following length categories (inches):

species	0-5	6-8	9-11	12-14	15-19	20-24	25-29	>30	Total
Black Bullhead	-	1	1	3	-	-	-	-	5
Black Crappie	16	52	28	-	-	-	-	-	108
Bluegill	11	20	1	-	-	-	-	-	32
Brown Bullhead	-	-	-	4	-	-	-	-	4
Largemouth Bass	-	1	-	-	-	-	-	-	1
Northern Pike	-	-	-	-	4	7	4	2	17
Pumpkin. Sunfish	-	4	-	-	-	-	-	-	4
White Sucker	-	1	-	2	3	-	-	-	6
Yellow Perch	3	12	-	-	-	-	-	-	17

Rock Lake

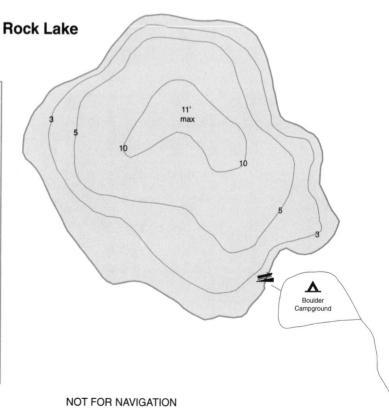

3

5

10

11' max

10

5

3

Boulder Campground

Rock Lake, Pine County

Map pg/coord: 17 / B,C-5
Watershed: Upper St. Croix
Mgmt. classification: Walleye
Surface area: 79 acres
Shorelength: NA
Max depth: 11 feet
Water clarity: 5.8 feet (2007)

Accessibility: State-owned public access with gravel ramp on southeast shore in campground; eight trailer spaces
Accommodations: Camping, picnicking, restroom

FISH STOCKING DATA			
year	species	size	# released
07	Walleye	Fingerling	2,926
09	Walleye	Fingerling	2,772
10	Walleye	Fingerling	1,872
11	Walleye	Fingerling	2,479

LENGTH OF SELECTED SPECIES SAMPLED FROM ALL GEAR
Survey Date: 09/04/2007   Survey method: gill net, trap net
Number of fish caught for the following length categories (inches):

species	0-5	6-8	9-11	12-14	15-19	20-24	25-29	>30	Total
Bluegill	204	49	2	-	-	-	-	-	259
Golden Shiner	3	-	-	-	-	-	-	-	3
Northern Pike	-	-	-	-	-	12	4	1	17
Walleye	-	-	-	1	1	4	-	-	6
White Sucker	-	-	-	-	2	-	-	-	2
Yellow Perch	36	17	-	-	-	-	-	-	55

NOT FOR NAVIGATION

Tamarack, McGowan & Kenney Lakes

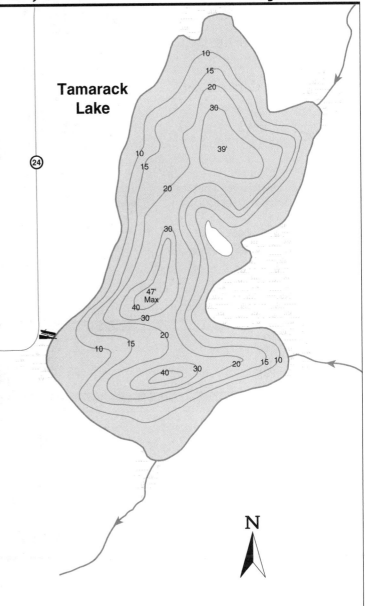

Tamarack Lake, Pine County

Map pg/coord: 17 / B-4
Watershed: Upper St. Croix
Mgmt. classification:
Centrarchid

Surface area: 70 acres
Shorelength: NA
Max depth: 47 feet
Water clarity: 12.1 feet (2009)

Accessibility: State-owned public access with concrete ramp on southwest shore; six trailer spaces
Accommodations: Restroom

FISH STOCKING DATA			
year	species	size	# released
05	Black Crappie	Fingerling	1,452
07	Black Crappie	Fingerling	8,700

LENGTH OF SELECTED SPECIES SAMPLED FROM ALL GEAR

Survey Date: 06/16/2009   **Survey method:** gill net, trap net

Number of fish caught for the following length categories (inches):

species	0-5	6-8	9-11	12-14	15-19	20-24	25-29	>30	Total
Black Crappie	2	-	2	-	-	-	-	-	4
Bluegill	186	193	-	-	-	-	-	-	385
Brown Bullhead	-	2	32	6	-	-	-	-	45
Largemouth Bass	-	2	-	2	-	-	-	-	4
Northern Pike	-	-	-	1	17	15	-	-	33
Pumpkin. Sunfish	-	5	-	-	-	-	-	-	5
White Sucker	-	-	-	-	1	-	-	-	1
Yellow Bullhead	-	-	2	-	-	-	-	-	2
Yellow Perch	1	4	-	-	-	-	-	-	6

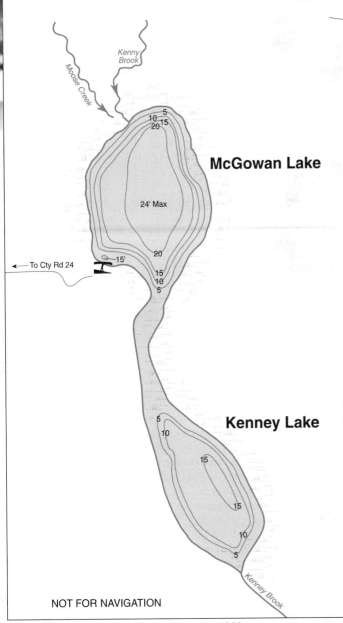

McGowan & Kenney Lakes, Pine County
Bordered by McGowan Wildlife Management Area

Map pg/coord: 17 / B,C-4
Watershed: Upper St. Croix
Mgmt. classification:
Centrarchid

Surface area:
McGowan - 21 acres
Kenney - 15 acres
Max depth: 24 feet; 15 feet
Water clarity: 6.0 feet (2003)

Accessibility: Carry-down access to west shore of McGowan off of County Road 24 (50-yard portage across marshy bog)
Accommodations: None

NO RECORD OF STOCKING

LENGTH OF SELECTED SPECIES SAMPLED FROM ALL GEAR

Survey Date: 08/25/2003   **Survey method:** gill net, trap net

Number of fish caught for the following length categories (inches):

species	0-5	6-8	9-11	12-14	15-19	20-24	25-29	>30	Total
Black Bullhead	-	-	4	1	-	-	-	-	5
Black Crappie	-	1	1	-	-	-	-	-	2
Bluegill	3	27	-	-	-	-	-	-	30
Brown Bullhead	-	-	4	-	-	-	-	-	4
Northern Pike	-	-	-	-	2	2	1	-	5
Pumpkin. Sunfish	-	1	-	-	-	-	-	-	1
Yellow Bullhead	-	-	4	-	-	-	-	-	4

NOT FOR NAVIGATION

LEWIS LAKE

LORY LAKE

Kanabec / Isanti Counties
Bordered by Stanchfield Wildlife Mgmt. Area

Area map page/coord: 19 / C-6
Watershed: Rum
Surface area: 178 acres
Shorelength: 3.5 miles
Maximum depth: 48 feet
Mean depth: 15 feet
Secchi disk (water clarity): 6.2 feet (2006)
Water color: Light green
Accessibility: State-owned public access with concrete ramp on east shore; eight trailer spaces
Accommodations: Dock
Shoreland zoning: Recreational dev.
Management class: Centrarchid
Ecological type: Centrarchid

Area map page/coord: 19 / C-6
Watershed: Rum
Surface area: 214 acres
Shorelength: 4.5 miles
Maximum depth: 21 feet
Mean depth: 7 feet
Secchi disk (water clarity): 4.0 feet (2009)
Water color: Green
Accessibility: County-owned public access with gravel ramp on west shore; parking on sides of road
Accommodations: None
Shoreland zoning: Recreational dev.
Management class: Centrarachid
Ecological type: Centrarchid

FISH STOCKING DATA

year	species	size	# released
10	Walleye	Fingerling	4,600
11	Walleye	Fingerling	2,398
11	Walleye	Adult	237
12	Walleye	Fingerling	8,288

NET CATCH DATA
Date: 08/21/2006

	Gill Nets		Trap Nets	
		avg. fish		avg. fish
species	# per net	weight (lbs.)	# per net	weight (lbs.)
Black Crappie	10.3	0.17	2.3	0.41
Bluegill	2.0	0.09	14.0	0.11
Brown Bullhead	0.2	1.76	1.0	1.42
Hybrid Sunfish	-	-	0.1	0.06
Largemouth Bass	0.3	1.37	0.3	1.22
Northern Pike	4.8	3.58	0.1	1.76
Pumpkin. Sunfish	-	-	0.4	0.13
Walleye	1.2	1.40	0.2	5.84
Yellow Perch	0.3	0.08	0.2	0.14

LENGTH OF SELECTED SPECIES SAMPLED FROM ALL GEAR
Number of fish caught for the following length categories (inches):

species	0-5	6-8	9-11	12-14	15-19	20-24	25-29	>30	Total
Black Crappie	39	24	16	-	-	-	-	-	83
Bluegill	98	34	-	-	-	-	-	-	138
Brown Bullhead	-	-	-	10	-	-	-	-	10
Hybrid Sunfish	1	-	-	-	-	-	-	-	1
Largemouth Bass	-	1	-	3	1	-	-	-	5
Northern Pike	-	-	-	-	3	18	5	3	30
Pumpkin. Sunfish	4	-	-	-	-	-	-	-	4
Walleye	-	-	-	4	2	2	1	-	9
Yellow Perch	2	2	-	-	-	-	-	-	4

FISH STOCKING DATA

year	species	size	# released
10	Walleye	Fingerling	6,900
11	Walleye	Fingerling	2,475
11	Walleye	Adult	105
12	Walleye	Fingerling	1,200

NET CATCH DATA
Date: 08/24/2009

	Gill Nets		Trap Nets	
		avg. fish		avg. fish
species	# per net	weight (lbs.)	# per net	weight (lbs.)
Black Crappie	35.3	0.26	1.3	0.26
Bluegill	12.3	0.24	9.4	0.19
Largemouth Bass	0.2	2.64	0.1	4.39
Northern Pike	2.7	3.42	-	-
Pumpkin. Sunfish	-	-	0.9	0.34
Walleye	1.5	3.38	-	-
Yellow Bullhead	1.0	0.54	0.1	0.79
Yellow Perch	1.7	0.15	0.7	0.29

LENGTH OF SELECTED SPECIES SAMPLED FROM ALL GEAR
Number of fish caught for the following length categories (inches):

species	0-5	6-8	9-11	12-14	15-19	20-24	25-29	>30	Total
Black Crappie	9	201	7	-	-	-	-	-	224
Bluegill	49	101	-	-	-	-	-	-	159
Brown Bullhead	-	-	12	32	-	-	-	-	45
Largemouth Bass	-	-	-	-	1	1	-	-	2
Northern Pike	-	-	-	-	-	9	3	4	16
Pumpkin. Sunfish	1	7	-	-	-	-	-	-	8
Walleye	-	-	-	-	-	8	1	-	9
Yellow Bullhead	-	-	7	-	-	-	-	-	7
Yellow Perch	1	11	2	-	-	-	-	-	16

FISHING INFORMATION: These are two small, but productive, lakes in the Braham area. **Lewis Lake** is a little smaller than Lory at 178 acres and more than twice as deep at 48 feet max. According to the latest DNR survey, the number and size of northerns have increased, with an average weight of 3.5 pounds and an average length of 22.9 inches. Try for them in shallows near the outlet at the northern end of the lake and in the narrows between the lake's two bays. Walleyes can be found, too. Fish for them with jig-and-minnow combinations while they're prowling for perch at weedlines in the northern bay. Crappies are in the same area. They are numerous and will usually hit a small minnow. Finally, don't forget to sample the bluegill fishing. Shallows at either end of the southern basin are the place to find these panfish. Worm chunks beneath a slip bobber are almost sure to get some action for the kids.

Small boat access to Lory Lake is located on the west side; for Lewis Lake, access is off County Road 47, on the east side.

Lory is the bigger of the two. It's only 214 acres, with a maximum depth of 21 feet, but it contains lots of good fish and gets its heaviest fishing pressure in winter. Largemouth bass are plentiful enough that they even occasionally show up in an ice angler's catch; sometimes they'll hit on jig-and-minnow combos. Locals say 3- and 4-pounders are common and an occasional 6-pounder is taken. Northern pike have been growing in numbers, and they're big, averaging around 23.6 inches and roughly 3 pounds. A #5 Mepps or a sucker minnow under a bobber should get some action. Walleyes are available, thanks to frequent stocking; they're of fair-to-medium size and can usually be taken on a jig-and-minnow or crankbait. The black crappie population is up, with decent size structure, too, according to the 2009 DNR survey. Bluegills are on the rebound as well. A nightcrawler chunk or worm should produce a few of these desirable panfish. Look for bluegills in shallows.

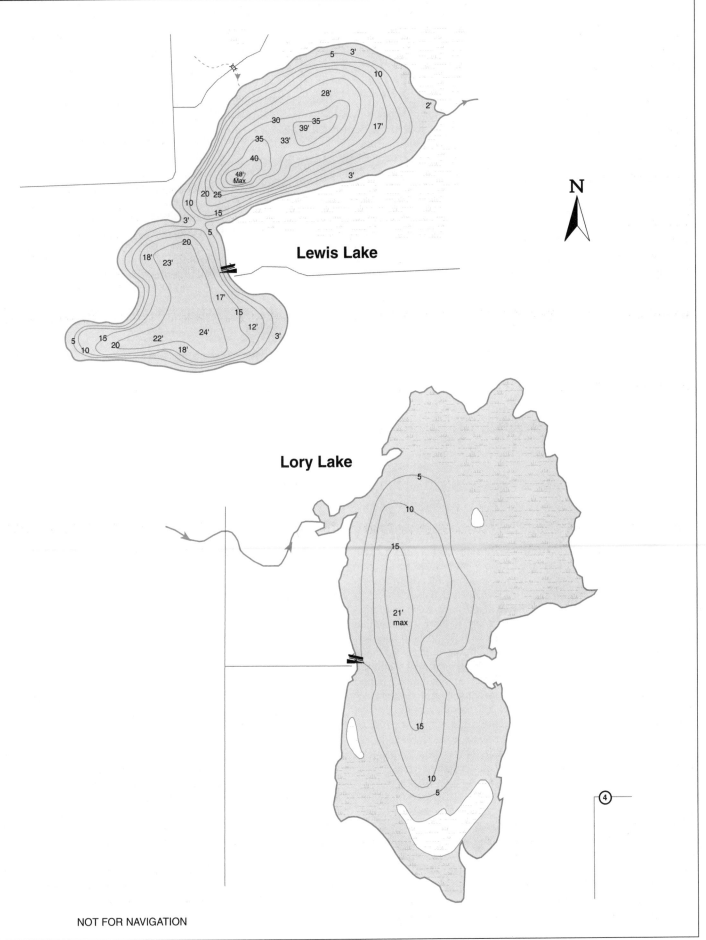

Lewis Lake

Lory Lake

N

④

NOT FOR NAVIGATION

NORTH STANCHFIELD LAKE
Isanti County

Area map page/coord: 19 / D-5
Watershed: Rum
Surface area: 143 acres
Maximum depth: 11 feet
Mean depth: 6 feet
Water clarity: 2.0 feet (1991)
Accessibility: Carry-down access from County Road right-of-way
Accommodations: None
Zoning: Natural environment
Management class: Roughfish-gamefish

SOUTH STANCHFIELD LAKE
Isanti County

Area map page/coord: 19 / D,E-5
Watershed: Rum
Surface area: 398 acres
Maximum depth: 17 feet
Mean depth: 9 feet
Water clarity: 1.8 feet (1991)
Accessibility: County-owned public access with gravel ramp on northeast shore
Accommodations: None
Zoning: Recreational development
Management class: Roughfish-gamefish

LITTLE STANCHFIELD LAKE
Isanti County

Area map page/coord: 20 / D,E-1
Watershed: Rum
Surface area: 138 acres
Maximum depth: 12 feet
Mean depth: 3.8 feet
Water clarity: 1.5 feet (2003)
Accessibility: State-owned public access with gravel ramp on south shore
Accommodations: None
Zoning: Natural environment
Management class: NA

North Stanchfield Lake

NO RECORD OF STOCKING SINCE 1987

NET CATCH DATA

Date: 07/29/1991	Gill Nets		Trap Nets	
species	# per net	avg. fish weight (lbs.)	# per net	avg. fish weight (lbs.)
Black Crappie	4.3	0.28	8.5	0.28
Bluegill	-	-	3.3	0.11
Northern Pike	5.3	3.08	0.3	1.50
Walleye	7.3	0.71	-	-
Yellow Perch	3.7	0.10	1.8	0.10

LENGTH OF SELECTED SPECIES SAMPLED FROM ALL GEAR

Number of fish caught for the following length categories (inches):

species	0-5	6-8	9-11	12-14	15-19	20-24	25-29	>30	Total
Black Bullhead	77	34	-	-	-	-	-	-	111
Black Crappie	-	42	5	-	-	-	-	-	47
Bluegill	9	4	-	-	-	-	-	-	13
Brown Bullhead	27	14	-	-	-	-	-	-	41
Northern Pike	-	-	-	-	1	11	5	-	17
Walleye	-	-	-	21	1	-	-	-	22
Yellow Perch	1	16	1	-	-	-	-	-	18

FISHING INFORMATION: North and South Stanchfield Lakes, northeast of Princeton, are winterkill lakes that provide some good crappie catches between freeze-outs. It is largely hit-and-miss fishing, however, and those who do try the lakes usually have them to themselves. South Stanchfield was used as a walleye rearing pond following the winterkill of 1988-89. Many of them migrated into North Stanchfield from South. However, North Stanchfield has very limited breeding grounds for walleyes. It is unlikely that any fish have survived since then, but one never really knows for sure. Northern pike and largemouth bass that find enough oxygenated water during tough winters to survive also provide decent fishing. Ice fishing for crappies is popular here.

Little Stanchfield Lake has little in common with the other Stanchfields, except the name. It has an area of 138 acres and a maximum depth of only 12 feet. Located a few miles north of Cambridge, this little lake is a backwater of the Rum River. As such, it avoids winterkill and provides a spawning area for crappies, bass and northern pike, as well as other species. Even though there are few residences on this lake, it does receive a high amount of fishing pressure. According to the DNR survey in 2003, northerns and largemouth bass are the primary targets of these anglers, and for good reason. Pike averaged 3.5 pounds, with sizes ranging from 20 to 36 inches. Bass caught during the survey measured 13 to 19 inches with a nice average weight of 2.2 pounds. Bluegills were abundant, but not very big. Shoreline seining found natural reproduction occurring for all gamefish, except walleyes, only one of which was found during the survey.

South Stanchfield Lake

FISH STOCKING DATA

year	species	size	# released
12	Walleye	Fry	2,000,000

NET CATCH DATA

Date: 07/30/1991	Gill Nets		Trap Nets	
species	# per net	avg. fish weight (lbs.)	# per net	avg. fish weight (lbs.)
Black Crappie	0.3	0.20	2.2	0.52
Bluegill	-	-	1.2	0.24
Brown Bullhead	18.5	0.11	1.0	0.50
Common Carp	26.5	1.08	5.5	1.72
Green Sunfish	-	-	0.3	0.10
Northern Pike	-	-	0.7	3.65
Walleye	4.2	1.16	0.2	0.20
White Sucker	0.5	0.37	1.3	1.04
Yellow Bullhead	0.2	0.20	0.5	0.67
Yellow Perch	19.3	0.14	1.3	0.13

LENGTH OF SELECTED SPECIES SAMPLED FROM ALL GEAR

Number of fish caught for the following length categories (inches):

species	0-5	6-8	9-11	12-14	15-19	20-24	25-29	>30	Total
Black Bullhead	27	97	-	-	-	-	-	-	124
Black Crappie	1	6	7	1	-	-	-	-	15
Bluegill	1	6	-	-	-	-	-	-	7
Brown Bullhead	38	35	5	1	-	-	-	-	79
Green Sunfish	2	-	-	-	-	-	-	-	2
Northern Pike	-	-	-	-	-	2	2	-	4
Walleye	-	-	9	5	10	-	-	-	24
Yellow Bullhead	-	1	2	1	-	-	-	-	4
Yellow Perch	31	80	-	-	-	-	-	-	111

Little Stanchfield Lake

NO RECORD OF STOCKING SINCE 1987

NET CATCH DATA

Date: 08/18/2003	Gill Nets		Trap Nets	
species	# per net	avg. fish weight (lbs.)	# per net	avg. fish weight (lbs.)
Black Crappie	14.5	0.45	24.7	0.41
Largemouth Bass	-	-	0.2	3.58
Northern Pike	11.5	2.12	6.8	3.97
Walleye	0.5	3.54	-	-

LENGTH OF SELECTED SPECIES SAMPLED FROM ALL GEAR

Number of fish caught for the following length categories (inches):

species	0-5	6-8	9-11	12-14	15-19	20-24	25-29	>30	Total
Black Bullhead	1	56	10	3	-	-	-	-	70
Black Crappie	1	43	37	-	-	-	-	-	81
Bluegill	13	40	-	-	-	-	-	-	53
Brown Bullhead	-	-	-	2	-	-	-	-	2
Largemouth Bass	-	-	-	2	2	-	-	-	2
Northern Pike	-	-	-	3	26	24	10	13	76
Pumpkin. Sunfish	1	2	-	-	-	-	-	-	3
Walleye	-	-	-	-	1	-	-	-	1
Yellow Bullhead	-	1	2	-	-	-	-	-	3
Yellow Perch	2	4	1	-	-	-	-	-	7

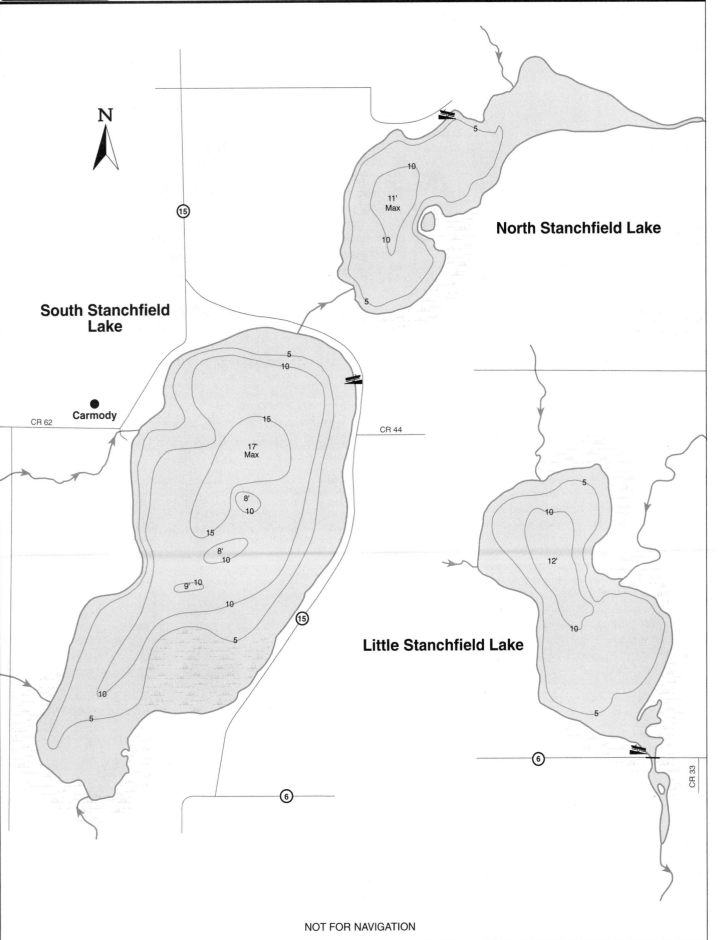

N

North Stanchfield Lake

11'
Max

South Stanchfield Lake

Carmody

CR 62

CR 44

17'
Max

8'

8'

9'

Little Stanchfield Lake

12'

CR 6

CR 33

Source: Minnesota Department of Natural Resources, USGS

POKEGAMA LAKE
Pine County

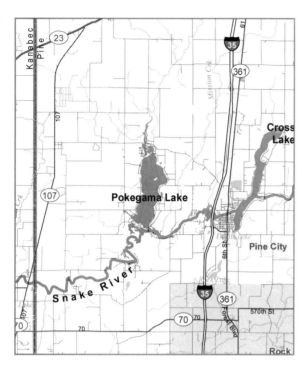

Area map pg / coord: 20 / A-2,3
Watershed: Snake
Secchi disk: 3.3 feet (2010)
Water color: Green

Surface area: 1,515 acres
Shorelength: 10.6 miles
Maximum depth: 25 feet
Mean depth: NA

Accessibility: 1) State-owned public access on south shore; 2) state-owned public access on northeastern shore
Boat ramp: 1) Concrete; 2) concrete
Parking: 1) Twelve trailer spaces; 2) seven to ten trailer spaces
Accommodations: 1) Dock, restroom; 2) dock

Shoreland zoning classification: General development
Management class: Walleye-centrarchid
Ecological type: Centrarchid

FISHING INFORMATION: Located just west of Pine City, Pokegama Lake is part of the Snake River flowage. The lake is highly fertile, yet rarely experiences any summer or winter fish kills. Nuisance algae blooms have been a problem on this lake since 1929. Due to the high algae blooms, there is limited deep aquatic vegetation with, most weed growth occurring in the upper 8 feet of the lake. The lake is managed primarily for walleyes and northern pike, with crappies and channel catfish as secondary species. The DNR annually stocks the lake with walleyes. There have been some good walleyes taken, including some in the 10-pound class, according to locals. However, according to DNR statistics, the average walleye caught here is closer to 1.5 pounds. The DNR is taking a close look at this lake to see if the natural walleye contribution to the lake's population is enough to sustain a suitable population. The south end of the lake, near the Snake River outlet, is good early in the season, when anglers catch walleyes using leeches or jigs and minnows.

Big northern pike also lurk in this flowage. The average weight, according to the DNR, was just over 3 pounds and measured 23.5 inches long. Locate the available weeds and you'll find pike. Keep your bait choice simple. Since water clarity isn't great, with an average of 3.3 feet of visibility, try using a brightly colored lure. Bright white, chartreuse or firetiger-colored jerkbaits or spinnerbaits will help northern pike find your hook. A basic cast and steady retrieve will work well, along with the occasional burst of speed.

Crappie fishing also is good. The northern-most bay is especially productive shortly after ice-out. Both black and white crappies are present in good numbers, and there are some real slabs. Small marabou jigs or tube jigs fished under a slip float early in the year over shallows can produce fish. Don't forget your small minnows and leeches. Bait is best when other methods fail.

Channel catfish offer a nice bonus fishery. According to the DNR, number and size distribution of this species are above normal for the area. Catfish are voracious feeders. Take advantage of this by offering them nightcrawlers, jumbo leeches, prepared bait or cut bait like shiners or suckers. Fish any of these offerings on or close to the bottom.

FISH STOCKING DATA			
year	species	size	# released
05	Walleye	Fingerling	19,545
07	Walleye	Fingerling	23,290
09	Walleye	Fingerling	25,635
10	Walleye	Fingerling	7,006
11	Walleye	Fingerling	15,324
12	Walleye	Fingerling	10,866
12	Walleye	Yearling	1,206

NET CATCH DATA				
Date: 07/12/2010	Gill Nets		Trap Nets	
species	# per net	avg. fish weight (lbs.)	# per net	avg. fish weight (lbs.)
Black Bullhead	-	-	0.1	1.01
Black Crappie	8.8	0.44	3.2	0.44
Bluegill	6.8	0.39	3.9	0.31
Channel Catfish	5.3	4.15	0.1	2.76
Largemouth Bass	0.1	1.06	-	-
Muskellunge	0.1	21.05	-	-
Northern Pike	1.8	3.57	0.6	3.50
Pumpkin. Sunfish	-	-	0.6	0.21
Walleye	0.9	1.44	0.1	0.99
White Bass	0.7	2.00	0.6	1.56
White Crappie	1.4	0.47	-	-
White Sucker	1.0	2.48	1.0	2.67
Yellow Bullhead	-	-	0.6	0.98
Yellow Perch	3.2	0.26	0.7	0.24

LENGTH OF SELECTED SPECIES SAMPLED FROM ALL GEAR								
Number of fish caught for the following length categories (inches):								
species	0-5	6-8	9-11	12-14	15-19	20-24	25-29	>30	Total
Black Bullhead	-	-	-	1	-	-	-	-	1
Black Crappie	2	49	84	-	-	-	-	-	141
Bluegill	11	107	3	-	-	-	-	-	124
Bowfin (Dogfish)	-	-	-	-	-	4	5	-	9
Channel Catfish	-	-	-	2	13	38	11	1	65
Common Carp	-	-	-	-	-	4	2	1	8
Largemouth Bass	-	-	-	1	-	-	-	-	1
Muskellunge	-	-	-	-	-	-	-	1	1
Northern Pike	-	-	-	1	4	8	6	3	27
Pumpkin. Sunfish	4	2	-	-	-	-	-	-	6
Walleye	-	-	2	6	3	1	-	-	12
White Bass	-	-	-	3	12	-	-	-	15
White Crappie	1	1	15	-	-	-	-	-	17
White Sucker	-	-	-	1	21	1	-	-	23
Yellow Bullhead	-	-	2	4	-	-	-	-	6
Yellow Perch	6	29	6	-	-	-	-	-	46

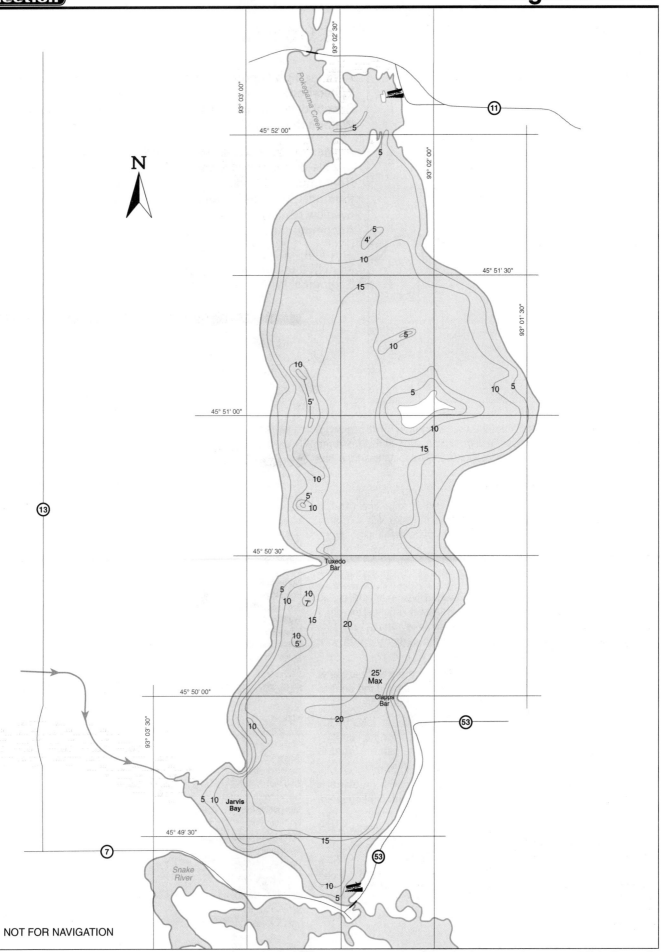

NOT FOR NAVIGATION

Source: Minnesota Department of Natural Resources, USGS

CROSS LAKE
Pine County

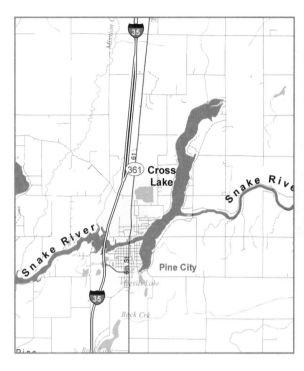

Area map pg / coord: 20 / A-3
Watershed: Snake
Secchi disk: 4.9 feet (2010)
Water color: Light brown

Surface area: 925 acres
Shorelength: 11.3 miles
Maximum depth: 30 feet
Mean depth: 12 feet

Accessibility: 1) State-owned public access on east shore by outlet; 2) state-owned public access on Snake River, in Pine City
Boat ramp: 1) Concrete; 2) two concrete plank ramps
Parking: 1) Twenty-five trailer spaces; 2) twenty trailer spaces with overflow parking available
Accommodations: 1) Dock, restroom; 2) two docks, restroom

Shoreland zoning classification: General development
Management class: Walleye-centrarchid
Ecological type: Centrarchid

FISHING INFORMATION: Cross Lake is another of those long, skinny bodies of water formed by damming a river, in this case the Snake. Located on the eastern outskirts of Pine City, this lake has lots of interesting structure to fish.

Walleyes are stocked annually by the DNR, and although they're tought to find, they're probably worth wetting your line. Try off Norway Point at the extreme northern end of the lake with a jig-and-minnow combination. Another good area to try is the sunken island only a few hundred yards off the end of Norway Point. The long, shallow bar just off the end of County Highway 10 is another quality spot. The average walleye in Cross weighs about 1.4 pounds.

Northern pike can be found at the Snake River inlet and outlet. Work these areas with a spinnerbait, crankbait, bucktail or other pike lure. Most of the northern pike in this lake range from 19.5 to 31.3 inches long. The latter-sized pike are certainly worth your time.

Largemouth bass can reach a nice size. Fish the weedy areas at either end of the lake with jigs and spinnerbaits early in the season and soft-plastic worms and tubes or surface baits later on.

Cross Lake has been designated as a muskellunge lake by the DNR, and these toothy critters have been stocked for the last several years. As muskie connoisseurs know, these fish are hard to catch. Try the bar located between the inlet and outlet.

Channel catfish are available in good numbers with an average fish weighing just over three pounds. Nightcrawlers and leeches are good baits to lure a cat to your hook.

Crappies are definitely worth your time at Cross Lake. Both numbers and size are about average according to DNR surveys. The typical crappie is about one-third of a pound. Use a jig-and-minnow combo or small minnow and slip bobber fished near the weed edges and off the sunken islands and bars.

FISH STOCKING DATA			
year	species	size	# released
09	Muskellunge	Fingerling	540
09	Walleye	Fingerling	14,325
10	Muskellunge	Fingerling	706
10	Walleye	Fingerling	3,937
11	Muskellunge	Fingerling	569
11	Walleye	Fingerling	9,277
12	Muskellunge	Fingerling	500
12	Walleye	Fingerling	6,274

NET CATCH DATA				
Date: 06/28/2010	Gill Nets		Trap Nets	
species	# per net	avg. fish weight (lbs.)	# per net	avg. fish weight (lbs.)
Black Crappie	3.6	0.32	1.4	0.30
Bluegill	2.1	0.27	10.1	0.30
Brown Bullhead	-	-	0.1	0.57
Channel Catfish	1.7	4.76	-	-
Golden Shiner	0.1	2.65	0.1	2.43
Lake Sturgeon	0.2	4.12	-	-
Northern Pike	1.1	6.24	0.3	3.43
Pumpkin. Sunfish	0.2	0.19	0.3	0.15
Smallmouth Bass	-	-	0.1	0.09
Walleye	0.8	2.30	0.1	0.15
White Bass	0.2	0.57	-	-
White Crappie	0.5	0.10	0.1	0.14
White Sucker	0.3	2.65	0.2	1.96
Yellow Perch	11.4	0.18	1.2	0.14

LENGTH OF SELECTED SPECIES SAMPLED FROM ALL GEAR								
Number of fish caught for the following length categories (inches):								
species	0-5	6-8	9-11	12-14	15-19	20-24	25-29	>30	Total
Black Bullhead	-	-	1	1	-	-	-	-	2
Black Crappie	6	38	16	-	-	-	-	-	60
Bluegill	15	129	-	-	-	-	-	-	146
Brown Bullhead	-	-	1	-	-	-	-	-	1
Channel Catfish	-	-	-	3	4	8	4	1	20
Common Carp	-	-	-	-	-	-	-	1	1
Lake Sturgeon	-	-	-	-	-	-	1	1	2
Northern Pike	-	-	-	-	3	4	3	6	17
Pumpkin. Sunfish	4	2	-	-	-	-	-	-	6
Smallmouth Bass	1	-	-	-	-	-	-	-	1
Walleye	-	1	1	2	2	5	-	-	11
White Bass	-	1	-	1	-	-	-	-	2
White Crappie	4	3	-	-	-	-	-	-	7
White Sucker	-	-	-	1	4	-	-	-	6
Yellow Perch	19	126	-	-	-	-	-	-	151

NOT FOR NAVIGATION

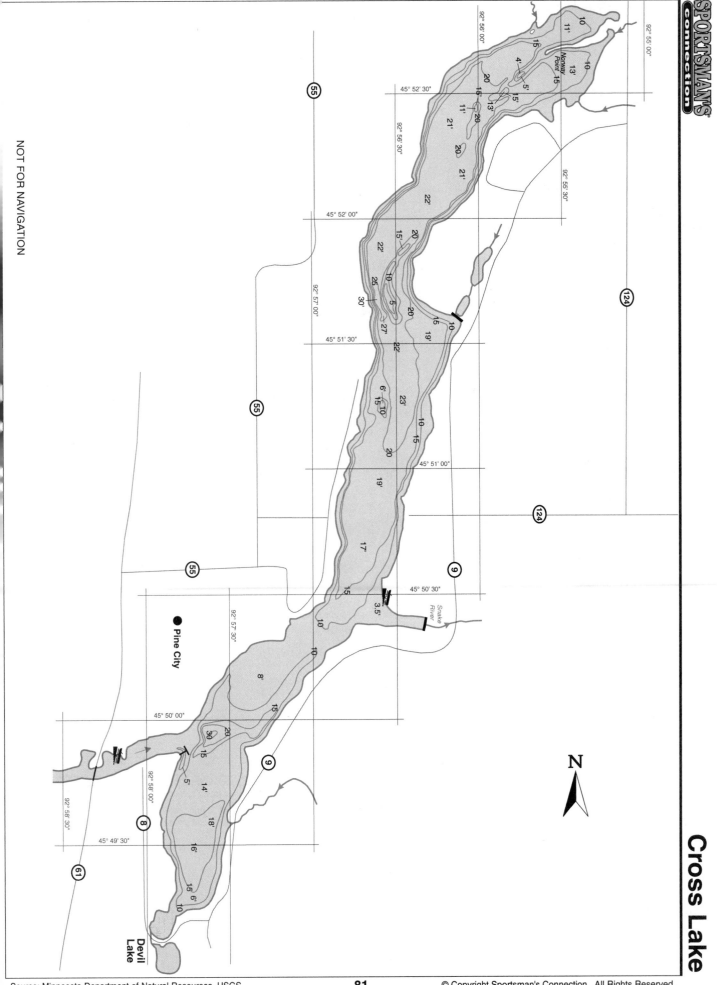

Cross Lake

81

WEST RUSH LAKE
Chisago County

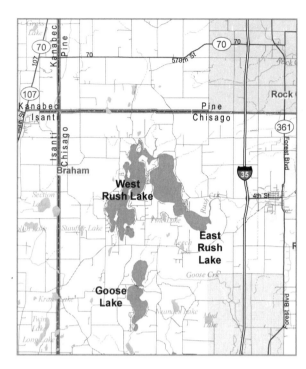

Area map pg / coord: 20 / C,D-2
Watershed: Lower St. Croix
Secchi disk: 2.8 feet (2007)
Water color: Stained

Surface area: 1,579 acres
Shorelength: NA
Maximum depth: 42 feet
Mean depth: NA

Accessibility: State-owned public access on west shore; also accessible via navigable channel from East Rush Lake
Boat ramp: Cement plank (both)
Parking: Thirty to forty trailer spaces
Accommodations: Resorts

Shoreland zoning classification: General development
Management class: Walleye-centrarchid
Ecological type: Centrarchid-walleye

FISHING INFORMATION: Located just outside of Rush City, Rush Lake is made up of two distinct basins, East Rush and West Rush. These are identified as separate lakes, but they're really one body of water separated in two by a boat channel. This double-lobed body of water is one of the premier fisheries in the east-central part of the state. West Rush Lake is the more interesting of the two basins; at least as far as structure fishing is concerned.

Shortly after ice-out in spring, crappies and bluegills move into the shallow bays, looking for warmer water. They will stay in these locations well into May, when crappies begin spawning. Bluegills, which spawn later than crappies, stay near shallow water a little longer. After the spawn, both species move out to deeper water.

Walleyes averaged 2.8 pounds and over 18 inches in length in the most recent DNR survey. Although the catch rate didn't meet the DNR lake management goal, the average size was good. There are numerous drop-offs and points to try throughout the lake. Trolling perch- or baitfish-colored crankbaits is a good way to find active fish. A slip bobber or a Lindy rig with a leech, minnow or crawler can lure the most lethargic walleye to bite.

Northern pike average just under 4 pounds here, with some fish measuring as much as 35 inches long. Look for pike to frequent the various bays and channels where submerged vegetation is present. Live minnows, jerkbaits, spoons and spinnerbaits will all work at times.

Yellow perch are the primary forage for both pike and walleyes. The perch population in West Rush Lake has been historically high, offering both forage for gamefish and decent-sized fish for anglers to catch.

Like many lakes in the areas, the largemouth bass population is solid. The average fish measures 10.8 inches long and weighs 0.8 pounds, down from 2002 averages. Bass are suckers for soft plastics fished along weed edges.

Muskie anglers will like this lake, and annual stocking helps bolster the population. Some nice muskies are caught every year.

FISH STOCKING DATA

year	species	size	# released
08	Walleye	Fingerling	25,508
09	Muskellunge	Fingerling	604
10	Muskellunge	Fingerling	316
10	Walleye	Fingerling	67,029
11	Muskellunge	Fingerling	575
11	Walleye	Fry	75,722
11	Walleye	Fingerling	30,068
11	Walleye	Yearling	471
12	Muskellunge	Fingerling	500
12	Walleye	Fingerling	17,549

NET CATCH DATA

Date: 08/20/2007

species	Gill Nets # per net	Gill Nets avg. fish weight (lbs.)	Trap Nets # per net	Trap Nets avg. fish weight (lbs.)
Black Crappie	28.0	0.28	4.3	0.33
Bluegill	3.7	0.20	7.4	0.20
Common Carp	0.1	0.04	0.1	14.33
Freshwater Drum	4.2	2.04	1.7	4.48
Golden Shiner	0.3	0.09	-	-
Hybrid Sunfish	0.1	0.28	-	-
Northern Pike	1.3	3.65	1.2	3.40
Pumpkin. Sunfish	-	-	1.0	0.12
Walleye	0.7	2.78	1.4	1.35
White Sucker	0.2	1.62	-	-
Yellow Bullhead	0.2	0.58	-	-
Yellow Perch	55.8	0.23	3.2	0.16

LENGTH OF SELECTED SPECIES SAMPLED FROM ALL GEAR
Number of fish caught for the following length categories (inches):

species	0-5	6-8	9-11	12-14	15-19	20-24	25-29	>30	Total
Black Crappie	8	327	32	-	-	-	-	-	379
Bluegill	53	60	-	-	-	-	-	-	118
Common Carp	1	-	-	-	-	-	-	1	2
Freshwater Drum	-	-	14	12	21	12	-	-	67
Golden Shiner	2	2	-	-	-	-	-	-	4
Hybrid Sunfish	-	1	-	-	-	-	-	-	1
Northern Pike	-	2	-	-	2	13	5	5	27
Pumpkinseed	9	1	-	-	-	-	-	-	10
Walleye	-	7	3	2	5	2	3	-	22
White Sucker	-	-	-	1	1	-	-	-	2
Yellow Bullhead	-	-	2	-	-	-	-	-	2
Yellow Perch	13	657	20	-	-	-	-	-	701

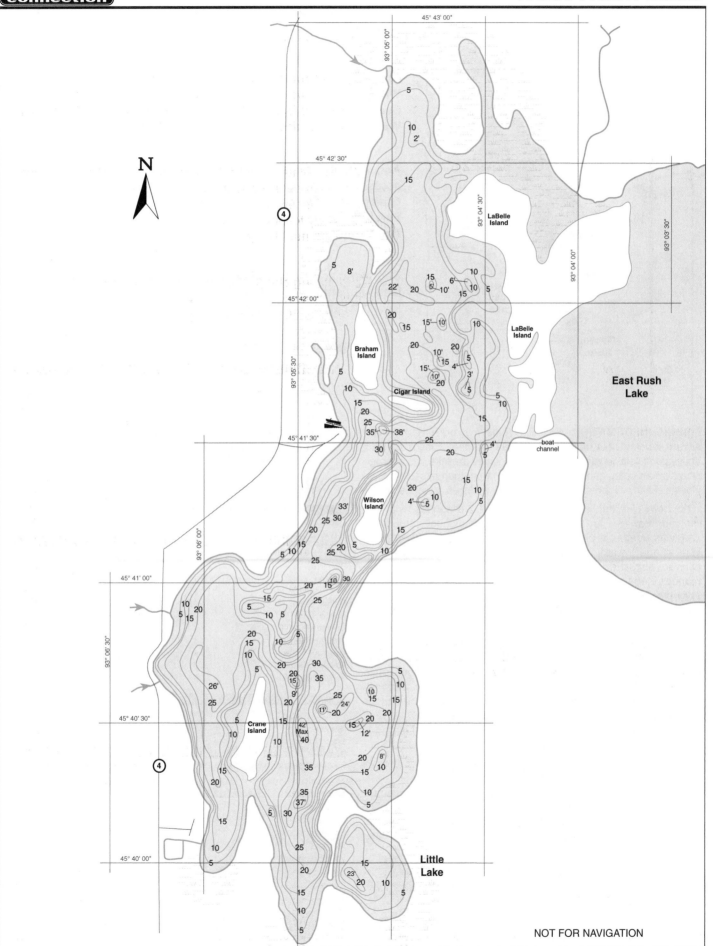

NOT FOR NAVIGATION

EAST RUSH LAKE
Chisago County

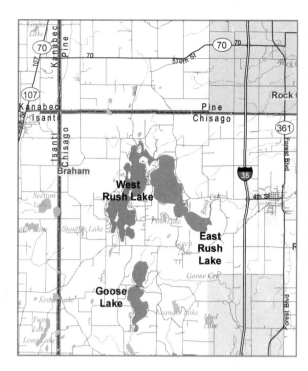

Area map pg / coord: 20 / C,D-2
Watershed: Lower St. Croix
Secchi disk: 2.4 feet (2011)
Water color: Green

Surface area: 1,481 acres
Shorelength: NA
Maximum depth: 24 feet
Mean depth: NA

Accessibility: State-owned public access on northeast shore; also accessible via navigable channel from West Rush Lake
Boat ramp: Two cement plank ramps
Parking: Thirty trailer spaces
Accommodations: None

Shoreland zoning classification: General development
Management class: Walleye-centrarchid
Ecological type: Centrarchid-walleye

FISH STOCKING DATA

year	species	size	# released
09	Muskellunge	Fingerling	620
10	Muskellunge	Fingerling	317
10	Walleye	Fingerling	72,367
11	Muskellunge	Fingerling	557
11	Walleye	Fry	72,576
11	Walleye	Fingerling	32,273
11	Walleye	Yearling	221
12	Muskellunge	Fingerling	500
12	Walleye	Fry	72,302

NET CATCH DATA

Date: 04/19/2011	Gill Nets		Trap Nets	
species	# per net	avg. fish weight (lbs.)	# per net	avg. fish weight (lbs.)
Black Crappie	23.8	0.12	-	-
Bluegill	3.3	0.23	-	-
Common Carp	0.3	0.07	-	-
Freshwater Drum	6.4	3.87	-	-
Golden Shiner	1.5	0.10	-	-
Hybrid Sunfish	0.1	0.29	-	-
Northern Pike	2.3	4.07	-	-
Pumpkin. Sunfish	0.4	0.25	-	-
Walleye	3.8	2.24	-	-
Yellow Bullhead	0.1	1.38	-	-
Yellow Perch	37.5	0.21	-	-

LENGTH OF SELECTED SPECIES SAMPLED FROM ALL GEAR

Number of fish caught for the following length categories (inches):

species	0-5	6-8	9-11	12-14	15-19	20-24	25-29	>30	Total
Black Crappie	200	68	7	-	-	-	-	-	285
Bluegill	11	24	-	-	-	-	-	-	35
Common Carp	4	-	-	-	-	-	-	-	4
Freshwater Drum	1	-	1	2	44	20	-	-	77
Golden Shiner	4	12	-	-	-	-	-	-	16
Hybrid Sunfish	-	1	-	-	-	-	-	-	1
Northern Pike	-	-	-	-	3	11	8	6	28
Pumpkin. Sunfish	1	3	-	-	-	-	-	-	4
Walleye	-	1	14	6	9	7	8	-	45
Yellow Bullhead	-	-	-	1	-	-	-	-	1
Yellow Perch	42	381	18	-	-	-	-	-	450

FISHING INFORMATION: East Rush Lake may not have the diversity of structure that its counterpart has, but that doesn't mean a shortage of fish. When the DNR last surveyed the lake, the average size of most of the gamefish was slightly larger than expected. East Rush Lake is managed for northern pike, walleyes and muskies.

Northern pike had an average weight of 3.6 pounds, with fish ranging from 18.4 to 37 inches long. The abundance of northern pike was normal. If pike are what you want to catch, then focus your efforts toward the weeds. This isn't a new revelation, but pike are almost always relating to submerged vegetation in some manner. Keep your lure and bait selection simple. Flashy spoons, spinnerbaits or crankbaits will attract pike. Bait choices should also include large minnows. Try whatever variety is available, but remember, these fish tend to prefer larger offerings.

The latest DNR survey showed the number of walleyes didn't meet the lake management goals. However, the fish were quality size, averaging 2.1 pounds, with one-third of the catch measuring more than 19.5 inches. Although the DNR stocks this lake with walleyes, there is also natural reproduction occurring. Fish the various points, submerged bars and weed edges to find walleyes. A fun and productive way to catch them during warm weather is to pitch jigs tipped with leeches or crawlers into the pockets and edges of submerged weeds. Pop your jig up and let it flutter back to the bottom. Walleyes will usually strike as the bait is descending.

Muskies are stocked annually to support the fishery. Search for these prized fish along the same deeper weed edges where you'll find northern pike. During summer, try a topwater bait to hook them. Also try a bucktail worked quickly across a weed flat during the early and late part of the day.

Bass busters can have a good time on this lake. Largemouth bass average just over 13 inches long here, with the average weight being 1.6 pounds. Work weed edges or deep into the thickest weeds with Texas-rigged soft plastics.

East Rush's access is on its northeast shore off County Road 1.

Eurasian milfoil is present, so be sure to check your boat carefully before and after launching it to make sure you remove any remnants of this invasive weed.

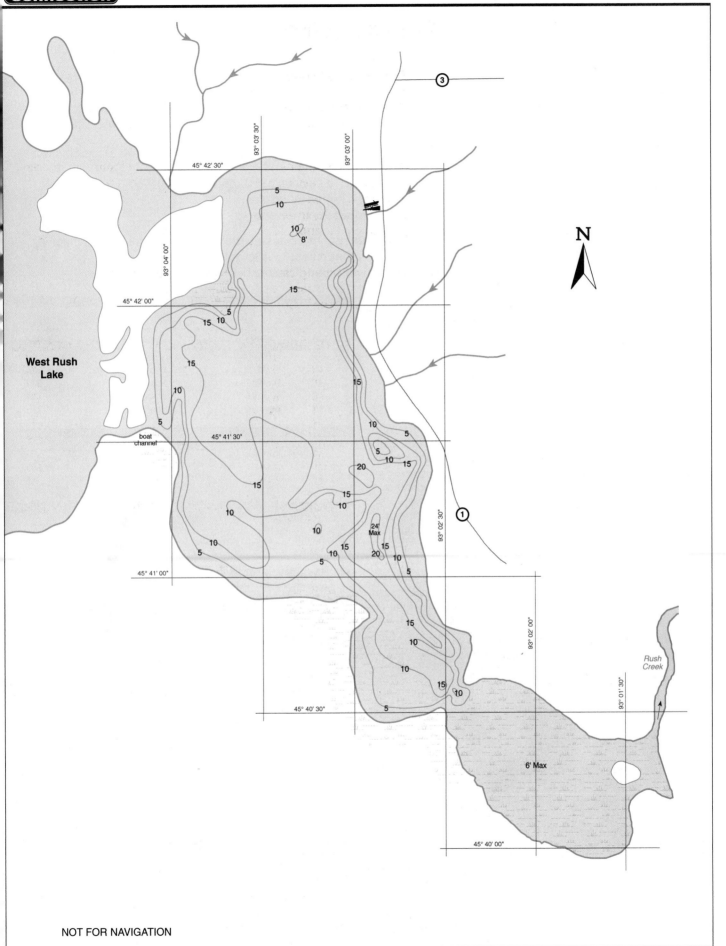

West Rush Lake

boat channel

24' Max

Rush Creek

6' Max

NOT FOR NAVIGATION

Source: Minnesota Department of Natural Resources, USGS

GOOSE LAKE
Chisago County

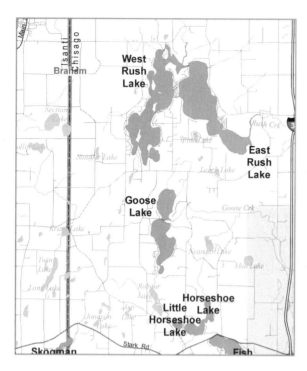

Area map pg / coord: 20 / D,E-2
Watershed: Lower St. Croix
Secchi disk: 6.9 feet (2007)
Water color: Light green

Surface area: 719 acres
Shorelength: 6.8 miles
Maximum depth: 55 feet
Mean depth: 15 feet

Accessibility: State-owned public access on east shore of northern basin
Boat ramp: Concrete ramp (on very shallow grade)
Parking: Ten trailer spaces
Accommodations: None

Shoreland zoning classification: Recreational development
Management class: Walleye-centrarchid
Ecological type: Centrarchid

FISH STOCKING DATA

year	species	size	# released
07	Walleye	Fingerling	12,640
09	Walleye	Fingerling	5,660
09	Walleye	Yearling	13
10	Walleye	Fingerling	5,382
11	Walleye	Fingerling	8,400
12	Walleye	Fingerling	2,189
12	Walleye	Yearling	733

NET CATCH DATA

Date: 07/16/2007

	Gill Nets		Trap Nets	
species	# per net	avg. fish weight (lbs.)	# per net	avg. fish weight (lbs.)
Black Bullhead	98.0	0.51	3.2	0.51
Black Crappie	4.2	0.23	8.3	0.37
Bluegill	1.8	0.25	15.3	0.30
Northern Pike	5.3	2.38	0.4	2.79
Walleye	1.7	2.70	0.2	3.03
Yellow Bullhead	6.7	0.68	0.6	0.94
Yellow Perch	6.2	0.20	-	-

LENGTH OF SELECTED SPECIES SAMPLED FROM ALL GEAR

Number of fish caught for the following length categories (inches):

species	0-5	6-8	9-11	12-14	15-19	20-24	25-29	>30	Total
Black Bullhead	13	31	864	-	-	-	-	-	911
Black Crappie	6	83	18	-	-	-	-	-	113
Bluegill	22	126	-	-	-	-	-	-	154
Northern Pike	-	-	-	-	8	34	9	-	52
Walleye	-	-	1	-	7	9	-	-	17
Yellow Bullhead	-	-	62	3	-	-	-	-	65
Yellow Perch	4	51	1	-	-	-	-	-	56

FISHING INFORMATION: This 719-acre lake southwest of Rush City doesn't get much fishing pressure, but it should. With good access and lots of fish lurking in its depths, it's a nice fishing experience waiting to happen. One word of caution, however, you may have to work a bit for your dinner. The lake has two basins connected by a narrow channel, which runs under a county road bridge. Fish the southern basin; it has some nice structure, and it's deep enough to avoid winterkill, something the northern basin can't do, with its bowl-like configuration and 9-foot maximum depth.

Walleyes are fairly numerous in the southern basin, and some are fairly large. Try the area just west of the sunken islands at mid-lake. The water drops off quickly there, and the fish can often be found suspended off weeds, where they wait for yellow perch or other forage fish to venture too far from cover. A jig-and-minnow combo will work well. There are several deep holes scattered throughout the southern basin where walleyes head as the water warms. A bottom rig and a leech or nightcrawler will get some action. You can also try trolling crankbaits or spinner rigs around the same structure, looking for suspended fish feeding on schools of small perch or other forage fish. During the last DNR survey of Goose Lake, the average walleye measured 15.6 inches long and weighed 1.6 pounds. The number of walleyes sampled met the lake's management goals at the time.

A fair number of northern pike, averaging 3 pounds or so, also prowl this lake. You'll find them in shallows, particularly in marshy areas toward the southern end of the lower basin. Northern pike were abundant in the last DNR sampling here. The lake's population was above expectations, with most of the pike in the 20-inch-plus class. Fast-moving lures will draw plenty of strikes from these toothy creatures. Try a spinnerbait, Rat-L-Trap or jerkbait in or around weeds. The old standby bobber and large shiner or sucker minnow will also work when the bite seems to slow down.

Of course, where you find northern pike, you'll often find largemouth bass. During the DNR's last survey, most largemouth bass measured longer than 12 inches, with an average weight of 1.6 pounds. The population is fast-growing, so there should be some truly large ones prowling the lake. Look for emergent weeds and flip soft plastics like tubes or worms or try a topwater offering early and late in day during the summer months. Don't pass up on fall fishing. While many anglers are pursuing other game, bass anglers can catch the biggest fish of the season using large spinnerbaits or jig-and-pig combos.

Goose Lake is supposed to contain a good number of bluegills and other sunfish, too. However, the bluegill population is down. Some of the bluegills sampled did measure as large as 9.3 inches. There are a fair number of black crappies in this lake. Goose Lake's crappies receive the highest amount of fishing pressure during winter and early spring. The basic bobber and minnow will work well here, as will a small jig tipped with or without a minnow. The public landing is on the northeast shore.

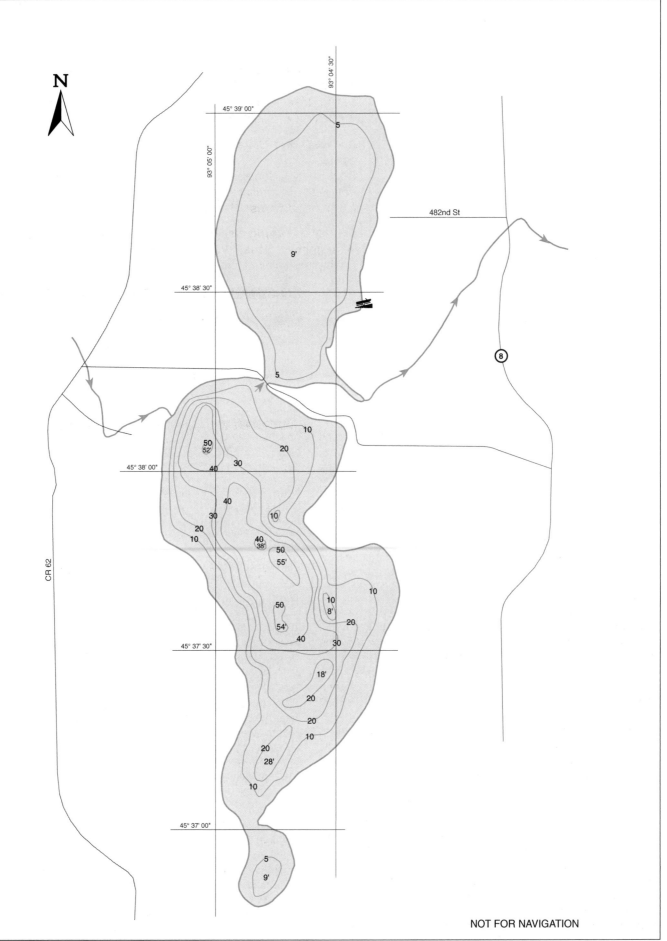

Source: Minnesota Department of Natural Resources, USGS

LONG LAKE

PICKEREL LAKE

Sherburne County

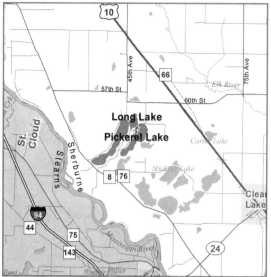

Area map page/coord: 22 / B-1,2

Watershed: Clearwater-Elk

Surface area: 174 acres

Shorelength: 3.4 miles

Maximum depth: 26 feet

Mean depth: 9 feet

Secchi disk (water clarity): 6.0 feet (2007)

Water color: Clear

Accessibility: Undeveloped state-owned public access on north shore

Accommodations: None

Shoreland zoning: Recreational dev.

Management class: Centrarchid

Ecological type: Centrarchid

Area map page/coord: 22 / B-1,2
Watershed: Clearwater-Elk

Surface area: 108 acres
Shorelength: 3.5 miles

Maximum depth: 21 feet
Mean depth: 4 feet
Secchi disk (water clarity): 11.75 feet
Water color: Clear

Accessibility: Only public access is through culvert from Round Lake and Long Lake
Accommodations: None

Shoreland zoning: Recreational dev.
Management class: Centrarchid
Ecological type: Unclassified

NO RECORD OF STOCKING

NET CATCH DATA

Date: 06/18/2007

species	Gill Nets # per net	Gill Nets avg. fish weight (lbs.)	Trap Nets # per net	Trap Nets avg. fish weight (lbs.)
Black Crappie	0.33	0.25	0.33	0.39
Bluegill	5.33	0.08	15.11	0.11
Largemouth Bass	1.00	0.99	-	-
Northern Pike	25.17	2.02	2.89	2.63
Pumpkin. Sunfish	5.83	0.11	3.89	0.12
Walleye	0.17	6.03	-	-
Yellow Perch	0.17	0.09	0.44	0.08

LENGTH OF SELECTED SPECIES SAMPLED FROM ALL GEAR

Number of fish caught for the following length categories (inches):

species	0-5	6-8	9-11	12-14	15-19	20-24	25-29	>30	Total
Black Crappie	-	3	2	-	-	-	-	-	5
Bluegill	117	50	-	-	-	-	-	-	168
Brown Bullhead	-	-	2	2	-	-	-	-	4
Largemouth Bass	-	-	4	2	-	-	-	-	6
Northern Pike	-	-	3	6	41	112	14	1	177
Pumpkin. Sunfish	58	12	-	-	-	-	-	-	70
Walleye	-	-	-	-	-	-	1	-	1
Yellow Bullhead	9	41	99	19	-	-	-	-	168
Yellow Perch	3	2	-	-	-	-	-	-	5

NO RECORD OF STOCKING

NET CATCH DATA

Date: 07/09/2007

species	Gill Nets # per net	Gill Nets avg. fish weight (lbs.)	Trap Nets # per net	Trap Nets avg. fish weight (lbs.)
Black Crappie	2.00	0.19	0.22	0.22
Bluegill	19.83	0.09	9.33	0.07
Largemouth Bass	0.67	1.59	0.22	0.07
Northern Pike	20.67	2.12	1.22	2.53
Pumpkin. Sunfish	8.83	0.12	4.67	0.10
Yellow Perch	0.17	0.20	0.33	0.12

LENGTH OF SELECTED SPECIES SAMPLED FROM ALL GEAR

Number of fish caught for the following length categories (inches):

species	0-5	6-8	9-11	12-14	15-19	20-24	25-29	>30	Total
Black Crappie	1	13	-	-	-	-	-	-	14
Bluegill	189	12	-	-	-	-	-	-	203
Northern Pike	-	-	1	3	30	88	12	-	135
Pumpkin. Sunfish	87	8	-	-	-	-	-	-	95
Yellow Bullhead	-	27	83	27	-	-	-	-	137
Yellow Perch	-	4	-	-	-	-	-	-	4

FISHING INFORMATION: Located north of the town of Clearwater, Long Lake is a 174-acre lake with maximum depths reaching 26 feet. Pickerel has 108 acres of surface area with maximum depths reaching 21 feet. It has decent water clarity, down to 9 feet. Shorelines of both lakes are heavily developed, and a lot of anglers crowd in for the bite. The fisheries seem to hold up pretty well, in spite of the pressure.

Long Lake and Pickerel Lake are popular with local anglers seeking panfish, especially during late ice conditions when action heats up for both crappies and bluegills. The most popular crappie bait to use in winter are small spoons or teardrop jigs tipped with crappie minnows worked near shoreline reeds. For bluegills, try teardrop jigs tipped with wax worms in the same areas. For warm-weather action, stick with a small slip bobber and a chunk of nightcrawler or wax worm to fool a few bluegills. Crappies will gobble up minnows, but don't forget to try a small leech as well.

Open-water anglers have some success fishing for northern pike by dangling big shiner minnows under bobbers. Of course, a fast-moving, flashy lure can draw some strikes, too. A gold- or silver-bladed spinnerbait or spoon will hook pike. During summer, try working a buzzbait along shoreline cover. The strikes can be explo-

sive. Make sure you bring along several buzzbaits; northern pike hit them with such ferocity, they'll often destroy the lure. Most colors will work, but black, white or chartreuse are the standard issue that work wherever pike live. Winter also sees some spear fishing. Most pike average 3 to 4 pounds, but at least one as large as 14 pounds was weighed by a local bait shop.

Largemouth bass are somewhat scarce, but those who know the lake have some success throwing spinnerbaits, crankbaits and other bass lures around shoreline weedbeds. Slow down and work soft-plastic lures along any visible cover. Try a floating worm or a Senko rigged with no weight. Let either of these lures fall slowly to the bottom. Most strikes will occur as the lure falls. When all else fails, switch over to a finesse approach and live bait. A large nightcrawler hooked once through the nose can draw plenty of attention from bass and other fish. Fish the crawler weightless and essentially let it squirm around with very little movement imparted by you. If you get a strike, feed the fish plenty of line before you set the hook.

Access to Long Lake is along the north shore. Pickerel's access is at the culvert from Round Lake and is strictly carry-in.

Long & Pickerel Lakes

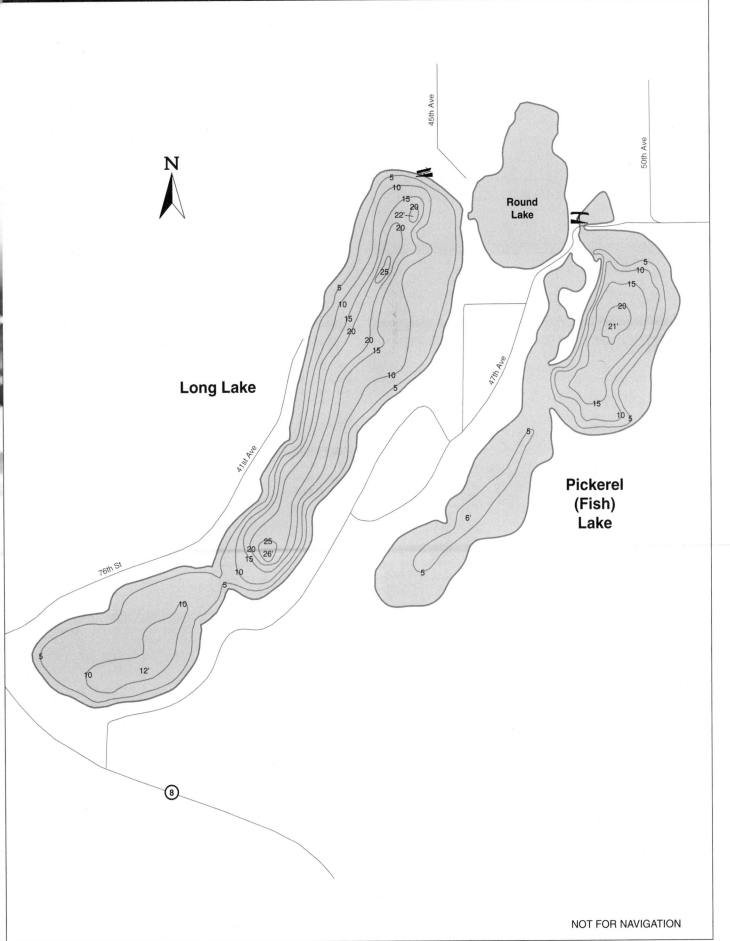

N

45th Ave

50th Ave

Round Lake

5
10
15
20
22'
20

25

5
10
15
20
15

20
15

10
5

Long Lake

41st Ave

76th St

25
20 26'
15

10

5

10

10

5

12'

8

5
10

6'

5

47th Ave

5

5
10
15

20
21'

15

10
5

Pickerel
(Fish)
Lake

NOT FOR NAVIGATION

Source: Minnesota Department of Natural Resources, USGS

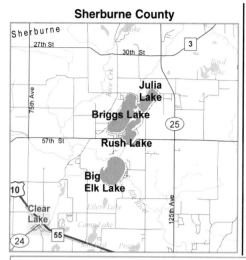

Sherburne County

	BRIGGS LAKE	JULIA LAKE	RUSH LAKE	BIG ELK LAKE
Area map page/coord:	22 / B-3	22 / B-3	22 / B-3	22 / B-3
Watershed:	Clearwater-Elk	Clearwater-Elk	Clearwater-Elk	Clearwater-Elk
Surface area:	404 acres	152 acres	161 acres	357 acres
Maximum depth:	25 feet	15 feet	11 feet	8 feet
Mean depth:	14 feet	NA	NA	7 feet
Water clarity:	1.7 feet (2009)	2.4 feet (2009)	1.2 feet (2009)	2.7 feet (2009)
Accessibility:	State-owned public access with concrete ramp on southwest shore; carry-down access on northwest shore	State-owned public access with concrete ramp on west shore	State-owned public access with concrete ramp on east shore, near outlet	State-owned public access with concrete ramp on east shore
Accommodations:	None	None	None	None
Zoning:	Recreational dev.	Recreational dev.	General dev.	Recreational dev.
Management class:	Walleye-centrarchid	Walleye-centrarchid	Roughfish-gamefish	Roughfish-gamefish

Briggs Lake

FISH STOCKING DATA

year	species	size	# released
06	Walleye	Fry	170,000
08	Walleye	Fry	170,000
10	Walleye	Fry	171,000
12	Walleye	Fry	170,000

LENGTH OF SELECTED SPECIES SAMPLED FROM ALL GEAR

Survey Date: 08/17/2009 **Survey method:** gill net, trap net

Number of fish caught for the following length categories (inches):

species	0-5	6-8	9-11	12-14	15-19	20-24	25-29	>30	Total
Black Bullhead	-	-	4	8	-	-	-	-	12
Black Crappie	34	80	19	1	-	-	-	-	134
Bluegill	54	37	-	-	-	-	-	-	91
Common Carp	-	-	-	-	-	1	4	2	7
Largemouth Bass	-	-	-	2	2	-	-	-	4
Northern Pike	-	-	-	-	3	2	3	2	10
Pumpkin. Sunfish	-	1	-	-	-	-	-	-	1
Walleye	-	3	15	7	45	12	4	-	86
White Crappie	6	5	2	-	-	-	-	-	13
White Sucker	-	3	19	24	81	-	-	-	127
Yellow Bullhead	-	-	14	15	-	-	-	-	29
Yellow Perch	33	162	8	-	-	-	-	-	203

Julia Lake

FISH STOCKING DATA

year	species	size	# released
06	Walleye	Fry	68,000
08	Walleye	Fry	68,000
10	Walleye	Fry	136,000
12	Walleye	Fry	136,000

LENGTH OF SELECTED SPECIES SAMPLED FROM ALL GEAR

Survey Date: 08/10/2009 **Survey method:** gill net, trap net

Number of fish caught for the following length categories (inches):

species	0-5	6-8	9-11	12-14	15-19	20-24	25-29	>30	Total
Black Bullhead	2	4	2	3	-	-	-	-	11
Black Crappie	8	12	1	-	-	-	-	-	21
Bluegill	194	13	-	-	-	-	-	-	207
Largemouth Bass	1	-	2	1	-	-	-	-	4
Northern Pike	-	-	-	-	4	4	4	1	13
Pumpkin. Sunfish	17	-	-	-	-	-	-	-	17
Smallmouth Bass	-	-	2	-	-	-	-	-	2
Walleye	-	2	18	1	11	2	-	-	34
White Crappie	61	19	4	-	-	-	-	-	84
White Sucker	-	7	16	4	5	-	-	-	32
Yellow Bullhead	-	-	4	3	1	-	-	-	8
Yellow Perch	13	10	-	-	-	-	-	-	23

Rush Lake

FISH STOCKING DATA

year	species	size	# released
10	Walleye	Fry	142,000
12	Walleye	Fry	142,000

LENGTH OF SELECTED SPECIES SAMPLED FROM ALL GEAR

Survey Date: 08/17/2009 **Survey method:** gill net, trap net

Number of fish caught for the following length categories (inches):

species	0-5	6-8	9-11	12-14	15-19	20-24	25-29	>30	Total
Black Bullhead	1	3	17	9	-	-	-	-	30
Black Crappie	23	25	1	-	-	-	-	-	49
Bluegill	6	20	-	-	-	-	-	-	26
Common Carp	-	-	-	-	1	-	6	-	7
Largemouth Bass	-	-	-	-	2	-	-	-	2
Northern Pike	-	-	-	-	15	7	-	1	23
Walleye	-	5	17	4	17	7	1	-	51
White Crappie	-	1	-	-	-	-	-	-	1
White Sucker	-	-	12	21	48	-	-	-	81
Yellow Perch	23	39	-	-	-	-	-	-	62

Big Elk Lake

FISH STOCKING DATA

year	species	size	# released
09	Walleye	Fry	100,000
12	Walleye	Fry	120,000

LENGTH OF SELECTED SPECIES SAMPLED FROM ALL GEAR

Survey Date: 06/22/2009 **Survey method:** gill net, trap net

Number of fish caught for the following length categories (inches):

species	0-5	6-8	9-11	12-14	15-19	20-24	25-29	>30	Total
Black Crappie	-	6	4	1	-	-	-	-	11
Bluegill	2	8	-	-	-	-	-	-	10
Walleye	-	5	1	2	15	4	6	-	33
White Sucker	-	-	12	54	137	-	-	-	205
Yellow Perch	10	20	2	-	-	-	-	-	32

FISHING INFORMATION: While homes and cabins line the shore on most of **Briggs Lake**, the eastern side of the lake has a small stretch of undeveloped, wooded land. You'll find fair numbers of walleyes, along with decent northern pike and panfish populations. The underwater point off the west shore is a place to look for walleyes. Try fishing weedlines for northern pike and panfish.

Julia is connected to Briggs and Rush Lakes via narrow, but navigable channels. It is a shallow lake, with maximum depths reaching 15 feet. It has little structure and vegetation. The DNR stocks walleye fry in all of these lakes. You'll find lots of small pike, crappies and bluegills. The DNR encourages anglers to harvest northern pike shorter than 22 inches in order to rebalance the fishery.

Rush Lake, a 161-acre fishery, has mostly developed shorelines and its bottom consists mostly of muck, sand and silt. The lake is stocked with walleye fry in even-numbered years. Harvest of small pike is encouraged. Largemouth bass numbers are average, but some as large as 20 inches are caught.

Walleye fry are stocked in **Big Elk Lake**, and other fish have migrated in from the Elk River and have decent numbers and an above-average growth rate. Black bullhead, northern pike, walleyes and white sucker are the most commonly caught species here.

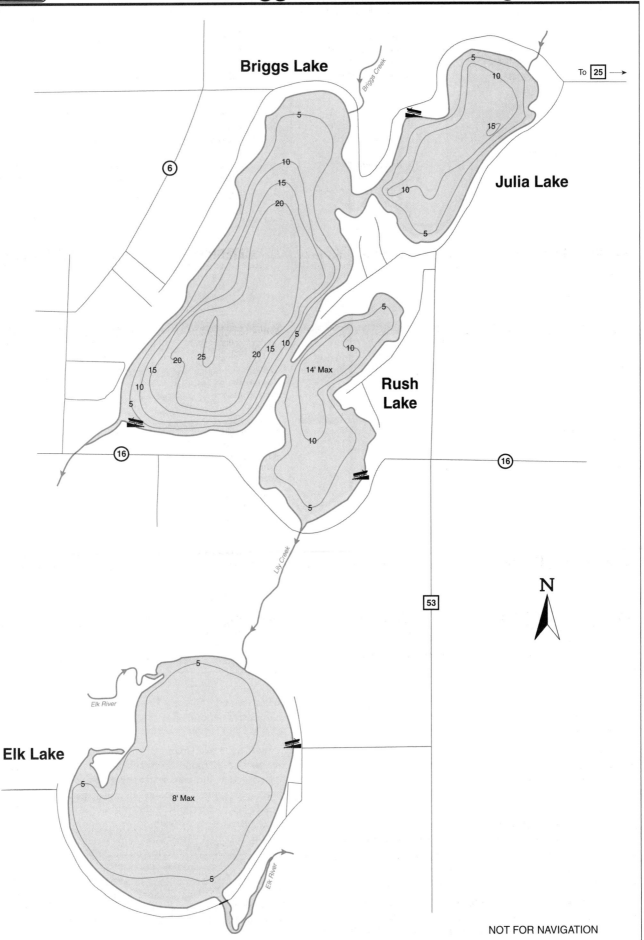

Briggs, Julia, Rush & Big Elk Lakes

Briggs Lake

Briggs Creek

To 25 →

Julia Lake

6

5

10

15

20

Rush Lake

14' Max

20 25 20 15 10

15

10

5

16

10

5

16

53

Lily Creek

N

Elk Lake

Elk River

5

8' Max

5

Elk River

NOT FOR NAVIGATION

LITTLE ELK LAKE

FREMONT LAKE

Sherburne County

Area map page/coord: 23 / B-6

Watershed: Clearwater-Elk

Surface area: 353 acres

Shorelength: 4.5 miles

Maximum depth: 14 feet

Mean depth: 10 feet

Secchi disk (water clarity): 2.5 feet (2002)

Water color: Brownish

Accessibility: State-owned public access with concrete ramp on south shore

Accommodations: None

Shoreland zoning: General dev.

Management class: Warm-water gamefish

Ecological type: Roughfish-gamefish

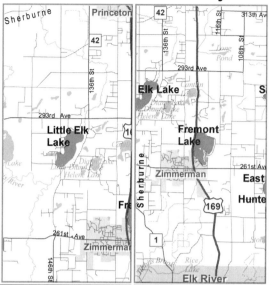

Area map page/coord: 23 / B,C-6

Watershed: Clearwater-Elk

Surface area: 486 acres

Shorelength: 3.9 miles

Maximum depth: 8 feet

Mean depth: 4 feet

Secchi disk (water clarity): 3.7 feet (2008)

Water color: Greenish-brown

Accessibility: City-owned public access with gravel ramp on southeast shore

Accommodations: None

Shoreland zoning: General dev.

Management class: Regular winterkill

Ecological type: Bullhead

FISH STOCKING DATA

year	species	size	# released
07	Walleye	Yearling	1,570
09	Walleye	Fry	350,000
09	Walleye	Fingerling	6,240
09	Walleye	Yearling	90
09	Walleye	Adult	68
11	Walleye	Fingerling	6,744

NET CATCH DATA

Date: 07/15/2012

	Gill Nets		Trap Nets	
species	# per net	avg. fish weight (lbs.)	# per net	avg. fish weight (lbs.)
Black Crappie	206.8	0.12	6.9	0.21
Bluegill	45.0	0.07	42.4	0.14
Common Carp	-	-	0.7	8.27
Largemouth Bass	0.2	1.04	0.7	2.01
Northern Pike	6.4	2.79	3.6	3.51
Pumpkin. Sunfish	0.2	0.15	1.3	0.09
Walleye	2.0	2.19	0.4	1.96
Yellow Perch	2.0	0.06	-	-

LENGTH OF SELECTED SPECIES SAMPLED FROM ALL GEAR

Number of fish caught for the following length categories (inches):

species	0-5	6-8	9-11	12-14	15-19	20-24	25-29	>30	Total
Black Crappie	741	336	7	-	-	-	-	-	1096
Bluegill	432	169	-	-	-	-	-	-	607
Common Carp	-	-	-	-	1	2	2	1	6
Largemouth Bass	-	2	-	2	3	-	-	-	7
Northern Pike	-	-	-	1	-	37	18	7	64
Pumpkin. Sunfish	12	1	-	-	-	-	-	-	13
Walleye	-	-	-	-	9	5	-	-	14
Yellow Bullhead	-	16	37	22	-	-	-	-	75
Yellow Perch	8	2	-	-	-	-	-	-	10

FISH STOCKING DATA

year	species	size	# released
09	Black Crappie	Adult	109
09	Bluegill	Adult	257
09	Yellow Perch	Adult	3,384
11	Bluegill	Adult	397
11	Largemouth Bass	Adult	6
11	Yellow Perch	Adult	397

NET CATCH DATA

Date: 06/09/2008

	Gill Nets		Trap Nets	
species	# per net	avg. fish weight (lbs.)	# per net	avg. fish weight (lbs.)
Black Bullhead	41.0	0.21	29.4	0.24
Black Crappie	2.5	0.14	0.2	0.14
Bluegill	-	-	0.3	0.41
Brown Bullhead	-	-	0.4	0.21
Common Carp	-	-	9.9	3.05
Golden Shiner	4.5	0.07	26.8	0.05
Northern Pike	7.0	2.42	0.1	2.76
Yellow Perch	26.8	-	1.4	0.05

LENGTH OF SELECTED SPECIES SAMPLED FROM ALL GEAR

Number of fish caught for the following length categories (inches):

species	0-5	6-8	9-11	12-14	15-19	20-24	25-29	>30	Total
Black Bullhead	-	345	-	-	-	-	-	-	347
Black Crappie	1	6	-	-	-	-	-	-	7
Bluegill	-	3	-	-	-	-	-	-	3
Common Carp	-	-	4	5	45	34	1	-	89
Golden Shiner	224	23	-	-	-	-	-	-	250
Northern Pike	-	-	-	-	-	14	1	-	15
Yellow Perch	2	2	-	-	-	--	-	-	4

FISHING INFORMATION: Elk Lake, or Little Elk Lake, as it is sometimes called, has received fairly regular plantings of walleyes from the DNR. Most of the lake is less than 8 feet deep with a maximum depth of 14 feet.

While the walleye stocking has resulted in some good numbers of fish, the average size walleye, according to the latest DNR survey, is 2.6 pounds, which is considered higher than normal. There is a general lack of structure on the lake, and many walleyes are caught near the point on the southwest shore, where there is a decent drop-off.

Crappies, both black and white, are also caught fairly regularly. Many are in the three-to-the-pound category, but some 2-pound crappies have been boated over the years. Bluegill numbers are good, but the average size is small. Northern pike numbers are in the normal range, with the average size being larger than normal, weighing 4.5 pounds with a couple of fish measuring longer than 37 inches caught in the last DNR survey. Largemouth bass numbers

are average for the area. Most of the bass sampled were small, but some measured nearly 19 inches in length. Good areas to try for all gamefish are points and drop-offs. There is a boat ramp with several parking spaces on the south end of the lake.

Fremont Lake, meanwhile, has a history of partial winterkills, but an aerator provided by the lake association has helped minimize this difficulty. Crappie fishing is a big attraction, and this lake has produced some 1.5-pound slabs in years past. Freeze-outs drove the average crappie size down to about 1/2 pound, but size should have rebounded. Anglers crowd the north shoreline after ice-out in spring, fishing maribou jigs and tube jigs tipped with small minnows. Some anglers anchor their boats near this area in order to escape the shoulder-to-shoulder congestion. Fish edges of the sunken timber. Later in the season, crappies will move out a little deeper along the north shore and in other areas where sunken timber or weeds appear. Sunfish are scattered and generally small. Public access is available on the southeast side of the lake.

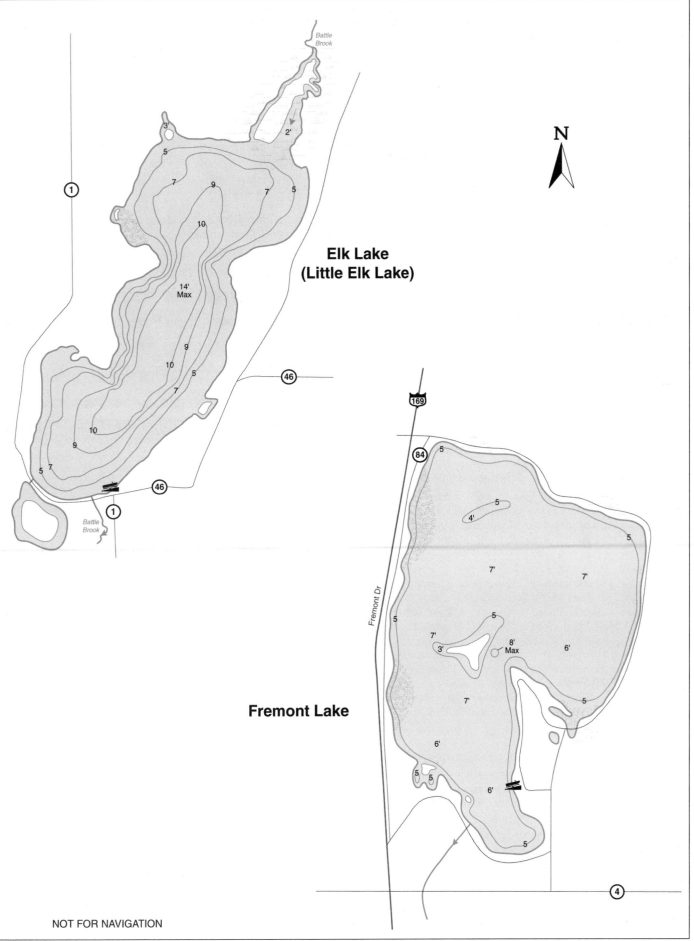

Source: Minnesota Department of Natural Resources, USGS

EAGLE LAKE
Sherburne County

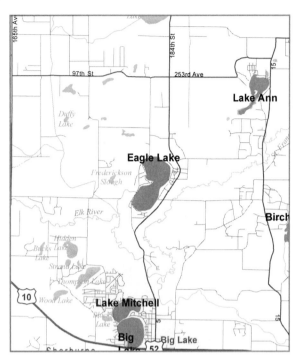

Area map pg / coord: 23 / C,D-5
Watershed: Clearwater-Elk
Secchi disk: 3.0 feet (2012)
Water color: Greenish-brown

Surface area: 381 acres
Shorelength: 5.4 miles
Maximum depth: 18 feet
Mean depth: 10 feet

Accessibility: State-owned public access on west shore of upper basin
Boat ramp: Concrete
Parking: Twelve trailer spaces
Accommodations: Fishing dock

Shoreland zoning classification: General development
Management class: Centrarchid
Ecological type: Centrarchid

FISH STOCKING DATA

year	species	size	# released
04	Walleye	Fingerling	2,600
07	Walleye	Fingerling	1,500
09	Walleye	Fingerling	1,064
10	Walleye	Fingerling	2,640
11	Walleye	Fingerling	1,400

NET CATCH DATA

Date: 08/12/2002

	Gill Nets		Trap Nets	
species	# per net	avg. fish weight (lbs.)	# per net	avg. fish weight (lbs.)
Black Bullhead	9.1	0.73	-	-
Black Crappie	45.8	0.25	1.0	0.29
Bluegill	5.8	0.14	12.7	0.09
Hybrid Sunfish	-	-	0.5	0.18
Largemouth Bass	0.8	1.22	0.3	1.95
Northern Pike	8.3	2.88	-	-
Walleye	3.6	1.79	0.3	2.68
White Sucker	3.0	1.10	0.2	1.09
Yellow Bullhead	0.8	0.81	0.3	1.11

LENGTH OF SELECTED SPECIES SAMPLED FROM ALL GEAR

Number of fish caught for the following length categories (inches):

species	0-5	6-8	9-11	12-14	15-19	20-24	25-29	>30	Total
Black Bullhead	-	17	42	14	-	-	-	-	73
Black Crappie	26	347	4	-	-	-	-	-	377
Bluegill	127	47	-	-	-	-	-	-	174
Hybrid Sunfish	3	2	-	-	-	-	-	-	5
Largemouth Bass	1	-	3	2	4	-	-	-	10
Northern Pike	-	-	-	-	15	31	14	6	66
Walleye	-	2	2	1	17	10	-	-	32
White Sucker	-	-	4	19	3	-	-	-	26
Yellow Bullhead	-	-	5	4	-	-	-	-	9

FISHING INFORMATION: Eagle Lake, located three miles north of the town of Big Lake in Sherburne County, has a reputation as a good panfish lake. However, this lake is primarily managed for largemouth bass and northern pike. It covers 381 acres and has a sand, silt and gravel substrate with an abundance of weeds.

Crappies, both black and white, make up most of the panfish population. There are many smaller crappies present; however, some real slabs are also taken. There was a report of a crappie weighing in excess of three pounds being caught. It was thought to be a hybrid of a black and white crappie. Fish for crappies near the feeder creeks and the outlet to Elk River early in the year and anywhere you find weeds or rushes. Concentrate on warm water, such as that found by inlets and outlets and along the northern shorelines, which receive southern sun exposure. Later in the season, move out to the deeper edges of the weedline and into open water where crappie schools will suspend. One reason that crappies can get big here are the number of northern pike present. These eating machines take their share of smaller crappies along with other forage. This helps the remaining crappies to grow larger, since there is less competition for food. The most recent DNR survey shows that crappies are abundant.

Try trolling or casting the weedbeds for pike, allowing for the inevitable hammer-handles that will take your bait between keepers. Large sucker or shiner minnows fished below a bobber are also a good strategy. A locally popular technique for catching pike is to troll a spinner rig baited with a strip of sucker or smelt. Casting any flashy lure can work. Spinnerbaits, crankbaits, and spoons can all attract pike. Most of the northerns will measure from 19 to 21 inches.

Largemouth bass are also found in Eagle Lake, and some of them reach 5 pounds, although the majority of the fish are smaller, with 12 to 15 inches being the average length. Focus your bass fishing efforts on shallow weeds. Both inside and outside weed edges will hold bass. Soft-plastic baits are best for catching fish during the summer months. Try a Texas-rigged tube, worm or creature bait.

Pitch this offering into pockets along weed edges or over the top of any matted weeds you find. Since most of the plant growth isn't much deeper than 5 feet, you can also break out your crankbaits and fish the deeper drop-offs and weed edges to locate big fish. Some bass will hang out in deeper water during the summer months. Use a deep-diving crankbait or a weighted plastic worm to reach these fish.

The sand bottom of the lake would suggest good walleye habitat, but the lake requires regular walleye fingerling stocking. However, there are some good-sized fish to be had, with many topping 20 inches. If you want to try your luck, fish deep weed edges with a slip bobber and a jumbo leech or a nightcrawler. Of course, there is a good chance you'll catch a panfish or two before you get a walleye when using live bait.

Eagle Lake

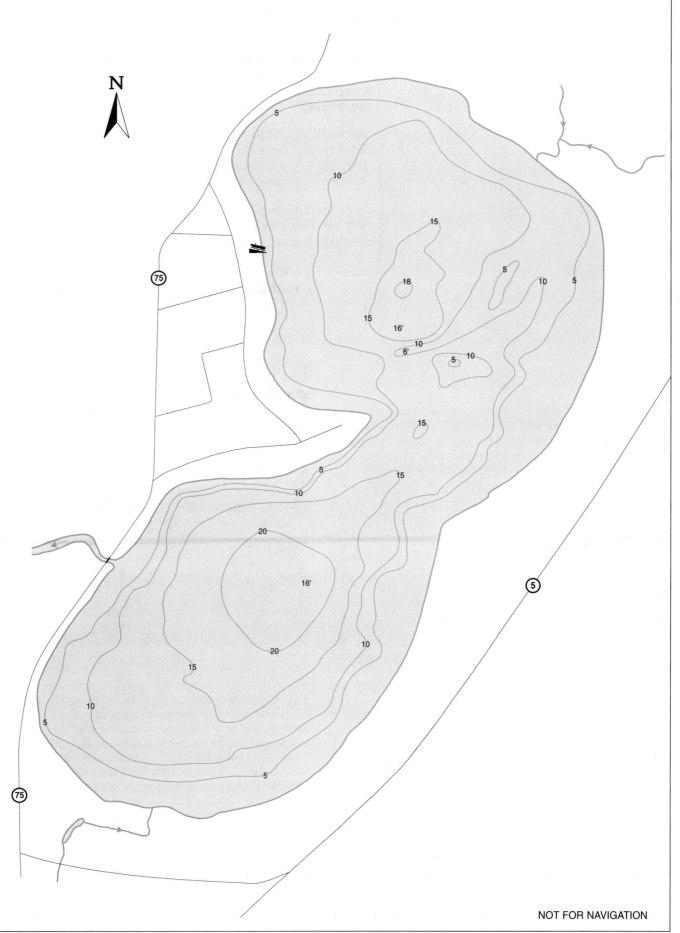

N

75

75

5

NOT FOR NAVIGATION

Source: Minnesota Department of Natural Resources, USGS

LAKE ANN
Sherburne County

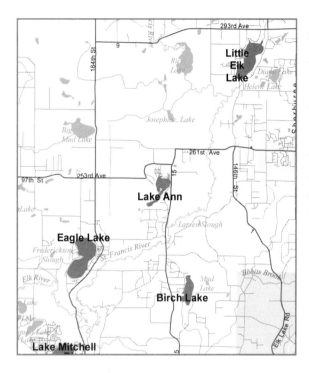

Area map pg / coord: 23 / C-5
Watershed: Clearwater-Elk
Secchi disk: 12 feet (2011)
Water color: Light green

Surface area: 184 acres
Shorelength: 4.3 miles
Maximum depth: 26 feet
Mean depth: 5 feet

Accessibility: Township-owned public access on north shore
Boat ramp: Concrete
Parking: Four trailer spaces
Accommodations: Restrooms

Shoreland zoning classification: Recreational development
Management class: Centrarchid
Ecological type: Centrarchid

NO RECORD OF STOCKING

NET CATCH DATA

Date: 06/27/2011	Gill Nets		Trap Nets	
species	# per net	avg. fish weight (lbs.)	# per net	avg. fish weight (lbs.)
Bluegill	18.5	0.12	130.8	0.13
Hybrid Sunfish	-	-	0.4	0.34
Largemouth Bass	0.17	3.64	-	-
Northern Pike	13.7	2.40	0.2	2.14
Pumpkin. Sunfish	1.0	0.07	1.2	0.21
Yellow Bullhead	34.0	0.47	4.1	0.64
Yellow Perch	0.7	0.12	0.1	0.07

LENGTH OF SELECTED SPECIES SAMPLED FROM ALL GEAR

Number of fish caught for the following length categories (inches):

species	0-5	6-8	9-11	12-14	15-19	20-24	25-29	>30	Total
Bluegill	998	286	-	-	-	-	-	-	1288
Hybrid Sunfish	-	4	-	-	-	-	-	-	4
Largemouth Bass	-	-	-	-	1	-	-	-	1
Northern Pike	-	-	1	3	15	51	14	-	84
Pumpkin. Sunfish	9	8	-	-	-	-	-	-	17
Yellow Bullhead	-	50	176	15	-	-	-	-	241
Yellow Perch	1	4	-	-	-	-	-	-	5

FISHING INFORMATION: Lake Ann, located a few miles west of Zimmerman in Sherburne County, is small in size at 184 acres, but big in fishing. The lake has good water clarity and supports a diverse plant community. The lake is managed for northern pike, largemouth bass and panfish. There has been a history of winter-kills in the past and an aeration system has been used with limited success.

The folks at Marv's Minnows, 25859 2nd St. E., Zimmerman, MN, (763) 856-4038, say crappies are caught along the weed edges in the northeast corner of the lake, especially through the ice. A small jig tipped with a crappie minnow is the preferred bait. You can either dabble this offering with or without a bobber. The DNR sampling of crappies shows the numbers to be low.

Panfish are similar in size and can be found in the same location, as well as near other weedbeds throughout the lake. During the 2001 DNR lake survey, bluegills were found to be highly abundant. In fact, they were more abundant than in previous lake surveys. The average size for a bluegill was 5.6 inches long. Lower bluegill abundance would most likely increase their overall size and growth.

Largemouth bass, many in the 3-pound range, seem to prefer the slop of weeds and timber along the west shoreline in front of the campground. Work a weedless lure like a Texas-rigged worm, tube or creature bait through thick vegetation for largemouths. You may want to try using a flipping stick and braided line. This heavy-duty gear will help you pull bass out of the thickest weeds. Peg your sinker at the top of your soft-plastic bait and pitch it into openings of the thickest weeds you can find. As soon as you suspect a hit, reel down, lower your rod tip and set the hook. Small fish will often be pulled right out of the water, but a larger opponent will try to bury itself in the weeds. You'll get them out with your heavy gear. Although locals report decent numbers of fish, the last DNR survey indicated bass numbers and size were below average for the area and their growth rate was slow. According to the DNR, the lake is difficult to sample and bass may be more abundant than their results indicate. The average length for a bass was 8.2 inches.

Northern pike are also pretty decent in size, with some heftier 4-

and 5-pound fish being mixed in among the little ones. Locals say a 17-pounder was pulled from Lake Ann a few years back. Use big shiners under a bobber for big pike. The point, sometimes referred to as The Island, on the northwest shore is good northern pike water. Pike were less abundant in the last DNR survey than in previous years; however the numbers and size were still above average for a lake of this type. The average size pike was 22.6 inches long and weighed 2.7 pounds. The DNR says pike grow slowly, which is likely due to their relatively high numbers and competition for food. Yellow perch are the preferred food fish for pike, but very few showed up in DNR survey results. This is probably due to heavy predation by the large number of northern pike.

The DNR suggest anglers can help improve this fishery by implementing selective harvesting of smaller pike, less than 24 inches, and releasing most bass. This may result in faster growth and a larger average size for pike and bluegills.

Access to Ann is on the north shore. The campground is on the west shore.

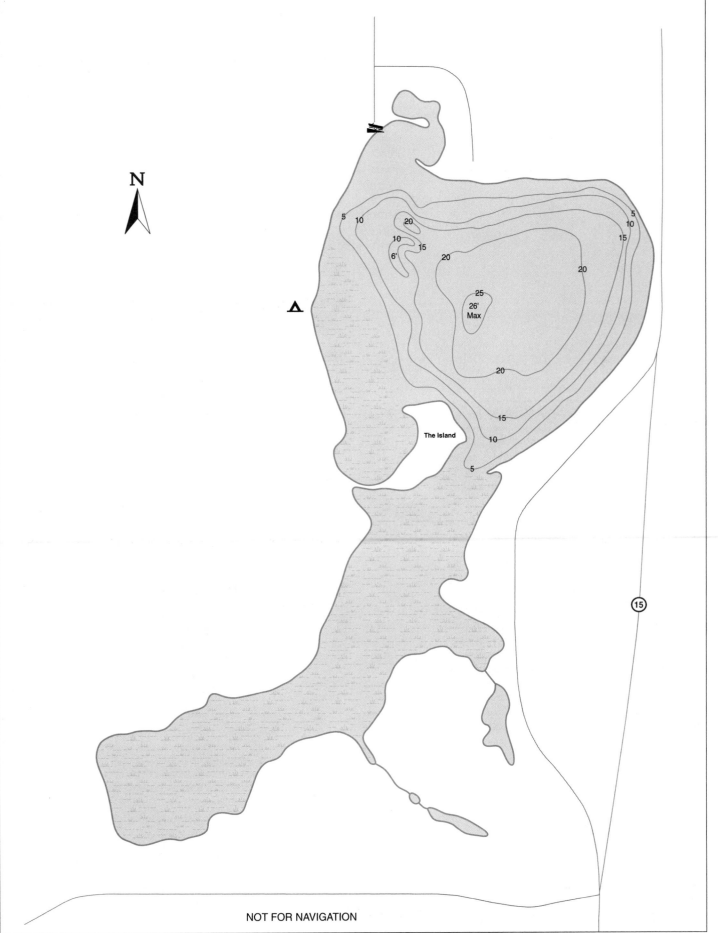

N

5 10
20
10
15
6'
20
25
26'
Max
20
15
10
5

The Island

5 10
15
20
20

15

NOT FOR NAVIGATION

BIRCH LAKE
Sherburne County

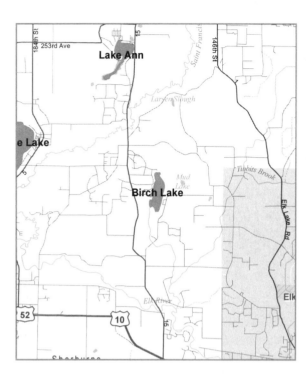

Area map pg / coord: 23 / D-5,6
Watershed: Clearwater-Elk
Secchi disk: 2.5 feet (2004)
Water color: Brownish

Surface area: 151 acres
Shorelength: 2.7 miles
Maximum depth: 18 feet
Mean depth: NA

Accessibility: Township-owned public access on west shore
Boat ramp: Concrete
Parking: Four trailer spaces
Accommodations: None

Shoreland zoning classification: Recreational development
Management class: Warm-water gamefish
Ecological type: Roughfish-gamefish

FISH STOCKING DATA			
year	species	size	# released
03	Walleye	Fry	100,000

NET CATCH DATA

Date: 06/14/2004

species	Gill Nets # per net	Gill Nets avg. fish weight (lbs.)	Trap Nets # per net	Trap Nets avg. fish weight (lbs.)
Black Bullhead	7.0	0.24	19.2	0.25
Black Crappie	26.5	0.08	43.2	0.18
Bluegill	1.0	0.05	179.8	0.08
Brown Bullhead	-	-	1.6	0.38
Common Carp	0.5	4.12	0.9	4.97
Golden Shiner	3.2	0.07	6.0	0.06
Green Sunfish	0.2	0.04	0.6	-
Hybrid Sunfish	0.3	0.04	8.4	0.08
Northern Pike	7.7	2.60	-	-
Pumpkin. Sunfish	1.2	0.05	5.3	0.05
Walleye	0.3	2.60	0.6	3.26
White Sucker	1.8	1.77	-	-
Yellow Bullhead	1.2	0.19	9.4	0.29
Yellow Perch	4.2	0.07	2.8	0.06

LENGTH OF SELECTED SPECIES SAMPLED FROM ALL GEAR
Number of fish caught for the following length categories (inches):

species	0-5	6-8	9-11	12-14	15-19	20-24	25-29	>30	Total
Black Bullhead	8	200	7	-	-	-	-	-	215
Black Crappie	161	151	2	2	-	-	-	-	316
Bluegill	209	38	-	-	-	-	-	-	247
Brown Bullhead	-	5	9	-	-	-	-	-	14
Green Sunfish	6	-	-	-	-	-	-	-	6
Hybrid Sunfish	71	7	-	-	-	-	-	-	78
Northern Pike	-	-	-	1	2	35	8	-	46
Pumpkin. Sunfish	55	-	-	-	-	-	-	-	55
Walleye	-	-	-	-	2	5	-	-	7
Yellow Bullhead	-	74	18	-	-	-	-	-	92
Yellow Perch	45	5	-	-	-	-	-	-	50

FISHING INFORMATION: Birch Lake is relatively shallow. The lake is subject to winterkill, so an aeration system has been installed to help prevent this from recurring. Since the last occurrence in 1997, the DNR has stocked walleyes, bass and crappies in hopes the fishery will return to its previous numbers. The DNR conducted a survey in 2004 to assess Birch Lake's comeback.

Northern pike fared the best, with a higher-than-average catch rate and relatively fast growth rates. Pike can be caught on spoons, spinnerbaits, crankbaits or live suckers. Work emergent vegetation early in the year, then move to deeper weed edges as water warms in summer. The standard early and late-in-the-day program works best, but overcast days can be productive at anytime.

The largemouth bass population appears to still be in a recovery phase from the winterkill, at least as of the latest survey in 2004. Electrofishing rates counted a mere 21 bass per hour, which is half the state average. Most of the bass were less than 12 inches and were 4 years old or younger. As the population matures, the DNR expects that size averages will increase. Practicing catch and release will help the population rebound. Get your practice in with a pitching stick and a supply of soft plastics and jigs. Target emergent vegetation early and late in the day. Try the outside weed edges when the sun is high. You can also hook a few largemouths with a spinnerbait; work through and around weeds. Since the water is not super clear, try a brightly colored spinnerbait. White, chartreuse, pink or firetiger will all work at times. If the water is slightly clearer when you're out, use a double-willowleaf model and use a fast and erratic retrieve. If water is more stained, use a double Colorado or single Colorado blade to provide more vibration. Use a steady retrieve with Colorado blades.

Crappies and bluegills are abundant, but tend toward the smaller side. Catch crappies near shoreline reeds. Small jigs and minnows under a slip bobber do the trick during the open-water season. Give a small spinner a try, too. You can fish this lure like you'd fish a spinnerbait for a bass or pike. Try a Beetle Spin or a Road Runner. Use wax worms through the ice, although crappie minnows also get some action when the lake has iced over. Sunfish aren't very common, and they are mostly small.

The walleye restocking efforts are only showing minimal success. Very few walleyes were caught in the survey and most of them were large, with a mean length of 21 inches. What used to be a decent walleye fishery is now struggling.

Good public access, with a concrete boat ramp, is available on the west shore, off 159th Street.

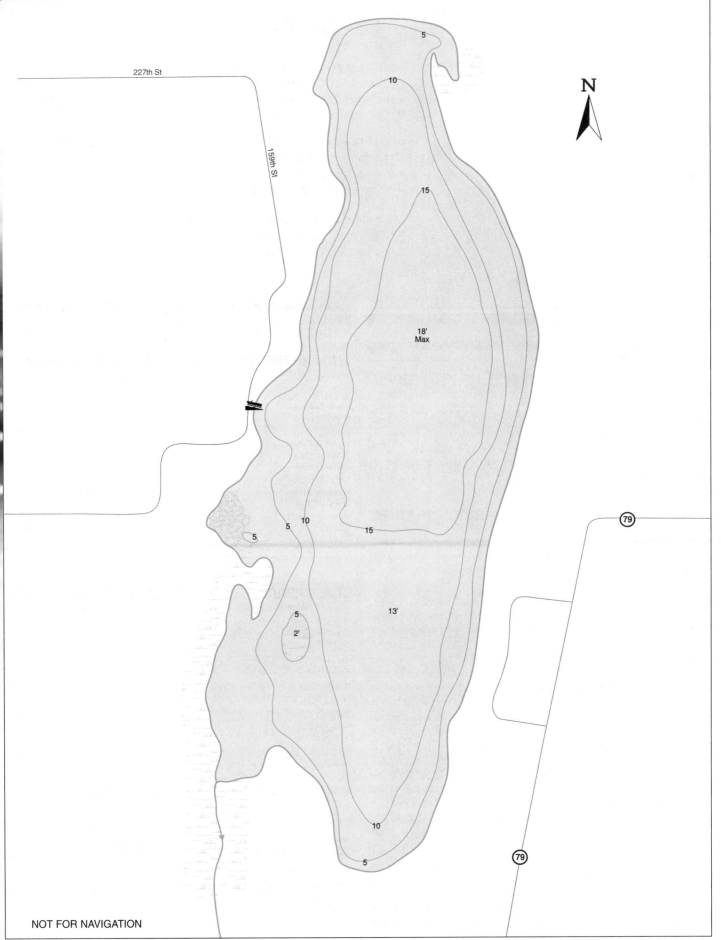

227th St

159th St

5

10

15

18'
Max

5

10

15

5

13'

5

2'

N

79

79

10

5

Source: Minnesota Department of Natural Resources, USGS

BIG LAKE

Bordered by Lakeside Municipal Park

Area map page/coord: 23 / D,E-4,5
Watershed: Clearwater-Elk
Surface area: 251 acres
Shorelength: 2.7 miles
Maximum depth: 48 feet
Mean depth: 18 feet
Secchi disk: 9.5 feet (2004)
Water color: Light green
Accessibility: City-owned public access with two concrete ramps on west shore in park (fee charged for parking); thirty trailer spaces
Accommodations: Park, fishing pier, picnicking, restrooms
Shoreland zoning: General dev.
Management class: Walleye-centrarchid
Ecological type: Centrarchid

LAKE MITCHELL

Sherburne County

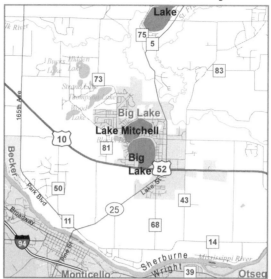

Area map page/coord: 23 / D,E-4,5
Watershed: Clearwater-Elk
Surface area: 170 acres
Shorelength: 2.6 miles
Maximum depth: 33 feet
Mean depth: 12 feet
Secchi disk: 10.5 feet (2004)
Water color: Light green
Accessibility: City-owned public access with concrete ramp on north shore (no parking); also access via navigable channel from Big Lake
Accommodations: None
Shoreland zoning: General dev.
Management class: Walleye-centrarchid
Ecological type: Centrarchid

NO RECORD OF STOCKING SINCE 1994

NET CATCH DATA

Date: 08/02/2004	Gill Nets		Trap Nets	
		avg. fish		avg. fish
species	# per net	weight (lbs.)	# per net	weight (lbs.)
Black Bullhead	12.5	1.00	-	-
Black Crappie	0.8	0.26	1.9	0.21
Bluegill	11.0	0.09	18.9	0.07
Hybrid Sunfish	0.2	0.05	1.4	0.15
Largemouth Bass	0.5	1.22	-	-
Northern Pike	15.5	2.42	0.7	2.62
Pumpkin. Sunfish	2.5	0.15	1.7	0.16
Walleye	2.7	4.11	0.1	1.95
White Sucker	0.2	3.53	0.2	3.38
Yellow Bullhead	9.8	0.74	3.2	0.80
Yellow Perch	0.8	0.09	0.6	0.07

LENGTH OF SELECTED SPECIES SAMPLED FROM ALL GEAR

Number of fish caught for the following length categories (inches):

species	0-5	6-8	9-11	12-14	15-19	20-24	25-29	>30	Total
Black Bullhead	-	7	38	29	-	-	-	-	74
Black Crappie	-	22	2	-	-	-	-	-	24
Bluegill	185	19	-	-	-	-	-	-	204
Hybrid Sunfish	8	7	-	-	-	-	-	-	15
Largemouth Bass	-	1	1	-	-	-	-	-	3
Northern Pike	-	-	-	-	10	79	11	-	100
Pumpkin. Sunfish	25	7	-	-	-	-	-	-	32
Walleye	-	-	-	-	1	14	2	-	17
Yellow Bullhead	-	7	64	20	-	-	-	-	91
Yellow Perch	6	5	-	-	-	-	-	-	11

NO RECORD OF STOCKING SINCE 1994

NET CATCH DATA

Date: 07/26/2004	Gill Nets		Trap Nets	
		avg. fish		avg. fish
species	# per net	weight (lbs.)	# per net	weight (lbs.)
Black Bullhead	14.7	0.79	0.2	0.98
Black Crappie	0.7	0.11	1.0	0.18
Bluegill	12.8	0.07	34.2	0.09
Hybrid Sunfish	0.5	0.20	2.9	0.23
Largemouth Bass	1.0	1.48	0.1	2.65
Northern Pike	13.3	1.81	0.7	2.21
Pumpkin. Sunfish	5.5	0.13	5.2	0.15
Walleye	2.0	4.94	-	-
Yellow Perch	-	-	0.2	0.10

LENGTH OF SELECTED SPECIES SAMPLED FROM ALL GEAR

Number of fish caught for the following length categories (inches):

species	0-5	6-8	9-11	12-14	15-19	20-24	25-29	>30	Total
Black Bullhead	-	4	81	5	-	-	-	-	90
Black Crappie	2	11	-	-	-	-	-	-	13
Bluegill	237	28	-	-	-	-	-	-	265
Hybrid Sunfish	10	19	-	-	-	-	-	-	29
Largemouth Bass	-	-	-	5	2	-	-	-	7
Northern Pike	-	-	-	2	40	39	3	1	85
Pumpkin. Sunfish	57	22	-	-	-	-	-	-	79
Walleye	-	-	-	-	-	10	2	-	12
Yellow Bullhead	1	11	79	13	-	-	-	-	104
Yellow Perch	1	1	-	-	-	-	-	-	2

FISHING INFORMATION: These two lakes, located off U.S. Highways 10 and 52, just outside the town of Big Lake, are very similar. They are connected by a narrow, but easily navigable channel. **Big Lake** is 251 acres and has a maximum depth of 48 feet, while its fraternal twin, **Mitchell Lake** measures 170 acres and has a maximum depth of 33 feet. They have little structure, except for a weedy bar jutting off the public beach on Big Lake. So similar are these two lakes that the DNR surveyed them as one in 2004. The statistics listed here are from that survey.

Catch rates for northern pike nearly doubled since the 1994 survey, which were double that of the lakes' management goals and were high compared to other typical lakes. Pike averaged 17 to 26 inches and 2.1 pounds. Particularly good spots to fish them are in shallows at either side of the channel connecting the two basins. A jig-and-minnow combination or #3 Mepps are attention-getters and should net some good specimens.

Walleyes have been stocked, but not recently. And since the lakes haven't been surveyed or stocked recently, the status of the walleye population is unknown. During the 2004 sampling, some of the walleyes caught were aged back to 1990, with one elder statesman celebrating his 18th birthday. He was from the class of 1986. While overall growth rates were slow, they varied among the fish caught,

The lakes have good water clarity, making them a largemouth bass haven. The bass population appears to be high and most fell in the 8- to 12-inch range. Bass are numerous along the weedy bar off the public beach on Big Lake, as they are all around the margins of these two lakes. Fish them in early summer with bottom-running crankbaits or jigs; in high summer, switch to plastic worms or surface baits.

Crappies can be found at weed edges throughout both of these lakes. Though they aren't numerous, they'll still provide good action on small minnows or jigs. Bluegill fishing is good generally. Try the southwest shore of Big Lake, near the public landing and also the north and east shores of Mitchell where water gets shallow. Don't neglect the shallows around the connecting channel, where the panfish action can become fast and furious.

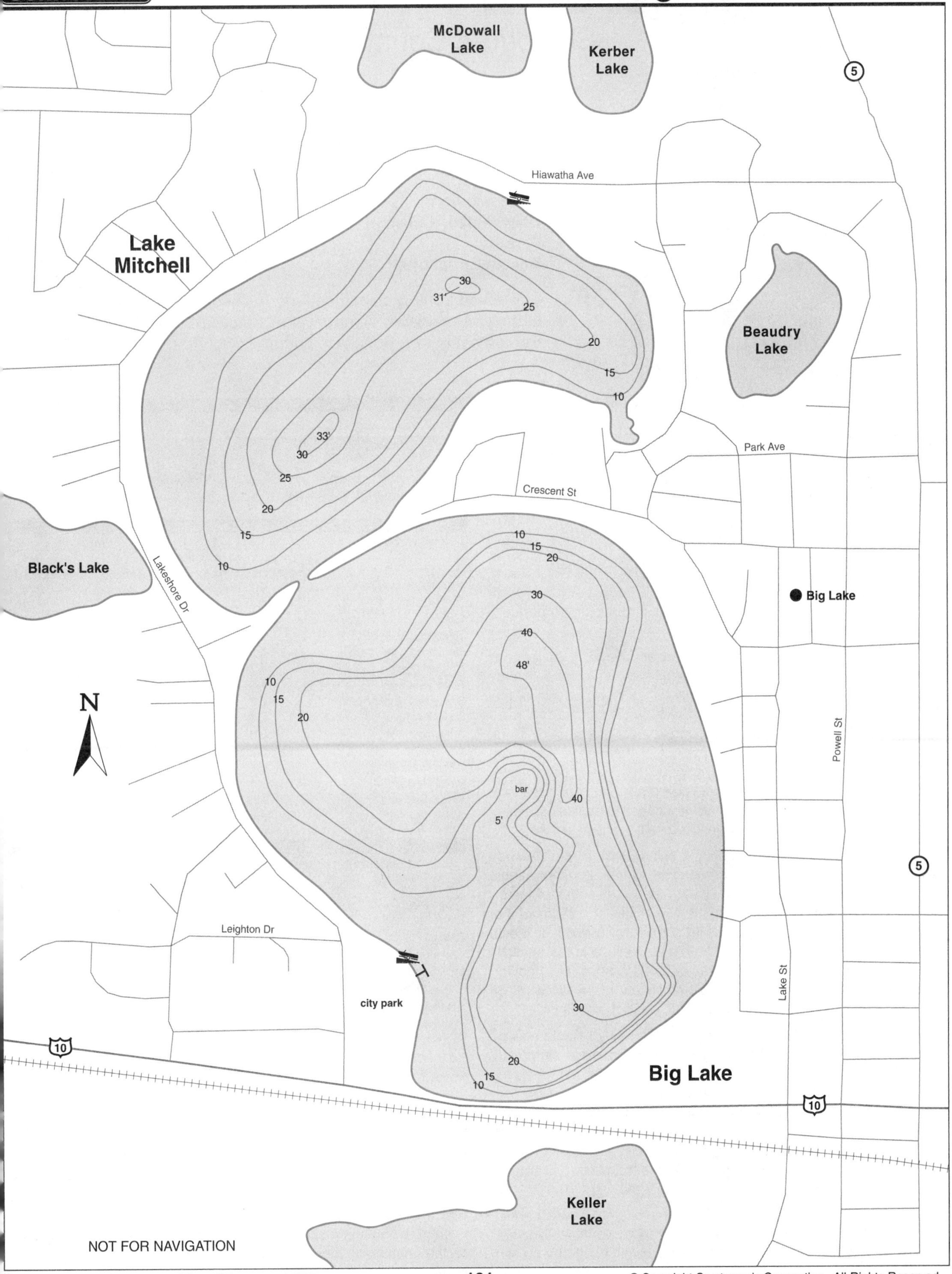

SPORTSMAN'S
connection

(5)

McDowall
Lake

Kerber
Lake

Hiawatha Ave

Lake
Mitchell

30
31'
25
20
15
10

Beaudry
Lake

Park Ave

33'
30
25
20
15
10

Crescent St

Black's Lake

Lakeshore Dr

10
15
20

● Big Lake

N

10
15
20

30
40
48'

bar
5'
40

Powell St

Leighton Dr

city park

30

Lake St

(5)

(10)

20
15
10

30

Big Lake

(10)

Keller
Lake

NOT FOR NAVIGATION

Source: Minnesota Department of Natural Resources, USGS

LAKE ORONO
Sherburne County

Bordered by Lake Orono Park

Area map pg / coord: 23 / E-6
Watershed: Clearwater-Elk
Secchi disk: 2 feet (2008)
Water color: Brownish

Surface area: 300 acres
Shorelength: 7.0 miles
Maximum depth: 18 feet
Mean depth: NA

Accessibility: City-owned public access on west shore in park
Boat ramp: Concrete
Parking: NA
Accommodations: Park, fishing pier, picnicking, restrooms

Shoreland zoning classification: General development
Management class: Warm-water gamefish
Ecological type: Roughfish-gamefish

FISH STOCKING DATA

year	species	size	# released
03	Black Crappie	Yearling	89
04	Bluegill	Adult	309
07	Bluegill	Adult	1,500
07	Black Crappie	Adult	1,000

NET CATCH DATA

Date: 08/04/2008

	Gill Nets		Trap Nets	
species	# per net	avg. fish weight (lbs.)	# per net	avg. fish weight (lbs.)
Black Bullhead	7.2	0.49	0.6	0.26
Black Crappie	1.7	0.19	4.2	0.21
Bluegill	-	-	1.1	0.06
Channel Catfish	-	-	0.2	0.12
Common Carp	1.0	5.12	1.1	5.34
Northern Pike	1.7	1.97	0.2	2.37
Rock Bass	1.3	0.36	0.6	0.14
Shorthead Redhorse	3.2	2.37	1.3	3.39
Silver Redhorse	1.0	2.96	4.8	2.80
Smallmouth Bass	1.0	1.46	-	-
Walleye	2.2	2.99	0.2	3.34
White Crappie	0.2	0.11	0.1	0.24
White Sucker	3.0	1.59	0.7	1.28
Yellow Bullhead	3.8	0.38	1.0	0.90
Yellow Perch	3.0	0.40	0.1	0.06

LENGTH OF SELECTED SPECIES SAMPLED FROM ALL GEAR

Number of fish caught for the following length categories (inches):

species	0-5	6-8	9-11	12-14	15-19	20-24	25-29	>30	Total
Black Bullhead	1	18	29	-	-	-	-	-	48
Black Crappie	20	25	2	1	-	-	-	-	48
Bluegill	9	1	-	-	-	-	-	-	10
Common Carp	-	-	-	-	1	14	1	-	16
Northern Pike	-	1	-	1	1	6	3	-	12
Silver Redhorse	-	1	1	-	29	18	-	-	49
Smallmouth Bass	-	-	2	1	3	-	-	-	6
Walleye	-	-	-	1	5	9	-	-	15
White Crappie	-	2	-	-	-	-	-	-	2
Yellow Bullhead	8	7	8	9	-	-	-	-	32
Yellow Perch	1	7	11	-	-	-	-	-	19

FISHING INFORMATION: Located in the city of Elk River, Lake Orono offers surprisingly good fishing for a body of water which is, for the most part, less than 5 feet deep and subject to periodic winterkill.

Northern pike are relatively numerous and large, with lengths running in the 20- to 26-inch range. A good location to fish for them is the eastern portion of the lake, at weedlines to either side of the dam. Of course, you can find them anywhere throughout the lake. When fishing for pike in thick weeds, make sure to use fairly stout tackle so you can safely get the fish out of the weeds. Medium-heavy-action casting gear and 20-pound line is a good starting point. Steel leaders will also prevent you from losing your lures to a pike's razor-sharp teeth. Flashy lures work best. Weedless spoons, spinnerbaits or large, soft-plastic jerkbaits will produce strikes.

Despite several years of stocking by the DNR in past years, walleyes aren't particularly numerous. The highest concentrations will be found near the deep hole beneath the Highway 53 bridge or drop-offs in the narrows separating the two southern portions of the lake. A split shot rig or jig tipped with a minnow, crawler or leech will work. Don't be surprised to find a bigger walleye in the shallow weeds from time to time. Bigger fish will often move into heavier cover in search of food. Jig-and-soft-plastic combos will work in thicker weeds. Just make sure to rig your plastics weedless.

Largemouth bass aren't numerous, but offer fairly reliable action. Toss soft plastics or spinnerbaits among the submerged stumps in the northwestern end of the lake, near the Elk River inlet. Also try a surface frog or mouse when you encounter thick mats of surface weeds. You may not catch a large number of bass, but the strikes you'll receive on a surface bait fished on top of matted weeds will be memorable. Just make sure to wait until you feel the fish before you set the hook. Most of the fish you'll miss will be due to setting the hook on the strike and not waiting to feel the fish.

Crappie action can be found where the original river channel forms slightly deeper areas. The deeper areas you're fishing for walleyes will also hold crappies. Small minnows fished under a slip bobber or on a lightweight jig work best. Try brightly colored jigs or colored hooks for added attraction. Crappies tend to be very active after dark.

Bluegills can be found in shallows throughout the lake. Fish for them with worm chunks, red worms or small leeches beneath a slip bobber.

Lake Orono has a public access and a fishing pier at the city park on the southwest shore, just off Highways 10 and 52.

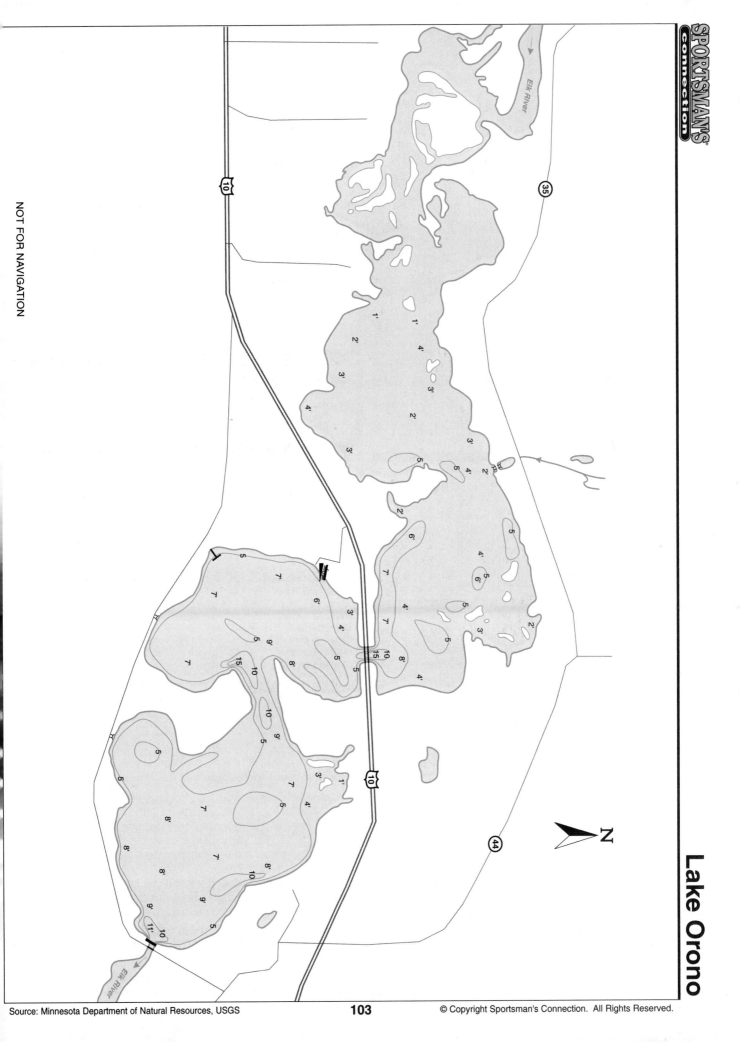

NOT FOR NAVIGATION

Lake Orono

N

Elk River

Elk River

GREEN LAKE

SPECTACLE LAKE

Isanti County

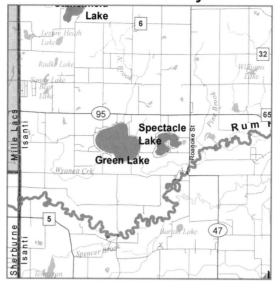

Area map page/coord: 24 / A-1,2

Watershed: Rum

Surface area: 833 acres

Shorelength: 4.4 miles

Maximum depth: 28 feet

Mean depth: 21 feet

Secchi disk: 5.0 feet (2007)

Water color: Green

Accessibility: State-owned public access with concrete ramp on east shore; twelve trailer spaces

Accommodations: Dock, restroom

Shoreland zoning: General dev.

Management class: Walleye-centrarchid

Ecological type: Centrarchid-walleye

Area map page/coord: 24 / A-1,2

Watershed: Rum

Surface area: 243 acres

Shorelength: 3.6 miles

Maximum depth: 51 feet

Mean depth: 12 feet

Secchi disk: 13.5 feet (2006)

Water color: Green tint

Accessibility: State-owned public access with concrete ramp on south shore; six trailer spaces

Accommodations: Dock, restroom

Shoreland zoning: General dev.

Management class: Centrarchid

Ecological type: Centrarchid

FISH STOCKING DATA

year	species	size	# released
10	Walleye	Fingerling	8,096
11	Walleye	Fingerling	5,015
12	Walleye	Fingerling	1,512
12	Walleye	Yearling	679

NET CATCH DATA

Date: 09/10/2007

	Gill Nets		Trap Nets	
species	# per net	avg. fish weight (lbs.)	# per net	avg. fish weight (lbs.)
Black Bullhead	2.0	1.14	0.6	1.57
Black Crappie	20.6	0.42	0.8	0.42
Bluegill	3.2	0.23	5.8	0.11
Largemouth Bass	0.1	0.87	0.2	0.43
Northern Pike	4.9	3.22	0.8	2.80
Pumpkin. Sunfish	-	-	0.6	0.29
Walleye	4.2	2.79	0.2	4.02
White Sucker	1.3	2.87	2.6	2.32
Yellow Bullhead	0.9	0.94	4.7	1.21
Yellow Perch	4.6	0.10	0.2	0.10

LENGTH OF SELECTED SPECIES SAMPLED FROM ALL GEAR

Number of fish caught for the following length categories (inches):

species	0-5	6-8	9-11	12-14	15-19	20-24	25-29	>30	Total
Black Bullhead	-	-	7	15	1	-	-	-	23
Black Crappie	2	130	51	-	-	-	-	-	192
Bluegill	54	24	-	-	-	-	-	-	81
Northern Pike	-	-	-	-	3	30	14	4	51
Pumpkin. Sunfish	-	5	-	-	-	-	-	-	5
Walleye	-	-	-	5	12	22	1	-	40
White Sucker	-	-	-	-	32	1	-	-	35
Yellow Bullhead	-	-	25	21	-	-	-	-	50
Yellow Perch	20	22	1	-	-	-	-	-	43

FISH STOCKING DATA

year	species	size	# released
10	Walleye	Fingerling	3,634
11	Walleye	Fingerling	2,174
12	Walleye	Fingerling	1,224

NET CATCH DATA

Date: 08/26/2006

	Gill Nets		Trap Nets	
species	# per net	avg. fish weight (lbs.)	# per net	avg. fish weight (lbs.)
Black Crappie	0.8	0.26	0.6	0.38
Bluegill	3.3	0.18	10.5	0.09
Hybrid Sunfish	-	-	0.1	0.19
Largemouth Bass	1.8	0.64	0.3	0.35
Northern Pike	6.8	2.01	0.8	1.52
Pumpkin. Sunfish	0.3	0.12	2.0	0.16
Walleye	2.5	2.33	0.9	0.87

LENGTH OF SELECTED SPECIES SAMPLED FROM ALL GEAR

Number of fish caught for the following length categories (inches):

species	0-5	6-8	9-11	12-14	15-19	20-24	25-29	>30	Total
Black Crappie	1	4	5	-	-	-	-	-	10
Bluegill	74	30	-	-	-	-	-	-	104
Brown Bullhead	2	17	133	16	-	-	-	-	240
Hybrid Sunfish	-	1	-	-	-	-	-	-	1
Largemouth Bass	-	1	9	3	-	-	-	-	13
Northern Pike	-	-	-	4	21	14	7	1	47
Pumpkin. Sunfish	9	9	-	-	-	-	-	-	18
Walleye	-	1	-	6	10	5	-	-	22
White Sucker	-	-	-	1	-	2	-	-	3
Yellow Bullhead	-	1	-	-	-	-	-	-	1

FISHING INFORMATION: Located just east of Princeton, these two lakes are popular with recreational boaters and anglers alike. As is the case with many lakes that receive heavy traffic, when you fish Green and Spectacle can be more important than where you fish. Largemouth bass seem to receive most of the attention on **Green Lake**. Anglers have success working the shoreline with spinnerbaits, crankbaits, plastic worms, tubes and other bass baits. Three-pound bass are not uncommon. Northern pike are also caught in these same areas, and there have been reports of pike up to 19 pounds being taken. Sucker minnows and crankbaits seem to attract larger fish. Walleyes are larger than on other lakes in this class, with a nice average of 2.8 pounds. The sunken island near the middle of the lake is a magnet for largemouth and walleyes, especially in fall. Panfish anglers seem to fare best in winter, especially during early and late ice, when big bluegills, some in the pound-class, and 1/2-pound crappies are caught. During the latest DNR survey, the bluegill population was normal compared to other lakes, but higher than the 20-year Green Lake average. Black crappie numbers were considered high for the lake class and were the highest recorded catch for the lake at the time. About 40% of the crappies caught measured over 8 inches in length.

Spectacle Lake is smaller and deeper than its neighbor and has more variations in structure. Largemouth bass and northern pike receive most of the attention here, too, and there are some nice ones to be caught. Work shorelines and ledges for both species, using soft plastics and jigs for bass, and crankbaits, spinnerbaits and topwater lures for both. A trench near the middle of the lake is a good spot to try during summer for bass and pike. Walleyes are scarce, but those caught are usually big. As in Green Lake, the panfish action in Spectacle seems to peak during winter, when crappies in the 1/2-pound range are found suspended in deeper water. Offer them wax worms or small minnows.

The public accesses to both lakes have good concrete ramps. Spectacle's is on the south side, off County Road 37, while Green's is on its east shore.

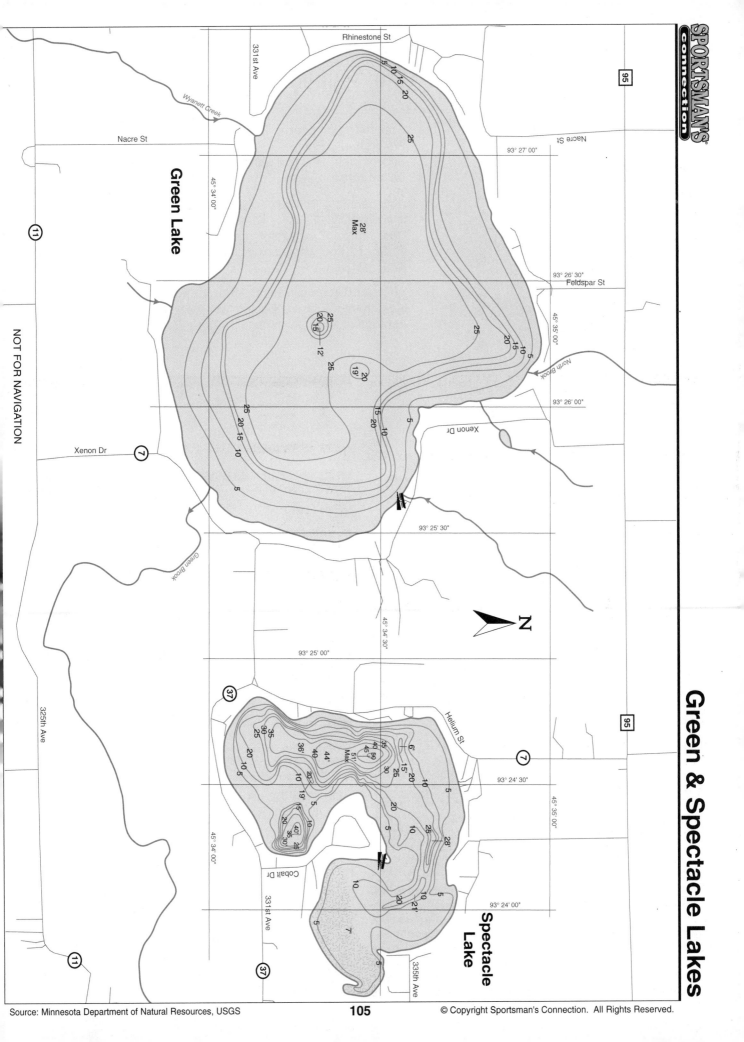

95

Green Lake

Spectacle Lake

NOT FOR NAVIGATION

28' Max

51' Max

N

Source: Minnesota Department of Natural Resources, USGS

105

BLUE LAKE
Isanti County

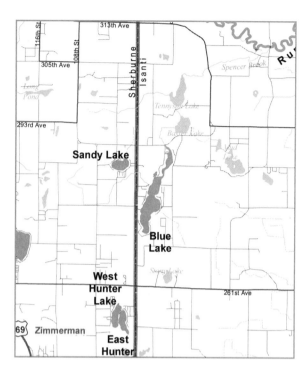

Area map pg / coord: 24 / B-1
Watershed: Rum
Secchi disk: 4.0 feet (2009)
Water color: Green

Surface area: 263 acres
Shorelength: 7.2 miles
Maximum depth: 31 feet
Mean depth: NA

Accessibility: Township-owned public access on northwest shore; township-owned public access on southeast shore
Boat ramp: Gravel (NW); asphalt (SE)
Parking: Four trailer spaces and six trailer spaces respectively
Accommodations: None

Shoreland zoning classification: Recreational development
Management class: Centrarchid
Ecological type: Centrarchid

FISH STOCKING DATA

year	species	size	# released
07	Walleye	Fingerling	7,000
09	Walleye	Fingerling	2,800
10	Walleye	Fingerling	3,082
11	Walleye	Fingerling	1,776
12	Walleye	Fingerling	1,056

NET CATCH DATA

Date: 08/17/2009

	Gill Nets		Trap Nets	
species	# per net	avg. fish weight (lbs.)	# per net	avg. fish weight (lbs.)
Black Crappie	9.8	0.42	0.8	0.25
Bluegill	11.8	0.28	11.8	0.17
Bowfin (Dogfish)	-	-	0.4	5.84
Brown Bullhead	3.2	1.39	0.7	1.55
Golden Shiner	-	-	0.1	-
Green Sunfish	-	-	0.1	0.11
Largemouth Bass	0.2	-	0.2	1.69
Northern Pike	1.0	2.79	0.1	1.52
Pumpkin. Sunfish	-	-	0.1	0.10
Walleye	2.7	4.25	0.3	3.73
Yellow Bullhead	6.5	0.59	1.1	0.78
Yellow Perch	33.8	0.18	1.1	0.16

LENGTH OF SELECTED SPECIES SAMPLED FROM ALL GEAR

Number of fish caught for the following length categories (inches):

species	0-5	6-8	9-11	12-14	15-19	20-24	25-29	>30	Total
Black Crappie	2	30	28	-	-	-	-	-	66
Bluegill	51	115	-	-	-	-	-	-	177
Bowfin (Dogfish)	-	-	-	-	-	2	2	-	4
Brown Bullhead	-	-	1	14	-	-	-	-	25
Green Sunfish	1	-	-	-	-	-	-	-	1
Largemouth Bass	-	2	-	-	1	-	-	-	3
Northern Pike	-	-	-	-	2	4	1	-	7
Pumpkin. Sunfish	1	-	-	-	-	-	-	-	
Walleye	-	-	1	-	3	11	4	-	19
Yellow Bullhead	-	11	32	3	-	-	-	-	49
Yellow Perch	27	173	8	-	-	-	-	-	213

FISHING INFORMATION: Blue Lake, near Princeton, is picturesque with its birch trees and sandy shoreline. It is also fairly popular, and its easy accessibility attracts both recreational boaters and anglers. Blue is a quality fishing lake, producing walleyes, northern pike, largemouth bass, crappies and panfish. Water clarity is moderate, with algae blooms more likely as summer progresses. In fact, boat navigation can be affected during early summer by dense stands of curled pondweed in shallower areas. Blue Lake is primarily managed for walleyes and largemouth bass.

Crappies are usually the first fish to get active on Blue Lake. Crappies in the 1/2- to 3/4-pound range are regularly caught just after ice-out. Slab-size, pound-plus crappies also are occasionally caught then. Crappie abundance is normal on this lake.

Bluegill numbers have declined a bit and the overall size isn't tremendous. The average bluegill on this lake measures just over 5 inches long. In addition to bluegills, there are hybrid sunfish and pumpkinseeds. Fish for any of these along shallow weedbeds. Use a chunk of nightcrawler, wax worm or small leech to hook a few panfish.

Walleyes can be found in decent numbers, in part because of DNR stocking. Many summertime anglers still-fish for walleyes with nightcrawlers or leeches under slip bobbers. Lindy rigs and jig-and-minnow combos also take their share of walleyes, which average a respectable 2 pounds. If live bait isn't working, try trolling crankbaits around shoreline drop-offs and sunken islands. Walleyes weren't overly abundant in the latest DNR survey, but the average fish weighed 2.6 pounds, with most fish measuring 20 inches or better.

The folks at Marv's Minnows, 25859 2nd St. E., Zimmerman, MN, (763) 856-4038, say Blue Lake has excellent largemouth bass fishing. Work the shoreline, especially early in the morning and again in evening, for largemouths. Bass anglers have good success by flipping plastic worms, tubes and jigs around docks. Make sure to try a few topwater lures in the low-light periods. Buzzbait and poppers produce fish. Most of the bass are small, but some are 3 pounds and up. During the 2004 DNR lake survey, the bass population was

considered abundant, with fish ranging in length from 7.6 to 20.5 inches. The average bass will measure 12 inches long and weigh 1.1 pounds. According to the DNR, the electrofishing results for the largemouth bass had never been better.

Blue Lake isn't known for its northern pike, but big ones are caught occasionally, along with some hammer-handles. Although the numbers are lower than normal for this type of lake, the size is large, with average fish measuring 24 inches long and weighing 4 pounds. Try casting a spinnerbait along deep weed edges. This is a very basic approach, but it can draw plenty of action.

Blue Lake

Source: Minnesota Department of Natural Resources, USGS

NOT FOR NAVIGATION

LAKE FRANCIS   # LONG LAKE

Isanti County

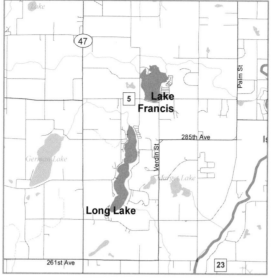

Area map page/coord: 24 / B-2,3
Watershed: Rum
Surface area: 301 acres
Shorelength: 3.8 miles
Maximum depth: 7 feet
Mean depth: 4.5 feet
Secchi disk: 1.4 feet (2003)
Water color: Brownish-green
Accessibility: County-owned public access with gravel ramp on east shore; three trailer spaces
Accommodations: None
Shoreland zoning: NA
Management class: Regular winterkill
Ecological type: Bullhead

Area map page/coord: 24 / B-2,3
Watershed: Rum
Surface area: 382 acres
Shorelength: 5.6 miles
Maximum depth: 15 feet
Mean depth: 5 feet
Secchi disk: 1.4 feet (2009)
Water color: Green
Accessibility: 1) State-owned public access with concrete ramp on northeast shore (twelve trailer spaces); 2) township-owned public access with sand ramp on west shore (parking along gravel road right-of-way)
Accommodations: None
Shoreland zoning: NA
Management class: Warm-water gamefish
Ecological type: Roughfish-gamefish

FISH STOCKING DATA

year	species	size	# released
07	Walleye	Fry	600,000
09	Walleye	Fry	600,000
10	Walleye	Fry	500,000

NET CATCH DATA

Date: 06/09/2003

	Gill Nets		Trap Nets	
species	# per net	avg. fish weight (lbs.)	# per net	avg. fish weight (lbs.)
Black Bullhead	87.8	0.28	34.0	0.49
Black Crappie	0.9	0.23	3.7	0.29
Bluegill	-	-	0.3	0.30
Hybrid Sunfish	-	-	0.1	0.31
Northern Pike	5.8	3.29	0.3	3.64
Walleye	-	-	0.2	5.80
Yellow Perch	10.1	0.20	13.7	0.25

LENGTH OF SELECTED SPECIES SAMPLED FROM ALL GEAR

Number of fish caught for the following length categories (inches):

species	0-5	6-8	9-11	12-14	15-19	20-24	25-29	>30	Total
Black Bullhead	1	152	67	2	-	-	-	-	222
Black Crappie	1	36	3	1	-	-	-	-	41
Bluegill	1	2	-	-	-	-	-	-	3
Hybrid Sunfish	-	1	-	-	-	-	-	-	1
Northern Pike	-	-	-	-	5	35	13	2	55
Walleye	-	-	-	-	-	1	1	-	2
Yellow Bullhead	-	-	3	-	-	-	-	-	3
Yellow Perch	19	47	56	-	-	-	-	-	122

FISH STOCKING DATA

year	species	size	# released
07	Walleye	Fry	600,000
09	Walleye	Fry	600,000
10	Walleye	Fry	500,000
11	Walleye	Fry	400,000

NET CATCH DATA

Date: 07/13/2009

	Gill Nets		Trap Nets	
species	# per net	avg. fish weight (lbs.)	# per net	avg. fish weight (lbs.)
Black Crappie	50.5	0.23	17.4	0.31
Largemouth Bass	-	-	0.4	3.12
Walleye	1.7	2.60	0.1	3.09

LENGTH OF SELECTED SPECIES SAMPLED FROM ALL GEAR

Number of fish caught for the following length categories (inches):

species	0-5	6-8	9-11	12-14	15-19	20-24	25-29	>30	Total
Black Bullhead	1	-	14	15	-	-	-	-	31
Black Crappie	107	308	15	-	-	-	-	-	442
Bluegill	8	110	-	-	-	-	-	-	118
Bowfin (Dogfish)	-	-	-	-	-	3	-	1	4
Brown Bullhead	-	-	16	28	-	-	-	-	46
Common Carp	-	-	-	2	1	2	-	-	5
Golden Shiner	-	1	-	-	-	-	-	-	1
Largemouth Bass	-	-	-	1	1	1	-	-	3
Northern Pike	-	-	-	3	24	36	9	7	80
Pumpkin. Sunfish	1	-	-	-	-	-	-	-	1
Walleye	-	-	-	2	5	3	1	-	11
White Sucker	-	-	2	2	8	-	-	-	13
Yellow Perch	22	19	-	-	-	-	-	-	41

FISHING INFORMATION: Both Francis and Long lakes have a history of winterkills. The 1995-1996 winter was hard on both lakes, as was the partial winterkill in 2001. As part of the DNR's lake management plan, gamefish are restocked after such an event. Now, both lakes seem to have rebounded well.

Lake Francis is shallow with low water clarity. Because the oxygen levels drop in winter, it is subject to some gamefish mortality. Even so, the northern pike population seems to be thriving. The DNR survey shows them averaging 23.7 inches and 3.3 pounds. With pike abundance on the rise, this is looking to be a decent fishery for northerns. Cast the usual array of flashy lures, like spoons, spinnerbaits and crankbaits to hook pike. Crappie numbers are high, with averages around 9 inches and some exceeding 12 inches. Like most lakes in the area, a small minnow or leech will get the most attention from crappies. Bluegills and largemouth bass don't fare as well here because of limited habitat and low levels of oxygen in winter. Overall angling pressure appeared to be somewhat light, according to the DNR.

Long Lake can be accessed on the northeast side of the lake and via a sandy ramp on the west-central side. Lake Francis has access on the southeast corner of the lake.

Long Lake has good bass numbers again, with largemouths averaging 11.6 inches long and 1 pound. This lake is subject to high algae blooms and has limited weeds. Fish the docks on the lake to find bass. With 211 residences here, there are plenty of places for bass to stay cool in summer. Work a topwater lure early and late in the day. Fish with tubes, jigs or plastic worms in shadowy areas under any dock. Try to skip your lure as far back under a dock as you can. Bass will congregate in shadows, waiting to attack any unsuspecting prey; hopefully your worm.

Crappies and bluegills were found in good numbers during the 2004 DNR survey, although their size tends to the smaller side. Northern pike were plentiful, with an average of 21.5 inches and 2.1 pounds. For both crappies and northern pike, use minnows and a slip float. Try small minnows for crappies and big minnows for pike. The black bullhead population remains high compared to similar lakes. The DNR thinks this is due to in part to the winterkill that occurred in 2001.

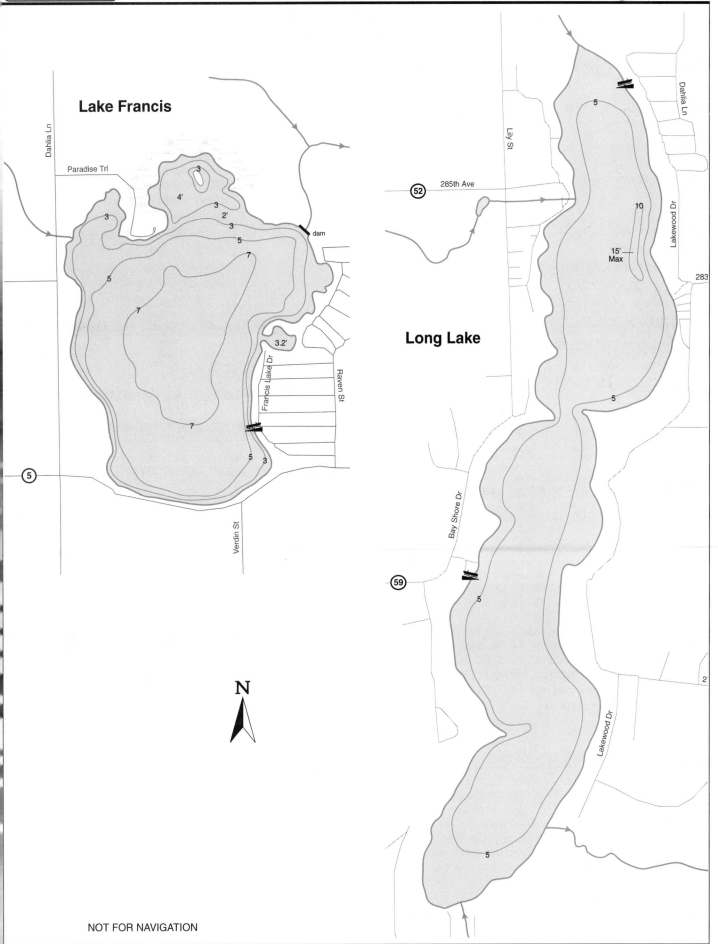

Lake Francis

Dahlia Ln

Paradise Trl

3

4'

3

2'

3

5

7

5

7

7

3.2'

Francis Lake Dr

Raven St

5

3

dam

(5)

Verdin St

Long Lake

Lily St

Dahlia Ln

(52) 285th Ave

5

10

15'
Max

Lakewood Dr

283

5

Bay Shore Dr

(59)

5

Lakewood Dr

5

N

NOT FOR NAVIGATION

Source: Minnesota Department of Natural Resources, USGS

SANDY LAKE
Sherburne County

Area map page/coord: 24 / B-1
Watershed: Rum
Surface area: 62 acres
Maximum depth: 41 feet
Mean depth: NA
Water clarity: 12 feet (2012)
Accessibility: Township-owned gravel access on south shore, earthen access on north shore
Accommodations: None
Zoning: Recreational development
Management class: Centrarchid

WEST HUNTER LAKE
Sherburne County

Area map page/coord: 24 / C-1
Watershed: Rum
Surface area: 60 acres
Maximum depth: 6 feet
Mean depth: NA
Water clarity: 6.0 feet (2007)
Accessibility: Township-owned public access with plank ramp on west shore
Accommodations: Dock
Zoning: Natural environment
Management class: Regular winterkill

EAST HUNTER LAKE
Sherburne County

Area map page/coord: 24 / C-1
Watershed: Rum
Surface area: 55 acres
Maximum depth: 7 feet
Mean depth: NA
Water clarity: 5.5 feet (2007)
Accessibility: From West Hunter
Accommodations: None
Zoning: Natural environment
Management class: Regular winterkill

Sandy Lake

NO RECORD OF STOCKING SINCE 1985

NET CATCH DATA

Date: 08/21/2012

species	Gill Nets # per net	Gill Nets avg. fish weight (lbs.)	Trap Nets # per net	Trap Nets avg. fish weight (lbs.)
Bluegill	2.3	0.07	3.0	0.11
Hybrid Sunfish	0.3	0.18	1.5	0.19
Largemouth Bass	0.3	1.91	0.3	0.35
Northern Pike	9.7	1.70	2.5	0.86
Pumpkinseed	0.7	0.04	0.6	0.18
Yellow Bullhead	8.3	0.42	3.8	0.95

LENGTH OF SELECTED SPECIES SAMPLED FROM ALL GEAR

Number of fish caught for the following length categories (inches):

species	0-5	6-8	9-11	12-14	15-19	20-24	25-29	>30	Total
Bluegill	26	5	-	-	-	-	-	-	31
Hybrid Sunfish	4	9	-	-	-	-	-	-	13
Largemouth Bass	-	1	1	1	-	-	-	-	3
Northern Pike	-	-	2	6	20	16	2	-	49
Pumpkin. Sunfish	3	4	-	-	-	-	-	-	7
Yellow Bullhead	-	9	29	18	-	-	-	-	56

FISHING INFORMATION: Sandy Lake is deep and sustains pretty fair populations of largemouth bass, northern pike and small panfish. Local anglers tend to come to this lake for the bass fishing. Bass average just over 12 inches long, and 5-pounders are not uncommon. Fish near weed points, especially in the southeast corner of the lake, using crankbaits such as Rat-L-Traps, Bandits or Lucky Crafts, or try a spinnerbait or soft-plastic presentation. Weekend boating activity can be heavy on nice days, so plan your outings accordingly. Many pike are caught in some of the same areas you find bass. Anywhere you find submerged weedbeds, you have a good chance of encountering a few pike. According to the latest DNR survey, the average pike measures 18.9 inches long and weighs 1.95 pounds. These measurements are average for pike in similar lakes. Float a large minnow or cast a large spinnerbait to attract a few toothy fish. Ice anglers spend some time chasing crappies, which suspend out over the 30- to 40-foot depths, but they run on the small side. There is a boat ramp on the south shore.

East and West Hunter Lakes are subject to frequent winterkill, making them very marginal fishing lakes. We include them here only because, in years between winterkills, they can offer some decent crappie fishing, along with a few largemouth bass. Crappies seem to rebound fairly well in winterkill lakes, and they grow fairly quickly. Judging from the DNR's test netting in years past, there have been some respectable-size crappies in these lakes. Access to the Hunter Lakes is on the west shore of West Hunter.

West Hunter Lake

FISH STOCKING DATA

year	species	size	# released
09	Bluegill	Adult	476
09	Largemouth Bass	Adult	24
09	Yellow Perch	Adult	1,230
11	Bluegill	Adult	358
11	Largemouth Bass	Adult	12
11	Yellow Perch	Adult	1,275

NET CATCH DATA

Date: 06/11/2007

species	Gill Nets # per net	Gill Nets avg. fish weight (lbs.)	Trap Nets # per net	Trap Nets avg. fish weight (lbs.)
Black Bullhead	-	-	4.2	0.43
Bluegill	-	-	29.8	0.10
Largemouth Bass	-	-	0.8	2.11
Pumpkin. Sunfish	-	-	23.4	0.19

LENGTH OF SELECTED SPECIES SAMPLED FROM ALL GEAR

Number of fish caught for the following length categories (inches):

species	0-5	6-8	9-11	12-14	15-19	20-24	25-29	>30	Total
Black Bullhead	-	7	14	-	-	-	-	-	21
Bluegill	122	27	-	-	-	-	-	-	149
Largemouth Bass	-	-	-	2	2	-	-	-	4
Pumpkin. Sunfish	41	76	-	-	-	-	-	-	117

East Hunter Lake

NO RECORD OF STOCKING SINCE 2001

NET CATCH DATA

Date: 06/11/2007

species	Gill Nets # per net	Gill Nets avg. fish weight (lbs.)	Trap Nets # per net	Trap Nets avg. fish weight (lbs.)
Black Bullhead	69.0	0.40	19.8	0.47
Black Crappie	9.5	0.13	-	-
Bluegill	37.5	0.09	28.2	0.10
Golden Shiner	19.5	0.11	-	-
Hybrid Sunfish	-	-	2.0	0.15
Largemouth Bass	1.5	1.23	1.0	2.31
Northern Pike	8.5	2.98	-	-
Pumpkin. Sunfish	58.5	0.18	18.0	0.21
White Sucker	1.0	2.09	-	-

LENGTH OF SELECTED SPECIES SAMPLED FROM ALL GEAR

Number of fish caught for the following length categories (inches):

species	0-5	6-8	9-11	12-14	15-19	20-24	25-29	>30	Total
Black Bullhead	-	85	151	-	-	-	-	-	237
Black Crappie	6	12	1	-	-	-	-	-	19
Bluegill	193	20	-	-	-	-	-	-	216
Golden Shiner	1	38	-	-	-	-	-	-	39
Hybrid Sunfish	6	4	-	-	-	-	-	-	10
Largemouth Bass	-	-	2	2	4	-	-	-	8
Northern Pike	-	1	1	-	1	7	6	1	17
Pumpkin. Sunfish	77	130	-	-	-	-	-	-	207
White Sucker	-	-	-	2	-	-	-	-	2

Sandy, West & East Hunter Lakes

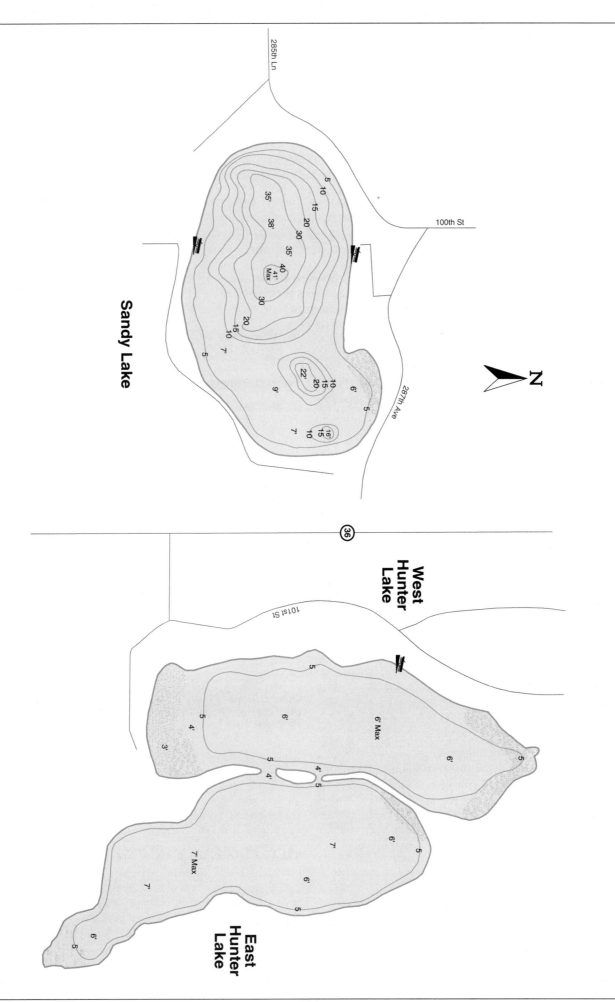

285th Ln

100th St

Sandy Lake

287th Ave

N

22'
41' Max

16'

NOT FOR NAVIGATION

36

West Hunter Lake

101st St

6' Max

East Hunter Lake

7' Max

LAKE GEORGE
Anoka County

Bordered by Lake George Regional Park

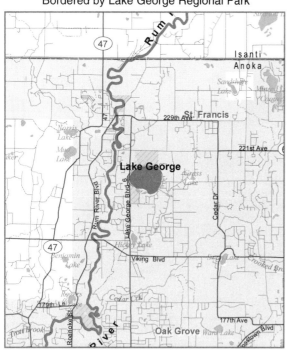

Area map pg / coord: 24 / D-2
Watershed: Rum
Secchi disk: 9.5 feet (2008)
Water color: Light blue-green

Surface area: 488 acres
Shorelength: 4.5 miles
Maximum depth: 32 feet
Mean depth: 9.5 feet

Accessibility: County-owned public access on north shore in park
Boat ramp: Concrete
Parking: Twenty-eight trailer spaces
Accommodations: Park, picnicking, restrooms

Shoreland zoning classification: General development
Management class: Centrarchid
Ecological type: Centrarchid

FISH STOCKING DATA

year	species	size	# released
09	Walleye	Fry	800,000
11	Walleye	Fry	800,000
12	Walleye	Fry	782,000

NET CATCH DATA

Date: 06/23/2008

	Gill Nets		Trap Nets	
species	# per net	avg. fish weight (lbs.)	# per net	avg. fish weight (lbs.)
Black Bullhead	1.8	0.63	0.2	0.71
Black Crappie	3.0	0.14	0.6	0.29
Bluegill	6.3	0.10	118.7	0.14
Hybrid Sunfish	-	-	1.9	0.20
Largemouth Bass	0.3	1.30	-	-
Northern Pike	21.3	2.00	0.4	1.30
Pumpkin. Sunfish	3.7	0.11	1.7	0.20
Yellow Bullhead	3.7	0.53	3.3	0.73
Yellow Perch	1.3	0.09	-	-

LENGTH OF SELECTED SPECIES SAMPLED FROM ALL GEAR

Number of fish caught for the following length categories (inches):

species	0-5	6-8	9-11	12-14	15-19	20-24	25-29	>30	Total
Black Bullhead	-	5	5	3	-	-	-	-	13
Black Crappie	11	10	2	-	-	-	-	-	23
Bluegill	588	514	-	-	-	-	-	-	1106
Bowfin (Dogfish)	-	-	-	-	-	13	7	-	20
Hybrid Sunfish	9	8	-	-	-	-	-	-	17
Largemouth Bass	-	-	-	2	-	-	-	-	2
Northern Pike	-	-	-	2	45	74	11	-	132
Pumpkin. Sunfish	28	9	-	-	-	-	-	-	37
Yellow Bullhead	1	9	32	10	-	-	-	-	52
Yellow Perch	3	5	-	-	-	-	-	-	8

FISHING INFORMATION: George is a round, clear lake that's easy to fish and full of panfish, northern pike and some largemouth bass. The water clarity is good, with visibility at times down to almost 10 feet. There is an abundance of weed growth, so make sure to remove any weeds clinging to your boat and trailer before you depart. This helps to prevent the additional spread of milfoil.

The most abundant fish in Lake George are bluegills, which is common for a lake of this type. The numbers of bluegills falls within the normal range, according to the DNR. Nearly 50% of the fish sampled in the 2008 DNR survey were longer than 6 inches. These aren't giants, but will provide you with plenty of fishing opportunities. Fishing for them is simple. Find shallow weeds and float a piece of crawler, a wax worm or leech under a bobber or weightless on a plain hook. Since the water is clear, put on a pair of polarized sunglasses and comb the shallows until you see a few bluegills. Once they're spotted, cast your offering in their general vicinity. They'll attack it in a hurry, if they're hungry.

The north end of the lake is most productive for early spring crappies, although the cabbage weeds anywhere along the shoreline can hold impressive schools. Small minnows and leeches are the best bait. Keep moving out toward the lake's center as the weather warms, working the weeds. By July and August, you can expect the few decent-size crappies to be suspended over deeper waters at mid-lake. According to the DNR survey, black crappie numbers were below average for a lake of this type.

Northerns can be found in weeds early, too; minnow-tipped jigs are good, as is a bobber and minnow. Spinnerbaits and spoons can be worked successfully later in the season. The northern pike in Lake George aren't particularly large, so smaller-than-usual lures will do well. Although there aren't any huge fish present, 2-foot-long pike can still put up a battle. Bring along a pair of longnose pliers to use for hook removal, and don't be surprised if you tie into a 5- or 6-pound pike; they're definitely out there.

The bars in the southeast quadrant of the lake are some of the better places to try for bass, and the north shoreline is often productive early in the year. The weeds are almost always good, and crankbaits and spinnerbaits are effective tools for hooking bass along weed edges. Topwater tactics can work early and late in the day during summer. Local anglers recommend night-fishing for finding bigger bass. The docks and rafts are good cover both at night and during the day. It's tough to beat a jig-and-pig flipped into the shadows during daylight. Try tossing a floating worm or Senko into the same areas. At night, the same slow-moving baits will work, but a large spinnerbait with a Colorado blade fished with a steady retrieve can really draw some attention from bass. Of course, a northern may decide to dine on it for a late-night snack, too.

Public launch facilities with good parking for 25 rigs or more can be found at the northern part of the lake, just off 217th Avenue NW. In addition, shore fishing is possible, starting at the regional park beach and heading along the north shore.

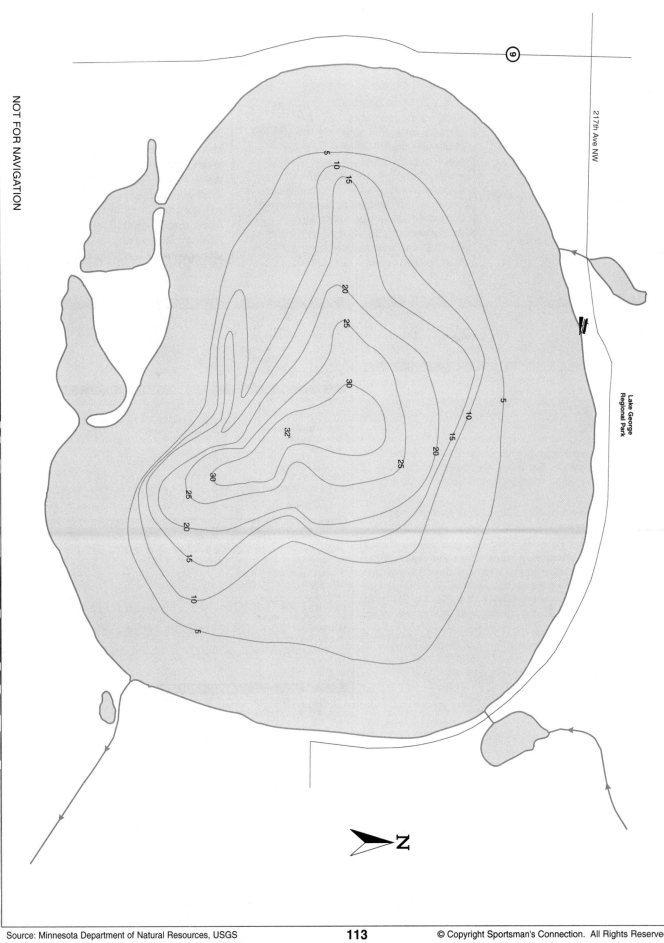

NOT FOR NAVIGATION

217th Ave NW

Lake George
Regional Park

N

Lake George

113

FLORENCE LAKE
Isanti County

Area map page/coord: 25 / A-4
Surface area: 141 acres
Maximum depth: 26 feet
Mean depth: NA
Water clarity: 5.0 feet (1991)
Accessibility: State-owned public access with gravel ramp on northwest shore
Accommodations: Restroom
Zoning: Recreational development
Management class: Centrarchid

FANNIE LAKE
Isanti County

Area map page/coord: 25 / A-4
Surface area: 354 acres
Maximum depth: 33 feet
Mean depth: 5 feet
Water clarity: 4.1 feet (2006)
Accessibility: State-owned public access with concrete ramp on northeast shore; carry-down access on east shore
Accommodations: None
Zoning: Recreational development
Management class: Centrarchid

SKOGMAN LAKE
Isanti County

Area map page/coord: 25 / A-4
Surface area: 221 acres
Maximum depth: 36 feet
Mean depth: 11 feet
Water clarity: 4.8 feet (2006)
Accessibility: State-owned public access with concrete ramp on east shore
Accommodations: Dock
Zoning: Recreational development
Management class: Centrarchid

Florence Lake

FISH STOCKING DATA

year	species	size	# released
07	Walleye	Fry	282,000
09	Walleye	Fry	282,000
11	Walleye	Fry	400,000

LAST SURVEY 1991

FISHING INFORMATION: Florence, Fannie and Skogman Lakes are like beads on a necklace, connected by tributary streams to the Rum River.

Florence Lake, at the western end of the necklace, is an irregular bowl without a whole lot of structure. It contains above-average numbers of small northerns, a few walleyes and largemouth bass, and a fair population of bluegills.

For walleyes, try the deep area off the Elms Lake inlet at the northeast corner with a jig-and-minnow combination. Northerns can be found during daytime off weedbeds in the same area.

Fannie offers a similar fishing experience. The entire western bay, near the outlet to Elms Lake and Florence, averages about 3.5 feet deep and is filled with weeds, making it a good area for small sunfish, perch and largemouth bass. For nice-sized walleyes, fish near the Skogman Lake inlet on the steep drop to the 33-foot level at the weedlines. Northerns hold there, too.

Skogman Lake is shallow at the margins, but drops off quickly to 36 feet, and has well-defined weedlines. These often hold walleyes. There's also a self-sustaining northern pike population, and 8- to 10-pounders can be caught on a bright spoon or #5 Mepps.

Fannie Lake

FISH STOCKING DATA

year	species	size	# released
06	Walleye	Fingerling	3,313
08	Walleye	Fingerling	10,857
10	Walleye	Fingerling	10,626
11	Walleye	Fingerling	2,881
12	Walleye	Fingerling	1,624

NET CATCH DATA

Date: 06/27/2006

	Gill Nets		Trap Nets	
species	# per net	avg. fish weight (lbs.)	# per net	avg. fish weight (lbs.)
Black Bullhead	76.2	0.19	10.3	0.25
Black Crappie	2.8	0.19	2.4	0.17
Bluegill	3.2	0.18	38.3	0.14
Brown Bullhead	1.8	1.02	2.2	0.80
Hybrid Sunfish	-	-	1.2	0.24
Northern Pike	5.5	2.90	0.8	3.25
Pumpkin. Sunfish	0.7	0.18	1.0	0.24
Walleye	2.0	2.91	0.1	0.26
Yellow Perch	8.0	0.08	-	-

LENGTH OF SELECTED SPECIES SAMPLED FROM ALL GEAR

Number of fish caught for the following length categories (inches):

species	0-5	6-8	9-11	12-14	15-19	20-24	25-29	>30	Total
Black Bullhead	3	502	36	-	-	-	-	-	550
Black Crappie	9	28	1	-	-	-	-	-	39
Bluegill	205	153	-	-	-	-	-	-	364
Hybrid Sunfish	2	7	-	-	-	-	-	-	11
Northern Pike	-	-	-	-	8	15	15	2	40
Pumpkin. Sunfish	7	3	-	-	-	-	-	-	13
Walleye	-	-	1	-	6	6	-	-	13
Yellow Perch	34	13	-	-	-	-	-	-	48

Skogman Lake

FISH STOCKING DATA

year	species	size	# released
06	Walleye	Fingerling	6,750
08	Walleye	Fingerling	6,345
10	Walleye	Fingerling	6,210
11	Walleye	Fingerling	1,701
11	Walleye	Adult	15
12	Walleye	Fingerling	2,085

LENGTH OF SELECTED SPECIES SAMPLED FROM ALL GEAR

Number of fish caught for the following length categories (inches):

species	0-5	6-8	9-11	12-14	15-19	20-24	25-29	>30	Total
Black Bullhead	-	115	3	-	-	-	-	-	121
Black Crappie	15	28	-	-	-	-	-	-	46
Bluegill	218	47	-	-	-	-	-	-	267
Brown Bullhead	-	3	9	1	-	-	-	-	13
Hybrid Sunfish	3	1	-	-	-	-	-	-	4
Northern Pike	-	-	-	-	2	2	6	1	11
Pumpkin. Sunfish	6	-	-	-	-	-	-	-	7
Walleye	-	-	-	-	3	3	-	-	6

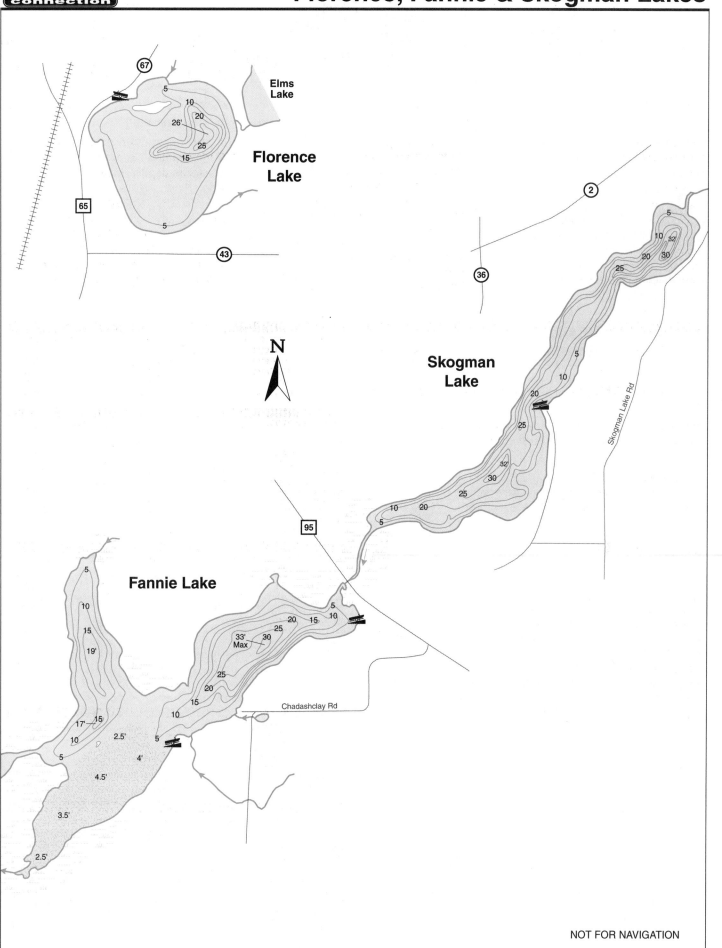

Elms Lake

Florence Lake

Skogman Lake

Skogman Lake Rd

N

Fannie Lake

33' Max

Chadashclay Rd

NOT FOR NAVIGATION

Source: Minnesota Department of Natural Resources, USGS

HORSESHOE LAKE LITTLE HORSESHOE LAKE
Chisago County

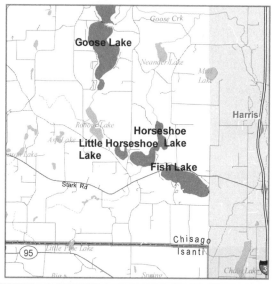

Area map page/coord: 25 / A-5

Watershed: Lower St. Croix

Surface area: 197 acres

Shorelength: 3.9 miles

Maximum depth: 53 feet

Mean depth: 13 feet

Secchi disk: 6.1 feet (2005)

Water color: Green tint

Accessibility: State-owned public access with concrete ramp on south shore; ten trailer spaces

Accommodations: None

Shoreland zoning: General dev.

Management class: Centrarchid

Ecological type: Centrarchid

Area map page/coord: 25 / A-5

Watershed: Lower St. Croix

Surface area: 36 acres

Shorelength: NA

Maximum depth: 42 feet

Mean depth: NA

Secchi disk: 4.0 feet (1990)

Water color: Light green

Accessibility: Public access with gravel ramp on east shore, off Cty. Rd. 8

Accommodations: None

Shoreland zoning: Recreational dev.

Management class: Centrarchid

Ecological type: Centrarchid

NO RECORD OF STOCKING SINCE 1995

NET CATCH DATA
Date: 06/21/2005

species	Gill Nets # per net	Gill Nets avg. fish weight (lbs.)	Trap Nets # per net	Trap Nets avg. fish weight (lbs.)
Black Bullhead	65.0	0.25	4.0	0.20
Black Crappie	2.5	0.18	0.1	0.13
Bluegill	8.8	0.14	36.1	0.14
Largemouth Bass	0.5	1.52	0.2	0.53
Northern Pike	5.8	2.62	0.2	2.39
Pumpkin. Sunfish	0.5	0.13	2.8	0.12
White Crappie	0.3	0.25	-	-
Yellow Bullhead	0.7	0.77	-	-
Yellow Perch	13.7	0.11	-	-

LENGTH OF SELECTED SPECIES SAMPLED FROM ALL GEAR
Number of fish caught for the following length categories (inches):

species	0-5	6-8	9-11	12-14	15-19	20-24	25-29	>30	Total
Black Bullhead	1	53	11	-	-	-	-	-	65
Black Crappie	1	15	-	-	-	-	-	-	16
Bluegill	87	66	-	-	-	-	-	-	153
Largemouth Bass	-	-	4	-	1	-	-	-	5
Northern Pike	-	-	-	2	5	18	11	1	37
Pumpkin. Sunfish	6	-	-	-	-	-	-	-	6
White Crappie	-	1	1	-	-	-	-	-	2
Yellow Bullhead	-	-	3	1	-	-	-	-	4
Yellow Perch	12	62	-	-	-	-	-	-	74

NO RECORD OF STOCKING SINCE 1993

NET CATCH DATA
Date: 08/15/1990

species	Gill Nets # per net	Gill Nets avg. fish weight (lbs.)	Trap Nets # per net	Trap Nets avg. fish weight (lbs.)
Black Crappie	2.3	0.11	0.7	ND
Bluegill	17.0	0.12	58.0	ND
Brown Bullhead	0.7	0.50	-	-
Golden Shiner	2.0	0.08	-	-
Hybrid Sunfish	0.7	0.10	2.7	ND
Northern Pike	0.7	2.55	-	-
Pumpkin. Sunfish	-	-	3.7	ND
Yellow Bullhead	1.7	0.46	1.7	0.36
Yellow Perch	1.7	0.06	0.3	0.10

LENGTH OF SELECTED SPECIES SAMPLED FROM ALL GEAR
Number of fish caught for the following length categories (inches):

species	0-5	6-8	9-11	12-14	15-19	20-24	25-29	>30	Total
Black Bullhead	-	-	4	-	-	-	-	-	4
Black Crappie	1	8	-	-	-	-	-	-	9
Bluegill	69	76	-	-	-	-	-	-	145
Brown Bullhead	-	-	2	-	-	-	-	-	2
Hybrid Sunfish	8	2	-	-	-	-	-	-	10
Northern Pike	-	-	-	-	-	2	-	-	2
Pumpkin. Sunfish	12	-	-	-	-	-	-	-	12
Yellow Bullhead	1	2	6	1	-	-	-	-	10
Yellow Perch	-	1	-	-	-	-	-	-	1

FISHING INFORMATION: Horseshoe Lake suffered from winterkill in 1991-92, according to the DNR. Since then, the lake has rebounded, and no stocking has taken place since 1995. Evidently, this relatively deep lake suffers partial winterkill during severe winters due, in part, to the heavy algae bloom that occurs during summer. When this vegetation decomposes later in the year, it consumes precious oxygen in the lake. A long winter with heavy snow cover prevents enough light from penetrating and the existing vegetation doesn't generate the oxygen it would otherwise. Consequently, oxygen levels drop and some fish die. Species have recovered, most notably northern pike, which are found in fair sizes. Crappies are still on the small side, but some keepers up to 1/2 pound do exist. Winter anglers jig deeper water with crappie minnows and wax worms for panfish. High numbers of bluegills are available in a wide variety of sizes. The bass population has increased dramatically, with some good-sized specimens in the lake.

Evidently, unlike its larger namesake, **Little Horseshoe Lake** escapes winterkill and provides a pretty good bass, panfish, and northern pike fishery. Bass anglers stress catch-and-release fishing practices here. Some hogs are present; 5- to 6-pounders are caught and released every season. Spinnerbaits and plastic worms fished along weedlines generate many of the strikes. Some 2-pound crappies are caught in Little Horseshoe, but the norm is closer to 1/2 pound. A slip bobber and a small minnow or leech are your friends if you want to catch a few crappies. Northerns most likely migrate through the channel to Horseshoe Lake, according to the DNR, although it appears as if a few maintain themselves on Little Horseshoe.

Boat traffic can get heavy on both of these lakes on a summer weekend, so plan accordingly. If you can get out during the weekdays, by all means, do it. There is generally lighter boat traffic then, resulting in less pressure on the fish. Also, make sure to shoot for an early morning arrival to get on the water at the most productive time of day for catching fish. Good public access sites are available on both lakes.

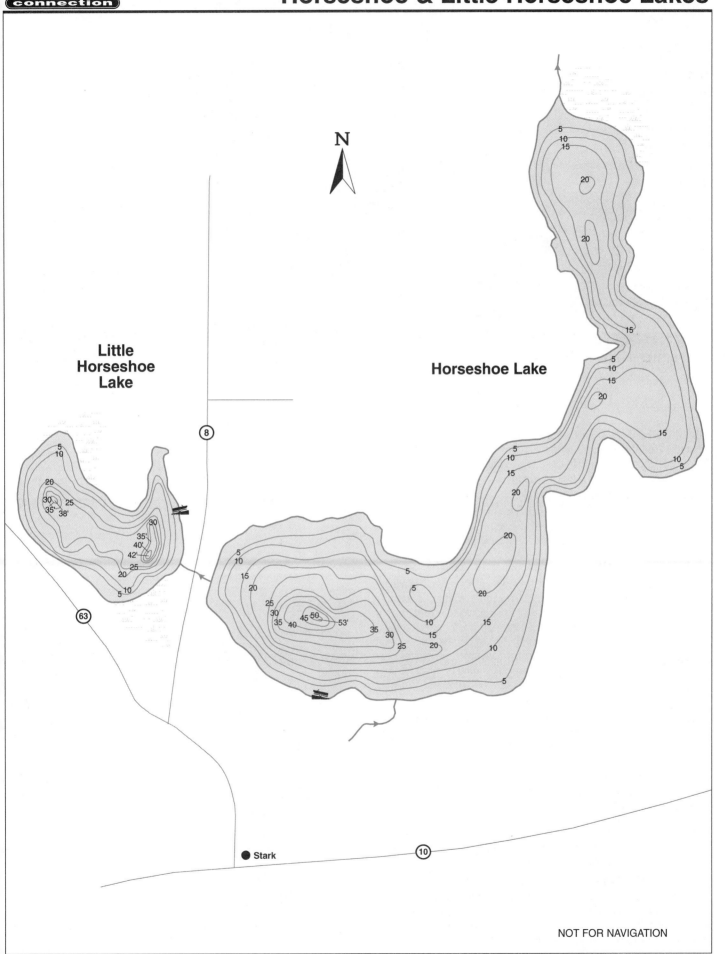

Little
Horseshoe
Lake

Horseshoe Lake

Stark

NOT FOR NAVIGATION

Source: Minnesota Department of Natural Resources, USGS

FISH LAKE
Chisago County

Bordered by Fish Lake County Park

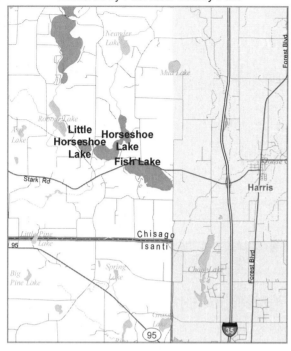

Area map pg / coord: 25 / A-5
Watershed: Lower St. Croix
Secchi disk: 7.9 feet (2011)
Water color: Green tint

Surface area: 314 acres
Shorelength: 3.2 miles
Maximum depth: 57 feet
Mean depth: 16 feet

Accessibility: County-owned public access on southeast shore
Boat ramp: Concrete
Parking: Twenty-five trailer spaces
Accommodations: Park, dock, picnicking, restrooms

Shoreland zoning classification: General development
Management class: Centrarchid
Ecological type: Centrarchid

FISH STOCKING DATA

year	species	size	# released
03	Walleye	Fingerling	21,700
05	Walleye	Fingerling	140,000
08	Walleye	Fingerling	21,333
10	Walleye	Fingerling	10,579

NET CATCH DATA

Date: 08/15/2011

	Gill Nets		Trap Nets	
species	# per net	avg. fish weight (lbs.)	# per net	avg. fish weight (lbs.)
Black Crappie	1.9	0.21	1.1	0.40
Bluegill	3.8	0.24	7.1	0.18
Largemouth Bass	1.0	1.48	0.3	1.27
Northern Pike	8.1	1.51	0.8	1.67
Pumpkin. Sunfish	0.7	0.23	1.4	0.21
Walleye	3.8	2.97	0.1	3.20
Yellow Bullhead	4.8	0.70	1.3	1.05

LENGTH OF SELECTED SPECIES SAMPLED FROM ALL GEAR

Number of fish caught for the following length categories (inches):

species	0-5	6-8	9-11	12-14	15-19	20-24	25-29	>30	Total
Black Crappie	10	6	10	-	-	-	-	-	26
Bluegill	31	59	-	-	-	-	-	-	91
Largemouth Bass	-	-	3	5	3	-	-	-	11
Northern Pike	-	-	-	6	45	21	5	-	80
Pumpkin. Sunfish	6	11	-	-	-	-	-	-	17
Walleye	-	-	-	-	18	15	2	-	35
Yellow Bullhead	-	8	28	17	-	-	-	-	53

FISHING INFORMATION: Fish Lake, located near Harris in Chisago County, receives a fair amount of fishing pressure, and that's with good reason. Fish Lake has become well known as a real fish producer. In fact, it's quite productive for walleyes, northerns and bass, along with some panfish action.

Walleye numbers are decent, and fish are large, weighing better than 2.5 pounds on average. Fish the sandbar on the southeast side with a jig-and-minnow combination or crankbait; then try the deeper sandbar on the north side, where the bottom drops away to 45 feet. Either area should offer good action. Make sure to give trolling a try when you're in search of old marble-eyes. Walleyes are usually on the lookout for baitfish. They often roam and are best located by trolling. Favorite lures include stickbaits, crankbaits or spinner rigs. You can either use a flatline approach out the back of the boat or place a planer board on your line to get the presentation away from your vessel. Once you find a concentration of walleyes, you can continue to troll for them. If you feel they're in an isolated area, cast to them with jigs, split shot and bait, crankbaits or slip bobber and bait rigs.

For northern pike, troll weedlines or bobber-fish with a large sucker minnow. Locals say both methods work well, but they also note that northerns are small; typically weighing less than two pounds. Pike are one of the best fish to pursue when the action slows for bass or walleyes. Although the fish aren't large here, they can provide you with some solid action. Use medium-weight gear and cast brightly colored spinnerbaits. White, chartreuse or other bright colors with similarly colored blades will draw strikes from these toothy predators. Fish your spinnerbait with a fast retrieve over the tops of weeds. The most action usually occurs early and late in the day, but smaller pike will often smack your lure any time of day.

Heavy weed growth makes the entire southern shoreline good bass habitat, and the largemouth population, while difficult to assess with typical survey methods, is believed to be quite large in this lake. According to the latest DNR survey, the largemouth bass population had exceeded the management goals for this lake,

with an average largemouth bass measuring 12.3 inches long and weighing 1.3 pounds. If you want to yank out a big bass from the heavy vegetation, break out your stout tackle and a few jig-and-pig combos, tubes or creature baits. Spool your reel with at least 20-pound line and work the thickest cover. In addition to these slower presentations, you can try a buzzbait in and around vegetation or a topwater plug fished slowly along outside edges of vegetation or along shoreline cover.

Crappies are present in Fish Lake, but numbers are low. However, according to the DNR survey, black crappies were fairly large. About 70% of the fish sampled measured over 8.5 inches. The catch rate was low, but the size was larger than expected. Fish weedlines with small minnows under a slip bobber. Also try a small Beetle Spin worked along shoreline cover both in early spring and again in fall.

Public access, for a fee, is at a county-owned park on the east shore. There's also a private landing on the west side.

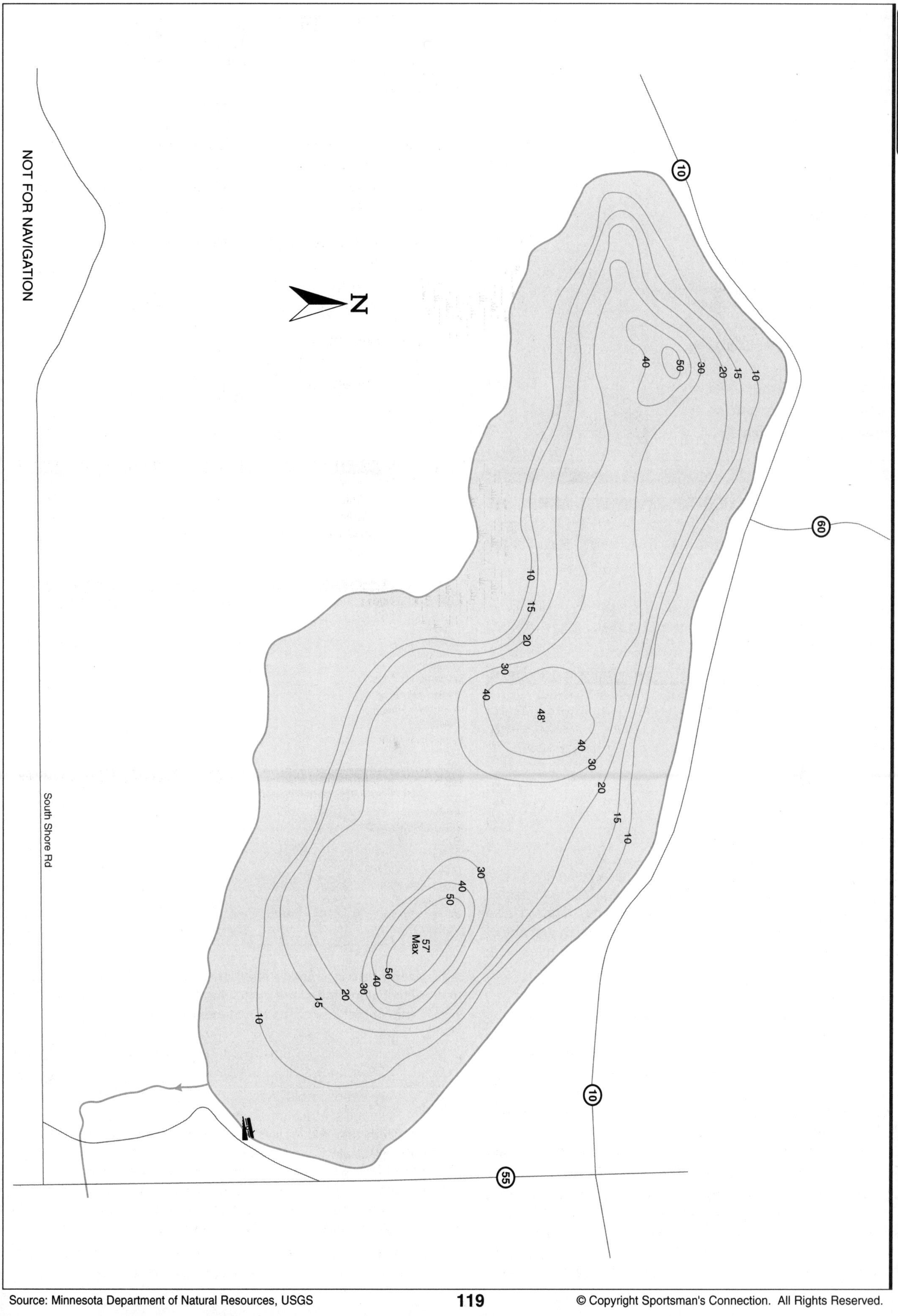

NOT FOR NAVIGATION

N

South Shore Rd

10

60

10

55

10

15

20

30

40

50

30

20

15

10

10

15

20

30

40

48'

40

30

20

15

10

30

40

50

57'
Max

50

40

30

20

15

10

Fish Lake

Source: Minnesota Department of Natural Resources, USGS

HAM LAKE

Bordered by Ham Lake County Park

Area map page/coord: 28 / A-1

Watershed: Twin Cities

Surface area: 168 acres

Shorelength: 2.4 miles

Maximum depth: 22 feet

Mean depth: 6 feet

Secchi disk: 4.9 feet (2010)

Water color: Green

Accessibility: County-owned public access with concrete ramp on southwest shore; five trailer spaces

Accommodations: Park, picnicking, restrooms

Shoreland zoning: Recreational dev.

Management class: Centrarchid

Ecological type: Centrarchid

Anoka County

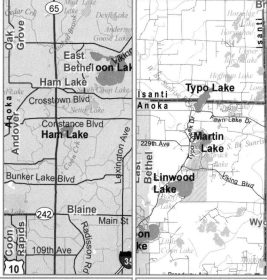

MARTIN LAKE

Bordered by Martin-Island-Linwood Lakes Regional Park

Area map page/coord: 25 / D-5

Watershed: Lower St. Croix

Surface area: 232 acres

Shorelength: 2.7 miles

Maximum depth: 17 feet

Mean depth: NA

Secchi disk: 2.0 feet (2009)

Water color: Brown tint

Accessibility: County-owned public access with concrete ramp on south shore in park; twelve trailer spaces

Accommodations: Park, picnicking, restrooms

Shoreland zoning: General dev.

Management class: Warm-water gamefish

Ecological type: Centrarchid

NO RECORD OF STOCKING

NET CATCH DATA

Date: 08/16/2010

species	Gill Nets # per net	Gill Nets avg. fish weight (lbs.)	Trap Nets # per net	Trap Nets avg. fish weight (lbs.)
Black Bullhead	3.3	1.22	-	-
Black Crappie	4.0	0.15	0.6	0.29
Bluegill	10.7	0.16	15.1	0.12
Hybrid Sunfish	-	-	1.0	0.08
Largemouth Bass	0.7	2.08	0.1	2.10
Northern Pike	11.3	1.94	0.6	2.69
Pumpkin.Sunfish	4.7	0.21	4.3	0.28
Yellow Bullhead	16.7	0.79	3.1	0.87

LENGTH OF SELECTED SPECIES SAMPLED FROM ALL GEAR

Number of fish caught for the following length categories (inches):

species	0-5	6-8	9-11	12-14	15-19	20-24	25-29	>30	Total
Black Bullhead	-	-	4	6	-	-	-	-	10
Black Crappie	3	12	1	-	-	-	-	-	16
Bluegill	79	54	-	-	-	-	-	-	138
Hybrid Sunfish	6	1	-	-	-	-	-	-	7
Largemouth Bass	-	-	1	-	2	-	-	-	3
Northern Pike	-	-	-	-	9	27	2	-	38
Pumpkin. Sunfish	13	31	-	-	-	-	-	-	44
Yellow Bullhead	-	6	45	21	-	-	-	-	72

FISH STOCKING DATA

year	species	size	# released
07	Walleye	Fry	1,180,000
08	Walleye	Fry	280,000
09	Walleye	Fry	300,000
10	Walleye	Fry	1,050,000
11	Walleye	Fry	280,000
12	Walleye	Fry	280,000

NET CATCH DATA

Date: 06/29/2009

species	Gill Nets # per net	Gill Nets avg. fish weight (lbs.)	Trap Nets # per net	Trap Nets avg. fish weight (lbs.)
Black Bullhead	0.5	0.78	0.6	0.95
Black Crappie	19.8	0.23	13.2	0.33
Bluegill	0.2	0.10	16.6	0.21
Common Carp	1.5	4.61	1.4	5.84
Northern Pike	0.3	2.86	0.4	6.84
Walleye	0.7	2.84	0.3	1.72
White Crappie	7.7	0.11	160.2	0.23
Yellow Perch	0.5	0.07	-	-

LENGTH OF SELECTED SPECIES SAMPLED FROM ALL GEAR

Number of fish caught for the following length categories (inches):

species	0-5	6-8	9-11	12-14	15-19	20-24	25-29	>30	Total
Black Bullhead	-	-	6	2	-	-	-	-	8
Black Crappie	11	204	20	-	-	-	-	-	238
Bluegill	38	112	-	-	-	-	-	-	150
Common Carp	-	-	-	-	6	11	5	-	22
Northern Pike	-	-	-	-	-	1	2	3	6
Walleye	-	-	1	2	1	3	-	-	7
White Crappie	28	1488	-	-	-	-	-	-	1,488
Yellow Perch	3	-	-	-	-	-	-	-	3

FISHING INFORMATION: Ham Lake is relatively shallow and a typical largemouth bass, bluegill, and northern pike lake with decent water quality. The latest DNR survey showed the northern pike average between 20 and 24 inches in length and weigh just shy of 2 pounds. Bluegills are abundant and young-of-the-year bass were present in good numbers.

Shoreline vegetation provides good spring fishing for panfish, as well as bass. Offer crappies a small minnow on a bare hook or, if it's a dark day, throw a small jig with the same bait. A good place to look for bass is near the island on the west side, especially near the small bridge. The bass hang around the lily pads, too; toss a jig-and-pig or plastic worm to them. Northerns roam the outside edges of emergent vegetation and you can do well at the lake's northwest corner or around the island.

Martin Lake is primarily managed for walleyes. The lake receives an annual stocking of walleyes. A DNR survey showed the average walleye in Martin measures just over 14 inches long. Northern pike are also available here. The average pike is 23.2 inches long and weighs 2.6 pounds. There's also the bonus largemouth bass cruising the weeds. Pitch a soft-plastic lure or a topwater to hook bass. Jig-and-minnow presentations work well for catching walleyes, as

do shallow-running cranks fished at weedlines. Toss a spinnerbait or crankbait along the same weedlines to hook a pike. One problem with Martin is that it's subject to periodic winterkill.

Typo Lake covers 298 acres and offers anglers the chance to catch bluegills, crappies, northern pike, walleyes and bullheads. Typo has an abundance of black crappies, and some of these fish reach a very respectable size, with some topping 15 inches on occasion. Bluegills are also abundant and good-sized. The average bluegill in this lake will measure about 7.5 inches. Over 80% of the bluegill captured in the DNR survey measured over 7 inches in length. Both walleyes and northern pike were not very abundant, but were of average size. The walleye population is supported with a stocking program that releases about 300,000 walleye fry into the lake every few years.

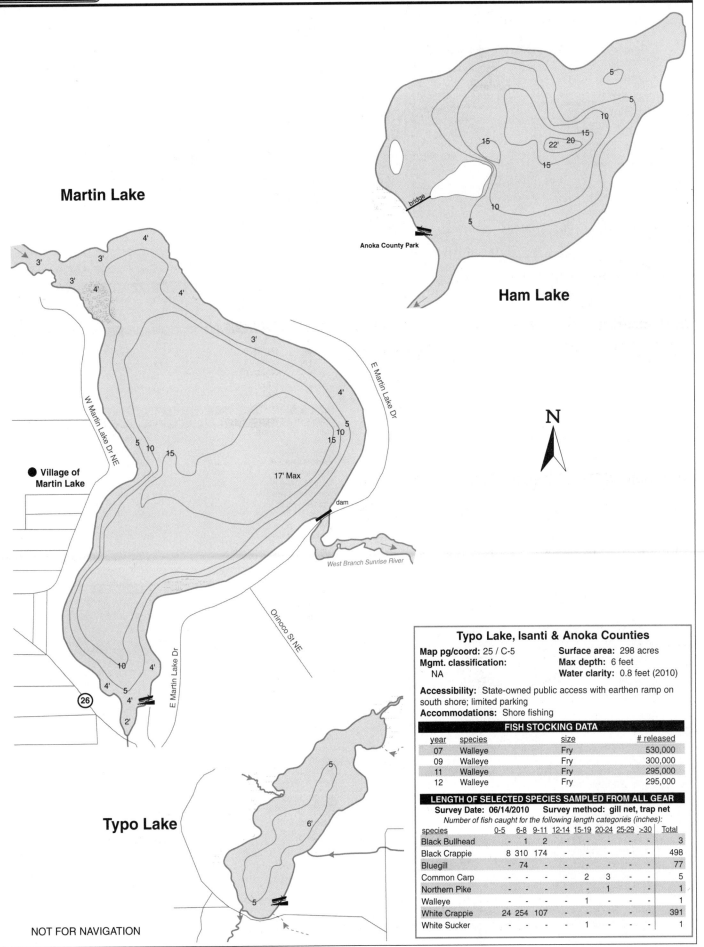

SPORTSMAN'S connection

Martin Lake

Ham Lake

N

- Village of Martin Lake

17' Max

W Martin Lake Dr NE

E Martin Lake Dr

dam

West Branch Sunrise River

Orinoco St NE

E Martin Lake Dr

26

bridge

Anoka County Park

Typo Lake

NOT FOR NAVIGATION

Typo Lake, Isanti & Anoka Counties

Map pg/coord: 25 / C-5
Mgmt. classification: NA
Surface area: 298 acres
Max depth: 6 feet
Water clarity: 0.8 feet (2010)

Accessibility: State-owned public access with earthen ramp on south shore; limited parking
Accommodations: Shore fishing

FISH STOCKING DATA			
year	species	size	# released
07	Walleye	Fry	530,000
09	Walleye	Fry	300,000
11	Walleye	Fry	295,000
12	Walleye	Fry	295,000

LENGTH OF SELECTED SPECIES SAMPLED FROM ALL GEAR
Survey Date: 06/14/2010   **Survey method:** gill net, trap net
Number of fish caught for the following length categories (inches):

species	0-5	6-8	9-11	12-14	15-19	20-24	25-29	>30	Total
Black Bullhead	-	1	2	-	-	-	-	-	3
Black Crappie	8	310	174	-	-	-	-	-	498
Bluegill	-	74	-	-	-	-	-	-	77
Common Carp	-	-	-	-	2	3	-	-	5
Northern Pike	-	-	-	-	-	1	-	-	1
Walleye	-	-	-	-	1	-	-	-	1
White Crappie	24	254	107	-	-	-	-	-	391
White Sucker	-	-	-	-	1	-	-	-	1

LINWOOD LAKE
Anoka County

Bordered by Linwood Lake Regional Park

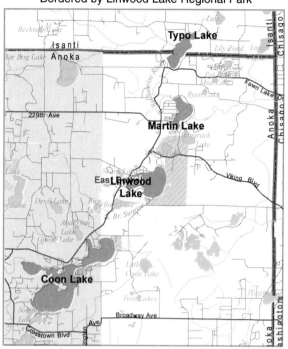

Area map pg / coord: 25 / D-5
Watershed: Lower St. Croix
Secchi disk: 3.3 feet (2009)
Water color: Brownish

Surface area: 572 acres
Shorelength: 4.1 miles
Maximum depth: 42 feet
Mean depth: 11 feet

Accessibility: County-owned public access on northeast shore
Boat ramp: Double concrete
Parking: Twenty-eight trailer spaces
Accommodations: Park, boat rental, picnicking, restrooms

Shoreland zoning classification: Recreational development
Management class: Walleye-centrarchid
Ecological type: Centrarchid

FISH STOCKING DATA

year	species	size	# released
07	Walleye	Fry	400,000
08	Walleye	Fry	1,250,000
08	Walleye	Fingerling	37,790
08	Walleye	Adult	95
10	Walleye	Fingerling	9,784
10	Walleye	Yearling	319
12	Walleye	Fingerling	11,400
12	Walleye	Yearling	659

NET CATCH DATA

Date: 07/06/2009

	Gill Nets		Trap Nets	
species	# per net	avg. fish weight (lbs.)	# per net	avg. fish weight (lbs.)
Black Bullhead	1.8	0.75	0.4	0.98
Black Crappie	31.5	0.11	0.3	0.22
Bluegill	11.0	0.07	28.9	0.15
Bowfin (Dogfish)	-	-	0.7	5.08
Common Carp	-	-	0.1	10.03
Hybrid Sunfish	-	-	1.3	0.20
Largemouth Bass	0.5	0.36	-	-
Northern Pike	13.0	2.88	0.3	10.14
Pumpkin. Sunfish	0.3	0.07	1.1	0.09
Walleye	1.5	3.91	-	-
White Crappie	0.2	0.10	0.1	0.56
Yellow Perch	1.3	0.08	-	-

LENGTH OF SELECTED SPECIES SAMPLED FROM ALL GEAR

Number of fish caught for the following length categories (inches):

species	0-5	6-8	9-11	12-14	15-19	20-24	25-29	>30	Total
Black Bullhead	1	1	5	7	-	-	-	-	14
Black Crappie	70	121	-	-	-	-	-	-	191
Bluegill	163	96	-	-	-	-	-	-	268
Bowfin (Dogfish)	-	-	-	-	-	3	2	-	5
Common Carp	-	-	-	-	-	-	1	-	1
Golden Shiner	2	-	-	-	-	-	-	-	2
Hybrid Sunfish	2	7	-	-	-	-	-	-	9
Largemouth Bass	-	1	2	-	-	-	-	-	3
Northern Pike	-	-	-	-	10	45	22	3	80
Pumpkin. Sunfish	9	1	-	-	-	-	-	-	10
Walleye	-	-	-	2	-	5	2	-	9
White Crappie	-	1	1	-	-	-	-	-	2
White Sucker	-	-	-	-	2	-	-	-	2
Yellow Bullhead	-	3	8	2	-	-	-	-	13
Yellow Perch	6	2	-	-	-	-	-	-	8

FISHING INFORMATION: Linwood is a somewhat murky lake that is short on structure, but long on panfish. This 572-acre lake has a maximum depth of 42 feet. Water clarity is a modest 3.3 feet.

While Linwood Lake is primarily managed for walleyes, this lake is known for its northern pike population. According to the 2009 DNR survey, there is an above-average population of pike in this lake, with good size structure. There are lots of fish in the 20-inch class or better, with three individuals captured 30 inches or longer.

There is also what anglers consider to be a decent largemouth bass population. The most recent DNR survey failed to substantiate claims of bass abundance, but netting isn't always the most reliable method of sampling for largemouth bass. Local anglers report decent catches of bass, so it's worth your time to fish for them. Bass can be found along most weedbeds near shore, although weeds on the east side are considered most productive by those who know the lake. Night fishing is recommended. Two sand bars, one on the east side of the lake, the other on the west, are good spots to bass bust during summer. Spinnerbaits or live baits, such as shiner minnows, are a good bet.

Crappies are rather abundant here, with 191 black crappies netted in the 2009 survey. Crappie abundance has actually dropped since the 1999 survey. They are on the small side, measuring only 7.1 inches and weighing 0.1 pound on average. Crappie fishing is good here, starting in spring, when fish spawn near the dam in the lake's northeast corner. Later, you'll find fish schooling along most of the shoreline, but particularly on the west side. The water is cloudy, so try bright jigs tipped with minnows under a slip bobber for easy depth adjustment.

Bluegills were netted at an all-time high rate since 1985, according to the survey. All in all, these were small, too, averaging 5.3 inches and 0.1 pound. Some decent-sized bluegills can be taken in the weeds, according to local anglers.

A few walleyes can be found in 10- to 15-foot depths along the bars and near the dam, although only nine were caught during the lake's assessment in 2009. During summer months, try fishing in the evening. A fun tactic to use is a slip bobber and jig or hook tipped with a jumbo leech. As walleyes move toward the shallows for their evening meal, a juicy leech swimming under your bobber will often attract a hungry walleye. If you prefer fishing during the day, try the same leech fished on a Lindy rig.

An asphalt-paved double ramp is available at Anoka County Park at the lake's northeast corner.

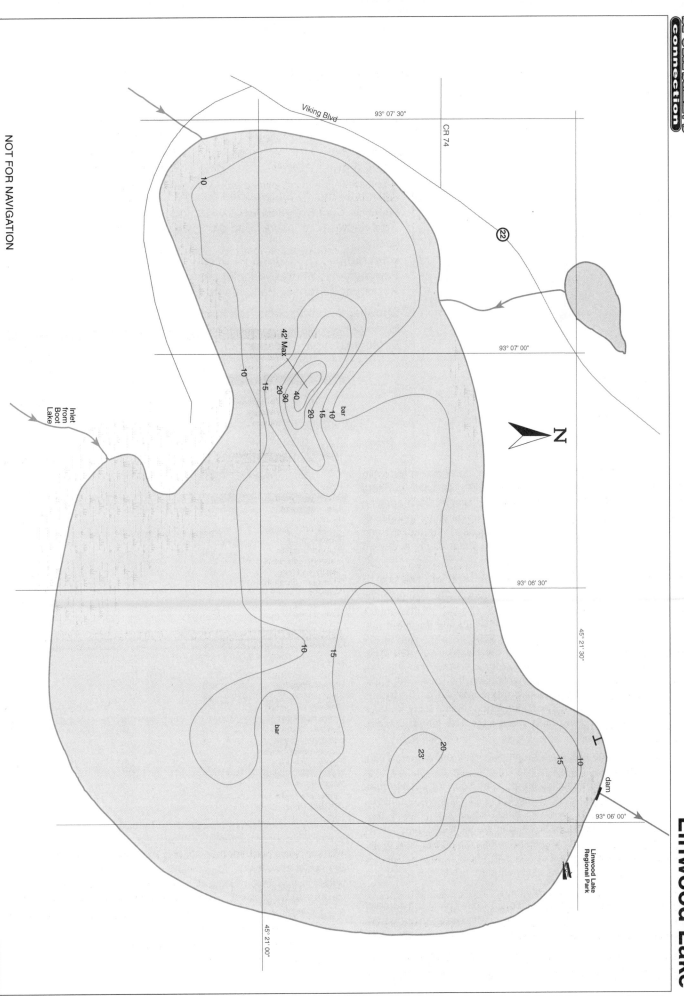

NOT FOR NAVIGATION

Viking Blvd

93° 07' 30"

CR 74

②②

93° 07' 00"

Inlet
from
Boot
Lake

10

42' Max

10

15

20

30 40

20 15 10

20

bar

N

93° 06' 30"

45° 21' 30"

10

15

bar

20

23'

15

10

dam

Linwood Lake
Regional Park

93° 06' 00"

45° 21' 00"

Linwood Lake

COON LAKE
Anoka County

Bordered by Coon Lake County Park

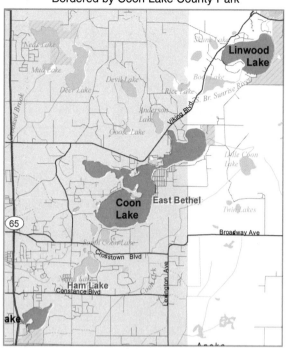

Area map pg / coord: 25 / E-4
Watershed: Twin Cities
Secchi disk: 7.75 feet (2005)
Water color: Clear

Surface area: 1,259 acres
Shorelength: 12.0 miles
Maximum depth: 27 feet
Mean depth: 10 feet

Accessibility: 1) State-owned public access on north shore of west basin; 2) County-owned fee access on east shore of east basin; 3) County-owned off gravel road on south side of channel between basins

Boat ramp: 1) Concrete; 2) Concrete; 3) Dirt
Parking: 1) Twenty-five trailer spaces; 2) Fifteen trailer spaces
Accommodations: Park, resort, camping, picnicking, restrooms

Shoreland zoning classification: General development
Management class: Centrarchid
Ecological type: Centrarchid

FISH STOCKING DATA			
year	species	size	# released
10	Walleye	Fingerling	1,388
10	Walleye	Yearling	284
11	Walleye	Fingerling	9,767
11	Walleye	Yearling	423
11	Walleye	Adult	4
12	Walleye	Fingerling	2,930
12	Walleye	Yearling	10

NET CATCH DATA				
Date: 06/20/2005	Gill Nets		Trap Nets	
species	# per net	avg. fish weight (lbs.)	# per net	avg. fish weight (lbs.)
Black Crappie	2.8	0.09	1.9	0.09
Bluegill	9.3	0.13	99.7	0.12
Hybrid Sunfish	0.1	0.20	1.9	0.17
Largemouth Bass	0.3	1.53	0.2	2.16
Northern Pike	17.1	2.11	1.3	1.96
Pumpkin. Sunfish	2.1	0.14	5.6	0.14
White Sucker	0.3	1.53	-	-
Yellow Bullhead	8.6	0.52	9.8	0.49
Yellow Perch	0.1	0.10	trace	0.33

LENGTH OF SELECTED SPECIES SAMPLED FROM ALL GEAR								
Number of fish caught for the following length categories (inches):								
species	0-5	6-8	9-11	12-14	15-19	20-24	25-29	>30	Total
Black Bullhead	-	2	35	10	1	-	-	-	48
Black Crappie	31	25	-	-	-	-	-	-	56
Bluegill	297	177	-	-	-	-	-	-	474
Brown Bullhead	-	1	21	17	1	-	-	-	40
Hybrid Sunfish	15	15	-	-	-	-	-	-	30
Largemouth Bass	-	1	-	2	3	-	-	-	6
Northern Pike	-	-	-	15	74	73	23	5	190
Pumpkin. Sunfish	80	25	-	-	-	-	-	-	105
Yellow Bullhead	8	85	114	26	-	-	-	-	233
Yellow Perch	1	1	-	-	-	-	-	-	2

FISHING INFORMATION: At 1,259 acres, Coon Lake offers room to fish, interesting structure and plenty of bluegills, bass, northern pike and some crappies. Coon isn't a deep lake; it needs aerating during the winter to assure fish survival. There is an abundance of plant growth, with most of the bottom comprised of sand, silt and muck. The maximum depth is 27 feet and water clarity is decent down to almost 8 feet.

The lake's eastern end is the deepest part, and you'll be able to find panfish schooling in the vegetation there in the spring. Small minnows on jigs, ice flies with worms or wax worms and small, bright maribou jigs are all worth trying until you find a pattern that produces well. The best way to present your offering is with a slip bobber. It allows you to change depth quickly, plus you can present your bait in a near vertical fashion for a precise presentation. Bluegills are the most abundant panfish on the lake. The most recent DNR survey showed bluegills range from 2.6 to 7.4 inches in length, with 33% of them measuring longer than 6 inches. Black crappie numbers are down from years past. The lengths ranged from 3.9 to 8.9 inches with only 10% longer than 8 inches.

Bass use the same areas as the panfish early on, although they seem to congregate at the lake's eastern end. Jigs and spinnerbaits tipped with pork or soft plastics are popular. Look for bass around cover, ranging from the deeper holes to the lake's docks and floats. Don't pass up the shallow-water bass action any time of day. Although many bass will move to deeper haunts, it's not uncommon to find good-sized bass holding under docks during the heat of the day. Flip a tube, creature bait or a Senko under a dock to see if a bass is there. The largemouth bass numbers are stable according to the latest DNR survey.

There's a big northern pike population in Coon Lake, and some of the fish are impressive. Trolling the weeds with sucker minnows will usually get attention; weedbeds in most parts of the lake are good. If bait isn't your bag then fire out a brightly colored spinnerbait, crankbait or spoon along deep weed edges or above submerged weeds. The DNR survey confirmed the abundance of northern pike

on this lake.

Walleyes, much less plentiful than other sport fish in Coon, also prefer the deeper eastern half of the lake. Fishing is good in spring with minnows near sand points and the deeper bay (20 feet) along the northeast shore.

Like so many lakes in the region, Eurasian milfoil is present. Make sure to remove any remnants of this weed from your boat before leaving the boat launch.

There's a public launch on the north shore, off Thielen Drive. Two fee launches are nearby at a local resort and campground. A county park on the far east shore also charges a fee.

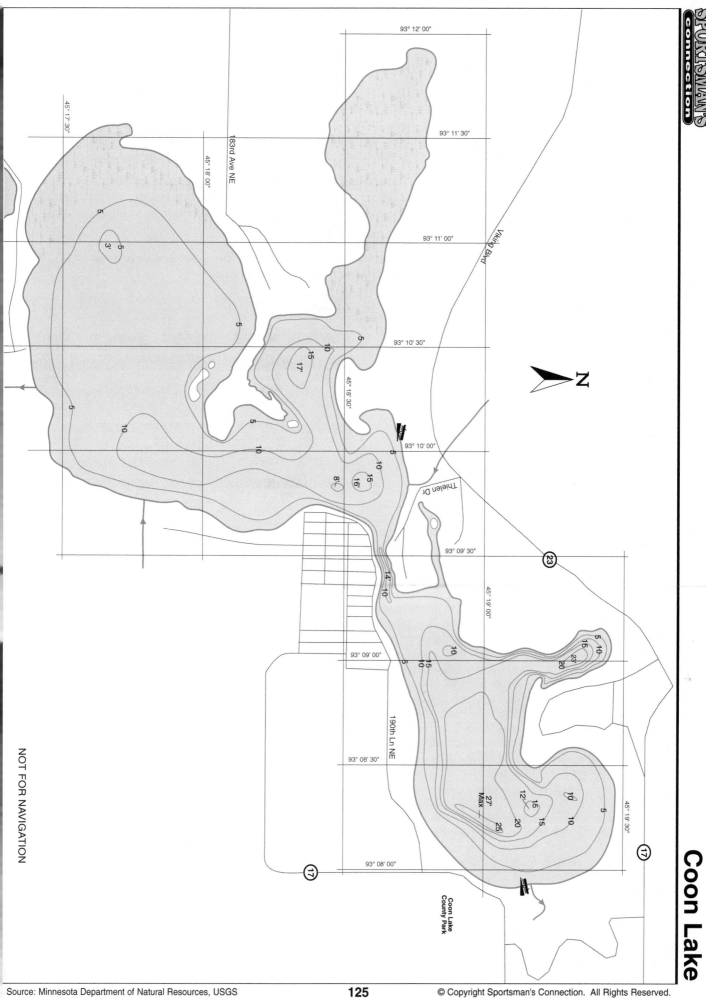

93° 12' 00"

93° 11' 30"

93° 11' 00"

93° 10' 30"

93° 10' 00"

93° 09' 30"

93° 09' 00"

93° 08' 30"

93° 08' 00"

45° 17' 30"

45° 18' 00"

45° 18' 30"

45° 19' 00"

45° 19' 30"

183rd Ave NE

Viking Blvd

Thielen Dr

190th Ln NE

Coon Lake County Park

N

5

3'

5

5

5

5

10

5

10

10

15

17'

16'

15

8'

10

14"

10

5

10

15

10

5

10

15

23'

20

5

10

15

5

10

10

15

15

20

25

27' Max

12'

26

23

17

17

NOT FOR NAVIGATION

BIG COMFORT LAKE
Chisago County

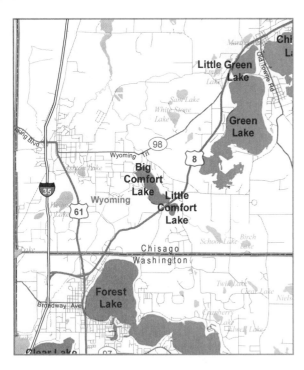

Area map pg / coord: 25 / E-6
Watershed: Lower St. Croix
Secchi disk: 10.0 feet (2010)
Water color: Light green

Surface area: 218 acres
Shorelength: 3.1 miles
Maximum depth: 47 feet
Mean depth: 21 feet

Accessibility: State-owned public access on north shore
Boat ramp: Concrete
Parking: Ten trailer spaces
Accommodations: NA

Shoreland zoning classification: General development
Management class: Centrarchid
Ecological type: Centrarchid

FISH STOCKING DATA

year	species	size	# released
07	Walleye	Fingerling	5,670
09	Walleye	Fingerling	3,798
10	Walleye	Fingerling	700
11	Walleye	Fingerling	2,010

NET CATCH DATA

Date: 06/14/2010

	Gill Nets		Trap Nets	
species	# per net	avg. fish weight (lbs.)	# per net	avg. fish weight (lbs.)
Black Bullhead	0.7	0.09	-	-
Black Crappie	22.3	0.13	34.3	0.19
Bluegill	2.8	0.20	54.2	0.18
Muskellunge	0.2	19.74	-	-
Northern Pike	3.0	2.69	0.1	0.89
Walleye	2.0	2.81	-	-

LENGTH OF SELECTED SPECIES SAMPLED FROM ALL GEAR

Number of fish caught for the following length categories (inches):

species	0-5	6-8	9-11	12-14	15-19	20-24	25-29	>30	Total
Black Bullhead	4	-	-	-	-	-	-	-	4
Black Crappie	104	321	3	-	-	-	-	-	443
Bluegill	161	338	-	-	-	-	-	-	505
Muskellunge	-	-	-	-	-	-	-	1	1
Northern Pike	-	-	1	1	7	4	5	1	19
Walleye	-	-	-	2	2	8	-	-	12
White Sucker	-	-	-	-	1	-	-	-	1
Yellow Perch	24	198	-	-	-	-	-	-	224

FISHING INFORMATION: If you are looking for a vast and varied fishing trip, take comfort in Big Comfort Lake's wide variety of species. From bluegills to carp, to walleyes to northern pike, this lake has 'em. While some species are more abundant than others, this lake offers hope to just about everyone. All of this fun is contained in a small-ish lake, boasting only 218 acres. It offers abundant plant growth down to 7 feet and has a bottom consisting of sand, silt and detritus. The maximum depth is 47 feet. The lake is fairly clear and has weeds, lily pads and reeds that can be fished successfully much of the year. The shoreline consists of (in order of abundance) lake/marshland, residential development, undeveloped forests/woodlands, crop land and livestock/pasture land.

Walleyes are considered to be of normal abundance for a lake of this size. Look for them near the sand bar off the southeast corner, the point on the northwest shore and the Sunrise River outlet on the north shore. Early in the season, get their attention with a bottom rig and minnow. As water warms, fish deeper spots near the center of the lake with a slip bobber and live bait. Be patient. Move vertically and jig until you find the depth where the fish are suspended. You can also take an aggressive approach and troll with crankbaits or spinner rigs. Sometimes the subtle approach doesn't work. Troll fairly fast to trigger walleyes into striking.

The north and south shores have always been good northern pike spots, according to locals. The point on the northwest side can be especially productive. Northerns average about 23 inches on this lake. Over the years, the numbers of northerns have decreased, but the average size of those caught has been on the rise. The decline in yellow perch populations may be a factor for the future of pike and walleyes on this lake, as yellow perch are a primary food source for these predators. Use a fairly large offering to tempt a big pike. A small muskie bucktail, large spinnerbait or jerkbait will draw the attention of an active pike. A large minnow with or without a bobber will work well too, especially during cold fronts or later in the year when the weather starts cooling down.

Crappies aren't everywhere, but most shorelines are good school-ing areas after the spawn. Float small minnows under a slip float to find them. Bass are difficult to find, but you can sometimes attract one near vegetation with topwater lures or spinnerbaits. Also try a Texas-rigged tube or worm to hook a bass in the weeds. Green pumpkin, black or junebug are good colors to try. There's a concrete ramp on the north shore and a carry-in area at the bridge at the south end of the lake.

Because of the connection to Sunrise River, Big Comfort Lake has two tall tales to tell, both of which are Loch Ness-like. One 39-inch muskellunge was caught from this lake, the only one ever recorded, and was probably just lost on the way to Forest Lake. The other tale is of a 106-pound sturgeon that washed up on shore here. The sturgeon was most likely a stray from the Sunrise River. The chances of these appearing again are slim, so don't bother fishing for these species here, or you'll be known as the local nut who is hunting for Nessie.

Big & Little Comfort Lakes

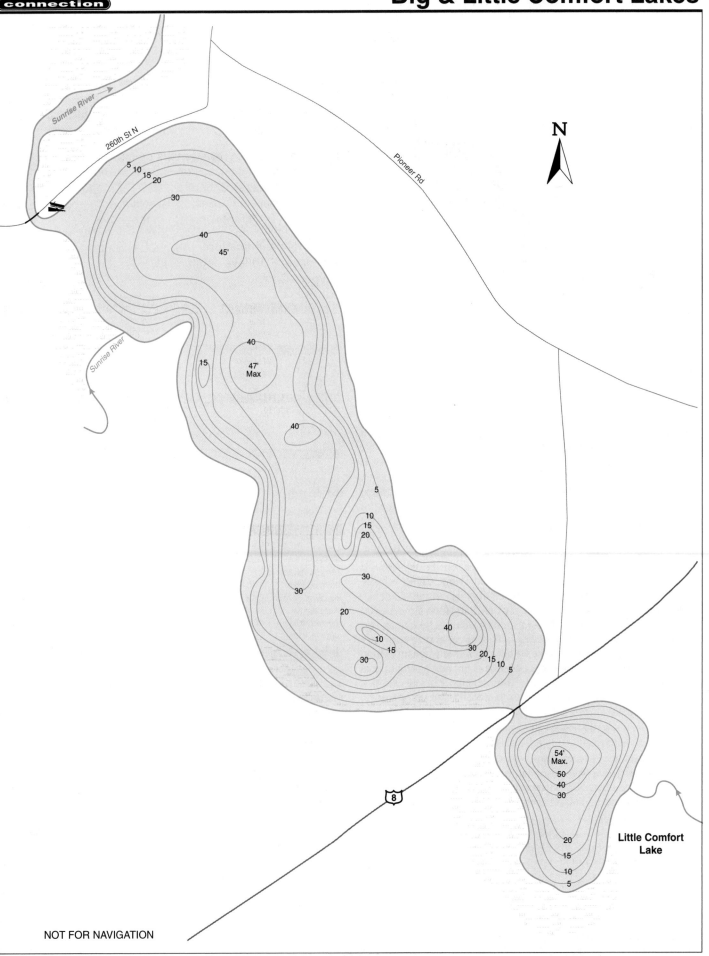

NOT FOR NAVIGATION

Source: Minnesota Department of Natural Resources, USGS

127

© Copyright Sportsman's Connection. All Rights Reserved.

GREEN LAKE
Chisago County

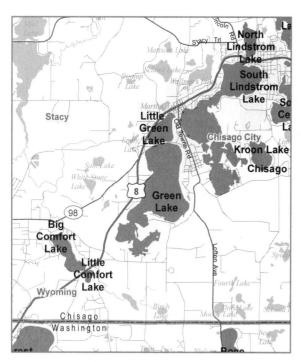

Area map pg / coord: 25 / D,E-6
Watershed: Lower St. Croix
Secchi disk: 3.4 feet (2011)
Water color: NA

Surface area: 1,809 acres
Shorelength: 12.0 miles
Maximum depth: 32 feet
Mean depth: 9 feet

Accessibility: 1) City-owned access on east shore of Little Green Lake; 2) State-owned public access on southeast shore of main lake
Boat ramp: 1) Concrete; 2) Concrete
Parking: 1) Fifteen trailers spaces; 2) Twenty-five trailer spaces
Accommodations: Boat rental, camping, restrooms

Shoreland zoning classification: General development
Management class: Walleye-centrarchid
Ecological type: Centrarchid-walleye

FISHING INFORMATION: Green Lake has a good reputation for producing walleyes. The lake also provides good fishing for northern pike, crappies, bluegills and largemouth bass. The lake is primarily managed for walleyes, northern pike and black crappies. The lake covers 1,809 acres, making it the largest lake in Chisago County.

Brad Dusenka of Frankie's Live Bait & Tackle, 10680 South Ave., Chisago City, MN, (651) 257-6334, says you can limit out on 17-inch walleyes and 9-inch crappies. The best spring-summer spots for walleyes, he says, are off Lindberg Point, on the lake's west shore, and at the steep break off the Girl Scout Camp, almost directly across from the point on the east shore. In fall, Dusenka says you'll find walleyes around the channel into North Green Lake. The north shore of the main lake has a nice weed edge that can be fished successfully at 5- to 15-feet in both summer and winter. You'll also find a hump near the southeast access that draws fish. During the last DNR survey, walleye populations met the management goal for size, but fell short in numbers. The sampled walleyes ranged from 9.3 to 29 inches. Walleye growth was normal compared to statewide averages.

Crappies hang around the lake's weedlines and in North Green Lake early in the season. Use brightly colored jigs tipped with minnows. Later in the season, crappies will suspend in deeper water and should be fished with minnows under a slip bobber. Start at 15 feet and work your way up slowly until you find fish. Crappies range from around 3.5 to 9.5 inches long according to DNR statistics.

Northern pike will go for sucker minnows around the points early, as well as in the entrance to the south bay. The DNR surveyed the pike population and found them to average around 24 inches long. They had a mean weight of 3.2 pounds.

Largemouth bass can be found in the weedy south bay, among other places. Cast Texas-rigged soft plastics like tubes or lizards or go weightless with a Senko or floating worm. Stick with colors such as watermelon, green pumpkin, black or pumpkinseed. A city-owned access area, with ramp and ample parking, lies on North (Little) Green Lake's east side. There is another public access on the southeast side of Green Lake.

FISH STOCKING DATA

year	species	size	# released
06	Walleye	Fingerling	38,369
08	Walleye	Fingerling	35,402
10	Walleye	Fingerling	30,080
11	Walleye	Fingerling	37,393
12	Walleye	Fingerling	20,612

NET CATCH DATA

Date: 07/25/2011

	Gill Nets		Trap Nets	
species	# per net	avg. fish weight (lbs.)	# per net	avg. fish weight (lbs.)
Black Bullhead	0.7	0.87	0.2	0.70
Black Crappie	8.8	0.19	7.5	0.20
Bluegill	40.8	0.16	58.5	0.17
Brown Bullhead	0.1	1.27	0.1	0.66
Common Carp	0.1	7.72	0.1	12.75
Hybrid Sunfish	0.4	0.15	0.7	0.16
Largemouth Bass	1.2	1.23	1.0	0.55
Northern Pike	5.3	3.73	1.3	3.68
Pumpkin. Sunfish	3.1	0.19	5.7	0.16
Walleye	3.2	2.23	0.6	0.21
Yellow Bullhead	4.9	0.96	1.9	1.01
Yellow Perch	0.3	0.13	0.1	0.08

LENGTH OF SELECTED SPECIES SAMPLED FROM ALL GEAR
Number of fish caught for the following length categories (inches):

species	0-5	6-8	9-11	12-14	15-19	20-24	25-29	>30	Total
Black Bullhead	-	-	8	4	-	-	-	-	13
Black Crappie	54	164	9	-	-	-	-	-	229
Bluegill	583	771	-	-	-	-	-	-	1368
Brown Bullhead	-	-	1	2	-	-	-	-	3
Common Carp	-	-	-	-	-	-	1	1	2
Hybrid Sunfish	11	5	-	-	-	-	-	-	16
Largemouth Bass	3	9	7	7	4	-	-	-	31
Northern Pike	-	-	-	2	12	38	24	9	96
Pumpkin. Sunfish	68	48	-	-	-	-	-	-	120
Walleye	-	6	9	8	17	7	7	-	56
Yellow Bullhead	-	-	37	59	-	-	-	-	98
Yellow Perch	2	4	-	-	-	-	-	-	6

Green & Little Green Lakes

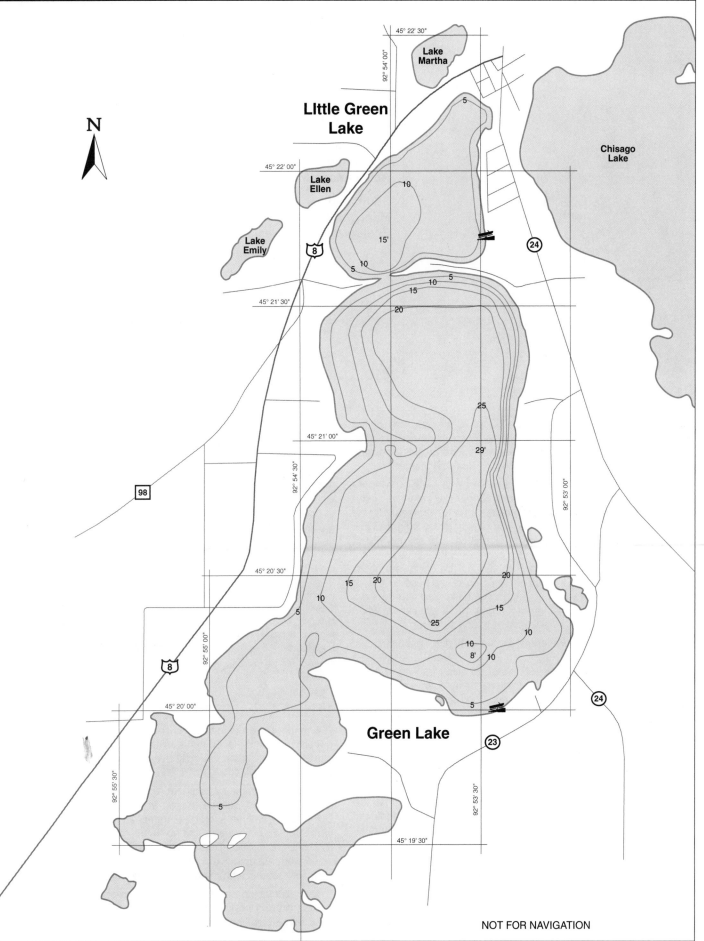

Lake Martha

Little Green Lake

Chisago Lake

N

45° 22' 30"
92° 54' 00"

Lake Ellen

Lake Emily

8

98

8

24

45° 22' 00"
45° 21' 30"
45° 21' 00"
45° 20' 30"
45° 20' 00"
45° 19' 30"

92° 54' 30"
92° 55' 00"
92° 55' 30"
92° 53' 00"
92° 53' 30"

5
10
15'
10
5
10
5
15
20
25
29'
20
15
10
5
25
15
10
10
8'
10
5
5

24
23

Green Lake

NOT FOR NAVIGATION

NORTH LINDSTROM LAKE
Chisago County

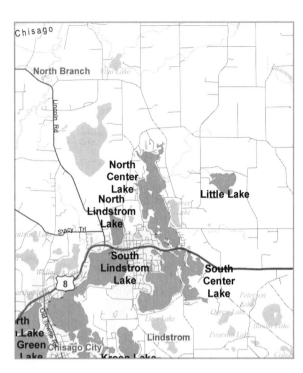

Area map pg / coord: 26 / C,D-1
Watershed: Lower St. Croix
Secchi disk: 6.1 feet (2010)
Water color: Green

Surface area: 142 acres
Shorelength: 2.2 miles
Maximum depth: 29 feet
Mean depth: 19 feet

Accessibility: City-owned on south side off city street,
Boat ramp: None
Accommodations: None

Shoreland zoning classification: General development
Management class: Centrarchid
Ecological type: Centrarchid

FISH STOCKING DATA SINCE 1992

NET CATCH DATA				
Date: 07/19/2010	Gill Nets		Trap Nets	
species	# per net	avg. fish weight (lbs.)	# per net	avg. fish weight (lbs.)
Black Bullhead	2.7	2.17	-	-
Black Crappie	2.8	0.26	2.0	0.26
Bluegill	54.8	0.22	36.2	0.19
Green Sunfish	-	-	0.3	0.09
Hybrid Sunfish	0.5	0.11	5.0	0.23
Largemouth Bass	0.5	0.95	0.1	0.10
Northern Pike	6.5	3.67	0.3	2.04
Pumpkin. Sunfish	2.2	0.32	4.6	0.16
Walleye	3.0	2.82	-	-

LENGTH OF SELECTED SPECIES SAMPLED FROM ALL GEAR								
Number of fish caught for the following length categories (inches):								
species	0-5	6-8	9-11	12-14	15-19	20-24	25-29	>30	Total
Black Bullhead	-	-	1	11	3	-	-	-	16
Black Crappie	2	30	2	-	-	-	-	-	35
Bluegill	166	472	-	-	-	-	-	-	655
Bowfin (Dogfish)	-	-	-	-	2	-	-	-	2
Brown Bullhead	-	1	-	2	-	-	-	-	3
Golden Shiner	-	3	-	-	-	-	-	-	3
Green Sunfish	3	-	-	-	-	-	-	-	3
Hybrid Sunfish	16	27	-	-	-	-	-	-	48
Largemouth Bass	-	1	1	2	-	-	-	-	4
Northern Pike	-	-	-	-	-	20	18	4	42
Pumpkin. Sunfish	27	25	-	-	-	-	-	-	54
Walleye	-	-	-	-	12	4	2	-	18
Yellow Bullhead	-	-	10	4	-	-	-	-	14
Yellow Perch	1	10	-	-	-	-	-	-	11

FISHING INFORMATION: This 142-acre lake is not one of the metro area's most popular fishing lakes. There is some first-class shore fishing though, especially near the bridge at the south end and at the northeast end near the County Road 20 bridge.

The largemouth bass population is doing well here, with abundance and sizes falling in the normal range. Bass can be found along both the east and west shorelines early in the season. Try for them with spinnerbaits, casting into weeds, or try a jig-and-pig. Later, when lily pads have filled the small bays at the north and south ends, go for largemouths with either weedless lures or bright plastic worms. There is also a good bar off the northwest shore that deserves attention in summer. The Senko has become one of the top lures to use for fooling largemouth bass. You can rig them weedless when you are fishing in weeds or try a whacky-rig when you are fishing outside of the weeds or in sparse cover.

Northern pike are more abundant now than in past surveys. Historically, this lake has fallen in the below-average to average range ever since abundance levels started being tracked in 1973. One of the reasons for the less-than-stellar numbers could lie on the shoulders of yellow perch. This pike food source is also falling off in abundance levels, which means fewer pike will be able to fill their bellies. Flashy lures are still best for taking northerns. A brightly colored spoon or spinnerbait will work well. A basic slip bobber with a plain hook and large minnow will also tempt them.

Crappies and bluegills will keep anglers busy on this lake. Look for panfish in weeds early in spring. Shore fishing the channel to Bowl Lake is popular, too. The water is clear, so you can get attention with worms or minnows on a plain hook before weeds get too thick. When water warms, panfish will be at edges of flats by deeper water. Later, they'll be suspended about 12 feet deep over the holes. Crappies love minnows and both species will take a small leech. If you're looking to fill your livewell with plenty of bluegills, then fish for them when they're on spawning beds. Of course, keep only what you'll eat, since they're easy targets at this time and try to select only the males. You can use almost anything to catch them, but a fun way to hook bluegills is with lightweight fly gear.

A 4-weight fly rod is ideal. Use small nymphs or try a leech or ant pattern. Anything placed in the middle of a bluegills bed will draw a strike. A popper fished directly overhead will get the attention of a protective bluegill, too.

Walleyes probably migrate into North Lindstrom from neighboring lakes. Measured walleye ranged from 16.3 to 27.2 inches in the DNR survey, with an average length of 20.6 inches. A good place to look for them is the bar at the north end. Use live bait, but use light line and small hooks. Don't hesitate to get down as deep as 25 feet when water warms. Favorite baits are leeches and crawlers during summer months, with minnows being best in fall.

Boat access isn't good here as there is only a city-owned street access with no parking. Navigation from South Lindstrom is possible with a small boat during normal water levels.

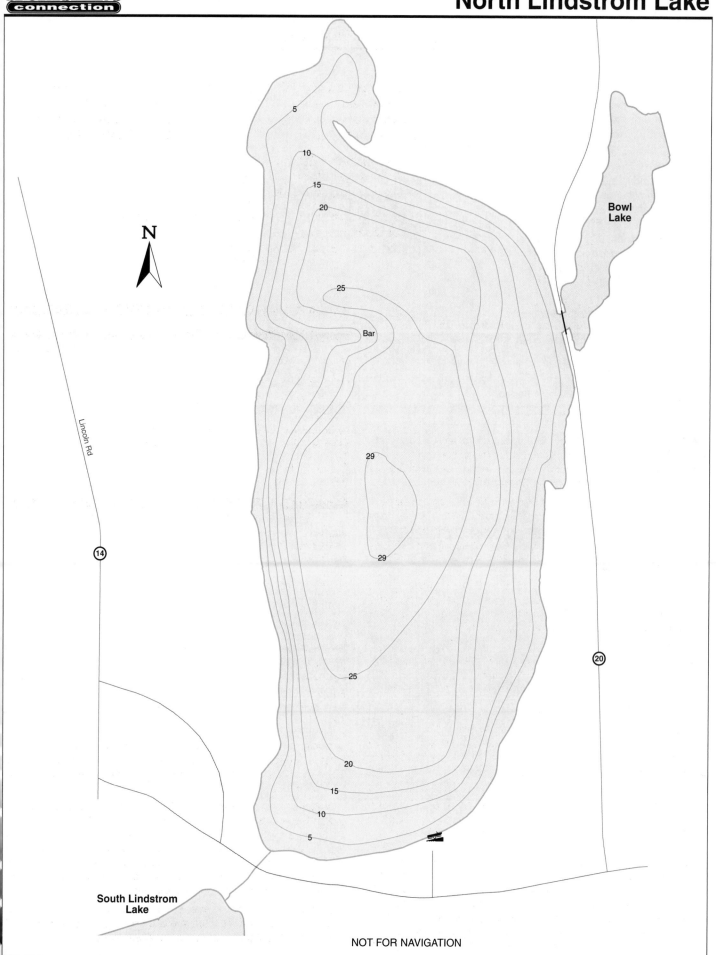

N

Bowl
Lake

Lincoln Rd

14

20

5

10

15

20

25

Bar

29

29

25

20

15

10

5

South Lindstrom
Lake

NOT FOR NAVIGATION

CHISAGO LAKE

Bordered by Paradise Park

Area map page/coord: 26 / D-1
Watershed: Lower St. Croix
Surface area: 897 acres
Shorelength: 11.5 miles
Maximum depth: 34 feet
Mean depth: 7 feet
Secchi disk: 3.2 feet (2010)
Water color: Green
Accessibility: State-owned public access with concrete ramp on west shore of channel to South Lindstrom; seventy trailer spaces
Accommodations: Park, fishing pier, resort, picnicking, restrooms
Shoreland zoning: General dev.
Management class: Walleye-centrarchid
Ecological type: Centrarchid-walleye

Chisago County

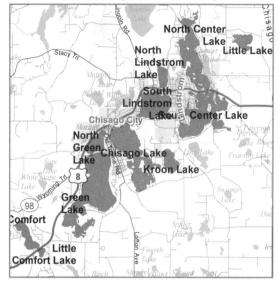

SO. LINDSTROM LAKE

Bordered by Russell Park

Area map page/coord: 26 / D-1
Watershed: Lower St. Croix
Surface area: 548 acres
Shorelength: 3.9 miles
Maximum depth: 34 feet
Mean depth: 12 feet
Secchi disk: 3.1 feet (2010)
Water color: Light green
Accessibility: 1) City-owned public access with concrete ramp on north shore in park; 2) State-owned public access with concrete ramp in the channel area on the SW end
Accommodations: Park, fishing pier, picnicking, restrooms
Shoreland zoning: General dev.
Management class: Walleye-centrarchid
Ecological type: Centrarchid-walleye

FISH STOCKING DATA

year	species	size	# released
10	Walleye	Fingerling	5,375
11	Walleye	Fingerling	11,451
12	Walleye	Fingerling	4,732
12	Walleye	Yearling	52

NET CATCH DATA

Date: 08/02/2010

	Gill Nets		Trap Nets	
species	# per net	avg. fish weight (lbs.)	# per net	avg. fish weight (lbs.)
Black Crappie	13.5	0.26	9.2	0.30
Bluegill	33.6	0.21	37.6	0.20
Largemouth Bass	1.4	1.45	0.7	1.90
Northern Pike	7.6	3.45	0.7	1.90
Pumkin. Sunfish	4.1	0.26	5.8	0.26
Walleye	6.5	2.63	0.2	3.78
Yellow Perch	13.9	0.13	-	-

LENGTH OF SELECTED SPECIES SAMPLED FROM ALL GEAR

Number of fish caught for the following length categories (inches):

species	0-5	6-8	9-11	12-14	15-19	20-24	25-29	>30	Total
Black Bullhead	-	-	-	7	-	-	-	-	7
Black Crappie	18	191	22	-	-	-	-	-	245
Bluegill	249	521	-	-	-	-	-	-	787
Bowfin (Dogfish)	-	-	-	-	-	14	1	3	19
Golden Shiner	2	69	1	-	-	-	-	-	77
Hybrid Sunfish	13	47	1	-	-	-	-	-	66
Largemouth Bass	-	-	4	7	11	-	-	-	22
Northern Pike	-	-	1	8	7	29	26	11	83
Pumpkin. Sunfish	21	85	-	-	-	-	-	-	111
Walleye	-	1	8	4	21	29	4	-	67
Yellow Bullhead	-	-	-	17	-	-	-	-	17
Yellow Perch	16	120	-	-	-	-	-	-	139

FISH STOCKING DATA

year	species	size	# released
10	Walleye	Fingerling	4,160
11	Walleye	Fingerling	4,384
12	Walleye	Fingerling	1,042
12	Walleye	Yearling	154

NET CATCH DATA

Date: 08/02/2010

	Gill Nets		Trap Nets	
species	# per net	avg. fish weight (lbs.)	# per net	avg. fish weight (lbs.)
Black Crappie	43.0	0.28	9.7	0.24
Bluegill	38.2	0.23	42.2	0.22
Largemouth Bass	2.5	1.10	0.1	0.61
Pumkin. Sunfish	5.3	0.27	10.1	0.28
Walleye	3.3	2.57	0.2	0.18

LENGTH OF SELECTED SPECIES SAMPLED FROM ALL GEAR

Survey Date: 07/26/2010   Survey method: gill net, trap net

Number of fish caught for the following length categories (inches):

species	0-5	6-8	9-11	12-14	15-19	20-24	25-29	>30	Total
Black Crappie	21	287	20	-	-	-	-	-	345
Bluegill	116	481	-	-	-	-	-	-	609
Hybrid Sunfish	12	29	-	-	-	-	-	-	42
Largemouth Bass	1	4	3	4	4	-	-	-	16
Northern Pike	-	-	-	7	8	5	6	10	37
Pumkin. Sunfish	18	100	-	-	-	-	-	-	123
Walleye	-	1	-	4	5	11	-	-	21
White Sucker	-	-	-	2	6	-	-	-	10
Yellow Perch	1	54	-	-	-	-	-	-	58

FISHING INFORMATION: While both South Lindstrom Lake and Chisago Lake have identical maximum depths of 34 feet, their surface areas are much different. Lindstrom is just shy of 550 acres and Chisago is over 890 acres. The two lakes are connected by a natural channel and share an abundance of fish. These two lakes are subject to major changes in water levels. There are bass, walleyes, panfish and northern pike in fairly good numbers, so you'll have plenty to do on these lakes while you're dodging the recreational boaters and water-skiers.

Due to a decline in size of the largemouth bass, both lakes have been selected for an experimental regulation research project. The DNR instituted a 12-inch maximum size limit on this species to allow the larger fish to keep growing.

Chisago Lake has some unique bass fishing opportunities in weeds and stumps along its north side, as well as in the smaller southeast bay. It's almost like fishing one of the big impoundments in the southern states. The weeded area at the south end of Chisago Lake is excellent for crappies and is as easily fished from shore as from a boat. The northwest end of Chisago is also a spring hot spot in the stump-filled shallows. Because vegetation becomes extremely heavy in summer, you will want to be in deeper water by mid-June. Look for northern pike along the narrow middle of Chisago Lake.

South Lindstrom Lake has a decent walleye population, thanks to the DNR's stocking efforts. Walleyes can be found in spring at the sand bars at the north and south ends of the lake. The deep water at the center of the lake is very good for slow trolling and slip bobber fishing.

Fish outside weed edges for northern pike early in the season, paying special attention to the channel between the lakes, as well as the bar along the north shore.

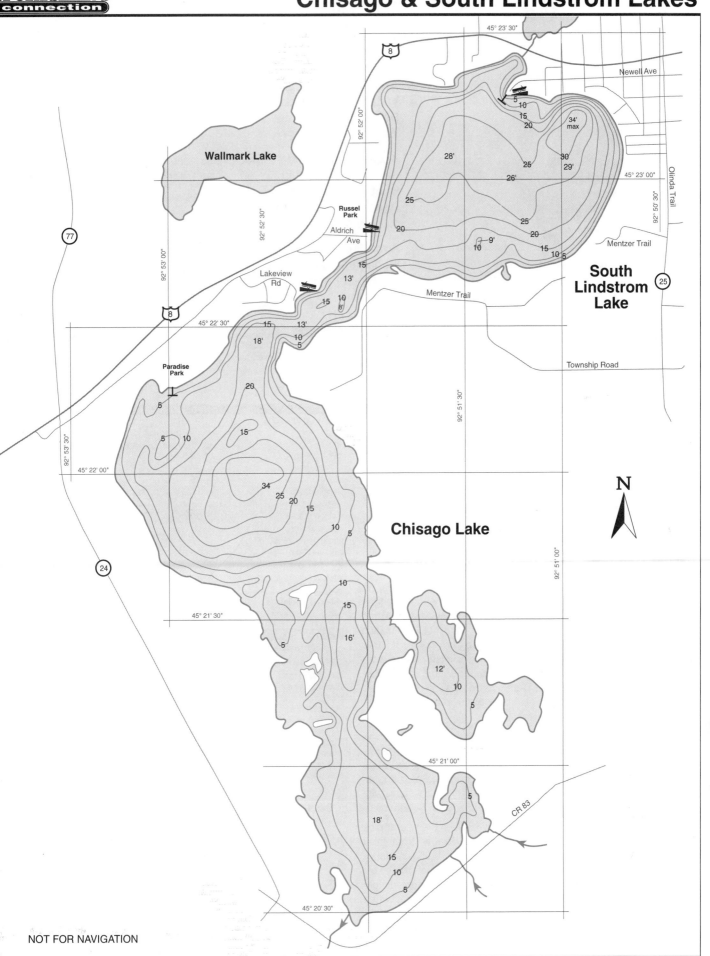

NOT FOR NAVIGATION

NORTH CENTER LAKE
Chisago County

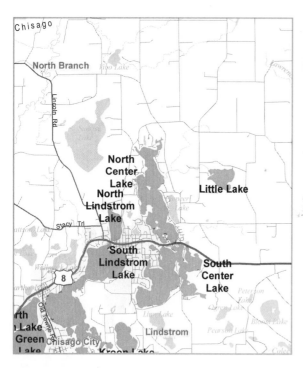

Area map pg / coord: 26 / C,D-1
Watershed: Lower St. Croix
Secchi disk: 3.4 feet (2005)
Water color: NA

Surface area: 725 acres
Shorelength: 11.2 miles
Maximum depth: 46 feet
Mean depth: 7 feet

Accessibility: State-owned public access on south shore; also via navigable channel from South Center Lake
Boat ramp: Concrete
Parking: Twenty-five trailer spaces
Accommodations: Camping, restrooms

Shoreland zoning classification: General development
Management class: Centrarchid
Ecological type: Centrarchid

FISH STOCKING DATA

year	species	size	# released
07	Walleye	Fingerling	19,323
09	Walleye	Fingerling	10,000
10	Walleye	Fingerling	9,780

NET CATCH DATA

Date: 08/01/2005

	Gill Nets		Trap Nets	
species	# per net	avg. fish weight (lbs.)	# per net	avg. fish weight (lbs.)
Black Bullhead	2.5	1.27	0.8	1.01
Black Crappie	44.6	0.27	10.4	0.30
Bluegill	29.4	0.23	12.6	0.25
Bowfin (Dogfish)	0.2	3.14	0.4	5.06
Common Carp	trace	4.46	-	-
Golden Shiner	10.6	0.24	trace	0.07
Hybrid Sunfish	-	-	0.2	0.29
Largemouth Bass	0.9	0.39	0.4	2.59
Northern Pike	2.8	5.43	-	-
Pumpkin. Sunfish	-	-	1.4	0.25
Walleye	1.7	2.81	trace	4.19
White Sucker	0.2	3.00	trace	3.97
Yellow Bullhead	0.3	1.28	0.5	1.07
Yellow Perch	11.2	0.15	-	-

LENGTH OF SELECTED SPECIES SAMPLED FROM ALL GEAR

Number of fish caught for the following length categories (inches):

species	0-5	6-8	9-11	12-14	15-19	20-24	25-29	>30	Total
Black Bullhead	-	-	3	24	-	-	-	-	27
Black Crappie	4	187	8	-	-	-	-	-	199
Bluegill	13	225	-	-	-	-	-	-	238
Hybrid Sunfish	-	2	-	-	-	-	-	-	2
Largemouth Bass	2	2	7	1	3	-	-	-	15
Northern Pike	-	-	-	1	-	6	14	12	33
Pumpkin. Sunfish	3	14	-	-	-	-	-	-	17
Walleye	-	-	3	1	5	12	-	-	21
Yellow Bullhead	-	-	2	4	-	-	-	-	6
Yellow Perch	3	85	-	-	-	-	-	-	88

FISHING INFORMATION: North Center Lake is a large lake covering 725 acres. The maximum depth is 46 feet with water clarity going down to a mere 3.4 feet. The lake is primarily managed for northern pike and walleyes. There are deep spots in the far south end and in the north end. These are good hiding places for many of the species after water warms. The thermocline runs to 25 feet, so you'll find fish in deeper water. Expect heavy fishing pressure at times, as well as crowded public access. Most anglers come here to fish for bass and panfish, but northern pike and walleyes are fun to hunt, too.

The northern pike population makes for exciting fishing on North Center Lake. Fish for these behemoths at outside edges of weedlines. Cast to weeds with spoons and spinnerbaits or troll flats with large sucker minnows. Also try a 5- to 7-inch soft-plastic jerkbait. There are a variety of these to choose from in your favorite tackle store. Light colors like white, pearl or a baitfish pattern work best. Use them like a hard jerkbait. The advantage to the soft plastic version is the capacity to fish them weedless. Work these lures through the edges of weeds where some of the real big pike wait for an easy meal to swim by.

Walleyes are large here, but not as abundant as they could be. The average walleye measured during the DNR survey was 22 inches and 2.8 pounds. Walleyes will be at gravel or sandy areas early in the year, which are located at the north end of the lake. Live bait or Shad Raps can be effective here. Try night fishing with original Rapalas in shallow areas near drop-offs for big walleyes.

This is a good panfish lake, heavy with smaller black crappies and bluegills. Lake structure is challenging. It ranges from thick weedbeds and islands to rocky points. One of the better spots for crappies is the small bay to the north of the peninsula on the lake's west side. Also try inside Nelson Island on the east shore. Bright jigs tipped with small minnows will be effective, especially when fished under a slip bobber.

Bass like to hang out off the peninsula and the islands in the south part of the lake. Stick with soft plastics during warm-weather months to hook the most bass. Tubes, creature baits, Senkos or plastic worms can all produce largemouths. Stick to weed edges or fish in dense weeds to find a few bass.

There's public access at the south end of the lake off U.S. 8, and there's fee access at a west-shore resort, which also offers bait and boat rentals.

N

Source: Minnesota Department of Natural Resources, USGS

SOUTH CENTER LAKE
Chisago County

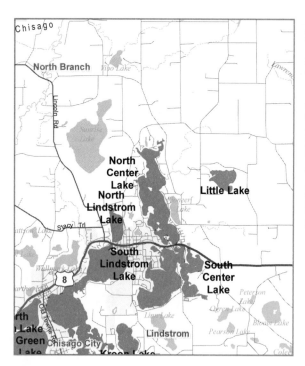

Area map pg / coord: 26 / D-1
Watershed: Lower St. Croix
Secchi disk: 5.2 feet (2010)
Water color: Green

Surface area: 898 acres
Shorelength: 7.6 miles
Maximum depth: 109 feet
Mean depth: 8 feet

Accessibility: State-owned public access on north shore of south-west bay; also via navigable channel from North Center Lake
Boat ramp: Concrete
Parking: Fifty trailer spaces
Accommodations: Resort, boat/motor rental, camping, restrooms

Shoreland zoning classification: General development
Management class: Walleye-centrarchid
Ecological type: Centrarchid

FISH STOCKING DATA

year	species	size	# released
07	Walleye	Fingerling	18,532
09	Walleye	Fingerling	12,675
10	Walleye	Fingerling	11,240
11	Walleye	Fingerling	15,375
12	Walleye	Fingerling	9,777

NET CATCH DATA

Date: 08/09/2010	Gill Nets		Trap Nets	
species	# per net	avg. fish weight (lbs.)	# per net	avg. fish weight (lbs.)
Black Crappie	15.4	0.26	7.5	0.26
Bluegill	22.3	0.19	55.3	0.17
Largemouth Bass	0.2	0.66	-	-
Northern Pike	1.8	5.52	0.3	3.22
Walleye	3.2	2.21	0.6	0.71

LENGTH OF SELECTED SPECIES SAMPLED FROM ALL GEAR
Number of fish caught for the following length categories (inches):

species	0-5	6-8	9-11	12-14	15-19	20-24	25-29	>30	Total
Black Bullhead	-	1	162	3	-	-	-	-	171
Black Crappie	7	248	7	-	-	-	-	-	275
Bluegill	276	646	-	-	-	-	-	-	930
Brown Bullhead	-	-	3	11	-	-	-	-	14
Common Carp	-	1	-	-	3	5	6	-	15
Golden Shiner	10	77	1	-	-	-	-	-	93
Hybrid Sunfish	7	4	-	-	-	-	-	-	11
Northern Pike	-	-	-	-	-	8	9	6	26
Pumpkin. Sunfish	9	44	-	-	-	-	-	-	53
Walleye	-	8	10	9	4	7	7	-	45
White Sucker	-	-	-	-	4	5	-	-	9
Yellow Bullhead	-	-	2	2	-	-	-	-	4
Yellow Perch	3	9	-	-	-	-	-	-	12

FISHING INFORMATION: South Center is an interesting lake to fish, full of small bays, points, sand bars and deep holes. This is one of the area's better fishing spots, with good populations of largemouth bass, northern pike, walleyes and panfish. With 898 acres and a maximum depth of 109 feet, it has plenty of places for fish to forage and frolic. The primary management species on this lake are walleyes and northern pike. Angling pressure is considered moderate to very high for all species.

South Center has an abundant walleye population. The fish are good-sized. with an average of 2.2 pounds and 16.3 inches. The size range of the fish caught during the 2010 DNR survey was between 8.5 and 27.1 inches. Anglers have their best shot at walleyes in spring along the northwest shore of the lake, the peninsula below the hill on the east side, and the sunken island in the middle of the lake's main bay. Use a jig, bumping your bait up the slopes. Locals say the south end of the lake can also be productive for walleyes. Work the steep drop-off at various depths until you locate a school. Oxygen runs deep in this lake, so fish down as far as 40 feet. Although using slow and precise methods like controlled drifting with live bait can be dull at times, it can sometimes be the ticket for bigger fish, especially in fall. Use a Lindy rig and bait your hook with a large fathead or chub. Fish deeper points and breaks. With large bait, make sure to feed the fish plenty of line after it strikes before you set your hook.

Northern pike were not as abundant as walleyes, but they were quality-sized, according to the DNR survey. Averages for pike were 4.8 pounds, with the largest caught measuring 36.8 inches. You can troll weedlines for northerns early in the season before the weeds get too thick. The area around Sunset Point, between the lake's two main bays, is usually productive; also try the flats in the east bay.

Largemouth bass are fairly numerous. Because there is good vegetation for bass along most of the shoreline, you'll want to try different techniques. Spinnerbaits, topwater lures and plastic worms are all good go-to baits. There is hardly a weedy area of South Center Lake that won't hold bass at one time or another throughout

the year. Change to plastic frogs, soft plastics and bright spoons as weather warms, because of the thickness of the weeds. The west shoreline, especially the southwest bay, is good then, as well as the narrow area between the lake's east and west bays.

While less abundant than in years past, crappies, bluegills and yellow perch are still plentiful. You can find bigger panfish, walleyes and some pike in deep holes at the south, middle and north ends of the big bay.

The state-owned access is located on the north shore of the southwest bay of the lake. The parking lot holds 50 vehicles with trailers. Even though that is a lot of spaces, it can be very busy at times, so plan your outing accordingly.

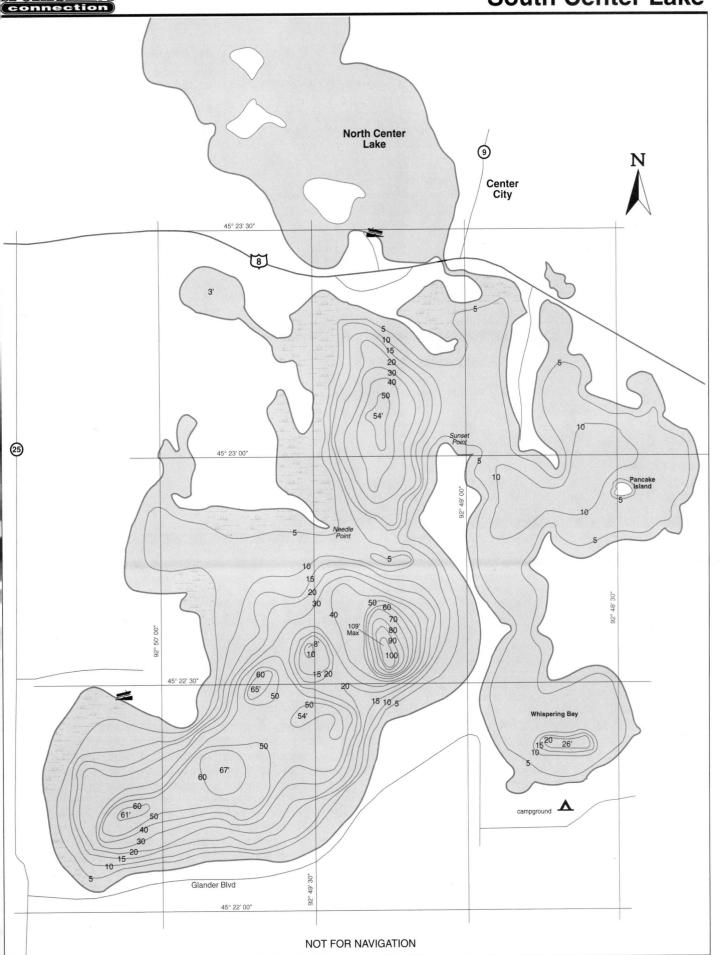

SPORTSMAN'S connection

North Center Lake

Center City

N

45° 23' 30"

8

25

3'

5

5
10
15
20
30
40
50
54'

5

Sunset Point

10

5

45° 23' 00"

10

Pancake Island

5

Needle Point

5

10

5

10

5

10
15
20
30
40
50 60
70
109' Max
80
90
100

8'
10

60
65'
50

15 20

50
54'

20

15 10 5

Whispering Bay

20 26'
15
10

5

50

67'
60

60
61'
50
40
30
20
15
10
5

campground

Glander Blvd

45° 22' 30"

45° 22' 00"

92° 50' 00"

92° 49' 30"

92° 49' 00"

92° 48' 30"

NOT FOR NAVIGATION

KROON LAKE

LITTLE LAKE

Chisago County

Area map page/coord: 26 / D-1

Watershed: Lower St. Croix

Surface area: 181 acres

Shorelength: 2.3 miles

Maximum depth: 30 feet

Mean depth: 5 feet

Secchi disk: 4.0 feet (2009)

Water color: Green

Accessibility: State-owned public access with concrete ramp on east shore; parking for ten trailers

Accommodations: None

Shoreland zoning: Recreational dev.

Management class: Centrarchid

Ecological type: Centrarchid

Area map page/coord: 26 / C-1

Watershed: Lower St. Croix

Surface area: 150 acres

Shorelength: 1.8 miles

Maximum depth: 23 feet

Mean depth: 9 feet

Secchi disk: 5.0 feet (2009)

Water color: Green

Accessibility: State-owned public access with concrete ramp on northeast shore; parking for six trailers

Accommodations: None

Shoreland zoning: Recreational dev.

Management class: Centrarchid

Ecological type: Centrarchid

NO RECORD OF STOCKING

NET CATCH DATA

Date: 06/22/2009

species	Gill Nets # per net	Gill Nets avg. fish weight (lbs.)	Trap Nets # per net	Trap Nets avg. fish weight (lbs.)
Black Crappie	6.0	0.20	1.0	0.23
Bluegill	10.2	0.20	15.2	0.15
Bowfin (Dogfish)	-	-	0.3	4.02
Brown Bullhead	1.0	1.52	4.2	0.97
Golden Shiner	0.8	0.13	-	-
Hybrid Sunfish	-	-	1.9	0.26
Largemouth Bas	1.2	1.69	0.4	0.60
Northern Pike	12.8	4.62	0.4	1.37
Pumpkin. Sunfish	1.6	0.31	4.7	0.26
Walleye	0.2	5.90	-	-

LENGTH OF SELECTED SPECIES SAMPLED FROM ALL GEAR

Number of fish caught for the following length categories (inches):

species	0-5	6-8	9-11	12-14	15-19	20-24	25-29	>30	Total
Black Crappie	6	30	1	-	-	-	-	-	39
Bluegill	58	124	-	-	-	-	-	-	188
Bowfin (Dogfish)	-	-	-	-	1	1	1	-	3
Brown Bullhead	-	-	19	24	-	-	-	-	43
Golden Shiner	-	4	-	-	-	-	-	-	4
Hybrid Sunfish	2	15	-	-	-	-	-	-	17
Largemouth Bass	-	1	4	3	2	-	-	-	10
Northern Pike	-	-	-	-	4	26	23	12	68
Pumpkin. Sunfish	2	45	-	-	-	-	-	-	50
Walleye	-	-	-	-	-	-	1	-	1

FISH STOCKING DATA

year	species	size	# released
06	Walleye	Fingerling	2,988
08	Walleye	Fingerling	3,176
10	Walleye	Fingerling	2,040

NET CATCH DATA

Date: 06/08/2009

species	Gill Nets # per net	Gill Nets avg. fish weight (lbs.)	Trap Nets # per net	Trap Nets avg. fish weight (lbs.)
Black Crappie	92.5	0.27	6.6	0.27
Bluegill	9.5	0.29	9.0	0.31
Bowfin (Dogfish)	-	-	0.9	6.57
Northern Pike	2.8	4.38	-	-
Pumpkin. Sunfish	0.2	0.45	0.8	0.37
Walleye	1.0	3.04	-	-
Yellow Bullhead	0.8	1.71	-	-
Yellow Perch	9.0	0.24	-	-

LENGTH OF SELECTED SPECIES SAMPLED FROM ALL GEAR

Number of fish caught for the following length categories (inches):

species	0-5	6-8	9-11	12-14	15-19	20-24	25-29	>30	Total
Black Crappie	-	565	13	-	-	-	-	-	608
Bluegill	10	117	-	-	-	-	-	-	129
Bowfin (Dogfish)	-	-	-	-	-	2	5	-	7
Northern Pike	-	-	-	-	-	6	11	-	17
Pumpkin. Sunfish	-	7	-	-	-	-	-	-	7
Walleye	-	-	-	1	-	5	-	-	6
Yellow Bullhead	-	-	-	5	-	-	-	-	5
Yellow Perch	3	45	1	-	-	-	-	-	54

FISHING INFORMATION: Kroon Lake is a fine place to fish for largemouth bass and northern pike, and it holds good numbers of smaller bluegills. Brad Dusenka of Frankie's Live Bait & Tackle, 10680 South Ave., Chisago City, MN, (651) 257-6334, says the good weedlines toward the lake's southern end are where you'll find bass early in the season. These weedbeds are thick, so try a weedless presentation. Before July, when the vegetation becomes extremely heavy, you can use a jig-and-minnow or jig-and-pig along weed edges. Northern pike often roam the same weedlines, typically on the prowl for bluegills. In spring, when water is clear, troll the outside edges with a sucker minnow. The flats along the south end, especially near the connecting creek to Boos Lake, should be trolled. The bottom drops fairly quickly to about 30 feet at mid-lake. Fish this center area after the first part of July. During the last DNR survey in 2009, it was noted that the largemouth bass, northern pike and bluegill populations were good. Bass averaged just shy of 12 inches, with an average weight of 0.8 pounds. About 41% of the bass sampled were longer than 12 inches. Most northerns (61%) were between 22 and 28 inches long. Although bluegills were abundant, very few of the fish sampled exceeded 7 inches in length.

Little Lake is subject to a degree of winterkill in severely cold years, but you'll find some good fishing, whatever the circumstances. Largemouth bass, northern pike and bluegills are the dominant species. Fish heavy weeds with weedless or topwater lures for bass. Dropping a jig with a minnow or worm will usually get some action, too. Northerns will be on the outer edges of the weeds, which expand dramatically as weather warms. Walleye numbers are only fair, but five of the six fish captured in the latest survery were bigger than 20 inches, so they're well worth pursuing. Try weed edges and the underwater point on the east side. During a 2009 DNR survey, largemouth bass numbers were good, although they were down from the 2004 survey. More than one-third of the bass sampled measured more than 13 inches long. Along with a good outlook for bass, the bluegill population was also solid with an average fish spanning 7.2 inches. Northern pike averaged 26.3 inches long with a weight of 4.4 pounds.

Kroon & Little Lakes

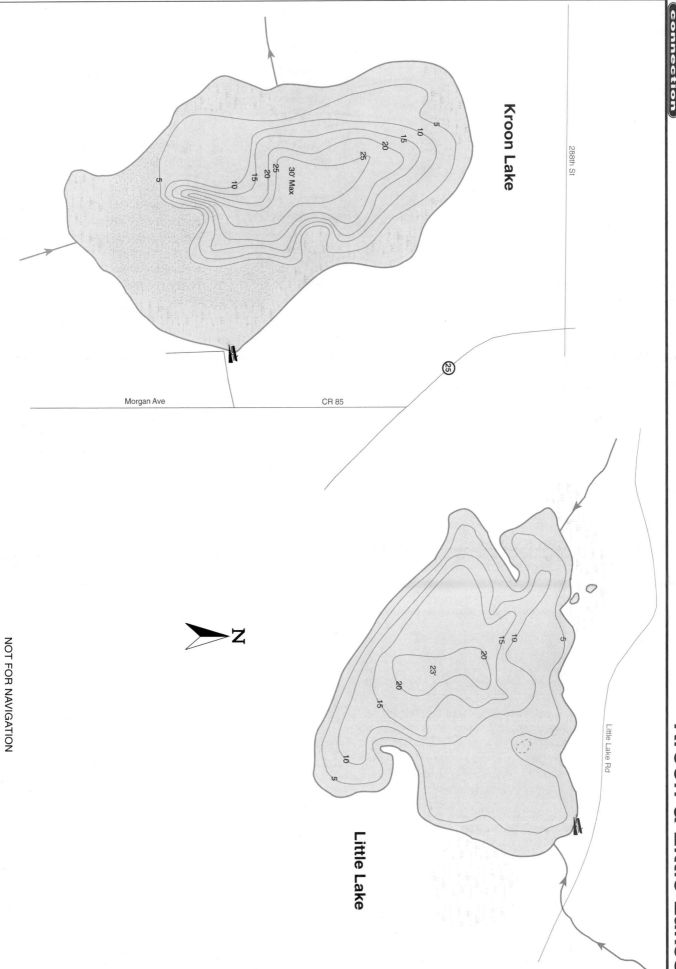

Kroon Lake

Little Lake

288th St

25

Morgan Ave

CR 85

Little Lake Rd

N

NOT FOR NAVIGATION

139

EAST TWIN LAKE

Bordered by East Twin Lake County Park

Area map page/coord: 24 / E-1
Watershed: Twin Cities
Surface area: 98 acres
Shorelength: NA
Maximum depth: 68 feet
Mean depth: NA
Secchi disk: 11.0 feet (2010)
Water color: Green tint
Accessibility: County-owned public access with earthen ramp on south shore in park; ten trailer spaces
Accommodations: Park, picnicking, restrooms
Shoreland zoning: Natural envt.
Management class: Centrarchid
Ecological type: Centrarchid

CROOKED LAKE

Anoka County

Bordered by Andover Park & Crooked Lake Park

Area map page/coord: 27 / B-6
Watershed: Twin Cities
Surface area: 118 acres
Shorelength: NA
Maximum depth: 26 feet
Mean depth: NA
Secchi disk: 8.5 feet (2009)
Water color: Green
Accessibility: State-owned public access with concrete ramp on north shore in park; ten trailer spaces
Accommodations: Parks, fishing piers, picnicking, restrooms
Shoreland zoning: Natural environment
Management class: Centrarchid
Ecological type: Centrarchid

FISH STOCKING DATA (East Twin Lake)

year	species	size	# released
03	Walleye	Fry	217,500
05	Walleye	Fry	218,000

NET CATCH DATA

Date: 07/19/2010

species	Gill Nets # per net	Gill Nets avg. fish weight (lbs.)	Trap Nets # per net	Trap Nets avg. fish weight (lbs.)
Black Bullhead	1.5	1.11	1.6	0.74
Black Crappie	-	-	0.4	0.27
Bluegill	8.5	0.13	56.6	0.13
Bowfin (Dogfish)	-	-	0.8	2.75
Hybrid Sunfish	-	-	2.6	0.12
Largemouth Bass	-	-	0.4	0.66
Northern Pike	-	-	0.8	1.79
Pumpkin. Sunfish	2.5	0.12	3.6	0.16
Yellow Bullhead	1.5	0.61	1.6	0.85

LENGTH OF SELECTED SPECIES SAMPLED FROM ALL GEAR

Number of fish caught for the following length categories (inches):

species	0-5	6-8	9-11	12-14	15-19	20-24	25-29	>30	Total
Black Bullhead	-	1	7	3	-	-	-	-	11
Black Crappie	-	2	-	-	-	-	-	-	2
Bluegill	192	105	-	-	-	-	-	-	300
Bowfin (Dogfish)	-	-	-	-	2	2	-	-	4
Hybrid Sunfish	10	3	-	-	-	-	-	-	13
Largemouth Bass	1	-	-	1	-	-	-	-	2
Northern Pike	-	-	-	2	5	6	2	2	17
Pumpkin. Sunfish	17	6	-	-	-	-	-	-	23
Yellow Bullhead	-	-	8	3	-	-	-	-	11

FISH STOCKING DATA (Crooked Lake)

year	species	size	# released
09	Channel Catfish	Yearling	1,598
09	Walleye	Fry	175,000
11	Channel Catfish	Yearling	2,601
11	Walleye	Fry	172,000
12	Walleye	Fry	172,000

NET CATCH DATA

Date: 07/20/2009

species	Gill Nets # per net	Gill Nets avg. fish weight (lbs.)	Trap Nets # per net	Trap Nets avg. fish weight (lbs.)
Black Crappie	6.5	0.14	0.3	0.27
Bluegill	76.5	0.13	81.0	0.10
Channel Catfish	4.5	1.55	-	-
Hybrid Sunfish	-	-	1.0	0.07
Largemouth Bass	1.0	1.58	0.3	1.96
Northern Pike	1.5	3.98	-	-
Pumpkin. Sunfish	-	-	0.8	0.09
Walleye	2.5	1.92	-	-
Yellow Perch	12.0	0.10	0.9	0.12

LENGTH OF SELECTED SPECIES SAMPLED FROM ALL GEAR

Number of fish caught for the following length categories (inches):

species	0-5	6-8	9-11	12-14	15-19	20-24	25-29	>30	Total
Black Crappie	3	12	-	-	-	-	-	-	15
Bluegill	552	244	-	-	-	-	-	-	801
Channel Catfish	-	-	4	3	-	1	1	-	9
Common Carp	-	-	-	-	1	-	-	-	1
Hybrid Sunfish	8	-	-	-	-	-	-	-	8
Largemouth Bass	-	2	-	-	2	-	-	-	4
Northern Pike	-	-	-	-	-	1	2	-	3
Pumpkin. Sunfish	5	1	-	-	-	-	-	-	6
Walleye	-	-	-	-	5	-	-	-	5
White Sucker	-	-	-	-	4	2	-	-	6
Yellow Bullhead	5	2	1	4	-	-	-	-	12
Yellow Perch	6	25	-	-	-	-	-	-	31

FISHING INFORMATION: East Twin is a fair lake for northern pike and also offers a whole bunch of bluegills and some largemouth bass. The water quality is good, with clarity to 11 feet. The north side of the lake below the access area is heavy with brush and dead trees, making it the obvious place to start looking for largemouth bass. Try spinnerbaits, jigs or plastic worms. The small bay on the north with an outlet is also productive, although it can be prohibitively shallow some years. Northerns tend to be at weedlines along the south shore, as well as around the trees and brush on the north side. In summer, pike go to deeper, cooler waters toward mid-lake; troll lip-hooked shiners to catch them. The bluegill population is healthy with catch rates above the normal range for this lake class. Pumpkinseed sunfish have a similar size structure as the bluegills, with an average pumpkinseed being 5.8 inches long. No walleye or yellow perch were captured during the 2010 DNR survey. Black bullhead, yellow bullhead and bowfin are also present.

Crooked Lake is a little larger than East Twin and holds a few northerns, plus lots of small bluegills and some nice bass. Sunfish are abundant in the lake's weedbeds. The average length is around 6 inches. The lake is fairly dark, so you may want to use a brightly colored jig tipped with a small minnow or worm. The northerns are generally at the outer edges of weeds in spring before moving to deeper water toward the south bay. Largemouth bass are present in average numbers and in decent sizes; fish for them in weeds and heavy cover. Channel cats are stocked in odd-numbered years and the fish have increased in abundance, with some fish larger than 25 inches long captured during the 2009 survey. Crooked Lake's access, with a good concrete ramp, is off County Road 16.

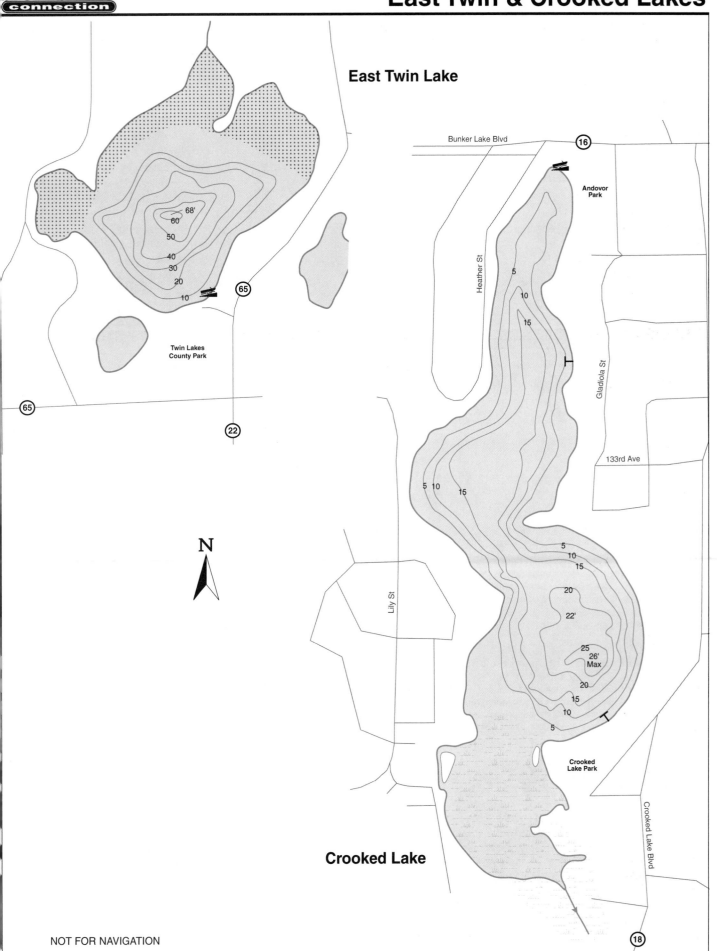

East Twin Lake

Bunker Lake Blvd

16

Andovor Park

Heather St

Gladiola St

133rd Ave

68'
60
50
40
30
20
10

65

Twin Lakes County Park

65

22

N

Lily St

5
10
15

5 10 15

5
10
15

20

22'

25 26' Max

20

15

10

5

Crooked Lake Park

Crooked Lake Blvd

Crooked Lake

NOT FOR NAVIGATION

18

Source: Minnesota Department of Natural Resources, USGS

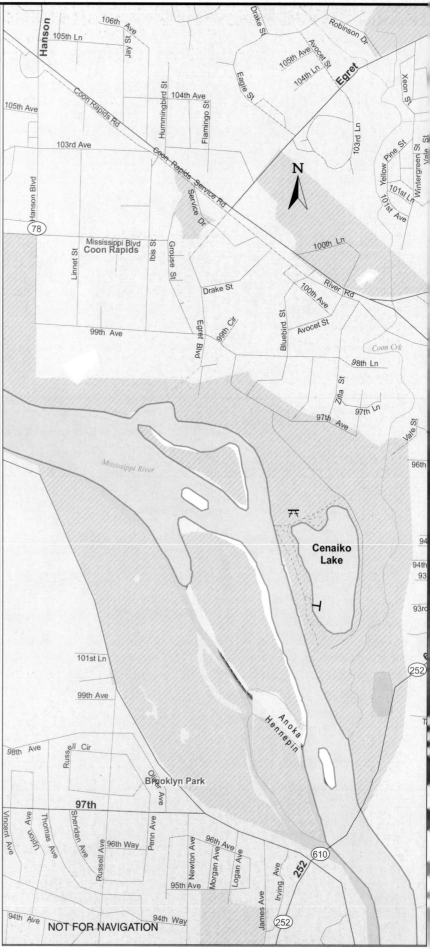

Anoka County
Located in Coon Rapids Dam Regional Park

Map page / coord: 27 / C-6

Nearest town: Coon Rapids
Surface water area: 29 acres
Max depth: 36 feet
Water clarity: 5.4 feet (2009)
Accessibility: County-owned public access
Accommodations: Park, fishing pier, picnicking

FISH STOCKING DATA

year	species	size	# released
07	Brook Trout	Adult	227
07	Rainbow Trout	Yearling	2,388
08	Brook Trout	Yearling	1,007
08	Rainbow Trout	Yearling	2,500
08	Rainbow Trout	Adult	139
09	Brown Trout	Adult	287
09	Rainbow Trout	Adult	75
09	Rainbow Trout	Yearling	2,445
10	Brook Trout	Yearling	221
10	Rainbow Trout	Yearling	2,500

LENGTH OF SELECTED SPECIES SAMPLED FROM ALL GEAR

Survey Date: 08/03/2009 **Survey method:** gill net, trap net

Number of fish caught for the following length categories (inches):

species	0-5	6-8	9-11	12-14	15-19	20-24	25-29	>30	Total
Black Crappie	-	-	1	-	-	-	-	-	1
Bluegill	16	4	-	-	-	-	-	-	20
Brown Trout	-	-	-	-	3	-	-	-	3
Common Carp	-	-	-	-	1	-	-	-	1
Green Sunfish	13	-	-	-	-	-	-	-	13
Hybrid Sunfish	64	2	-	-	-	-	-	-	66
Pumpkin. Sunfish	-	1	-	-	-	-	-	-	1
Smallmouth Bass	-	-	2	-	-	-	-	-	2
White Crappie	6	5	1	-	-	-	-	-	12
White Sucker	-	-	2	-	4	-	-	-	6

Notes: Cenaiko Lake is located in Coon Rapids Regional Park in Coon Rapids. It's a very small body of water covering only 29 acres. It's been designated a stream trout lake by the DNR. Rainbow and brook trout are stocked annually, along with occasional brown trout stockings. The lake receives large amounts of fishing pressure when trout seasons opens. Anglers also frequent this small lake during the winter months.

Use jigs or bobbers to present single kernels of corn, small pieces of Power Bait or pieces of nightcrawler to the trout. Casting small spinners or spoons will also catch a few of the larger adult trout that have been stocked.

Along with trout, hybrid sunfish are abundant, although small. White crappies are also available in average abundance, but small, although some are in excess of 10 inches in length. Carp and black bullhead are also present.

Source: Minnesota Department of Natural Resources, USGS

MINNESOTA STATE RECORD FISH

Species	Weight (lbs. - oz.)	Length/girth (inches)	Lake where caught	County	Date
Bass, Largemouth	8 lbs., 15 oz.	23.5 / 18	Auburn Lake	Carver	10/05/2005
Bass, Rock (tie)	2 lbs., 0 oz.	13.5 / 12.5	Osakis Lake	Todd	05/10/1998
	2 lbs., 0 oz.	12.6 / 12.4	Lake Winnibigoshish	Cass	08/30/2004
Bass, Smallmouth	8 lbs., 0 oz.	n/a	West Battle Lake	Otter Tail	1948
Bass, White	4 lbs., 2.4 oz.	18.5 / 15.1	Mississippi River Pool 5	Wabasha	05/04/2004
Bluegill	2 lbs., 13 oz.	n/a	Alice Lake	Hubbard	1948
Bowfin (tie)	11 lbs., 4 oz.	35 / 20	St. Croix River	Washington	10/07/2008
Buffalo, Bigmouth	41 lbs., 11 oz.	38.5 / 29.5	Mississippi River	Goodhue	05/07/1991
Buffalo, Black	20 lbs., 0.5 oz.	34.2 / 20	Minnesota River	Nicollet	06/26/1997
Buffalo, Smallmouth	20 lbs., 0 oz.	32 / 23-3/4	Big Sandy	Aitkin	09/20/2003
Bullhead, Black	3 lbs., 13.12 oz.	17.17 / 14.96	Reno Lake	Pope	06/08/1997
Bullhead, Brown	7 lbs., 1 oz.	24.4 / n/a	Shallow Lake	Itasca	05/21/1974
Bullhead, Yellow	3 lbs., 10.5 oz.	17 7/8 / 11 3/4	Osakis Lake	Todd	08/05/2002
Burbot	19 lbs., 3 oz.	36 1/4 / 22 3/4	Lake of the Woods	Lake of the Woods	02/17/2001
Carp	55 lbs., 5 oz.	42 / 31	Clearwater Lake	Wright	07/10/1952
Carpsucker, River	3 lbs., 15 oz.	19.5 / 14	Mississippi River	Ramsey	03/09/1991
Catfish, Channel	38 lbs., 0 oz.	44 / n/a	Mississippi River	Hennepin	1975
Catfish, Flathead	70 lbs., 0 oz.	n/a	St. Croix River	Washington	1970
Crappie, Black	5 lbs., 0 oz.	21 / n/a	Vermillion River	Dakota	1940
Crappie, White	3 lbs., 15 oz.	18 / 16	Lake Constance	Wright	07/28/2002
Drum, Freshwater (Sheepshead)	35 lbs., 3.2 oz.	36 / 31	Mississippi River	Winona	10/05/1999
Eel, American	6 lbs., 9 oz.	36 / 14	St. Croix River	Washington	08/08/1997
Gar, Longnose	16 lbs., 12 oz.	53 / 16.5	St. Croix River	Washington	05/04/1982
Gar, Shortnose	4 lbs., 9.6 oz.	34.6 / 10	Mississippi River	Hennepin	07/22/1984
Goldeye	2 lbs., 13.1 oz.	20.1 / 11.5	Root River	Houston	06/10/2001
Hogsucker, Northern	1 lb., 15 oz.	14.25 / 7 1/8	Sunrise River	Chisago	08/16/1982
Mooneye	1 lb., 15 oz.	16.5 / 9.75	Minnesota River	Redwood	06/18/1980
Muskellunge	54 lbs., 0 oz.	56 / 27.8	Lake Winnibigoshish	Itasca	1957
Muskellunge, Tiger	34 lbs., 12 oz.	51 / 22.5	Lake Elmo	Washington	07/07/1999
Perch, Yellow	3 lbs., 4 oz.	n/a	Lake Plantaganette	Hubbard	1945
Pike, Northern	45 lbs., 12 oz.	n/a	Basswood Lake	Lake	05/16/1929
Pumpkinseed	1 lbs., 5.6 oz.	10.1 / 12 1/8	Leech Lake	Cass	06/06/1999
Quillback	7 lbs., 4.5 oz.	22.58 / 18	Upper Red Lake	Beltrami	08/09/2010
Redhorse, Golden	3 lbs., 15.5 oz.	20.125 / 12.375	Root River	Fillmore	04/30/2007
Redhorse, Greater	12 lbs., 11.5 oz.	28.5 / 18.5	Sauk River	Stearns Wing	05/20/2005
Redhorse, River	12 lbs., 10 oz.	28.38 / 20	Kettle River	Pine	05/20/2005
Redhorse, Shorthead	7 lbs., 15 oz.	27 / 15	Rum River	Anoka	08/05/1983
Redhorse, Silver	9 lbs., 15 oz.	26.6 / 16 7/8	Big Fork River	Koochiching	04/16/2004
Salmon, Atlantic	12 lbs., 13 oz.	35.5 / 16.5	Baptism River	Lake	10/12/1991
Salmon, Chinook (King) (tie)	33 lbs., 4 oz.	44.75 / 25.75	Poplar River	Cook	09/23/1989
	33 lbs., 4 oz.	42.25 / 26.13	Lake Superior	St. Louis	10/12/1989
Salmon, Coho	10 lbs., 6.5 oz.	27.3 / n/a	Lake Superior	Lake	11/07/1970
Salmon, Kokanee	2 lbs., 15 oz.	20 / 11.5	Caribou Lake	Itasca	08/06/1971
Salmon, Pink	4 lbs., 8 oz.	23.5 / 13.2	Cascade River	Cook	09/09/1989
Sauger	6 lbs., 2.75 oz.	23 7/8 / 15	Mississippi River	Goodhue	05/23/1988
Splake	13 lbs., 5.44 oz.	33 1/2 / 19	Larson Lake	Itasca	02/11/2001
Sturgeon, Lake	94 lbs., 4 oz.	70 / 26.5	Kettle River	Pine	09/05/1994
Sturgeon, Shovelnose	5 lbs., 9 oz.	36 / 11-7/8	Mississippi River	Goodhue	06/04/2007
Sucker, Blue	14 lbs., 3 oz.	30.4 / 20.2	Mississippi River	Wabasha	02/28/1987
Sucker, Longnose	3 lbs., 10.6 oz.	21 / 10.25	Brule River	Cook	05/19/2005
Sucker, White	9 lbs., 1 oz.	24.25 / 16.25	Big Fish Lake	Stearns	05/01/1983
Sunfish, Green	1 lbs., 4.8 oz.	10.25 / 10.625	North Arbor Lake	Hennepin	06/14/2005
Sunfish, Hybrid	1 lb., 12 oz.	11.5 / 12	Zumbro River	Olmsted	07/09/1994
Trout, Brook	6 lbs., 5.6 oz.	24 / 14.5	Pigeon River	Cook	09/02/2000
Trout, Brown	16 lbs., 12 oz.	31.4 / 20.6	Lake Superior	St. Louis	06/23/1989
Trout, Lake	43 lbs., 8 oz.	n/a	Lake Superior	Cook	05/30/1955
Trout, Rainbow (Steelhead)	16 lbs. 6 oz.	33 / 19.5	Devil Track River	Cook	04/27/1980
Trout, Tiger	2 lbs., 9.12 oz.	20 / 9 5/8	Mill Creek	Olmsted	08/07/1999
Tullibee (Cisco)	5 lbs., 11.8 oz.	20.45 / 16.40	Little Long Lake	St. Louis	04/16/2002
Walleye	17 lbs., 8 oz.	35.8 / 21.3	Seagull River	Cook	05/13/1979
Walleye-Sauger Hybrid	9 lbs., 13.4 oz.	27 / 17 3/4	Mississippi River	Goodhue	03/20/1999
Whitefish, Lake	12 lbs., 4.5 oz.	28.5 / 20	Leech Lake	Cass	03/21/1999
Whitefish, Menominee (Round)	2 lbs., 7.5 oz.	21 / 9.1	Lake Superior	Cook	04/27/1987

LONG LAKE
Ramsey County

Bordered by Long Lake Regional Park

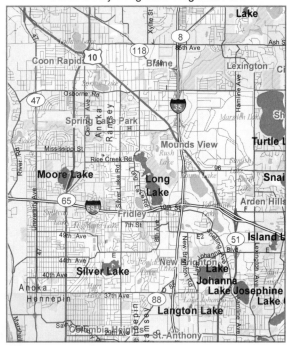

Area map pg / coord: 28 / D-1
Watershed: Twin Cities
Secchi disk: 6.0 feet (2008)
Water color: Green

Surface area: 173 acres
Shorelength: NA
Maximum depth: 30 feet
Mean depth: NA

Accessibility: City-owned public access in park on south shore
Boat ramp: Double concrete ramp
Parking: Twelve car and trailer spaces
Accommodations: Park, fishing pier

Shoreland zoning classification: General development
Management class: Centrarchid
Ecological type: Centrarchid

FISH STOCKING DATA

year	species	size	# released
07	Walleye	Fry	110,000
08	Walleye	Fry	110,000
09	Northern Pike	Adult	736
09	Walleye	Fry	150,000
10	Walleye	Fry	110,000
11	Walleye	Fry	110,000
12	Walleye	Fry	110,000

NET CATCH DATA

Date: 07/07/2008

	Gill Nets		Trap Nets	
species	# per net	avg. fish weight (lbs.)	# per net	avg. fish weight (lbs.)
Black Bullhead	38.8	0.30	0.8	0.25
Black Crappie	5.8	0.22	4.8	0.23
Bluegill	-	-	8.0	0.16
Bowfin (Dogfish)	-	-	0.1	2.02
Common Carp	5.2	2.08	12.8	2.09
Freshwater Drum	-	-	0.1	1.41
Hybrid Sunfish	-	-	0.1	0.22
Northern Pike	2.8	3.47	0.4	2.75
Smallmouth Buffalo	0.2	3.09	0.3	2.45
Walleye	0.2	3.42	0.1	0.76
White Sucker	-	-	0.1	1.68
Yellow Bullhead	-	-	0.1	0.25
Yellow Perch	0.6	0.07	-	-

LENGTH OF SELECTED SPECIES SAMPLED FROM ALL GEAR

Number of fish caught for the following length categories (inches):

species	0-5	6-8	9-11	12-14	15-19	20-24	25-29	>30	Total
Black Bullhead	4	186	10	-	-	-	-	-	200
Black Crappie	8	58	1	-	-	-	-	-	67
Bluegill	34	26	-	-	-	-	-	-	64
Bowfin (Dogfish)	-	-	-	-	1	-	-	-	1
Common Carp	-	-	-	55	62	10	1	-	128
Freshwater Drum	-	-	-	-	1	-	-	-	1
Hybrid Sunfish	-	1	-	-	-	-	-	-	1
Northern Pike	-	-	-	-	-	10	6	1	17
Smallmouth Buffalo	-	-	-	-	3	-	-	-	3
Walleye	-	-	-	1	-	1	-	-	2
White Sucker	-	-	-	-	1	-	-	-	1
Yellow Bullhead	-	1	-	-	-	-	-	-	1
Yellow Perch	3	-	-	-	-	-	-	-	3

FISHING INFORMATION: When the Locke Dam was being repaired, fish entered into the Rice Creek Watershed from the Mississippi River. This accounts for the wide variety of fish that are available on Long Lake. This 173-acre impoundment is stocked regularly with walleyes, which are the primary management species. This lake in New Brighton has a heavy algae bloom during summer. Black bullheads and carp are abundant.

In the 2008 survey, 33% of the northern pike were 26 inches or longer. The inlet from small Pike Lake, at the west side of the south bay, is a good place to start looking for them in spring. Other spots are near the fishing dock on the south side and near the Rice Creek outlet at the northwest corner of the lake. Troll with a live-bait rig and shiner minnow in flats in both bays, although the south bay is usually more productive. Burning, or reeling really fast, a brightly colored spinnerbait along shoreline cover is an excellent way to entice a strike from a pike during summer months, especially during low-light periods. Also try a buzzbait in late summer and early fall. Pike will often explode on these noisy lures. Many of the strikes produce no hook-ups, but it's an exciting way to hook a pike or two.

Black crappies are at a normal level of abundance, with sizes averaging 7.1 inches and five fish per pound. Crappies use the areas around Rice Creek as spawning beds, and you can get lucky there with bright jigs tipped with minnows. They will head for deep water in summer. Go down about 10 feet with a slip bobber at the deep holes in both the south and north bays. Small leeches or minnows are the top baits for fooling specks in summer months.

Low-light periods are preferred for catching walleyes during the heat of summer, but a nice overcast day can be quite productive as well. Walleyes are stocked annually, although their catch numbers were low during the 2008 assessment. You'll do well in spring to put a shiner or leech on a Lindy rig and work along the lake's sandy bottom near drop-offs. The south end, near the pier and Pike Lake Creek can also be productive at that time of year. Walleyes suspend at the north and south holes during warm weather. Try trolling with a spinner rig or a crankbait when fish are suspended.

Bluegill numbers and overall size were down, with just 3% of the fish measuring 7 inches or bigger. Still, Long Lake bluegills are fun to fish and to fry. Stick with bluegill basics. A bobber, small hook and a chunk of crawler or a small leech are good tools to fool bluegills.

Public access, with concrete ramp and fishing pier, is at the south end of the lake off I-694. Long Lake Regional Park borders the east shoreline.

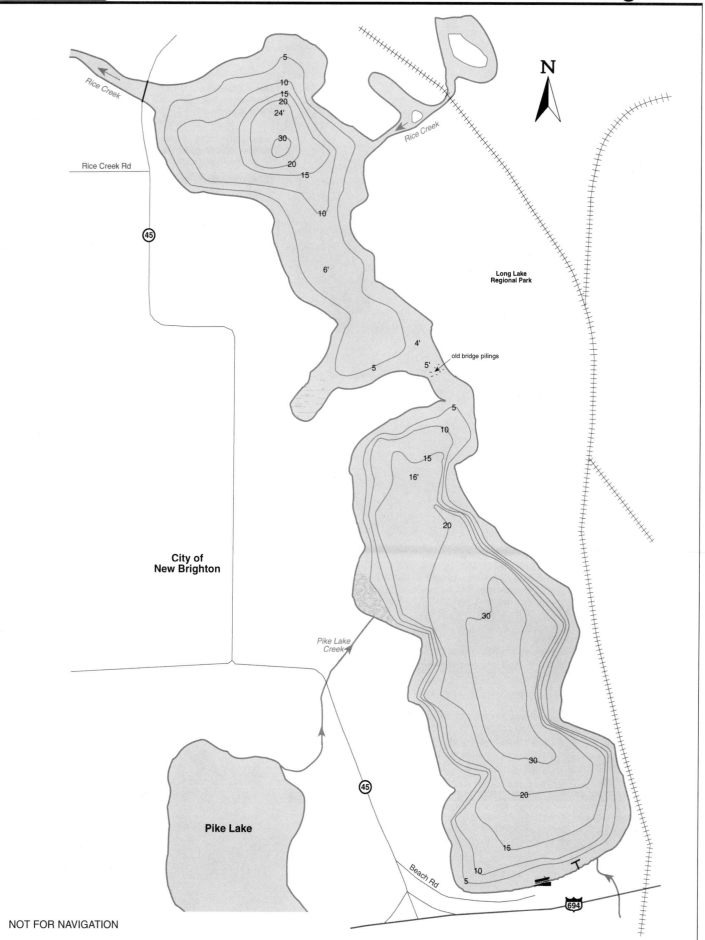

Rice Creek

Rice Creek

5
10
15
20
24'
30
20
15
10
6'

Rice Creek Rd

45

4'

old bridge pilings

5
5'

Long Lake
Regional Park

N

5
10
15
16'
20

City of
New Brighton

Pike Lake
Creek

30

45

30

20

Pike Lake

15

10
5

Beach Rd

694

NOT FOR NAVIGATION

Snail & Island Lakes

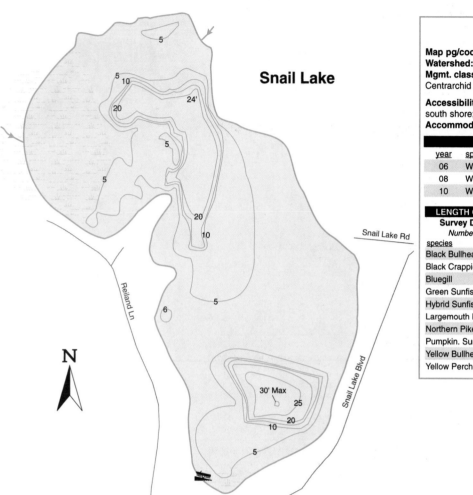

Snail Lake, Ramsey County
Bordered by Snail Lake Regional Park

Map pg/coord: 28 / D-1,2 **Surface area:** 156 acres
Watershed: Twin Cities **Shorelength:** NA
Mgmt. classification: Centrarchid **Max depth:** 30 feet
Water clarity: 10.0 feet (2010)

Accessibility: County-owned public access with concrete ramp on south shore; parking for twenty-five trailers
Accommodations: Park, shore fishing, picnicking, restrooms

FISH STOCKING DATA
year	species	size	# released
06	Walleye	Fry	260,000
08	Walleye	Fry	260,000
10	Walleye	Fry	260,000

LENGTH OF SELECTED SPECIES SAMPLED FROM ALL GEAR
Survey Date: 07/06/2010 Survey method: gill net, trap net
Number of fish caught for the following length categories (inches):

species	0-5	6-8	9-11	12-14	15-19	20-24	25-29	>30	Total
Black Bullhead	-	-	4	-	-	-	-	-	4
Black Crappie	-	7	1	-	-	-	-	-	8
Bluegill	152	30	-	-	-	-	-	-	188
Green Sunfish	4	-	-	-	-	-	-	-	4
Hybrid Sunfish	13	21	-	-	-	-	-	-	34
Largemouth Bass	-	3	1	2	-	-	-	-	6
Northern Pike	-	-	-	1	8	20	-	1	30
Pumpkin. Sunfish	38	20	-	-	-	-	-	-	58
Yellow Bullhead	-	-	14	9	-	-	-	-	23
Yellow Perch	1	-	-	-	-	-	-	-	1

Island Lake, Ramsey County
Bordered by Island Lake County Park

Map pg/coord: 28 / D-1,2 **Surface area:** 59 acres
Watershed: Twin Cities **Shorelength:** NA
Mgmt. classification: Centrarchid **Max depth:** 11 feet
Water clarity: 4.8 ft. (2009)

Accessibility: County-owned public access with earthen ramp on north shore; parking for ten trailers
Accommodations: Park, fishing pier, picnicking, restrooms

FISH STOCKING DATA
year	species	size	# released
09	Channel Catfish	Yearling	3,058
09	Yellow Perch	Yearling	1,200
09	Yellow Perch	Adult	1,703
10	Channel Catfish	Yearling	1,990
11	Channel Catfish	Yearling	1,797
11	Walleye	Fry	120,000
12	Channel Catfish	Yearling	1,989
12	Walleye	Fry	120,000

LENGTH OF SELECTED SPECIES SAMPLED FROM ALL GEAR
Survey Date: 08/10/2009 Survey method: gill net, trap net
Number of fish caught for the following length categories (inches):

species	0-5	6-8	9-11	12-14	15-19	20-24	25-29	>30	Total
Black Crappie	16	10	-	-	-	-	-	-	26
Bluegill	382	-	-	-	-	-	-	-	382
Channel Catfish	2	-	1	2	2	1	-	-	8
Golden Shiner	-	3	-	-	-	-	-	-	3
Hybrid Sunfish	26	-	-	-	-	-	-	-	26
Pumpkin. Sunfish	3	-	-	-	-	-	-	-	3
Tiger Muskellunge	-	-	1	-	1	-	-	-	2
Walleye	-	-	-	6	3	-	-	-	9

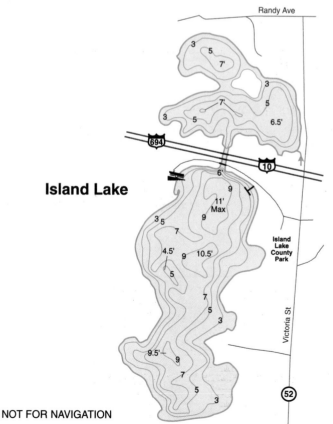

Island Lake

NOT FOR NAVIGATION

Snail Lake

N

146

Source: Minnesota Department of Natural Resources, USGS © Copyright Sportsman's Connection. All Rights Reserved.

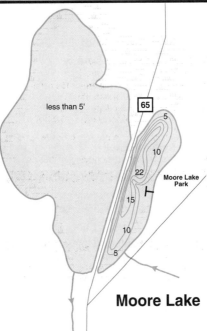

less than 5'

65

5

10

22

15

10

5

Moore Lake Park

Moore Lake

Moore Lake, Anoka County
Bordered by Moore Lake Park

Map pg/coord: 28 / D-1
Watershed: Twin Cities
Mgmt. classification: Centrarchid

Surface area: 28 acres (East)
Shorelength: NA
Max depth: 22 feet
Water clarity: 4.9 ft. (2009)

Accessibility: Carry-down public access in city park on east shore; parking for seventy-five vehicles
Accommodations: Park, fishing pier, restrooms

FISH STOCKING DATA			
year	species	size	# released
07	Channel Catfish	Yearling	1,316
08	Black Crappie	Adult	279
08	Bluegill	Adult	126
08	Channel Catfish	Yearling	1,324
08	Largemouth Bass	Adult	20
09	Channel Catfish	Yearling	1,328

Silver Lake, Ramsey County
Bordered by Silver Lake County Park & Joy Park

Map pg/coord: 28 / E-3
Watershed: Twin Cities
Mgmt. classification: Centrarchid

Surface area: 72 acres
Shorelength: NA
Max depth: 18 feet
Water clarity: 3 ft. (2012)

Accessibility: County-owned public access with concrete ramp on north shore in park; parking for fifteen trailers
Accommodations: Parks, fishing pier, shore fishing, restrooms

FISH STOCKING DATA			
year	species	size	# released
08	Tiger Muskellunge	Fingerling	107
08	Yellow Perch	Adult	625
09	Walleye	Fry	150,000
09	Yellow Perch	Adult	1,618
11	Walleye	Fry	142,000
12	Walleye	Fry	142,000

LENGTH OF SELECTED SPECIES SAMPLED FROM ALL GEAR
Survey Date: 07/24/2012   **Survey method:** gill net, trap net
Number of fish caught for the following length categories (inches):

species	0-5	6-8	9-11	12-14	15-19	20-24	25-29	>30	Total
Black Bullhead	-	3	35	3	-	-	-	-	41
Black Crappie	33	89	1	-	-	-	-	-	126
Bluegill	539	6	-	-	-	-	-	-	545
Hybrid Sunfish	44	7	-	-	-	-	-	-	51
Northern Pike	-	-	-	-	-	7	5	1	13
Tiger Musky	-	-	-	-	-	-	-	1	1

Silver Lake

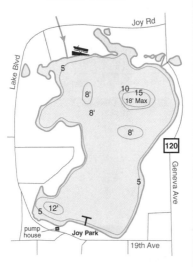

Joy Rd

Lake Blvd

5

8'

10 15 18' Max

8'

8'

120

Geneva Ave

5

5 12'

pump house

Joy Park

19th Ave

McCarron Lake

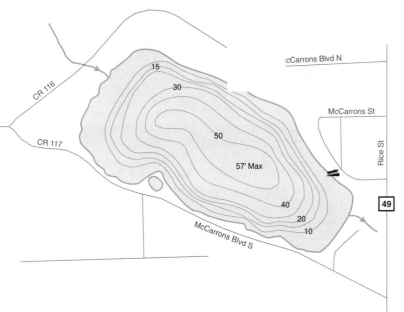

cCarrons Blvd N

15

30

CR 116

50

CR 117

57' Max

McCarrons St

40

20

10

Rice St

McCarrons Blvd S

49

McCarron Lake, Ramsey County
Bordered by McCarrons County Park

Map pg/coord: 30 / A-1,2
Watershed: Twin Cities
Mgmt. classification: Centrarchid

Surface area: 73 acres
Shorelength: NA
Max depth: 57 feet
Water clarity: 14.0 ft. (2010)

Accessibility: County-owned public access, with asphalt ramp, in park on east shore; parking for twenty-five trailers
Accommodations: Fishing pier, park, restrooms

FISH STOCKING DATA			
year	species	size	# released
05	Northern Pike	Yearling	124
07	Black Crappie	Adult	630
09	Northern Pike	Adult	80

LENGTH OF SELECTED SPECIES SAMPLED FROM ALL GEAR
Survey Date: 06/16/2008   **Survey method:** gill net, trap net
Number of fish caught for the following length categories (inches):

species	0-5	6-8	9-11	12-14	15-19	20-24	25-29	>30	Total
Black Crappie	-	3	2	-	-	-	-	-	5
Bluegill	41	340	-	-	-	-	-	-	381
Hybrid Sunfish	7	6	-	-	-	-	-	-	13
Largemouth Bass	-	1	1	-	-	-	-	-	2
Pumpkin. Sunfish	4	-	-	-	-	-	-	-	4
Yellow Bullhead	-	1	7	3	-	-	-	-	11

NOT FOR NAVIGATION

LAKE JOHANNA

Bordered by Schmidt County Park

Area map page/coord: 28 / E-1
Watershed: Twin Cities
Surface area: 212 acres
Shorelength: 2.9 miles
Maximum depth: 43 feet
Mean depth: 20 feet
Secchi disk: 3.9 feet (2008)
Water color: Green tint
Accessibility: County-owned public access with concrete ramp on north shore in park; fifteen trailer spaces
Accommodations: Shore fishing, fishing pier
Shoreland zoning: Recreational development
Management class: Centrarchid
Ecological type: Centrarchid

Ramsey County

LAKE JOSEPHINE

Bordered by Lake Josephine County Park

Area map page/coord: 28 / E-1,2
Watershed: Twin Cities
Surface area: 116 acres
Shorelength: NA
Maximum depth: 44 feet
Mean depth: NA
Secchi disk: 5.5 feet (2012)
Water color: Green-brown
Accessibility: County-owned public access with concrete ramp on east shore in park; six trailer spaces
Accommodations: Shore fishing
Shoreland zoning: General development
Management class: Centrarchid
Ecological type: Centrarchid

FISH STOCKING DATA

year	species	size	# released
08	Tiger Muskellunge	Fingerling	426
09	Tiger Muskellunge	Fry	22,824
09	Walleye	Yearling	1,375
10	Tiger Muskellunge	Fingerling	426
11	Walleye	Fingerling	9,450
12	Tiger Muskellunge	Fingerling	432

NET CATCH DATA

Date: 06/30/2008

	Gill Nets		Trap Nets	
species	# per net	avg. fish weight (lbs.)	# per net	avg. fish weight (lbs.)
Black Crappie	5.8	0.14	2.2	0.15
Bluegill	8.7	0.10	115.3	0.10
Hybrid Sunfish	-	-	2.3	0.12
Largemouth Bass	0.3	0.23	-	-
Northern Pike	4.8	4.21	-	-
Pumpkin. Sunfish	1.3	0.15	5.9	0.12
Walleye	1.5	2.53	0.1	0.06
White Sucker	0.3	2.30	-	-
Yellow Bullhead	0.3	1.16	0.6	0.81
Yellow Perch	15.3	0.11	0.3	0.07

LENGTH OF SELECTED SPECIES SAMPLED FROM ALL GEAR

Number of fish caught for the following length categories (inches):

species	0-5	6-8	9-11	12-14	15-19	20-24	25-29	>30	Total
Black Bullhead	-	-	-	3	-	-	-	-	3
Black Crappie	5	50	-	-	-	-	-	-	55
Bluegill	861	224	-	-	-	-	-	-	1090
Green Sunfish	19	-	-	-	-	-	-	-	19
Hybrid Sunfish	15	6	-	-	-	-	-	-	21
Largemouth Bass	-	2	-	-	-	-	-	-	2
Northern Pike	-	-	-	-	12	14	3	-	29
Pumpkin. Sunfish	48	13	-	-	-	-	-	-	61
Walleye	-	1	-	5	4	-	-	-	10
Yellow Bullhead	-	-	4	3	-	-	-	-	7
Yellow Perch	23	72	-	-	-	-	-	-	95

FISH STOCKING DATA

year	species	size	# released
07	Walleye	Fingerling	95
07	Walleye	Yearling	251
09	Walleye	Fingerling	7,648
09	Walleye	Yearling	18
11	Walleye	Fry	81,000
12	Walleye	Fry	81,000

NET CATCH DATA

Date: 07/23/2012

	Gill Nets		Trap Nets	
species	# per net	avg. fish weight (lbs.)	# per net	avg. fish weight (lbs.)
Black Crappie	3.5	0.15	13.6	0.19
Bluegill	7.0	0.12	93.6	0.15
Common Carp	0.3	3.31	0.3	3.22
Green Sunfish	-	-	0.2	0.12
Hybrid Sunfish	-	-	2.2	0.22
Largemouth Bass	-	-	0.2	1.28
Northern Pike	11.0	2.94	0.3	0.97
Pumpkin. Sunfish	4.5	0.08	2.3	0.12
Walleye	2.5	2.69	0.1	5.07
Yellow Bullhead	12.0	0.46	3.8	0.55

LENGTH OF SELECTED SPECIES SAMPLED FROM ALL GEAR

Number of fish caught for the following length categories (inches):

species	0-5	6-8	9-11	12-14	15-19	20-24	25-29	>30	Total
Black Crappie	4	137	5	-	-	-	-	-	150
Bluegill	685	270	3	-	-	-	-	-	964
Common Carp	-	-	-	-	4	-	-	-	4
Green Sunfish	1	1	-	-	-	-	-	-	2
Hybrid Sunfish	5	17	-	-	-	-	-	-	12
Largemouth Bass	-	1	-	-	1	-	-	-	2
Northern Pike	-	-	-	1	3	33	10	-	47
Pumpkin. Sunfish	38	2	-	-	-	-	-	-	40
Walleye	-	-	-	1	6	3	1	-	11
Yellow Bullhead	-	38	39	9	-	-	-	-	86

FISHING INFORMATION: Lake Johanna has a lot of recreational boating that can make fishing tough. However, good fishing for northern pike, panfish, largemouth bass, tiger muskies and a few walleyes can be found once you get past all the churning props.

Northerns and muskies are at the lake's weedlines. The island just off the south shore is considered a hot spot by veteran anglers. There is also an underwater hump toward the middle of the lake that is usually productive. Northerns at Johanna average 25.9 inches long and weigh 4.21 pounds.

Bluegills are quite abundant, although not very large, with an average 'gill barely longer than 5 inches. Pumpkinseed and hybrid sunfish are also available in high numbers.

For bass, try plastic worms in the small bays at the southwest and

northeast corners. Many docks line the shore, and lots of these are good fishing spots early in the morning or at dusk.

During the last DNR survey, walleyes were in the lake in average numbers, with half of the fish sampled measuring over 20 inches long. Fish humps, drop-offs or deep weedlines.

In **Lake Josephine**, you'll find a fair number of northerns and bluegills. Northerns can be found at the south end of the lake. Fish outside the weedlines there and follow the west shoreline to the point. Northerns may also be found near the east side access. During the most recent DNR survey, northern pike averaged just over 22 inches long, with 17% of the fish sampled measuring longer than 25 inches.

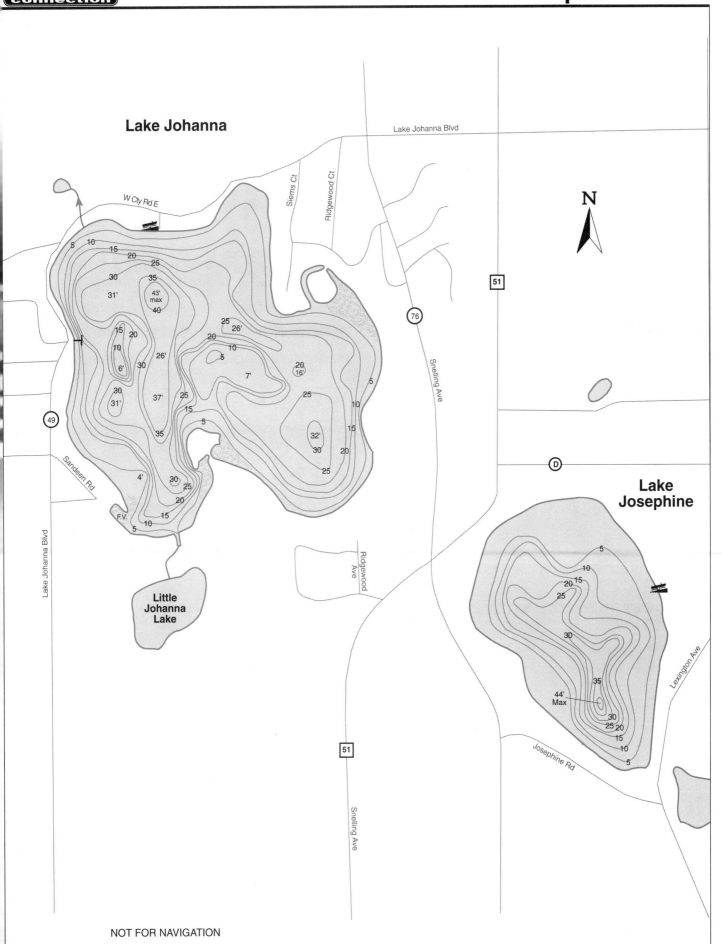

Lake Johanna

Little Johanna Lake

Lake Josephine

N

NOT FOR NAVIGATION

LAKE OWASSO

Bordered by Lady Slipper Park &
Lake Owasso County Park

Area map page/coord: 28 / E-2
Watershed: Twin Cities
Surface area: 375 acres
Shorelength: 4.9 miles
Maximum depth: 37 feet
Mean depth: NA
Secchi disk: 3.3 feet (2006)
Water color: NA
Accessibility: County-owned public access with concrete ramp on north shore in park; parking for seven trailers
Accommodations: Parks, shore fishing, marina, boat rental, picnicking, restrooms
Shoreland zoning: General development
Management class: Centrarchid
Ecological type: Centrarchid

Ramsey County

LAKE WABASSO

Bordered by Lake Wabasso Park

Area map page/coord: 28 / E-2
Watershed: Twin Cities
Surface area: 46 acres
Shorelength: NA
Maximum depth: 66 feet
Mean depth: NA
Secchi disk (water clarity): 13.0 feet
Water color: NA

Accessibility: County-owned public access with earthen ramp in park on south shore; parking for four trailers
Accommodations: Park, shore fishing, restrooms

Shoreland zoning: General development
Management class: Centrarchid
Ecological type: Centrarchid

FISH STOCKING DATA

year	species	size	# released
08	Muskellunge	Fingerling	379
08	Walleye	Fingerling	44,819
08	Walleye	Adult	3
10	Muskellunge	Fingerling	423
10	Walleye	Fingerling	32,280
12	Muskellunge	Yearling	100
12	Walleye	Fingerling	18,681
12	Walleye	Yearling	1,324
12	Walleye	Adult	69

NET CATCH DATA

Date: 06/25/2012

species	Gill Nets # per net	Gill Nets avg. fish weight (lbs.)	Trap Nets # per net	Trap Nets avg. fish weight (lbs.)
Black Crappie	3.0	0.09	19.2	0.18
Bluegill	29.5	0.06	103.4	0.11
Golden Shiner	-	-	2.0	trace
Hybrid Sunfish	-	-	0.6	0.26
Largemouth Bass	-	-	0.5	trace
Northern Pike	7.3	5.55	0.2	trace
Pumpkin. Sunfish	-	-	2.8	0.14
Walleye	6.3	2.84	0.2	trace
Yellow Bullhead	-	-	0.2	trace
Yellow Perch	29.0	0.11	0.2	trace

LENGTH OF SELECTED SPECIES SAMPLED FROM ALL GEAR

Number of fish caught for the following length categories (inches):

species	0-5	6-8	9-11	12-14	15-19	20-24	25-29	>30	Total
Black Crappie	23	168	6	-	-	-	-	-	204
Bluegill	958	188	-	-	-	-	-	-	1152
Golden Shiner	-	-	-	-	-	-	-	-	20
Hybrid Sunfish	2	4	-	-	-	-	-	-	6
Largemouth Bass	-	-	-	-	-	-	-	-	5
Northern Pike	-	-	-	1	-	9	10	8	31
Pumpkin. Sunfish	22	6	-	-	-	-	-	-	28
Walleye	-	-	-	6	5	11	3	-	27
Yellow Bullhead	-	-	-	-	-	-	-	-	2
Yellow Perch	29	83	-	-	-	-	-	-	118

NO FISH STOCKING DATA SINCE 2002

NET CATCH DATA

Date: 06/20/2005

species	Gill Nets # per net	Gill Nets avg. fish weight (lbs.)	Trap Nets # per net	Trap Nets avg. fish weight (lbs.)
Black Bullhead	26.0	0.13	1.2	0.42
Black Crappie	-	-	2.3	0.22
Bluegill	1.5	0.21	54.8	0.13
Common Carp	0.5	5.04	-	-
Largemouth Bass	-	-	0.5	0.68
Northern Pike	5.0	3.05	0.5	1.96
Pumpkin. Sunfish	-	-	0.8	0.07
White Sucker	0.5	4.41	-	-
Yellow Bullhead	0.5	0.63	0.8	0.93
Yellow Perch	0.5	0.09	-	-

LENGTH OF SELECTED SPECIES SAMPLED FROM ALL GEAR

Number of fish caught for the following length categories (inches):

species	0-5	6-8	9-11	12-14	15-19	20-24	25-29	>30	Total
Black Bullhead	47	2	10	-	-	-	-	-	59
Black Crappie	1	12	1	-	-	-	-	-	14
Bluegill	71	24	-	-	-	-	-	-	95
Largemouth Bass	1	-	1	1	-	-	-	-	3
Northern Pike	-	-	-	-	4	5	4	-	13
Pumpkin. Sunfish	5	-	-	-	-	-	-	-	5
Yellow Bullhead	-	-	3	3	-	-	-	-	6
Yellow Perch	-	1	-	-	-	-	-	-	1

shiner or sucker minnows just outside weedlines. The bay on the northwest side with the channel into Lake Wabasso is also very good. Fishing from there southward along the west bank to mid-lake is also a favorite for local anglers. Most of the lake's weedy shoreline is good for panfish, with the best fishing in spring at the south end in heavy bulrushes. As water warms, find bluegills and crappies in the deeper, northeast part of the lake.

There are some largemouth bass to be found, too, but not a lot of them. Weedbeds are their favorite places. The south end of the lake is a good spring location, although most shoreline areas with emergent vegetation will offer decent June fishing. Try plastic worms in the breaks. Muskies are very likely hanging around flats in the northeast end of the lake.

Lake Wabasso is very small, and is connected by a channel with Owasso. It is full of bluegills, has some decent northern pike and a few crappies.

Whichever lake you fish, make sure to remove all weeds from your boat and trailer prior to entering and when exiting the water to help prevent the spread of Eurasian milfoil.

FISHING INFORMATION: Lake Owasso in Little Canada is another of the metro lakes that gets a lot of recreational boating use. It has panfish, northern pike, walleyes and enough muskellunge to make fishing more than interesting. Bluegills were the most abundant species in the 2012 DNR survey of the lake, although they tended to be on the small side, with only one bluegill exceeding 7 inches out of the 1,152 caught. Walleye numbers were at an all-time high in 2012, with the average fish measuring 19.2 inches. Northern pike size was strong, with the average fish weighing more than 5 pounds. Some of the better spots for northerns in spring are along the lake's north shore. There are two holes there; fish the areas between them and the shoreline. The lake is quite clear, so you can do well offering

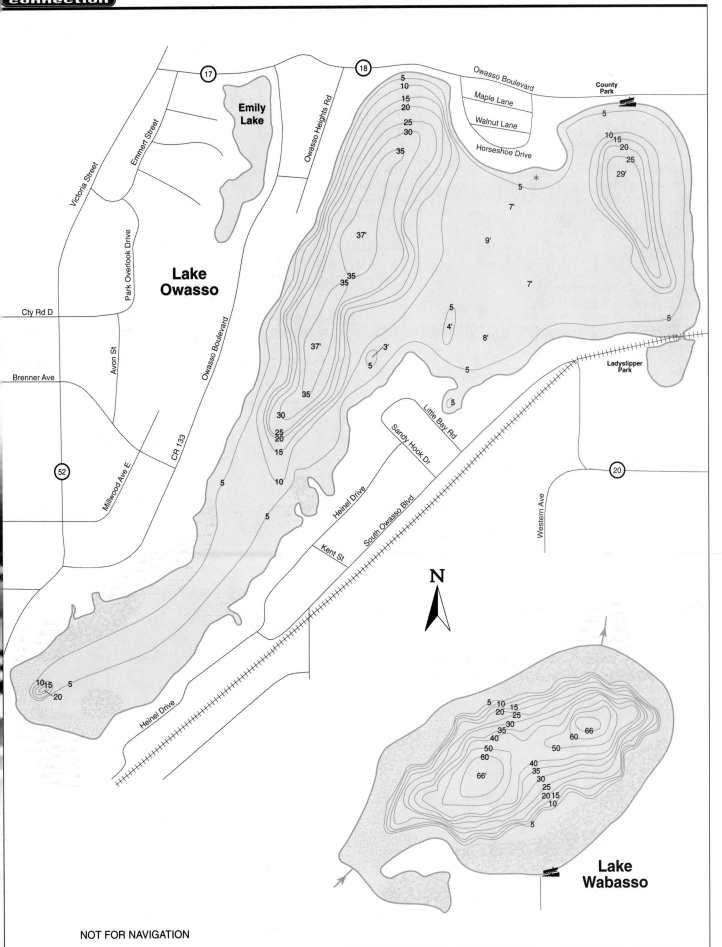

NOT FOR NAVIGATION

Source: Minnesota Department of Natural Resources, USGS

TURTLE LAKE
Ramsey County

Bordered by Turtle Lake Park

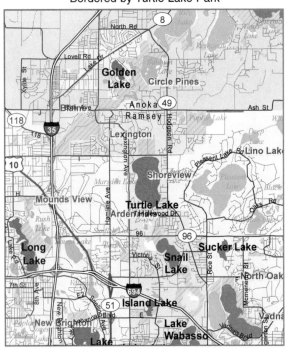

Area map pg / coord: 28 / D-1,2
Watershed: Twin Cities
Secchi disk: 8.5 feet (2007)
Water color: NA

Surface area: 450 acres
Shorelength: NA
Maximum depth: 28 feet
Mean depth: NA

Accessibility: State-owned public access in county park on east shore
Boat ramp: Concrete
Parking: Twenty-seven trailer spaces
Accommodations: Shore fishing, picnicking, restrooms

Shoreland zoning classification: General development
Management class: Centrarchid
Ecological type: Centrarchid

FISH STOCKING DATA

year	species	size	# released
06	Walleye	Fry	790,000
08	Walleye	Fry	490,000
10	Walleye	Fry	490,000
12	Walleye	Fry	490,000

NET CATCH DATA

Date: 07/23/2007

species	Gill Nets # per net	Gill Nets avg. fish weight (lbs.)	Trap Nets # per net	Trap Nets avg. fish weight (lbs.)
Black Crappie	1.5	0.26	1.9	0.34
Bluegill	0.8	0.12	20.3	0.13
Hybrid Sunfish	-	-	0.9	0.10
Largemouth Bass	1.8	0.88	1.3	1.17
Northern Pike	7.3	1.79	0.6	1.30
Pumpkin. Sunfish	0.1	0.18	1.0	0.10
Walleye	7.0	1.26	0.2	0.40
White Crappie	0.1	0.83	0.1	0.04
White Sucker	1.8	1.77	0.1	1.90
Yellow Bullhead	0.3	0.94	0.1	0.90
Yellow Perch	-	-	0.1	0.20

LENGTH OF SELECTED SPECIES SAMPLED FROM ALL GEAR

Number of fish caught for the following length categories (inches):

species	0-5	6-8	9-11	12-14	15-19	20-24	25-29	>30	Total
Black Crappie	6	14	9	-	-	-	-	-	29
Bluegill	118	66	-	-	-	-	-	-	190
Common Carp	-	1	1	-	-	3	-	-	5
Hybrid Sunfish	6	2	-	-	-	-	-	-	8
Largemouth Bass	-	3	7	10	6	-	-	-	26
Northern Pike	-	-	-	-	46	11	2	4	63
Pumpkin. Sunfish	8	2	-	-	-	-	-	-	10
Walleye	-	-	8	6	42	2	-	-	58
White Crappie	1	-	1	-	-	-	-	-	2
White Sucker	-	-	1	2	10	-	-	-	15
Yellow Bullhead	-	-	1	2	-	-	-	-	3
Yellow Perch	-	1	-	-	-	-	-	-	1

FISHING INFORMATION: Turtle Lake is probably best known for its good northern pike population. It also offers decent crappie and bluegill action, some pretty good largemouth bass, and an occasional walleye. The bottom substrate is comprised primarily of sand, marl and silt and there is an abundance of weed growth.

The northerns can get large, and there are a fair number of them. Local anglers say that the best place to try for a big pike is at the aeration pump near the park at the lake's southeast corner. They also recommend the underwater island near the center of the lake, where you can anchor near the weeds in warm weather and drop down a sucker minnow. According to the most recent DNR survey, northern pike abundance is high, although the majority of the captured fish were less than 20 inches long.

Look for bass in the bulrushes at the south end of the lake or on the flats in the northwest corner. Use a plastic worm or a small jig. If you aren't getting much action, try a live bait setup. Use light line and a lightweight hook, in size 6 or 8. Use a whole nightcrawler or jumbo leech. Hook the crawler through the pointed section and the leech through the sucker. Fish this rig weightless along deeper weed edges or over the top of shallow vegetation. Bass will often devour this offering when all else fails. The southeast end of the lake has a lot of rocks that bass are often attracted to in summer. Largemouths will move into deep water off the bars as summer turns into fall.

Crappies, bluegills and assorted sunfish will be in weedlines. The traditional offering of a minnow or worm on a bare hook will probably work, but you may want to use an ice fly or bright marabou jig if the water has turned cloudy. Bluegills and sunfish will readily take red worms, a piece of nightcrawler or a small leech. Ice fishermen work the north end for plump crappies. Both black and white crappies are present, but black crappies are predominant. They are of normal abundance, with more than 60% of the fish surveyed being larger than 8 inches, and nearly 24% of the fish being larger than 10 inches. Bluegills were the most abundant fish in the lake, but

they're small. The average size was slightly better than 5 inches long, although some up to 8 inches were caught.

Walleyes are present in the lake, and they have a nice average size. Walleye fry are stocked in even-numbered years. Basic presentations like live-bait rigs or a slip bobber will usually work best. Stick with leeches and nightcrawlers during the warm-weather months and minnows in the fall.

There's a county-owned access with concrete ramps and parking on Highway 49 at Turtle Lake Park, on the lake's southeast shore.

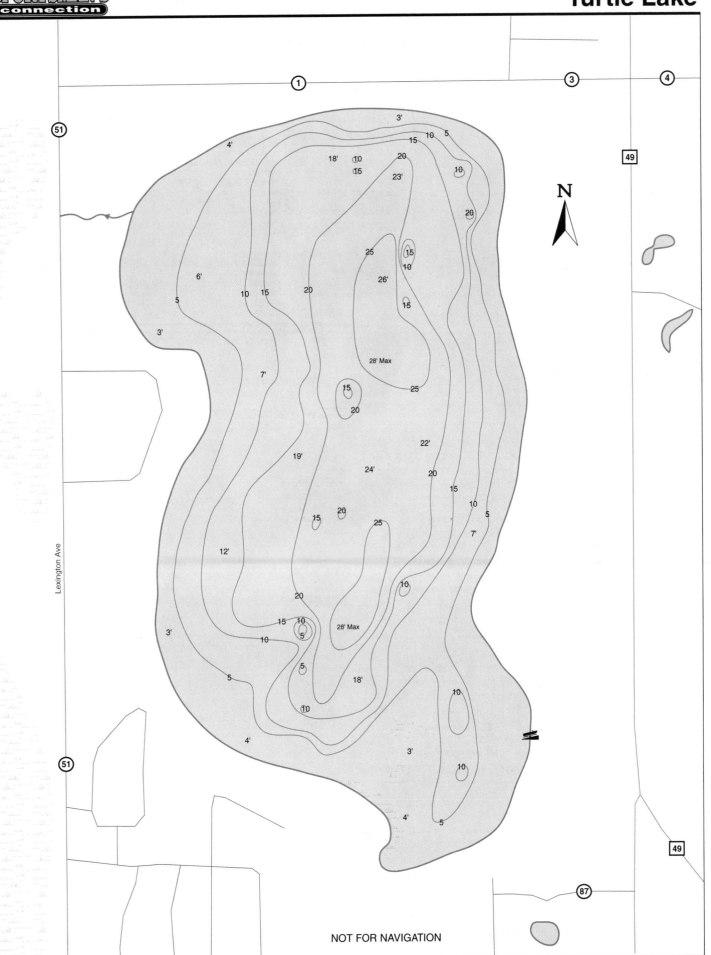

Source: Minnesota Department of Natural Resources, USGS

SPORTSMAN'S
connection

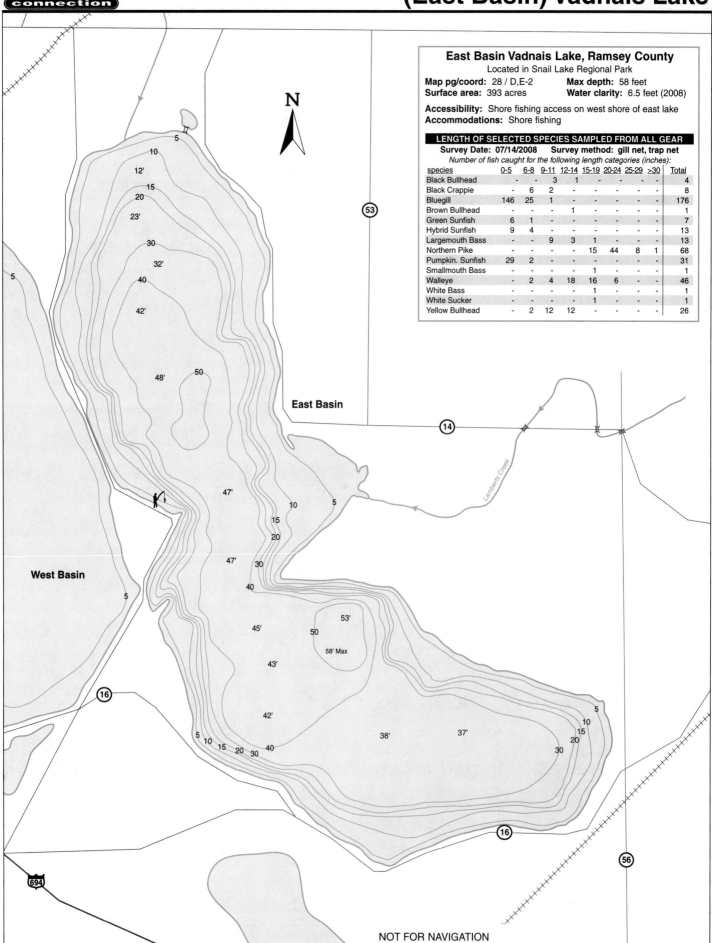

East Basin Vadnais Lake, Ramsey County
Located in Snail Lake Regional Park
Map pg/coord: 28 / D,E-2   **Max depth:** 58 feet
Surface area: 393 acres   **Water clarity:** 6.5 feet (2008)

Accessibility: Shore fishing access on west shore of east lake
Accommodations: Shore fishing

LENGTH OF SELECTED SPECIES SAMPLED FROM ALL GEAR
Survey Date: 07/14/2008   **Survey method:** gill net, trap net
Number of fish caught for the following length categories (inches):

species	0-5	6-8	9-11	12-14	15-19	20-24	25-29	>30	Total
Black Bullhead	-	-	3	1	-	-	-	-	4
Black Crappie	-	6	2	-	-	-	-	-	8
Bluegill	146	25	1	-	-	-	-	-	176
Brown Bullhead	-	-	-	1	-	-	-	-	1
Green Sunfish	6	1	-	-	-	-	-	-	7
Hybrid Sunfish	9	4	-	-	-	-	-	-	13
Largemouth Bass	-	-	9	3	1	-	-	-	13
Northern Pike	-	-	-	-	15	44	8	1	68
Pumpkin. Sunfish	29	2	-	-	-	-	-	-	31
Smallmouth Bass	-	-	-	-	1	-	-	-	1
Walleye	-	2	4	18	16	6	-	-	46
White Bass	-	-	-	-	1	-	-	-	1
White Sucker	-	-	-	-	1	-	-	-	1
Yellow Bullhead	-	2	12	12	-	-	-	-	26

N

East Basin

West Basin

Lamberts Creek

5
10
12'
15
20
23'
30
32'
40
42'
48'
50
47'
10
15
20
30
40
47'
53'
45'
50
58' Max
43'
42'
38'
37'
5
10
15
20
30
5
10
15
20
30
40
15

53
14
16
16
56
694

NOT FOR NAVIGATION

![SPORTSMAN'S connection]

96

5
10
20
15
5
20
26' Max
15
10
5
5

Sucker Lake

Sucker Lake, Ramsey County
Bordered by Snail Lake Regional Park

Map pg/coord: 28 / D-2 **Max depth:** 26 feet
Surface area: 61 acres **Water clarity:** 6.5 feet (2005)

Accessibility: Shore fishing access
Accommodations: Shore fishing

FISH STOCKING DATA			
year	species	size	# released
09	White Bass	Adult	233
10	White Bass	Adult	185
11	White Bass	Adult	39

LENGTH OF SELECTED SPECIES SAMPLED FROM ALL GEAR
Survey Date: 07/25/2005 **Survey method:** gill net, trap net
Number of fish caught for the following length categories (inches):

species	0-5	6-8	9-11	12-14	15-19	20-24	25-29	>30	Total
Black Crappie	2	-	-	-	-	-	-	-	2
Bluegill	89	58	1	-	-	-	-	-	148
Hybrid Sunfish	6	-	-	-	-	-	-	-	6
Northern Pike	-	-	-	-	8	11	3	-	22
Pumpkin. Sunfish	12	-	-	-	-	-	-	-	12
Walleye	-	-	-	-	3	1	-	-	4
Yellow Bullhead	-	8	45	9	-	-	-	-	62
Yellow Perch	37	4	-	-	-	-	-	-	41

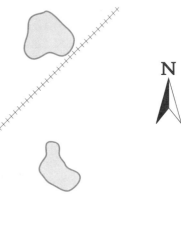

N

Hanlos Pond, Ramsey County
Located in Lakewood Hills Park

Map pg/coord: 28 / D,E-3 **Max depth:** 7 feet
Surface area: 7.7 acres **Water clarity:** NA

Accessibility: Fishing pier in park
Accommodations: Park, fishing pier

FISH STOCKING DATA			
year	species	size	# released
07	Black Crappie	Adult	1,028
07	Bluegill	Adult	751
08	Bluegill	Adult	945

LENGTH OF SELECTED SPECIES SAMPLED FROM ALL GEAR
Survey Date: 06/03/1997 **Survey method:** gill net, trap net
Number of fish caught for the following length categories (inches):

species	0-5	6-8	9-11	12-14	15-19	20-24	25-29	>30	Total
Black Bullhead	49	58	4	-	-	-	-	-	111
Black Crappie	14	174	-	-	-	-	-	-	188
Bluegill	89	92	-	-	-	-	-	-	181
Green Sunfish	2	-	-	-	-	-	-	-	2
Hybrid Sunfish	1	1	-	-	-	-	-	-	2
Pumpkin. Sunfish	3	3	-	-	-	-	-	-	6

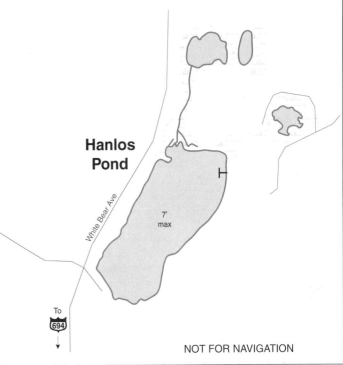

Hanlos Pond

White Bear Ave

7' max

To
694

NOT FOR NAVIGATION

GERVAIS LAKE
Ramsey County

Bordered by Gervais Lake County Park

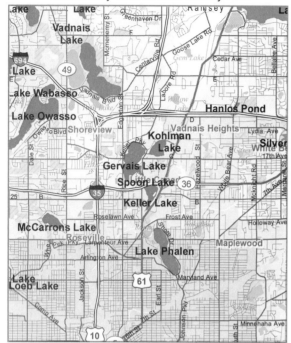

Area map pg / coord: 28 / E-2
Watershed: Twin Cities
Secchi disk: 10.5 feet (2011)
Water color: Green

Surface area: 234 acres
Shorelength: 2.8 miles
Maximum depth: 41 feet
Mean depth: 18 feet

Accessibility: Via navigable channel from Spoon Lake; concrete ramp on south shore in park on Spoon Lake
Boat ramp: Concrete ramp on Spoon Lake
Parking: Parking for ten trailers at access site on Spoon Lake
Accommodations: Shore fishing, park, restroom

Shoreland zoning classification: General development
Management class: Centrarchid
Ecological type: Centrarchid

FISHING INFORMATION: Gervais offers the best fishing out of the small chain of lakes it belongs to. The other lakes in the chain, Spoon, Keller, Kohlman and Round, are not as productive, according to local anglers. Gervais isn't very clear, but it has good bars, deep holes and a nice weedline. Bluegills, black crappies, northern pike and largemouth bass are all present. Tiger muskies have been stocked for some time, too.

According to the latest DNR survey of Gervais Lake, the most abundant fish captured were bluegills. The average fish was 5.9 inches, with only 3% of the 'gills surveyed being 7 inches or larger. The bluegills at the time of the survey exhibited average growth patterns.

Black crappies were small, with only a few over 8 inches captured. The numbers were below average for this type of lake in Minnesota.

Gervais Lake's channels heading into Kohlman and Keller are good places to fish early season bluegills and crappies. The south channel at Spoon Lake Park is also one of the metro area's better shore fishing spots. You can do very well with crappies by fishing the northeast channel south along the weeds. The east-side vegetation can be fished south with jigs and worms or minnows. When all else fails, use a slip bobber and small leech to lure a finicky bluegill or crappie.

Walleyes were captured in good numbers, with an average length of 19.8 inches and weight of 3.4 pounds. About 30% of the fish were at least 24 inches long. Use a basic live-bait or trolling approach to find active walleyes. Fish points and drop-offs. A bottom bouncer rigged with the "Slow Death" approach may work well. The "Slow Death" method is simply using a half nightcrawler rigged on a size 1 or 2 long-shank hook that's been bent slightly or already has a bend in it. You tie this to your bottom bouncer and slowly work along the bottom. The crawler will gradually twist through the water, often enticing strikes when other methods fail.

Northern pike were low in numbers, as were tiger muskies. You

	FISH STOCKING DATA		
year	species	size	# released
08	Walleye	Fingerling	7,617
08	Walleye	Yearling	40
09	Tiger Muskellunge	Fingerling	574
10	Walleye	Fingerling	20
10	Walleye	Yearling	900
10	Walleye	Adult	5
10	Tiger Muskellunge	Fry	26,250
11	Tiger Muskellunge	Fry	18,810
11	Tiger Muskellunge	Fingerling	234
12	Walleye	Fingerling	1,278
12	Walleye	Adult	54

NET CATCH DATA				
Date: 06/27/2011	Gill Nets		Trap Nets	
species	# per net	avg. fish weight (lbs.)	# per net	avg. fish weight (lbs.)
Black Crappie	-	-	4.7	0.20
Bluegill	9.6	0.18	116.2	0.24
Largemouth Bass	0.8	0.11	0.6	0.41
Northern Pike	6.2	4.21	-	-
Walleye	2.0	0.79	0.1	0.23
Yellow Bullhead	-	-	1.3	0.69
Yellow Perch	29.4	0.16	0.8	0.15

LENGTH OF SELECTED SPECIES SAMPLED FROM ALL GEAR									
Number of fish caught for the following length categories (inches):									
species	0-5	6-8	9-11	12-14	15-19	20-24	25-29	>30	Total
Black Crappie	5	36	1	-	-	-	-	-	42
Bluegill	81	1008	-	-	-	-	-	-	1094
Largemouth Bass	4	3	1	1	-	-	-	-	9
Northern Pike	-	-	-	-	1	13	15	2	31
Walleye	-	-	5	5	1	-	-	-	11
Yellow Bullhead	-	4	6	2	-	-	-	-	12
Yellow Perch	21	132	1	-	-	-	-	-	154

can find northerns by trolling outer edges of weedbeds, the east-side point, and the rocky bar just above it. Offer a shiner minnow on sunny days; try bright lures at dawn and dusk, as well as on overcast days. You may run across a muskie in these same spots.

Largemouth bass were available in moderate numbers according to the DNR survey. Not many big fish were caught, but there were bass up to 18.3 inches measured. Bass are in weedlines; the north and south ends are bass hotspots early in the season.

Boat access to Gervais Lake and the rest of the chain is available from a Ramsey County Park on Spoon Lake. The access has parking for about 10 rigs.

Gervais, Spoon, Keller & Kohlman Lakes

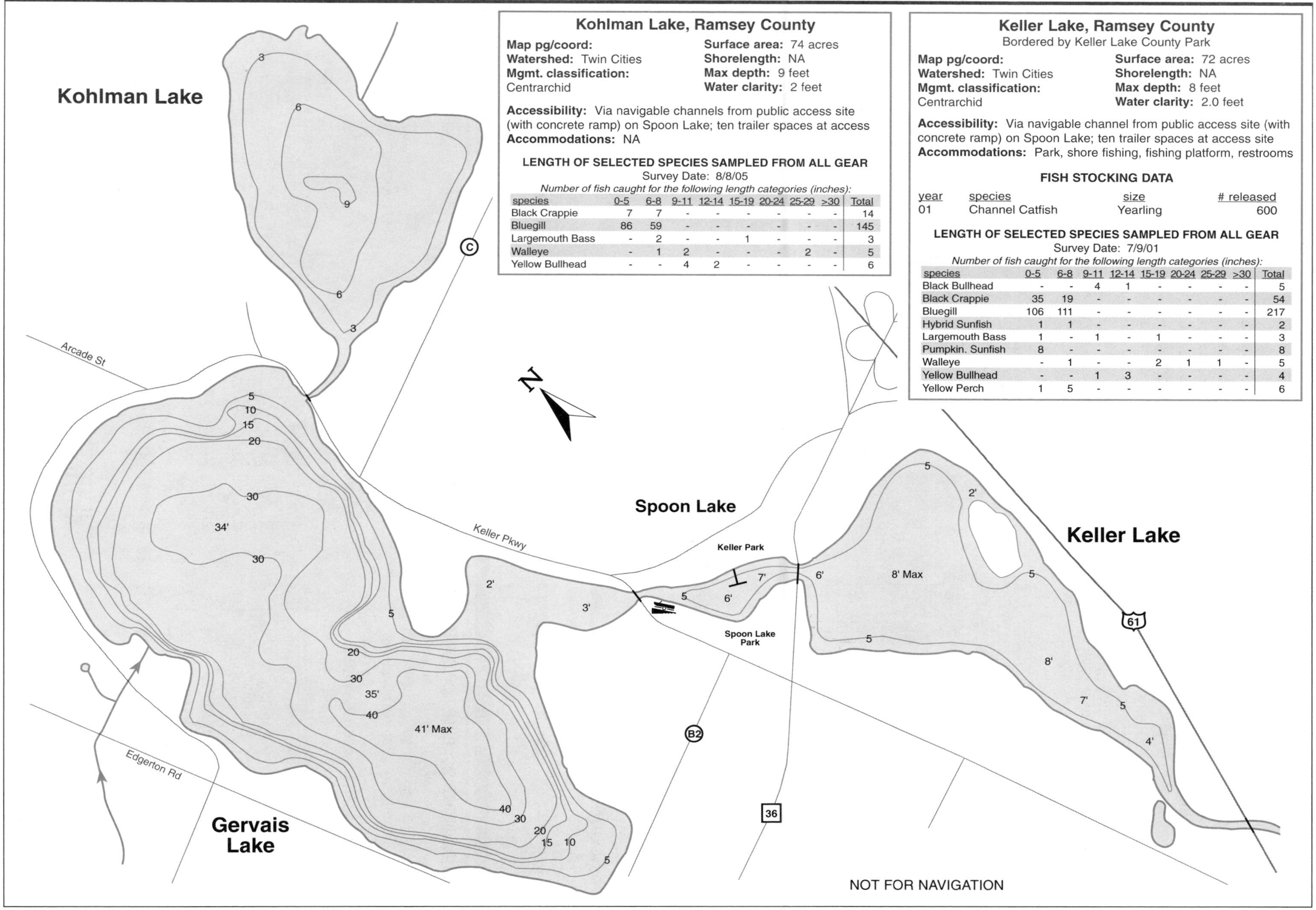

Kohlman Lake

Gervais Lake

Spoon Lake

Keller Lake

Keller Park

Spoon Lake Park

Arcade St

Edgerton Rd

Keller Pkwy

NOT FOR NAVIGATION

41' Max

34'

8' Max

N

Kohlman Lake, Ramsey County

Map pg/coord:
Watershed: Twin Cities
Mgmt. classification:
Centrarchid
Surface area: 74 acres
Shorelength: NA
Max depth: 9 feet
Water clarity: 2 feet

Accessibility: Via navigable channels from public access site (with concrete ramp) on Spoon Lake; ten trailer spaces at access

Accommodations: NA

LENGTH OF SELECTED SPECIES SAMPLED FROM ALL GEAR
Survey Date: 8/8/05

Number of fish caught for the following length categories (inches):

species	0-5	6-8	9-11	12-14	15-19	20-24	25-29	>30	Total
Black Crappie	7	7	-	-	-	-	-	-	14
Bluegill	86	59	-	-	-	-	-	-	145
Largemouth Bass	-	2	-	1	-	-	-	-	3
Walleye	-	-	1	2	-	-	-	-	3
Yellow Bullhead	-	-	4	2	-	-	-	-	6

Keller Lake, Ramsey County
Bordered by Keller Lake County Park

Map pg/coord:
Watershed: Twin Cities
Mgmt. classification:
Centrarchid
Surface area: 72 acres
Shorelength: NA
Max depth: 8 feet
Water clarity: 2.0 feet

Accessibility: Via navigable channel from public access site (with concrete ramp) on Spoon Lake; ten trailer spaces at access site

Accommodations: Park, shore fishing, fishing platform, restrooms

FISH STOCKING DATA

year	species	size	# released
01	Channel Catfish	Yearling	600

LENGTH OF SELECTED SPECIES SAMPLED FROM ALL GEAR
Survey Date: 7/9/01

Number of fish caught for the following length categories (inches):

species	0-5	6-8	9-11	12-14	15-19	20-24	25-29	>30	Total
Black Bullhead	-	-	4	1	-	-	-	-	5
Black Crappie	35	19	-	-	-	-	-	-	54
Bluegill	106	111	-	-	-	-	-	-	217
Hybrid Sunfish	1	1	-	-	-	-	-	-	2
Largemouth Bass	-	1	1	1	-	-	-	-	3
Pumpkin. Sunfish	8	-	-	-	-	-	-	-	8
Walleye	-	-	1	2	-	1	-	-	4
Yellow Bullhead	-	1	3	-	-	-	-	-	4
Yellow Perch	1	5	-	-	-	-	-	-	6

Source: Minnesota Department of Natural Resources, USGS

PELTIER LAKE

CENTERVILLE LAKE

Anoka County

Bordered by Centerville Lake Park

Area map page/coord: 28 / B-2
Watershed: Twin Cities
Surface area: 579 acres
Shorelength: 8.8 miles
Maximum depth: 18 feet
Mean depth: 7 feet
Secchi disk: 2.5 feet (2007)
Water color: Green
Accessibility: County-owned public access with concrete ramp on southwest shore next to the outlet dam; parking for twenty-nine trailers
Accommodations: Fishing pier, restrooms
Shoreland zoning: Nat. Environment
Management class: Warm-water gamefish
Ecological type: Roughfish-gamefish

Area map page/coord: 28 / B,C-2
Watershed: Twin Cities
Surface area: 474 acres
Shorelength: 4.1 miles
Maximum depth: 19 feet
Mean depth: 12 feet
Secchi disk: 2.1 feet (2007)
Water color: Green
Accessibility: County-owned public access with concrete ramp on west shore in park; parking for twenty-nine trailers
Accommodations: Park, shore fishing, camping
Shoreland zoning: Recreational dev.
Management class: Warm-water gamefish
Ecological type: Roughfish-gamefish

FISH STOCKING DATA

year	species	size	# released
07	Channel Catfish	Fingerling	38,253
07	Channel Catfish	Yearling	2,500
08	Walleye	Fry	465,000
09	Channel Catfish	Yearling	4,649
09	Walleye	Fry	1,030,000
11	Walleye	Fry	1,030,000

FISH STOCKING DATA

year	species	size	# released
08	Walleye	Fry	828,000
09	Walleye	Fry	1,000,000
10	Walleye	Fry	1,528,000
11	Walleye	Fry	528,000
12	Walleye	Fry	828,000

NET CATCH DATA

Date: 07/30/2007

species	Gill Nets # per net	Gill Nets avg. fish weight (lbs.)	Trap Nets # per net	Trap Nets avg. fish weight (lbs.)
Black Bullhead	11.5	1.11	0.6	0.80
Black Crappie	90.3	0.16	32.2	0.22
Bluegill	2.5	0.13	26.9	0.21
Bowfin (Dogfish)	0.8	4.67	1.9	3.48
Brown Bullhead	2.0	1.51	0.1	0.60
Common Carp	-	-	0.6	5.70
Golden Shiner	10.3	0.10	-	-
Largemouth Bass	0.3	0.66	0.2	0.43
Northern Pike	10.0	1.85	1.3	2.98
Pumpkin. Sunfish	-	-	0.8	0.11
White Sucker	1.3	2.40	0.3	2.66
Yellow Bullhead	-	-	0.3	0.81
Yellow Perch	7.5	0.09	0.2	0.09

NET CATCH DATA

Date: 07/30/2007

species	Gill Nets # per net	Gill Nets avg. fish weight (lbs.)	Trap Nets # per net	Trap Nets avg. fish weight (lbs.)
Black Bullhead	7.5	1.38	0.3	1.29
Black Crappie	62.8	0.27	35.4	0.29
Bluegill	38.5	0.19	43.8	0.19
Common Carp	-	-	0.3	5.73
Golden Shiner	4.3	0.17	-	-
Hybrid Sunfish	0.3	0.28	0.4	0.26
Largemouth Bass	0.5	0.17	0.8	1.84
Northern Pike	9.8	3.81	1.0	4.77
Pumpkin. Sunfish	-	-	0.3	0.37
Walleye	4.0	3.12	0.1	2.54
White Sucker	1.0	3.35	0.3	4.55
Yellow Bullhead	1.0	0.96	1.1	0.78
Yellow Perch	8.0	0.10	0.4	0.09

LENGTH OF SELECTED SPECIES SAMPLED FROM ALL GEAR

Number of fish caught for the following length categories (inches):

species	0-5	6-8	9-11	12-14	15-19	20-24	25-29	>30	Total
Black Bullhead	-	2	20	28	1	-	-	-	51
Black Crappie	128	496	18	-	-	-	-	-	651
Bluegill	81	165	-	-	-	-	-	-	252
Bowfin (Dogfish)	-	-	-	-	6	13	1	-	20
Golden Shiner	5	36	-	-	-	-	-	-	41
Largemouth Bass	-	1	2	-	-	-	-	-	3
Northern Pike	-	-	-	1	22	23	5	1	52
Pumpkin. Sunfish	6	1	-	-	-	-	-	-	7
White Sucker	-	-	-	-	8	-	-	-	8
Yellow Bullhead	-	-	1	2	-	-	-	-	3
Yellow Perch	24	8	-	-	-	-	-	-	32

LENGTH OF SELECTED SPECIES SAMPLED FROM ALL GEAR

Number of fish caught for the following length categories (inches):

species	0-5	6-8	9-11	12-14	15-19	20-24	25-29	>30	Total
Black Bullhead	-	1	4	24	3	-	-	-	32
Black Crappie	7	508	13	-	-	-	-	-	534
Bluegill	161	335	-	-	-	-	-	-	504
Golden Shiner	-	17	-	-	-	-	-	-	17
Hybrid Sunfish	-	4	-	-	-	-	-	-	4
Largemouth Bass	3	3	-	-	3	-	-	-	9
Northern Pike	-	-	-	-	8	21	4	14	47
Pumpkin. Sunfish	-	2	-	-	-	-	-	-	2
Walleye	-	-	-	-	6	11	-	-	17
Yellow Bullhead	-	2	6	5	-	-	-	-	13
Yellow Perch	10	25	-	-	-	-	-	-	35

FISHING INFORMATION: Peltier needs an aerator to prevent winterkill and to assure anglers of a healthy supply of northerns, crappies, panfish and walleyes. Panfish are at both the south and north ends of the lake, as well as around the island at the north end. Crappies move to deeper water in summer. Try fishing for crappies with small minnows under a slip float. Northerns, which are plentiful in Peltier, stay fairly close to shorelines in spring. The best fishing for them is in the southern part of the lake. Cast spinnerbaits and spoons to hook active fish. There are good walleyes here, too. Try the weed edges and around the island with live bait.

Centerville is a shallow lake saved from winterkill in recent years by an aerator. Now it is able to support populations of good-sized walleyes, average northern pike and some truly impressive crappies. There aren't many mysteries to this lake. It's almost round, with shorelines that drop gradually over a sand bottom to about 19 feet. The water is cloudy, so use bright lures. Walleyes are active in spring along the southeast shore near the protruding point. It's shallow there, so move deeper as the season progresses. Leeches work well around 10 feet. Northerns like the corner, too, but they'll be moving around the vegetation. Fish green weeds with spoons or suckers. Panfish are abundant in Centerville and can be fished from shore or from boats. Crappies and sunfish can be taken along shorelines, but pickings are easiest along the southeast shore where the panfish tend to school near the pumphouse, and along the north shore, close to the Parkway Road Bridge between Centerville and Peltier Lakes. There are a few bass in the lake, mostly down in the south end, near the small islands and around the south point.

Peltier & Centerville Lakes

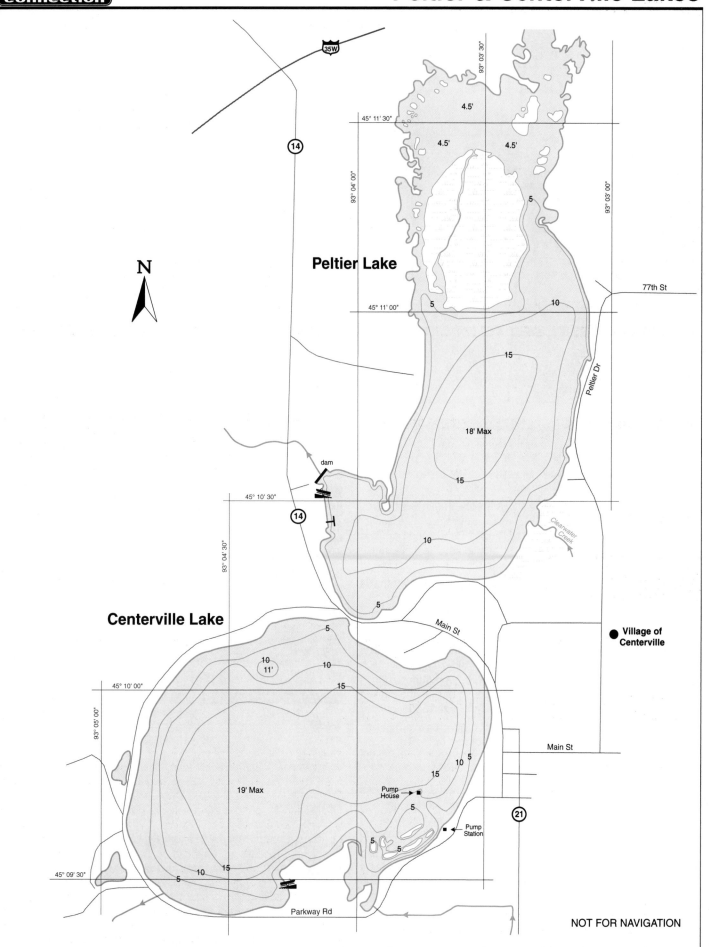

N

35W

14

45° 11' 30"

93° 04' 00"

93° 03' 30"

93° 03' 00"

4.5'

4.5'   4.5'

5

Peltier Lake

5

45° 11' 00"

5   10   77th St

15

Peltier Dr

18' Max

dam

15

45° 10' 30"

10

14

Clearwater Creek

93° 04' 30"

5

10

● Village of Centerville

Centerville Lake

5

Main St

5

10   10

11'

15

45° 10' 00"

93° 05' 00"

Main St

15

10   5

19' Max   15

Pump House → ■

5

■ → Pump Station

21

5

10   15

45° 09' 30"   5

Parkway Rd

NOT FOR NAVIGATION

CLEAR LAKE
Washington County

Bordered by Clear Lake Park

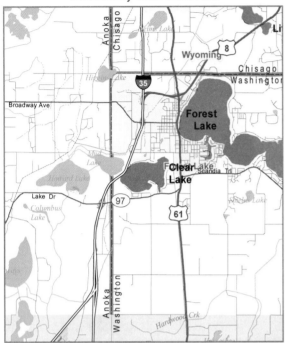

Area map pg / coord: 28 / A-3
Watershed: Twin Cities
Secchi disk: 5.1 feet (2009)
Water color: NA

Surface area: 429 acres
Shorelength: 3.9 miles
Maximum depth: 28 feet
Mean depth: 12 feet

Accessibility: State-owned public access on west shore
Boat ramp: Concrete
Parking: Twenty trailer spaces
Accommodations: Park, shore fishing, picnicking, restrooms

Shoreland zoning classification: General development
Management class: Walleye-centrarchid
Ecological type: Centrarchid

FISHING INFORMATION: Drivers rushing north on I-35 will notice all the marshes around and can easily mistake Clear Lake for one of those. Back behind the rushes, though, there really is a pretty good lake for bluegills and especially, for walleyes. The primary management focus for this lake is walleyes.

Brad Dusenka of Frankie's Live Bait & Tackle, 10680 South Ave., Chisago City, MN, (651) 257-6334, says walleyes are quite decent in this lake; some, in fact, are getting "huge." Good sand bars and plenty of forage provide nearly ideal habitat for them. Dusenka says spring hotspots for walleyes include the bar in the middle of the western bay, the sunken island at mid-lake and the sand bar and rocks along the west shore. A Lindy rig with a minnow or leech retrieved along the bottom near the sand bars is effective. You can also do fairly well trolling crankbaits. In summer, says Dusenka, your best bets are off the weedline on the north side and on the deep side of the sand bar heading northwest from the south-side point. The northeast corner also offers a fairly deep hole with steeply descending sides, and walleyes will hang out there during daylight hours. Later in the day, they often head back to the sunken island. Walleye have been stocked annually for nearly 20 years.

Tiger muskies are also stocked regularly. Clear Lake's muskies aren't huge, but there are good numbers of fish in the 24- to 26-inch range. Try for tigers at mid-lake humps or in pads on the south and west.

Bluegills and some crappies are also in thick weeds. Try the rocks at the west end, the small bay in the southeast corner and the sunken island. Bluegills are relatively abundant, with an average fish about 5.3 inches long. Black crappies were sampled above the median levels, while white crappie numbers were much lower.

There are some northern pike in Clear Lake, too. Try for them along the outside edges of weedlines. The pike population was in the normal range during the DNR sampling, although it was slightly lower than the previous survey. The average pike measured 24.7 inches long and weighed 3.7 pounds.

FISH STOCKING DATA			
year	species	size	# released
08	Walleye	Adult	4
09	Tiger Muskellunge	Fingerling	401
09	Walleye	Fingerling	13,558
09	Walleye	Yearling	13
10	Walleye	Fingerling	5,868
11	Tiger Muskellunge	Fingerling	401
11	Walleye	Fingerling	9,444
12	Black Crappie	Adult	11
12	Walleye	Fingerling	14,470
12	Walleye	Adult	8

NET CATCH DATA				
Date: 06/08/2009	Gill Nets		Trap Nets	
species	# per net	avg. fish weight (lbs.)	# per net	avg. fish weight (lbs.)
Black Crappie	11.5	0.15	0.8	0.20
Bluegill	6.5	0.08	69.1	0.12
Hybrid Sunfish	-	-	1.0	0.04
Largemouth Bass	0.2	1.86	-	-
Northern Pike	3.8	3.67	0.3	5.86
Pumpkin. Sunfish	-	-	0.7	0.04
Tiger Muskellunge	1.5	4.20	-	-
Walleye	5.0	2.05	0.4	1.67
White Crappie	0.8	0.34	1.1	0.40
White Sucker	0.2	1.94	-	-
Yellow Bullhead	0.2	1.29	1.7	1.10
Yellow Perch	40.7	0.09	1.6	0.09

LENGTH OF SELECTED SPECIES SAMPLED FROM ALL GEAR									
Number of fish caught for the following length categories (inches):									
species	0-5	6-8	9-11	12-14	15-19	20-24	25-29	>30	Total
Black Crappie	14	62	-	-	-	-	-	-	76
Bluegill	606	54	-	-	-	-	-	-	661
Common Carp	-	-	-	-	3	5	-	-	8
Hybrid Sunfish	9	-	-	-	-	-	-	-	9
Northern Pike	-	-	-	-	1	10	13	2	26
Pumpkin. Sunfish	6	-	-	-	-	-	-	-	6
Tiger Muskellunge	-	-	-	-	1	4	1	3	9
Walleye	-	1	6	10	7	8	2	-	34
White Crappie	-	10	4	1	-	-	-	-	15
White Sucker	-	-	-	1	-	-	-	-	1
Yellow Bullhead	-	-	9	7	-	-	-	-	16
Yellow Perch	103	155	-	-	-	-	-	-	258

A concrete ramp and 20 parking spaces can be found on the northwest shore. There's no launch fee.

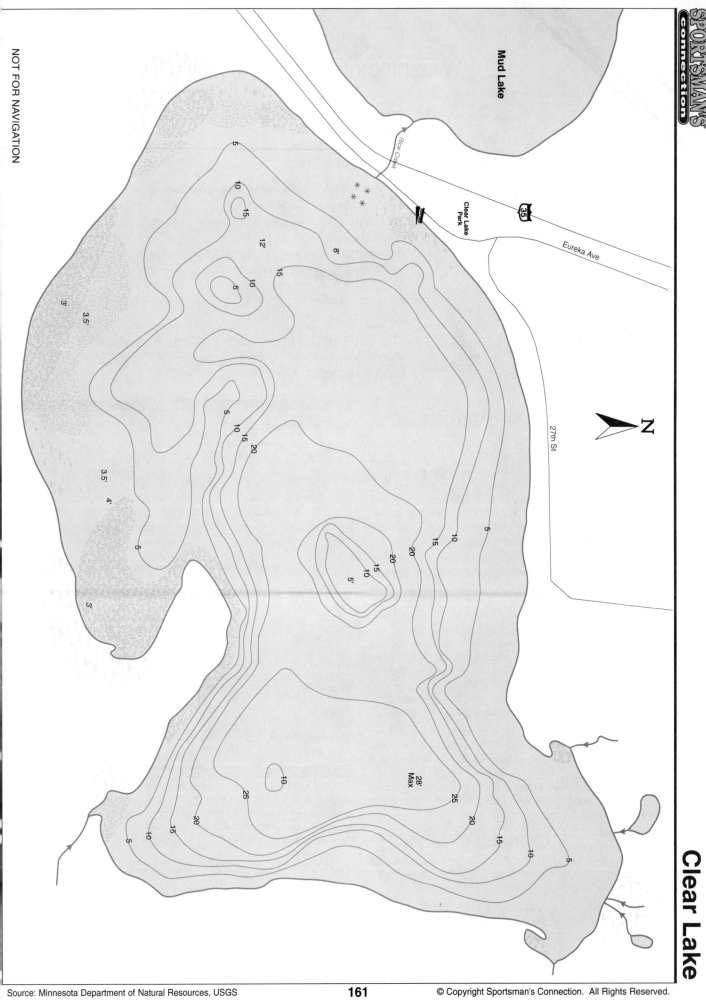

Clear Lake

Mud Lake

Clear Lake Park

35

Eureka Ave

27th St

Rice Creek

N

NOT FOR NAVIGATION

28' Max

FOREST LAKE
Washington County

Bordered by Lakeside Memorial Park

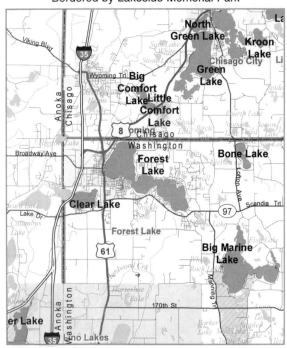

Area map pg / coord: 28 / A-3
Watershed: Lower St. Croix
Secchi disk: 5.5 feet (2009)
Water color: Green

Surface area: 2,271 acres
Shorelength: 6.6 miles
Maximum depth: 37 feet
Mean depth: 11 feet

Accessibility: 1) State-owned public access on west shore of Lake One in Lakeside Memorial Park; 2) State-owned public access on north shore of Lake Two; 3) State-owned public access on east shore of Lake Three

Boat ramp: All ramps at above launch sites are concrete
Parking: 1) Twenty trailer spaces; 2) Eleven trailer spaces; 3) Fifteen trailer spaces
Accommodations: Park, fishing piers, shore fishing, boat rental, picnicking, restrooms

Shoreland zoning classification: General development
Management class: Centrarchid
Ecological type: Centrarchid

FISHING INFORMATION: Walleyes, northern pike and panfish are the staples for anglers here, and there are also quite a few largemouth bass. No wonder Forest is a busy lake nearly year-round, especially when you factor in the expanding muskie population. The primary management species on the lake are walleyes and muskies. Both species are stocked reglarly. The lake itself is made up of three basins called One, Two and Three, which run west to east.

The walleyes, stocked by the DNR, are found in all the basins and average around 16 inches, says Brad Dusenka of Frankie's Live Bait & Tackle, 10680 South Ave., Chisago City, MN, (651) 257-6334. In basin One, the bar on the north side is a spring hot spot, as is the bar on the southeast corner of Two. The point along the northeast shore of Three is good, too. Use a jig with a minnow or leech, bouncing it along as you retrieve. Later in the season, try slowly trolling deeper spots. The good news for walleyes, based on the last DNR survey, was that their numbers are above median levels in all three lake basins. The average walleye measured 18.2 inches long and weighed 2.67 pounds, with 12% of the walleyes captured measuring 24 inches long or more. Walleye growth rates are fair.

There's a good chance of catching a muskie in this lake, and there are several good spots to try for them. The rock bar off the north shore of Lake One is a good spot, as is the nice drop off Willow Point in Lake Two. Dusenka says you might also try the bar toward the southern shore of Lake Three, almost directly south of Shadyland Point. The muskie population was sampled and found to be at the median level for a lake of this type.

During spring, northern pike will be in weeds or cruising outside edges. Pike will also be found on most of the points and in the channels connecting the basins. The latest DNR survey showed the pike population to be at the median level for abundance. The average pike measured 20.9 inches long and weighed 2.05 pounds.

This is a productive largemouth bass lake, and the rocks toward the southeast end of Lake One are good places to try. According to the DNR survey, you'll find the average bass measuring 11.5 inches long and weighing 0.9 pounds.

FISH STOCKING DATA

year	species	size	# released
07	Walleye	Fingerling	33,605
08	Muskellunge	Fingerling	2,241
09	Muskellunge	Fingerling	1,498
09	Walleye	Fingerling	54,513
09	Walleye	Yearling	1,833
09	Walleye	Adult	59
10	Muskellunge	Fingerling	752
11	Walleye	Fingerling	72,645
11	Walleye	Yearling	118
11	Walleye	Adult	2
12	Muskellunge	Fingerling	1,308

NET CATCH DATA

Date: 07/13/2009

species	Gill Nets # per net	Gill Nets avg. fish weight (lbs.)	Trap Nets # per net	Trap Nets avg. fish weight (lbs.)
Black Crappie	10.3	0.13	3.1	0.19
Bluegill	17.5	0.09	118.5	0.16
Green Sunfish	-	-	0.1	0.04
Largemouth Bass	0.6	0.91	0.1	0.85
Muskellunge	0.4	13.30	0.1	0.26
Northern Pike	6.8	2.05	0.4	1.83
Rock Bass	-	-	2.4	0.46
Walleye	3.3	2.67	0.2	3.56
White Crappie	0.3	0.70	0.1	0.23
Yellow Perch	7.1	0.11	0.4	0.23

LENGTH OF SELECTED SPECIES SAMPLED FROM ALL GEAR

Number of fish caught for the following length categories (inches):

species	0-5	6-8	9-11	12-14	15-19	20-24	25-29	>30	Total
Black Crappie	41	90	4	-	-	-	-	-	135
Bluegill	1284	864	-	-	-	-	-	-	2154
Green Sunfish	2	-	-	-	-	-	-	-	2
Hybrid Sunfish	43	207	-	-	-	-	-	-	254
Largemouth Bass	-	1	4	1	1	-	-	-	7
Muskellunge	-	-	1	-	-	-	-	3	4
Northern Pike	-	-	-	1	30	22	6	1	60
Pumpkin. Sunfish	178	145	-	-	-	-	-	-	327
Rock Bass	4	30	6	-	-	-	-	-	40
Walleye	-	-	3	4	9	9	4	-	29
White Crappie	-	2	-	1	-	-	-	-	3
Yellow Perch	13	49	1	-	-	-	-	-	63

Forest Lake

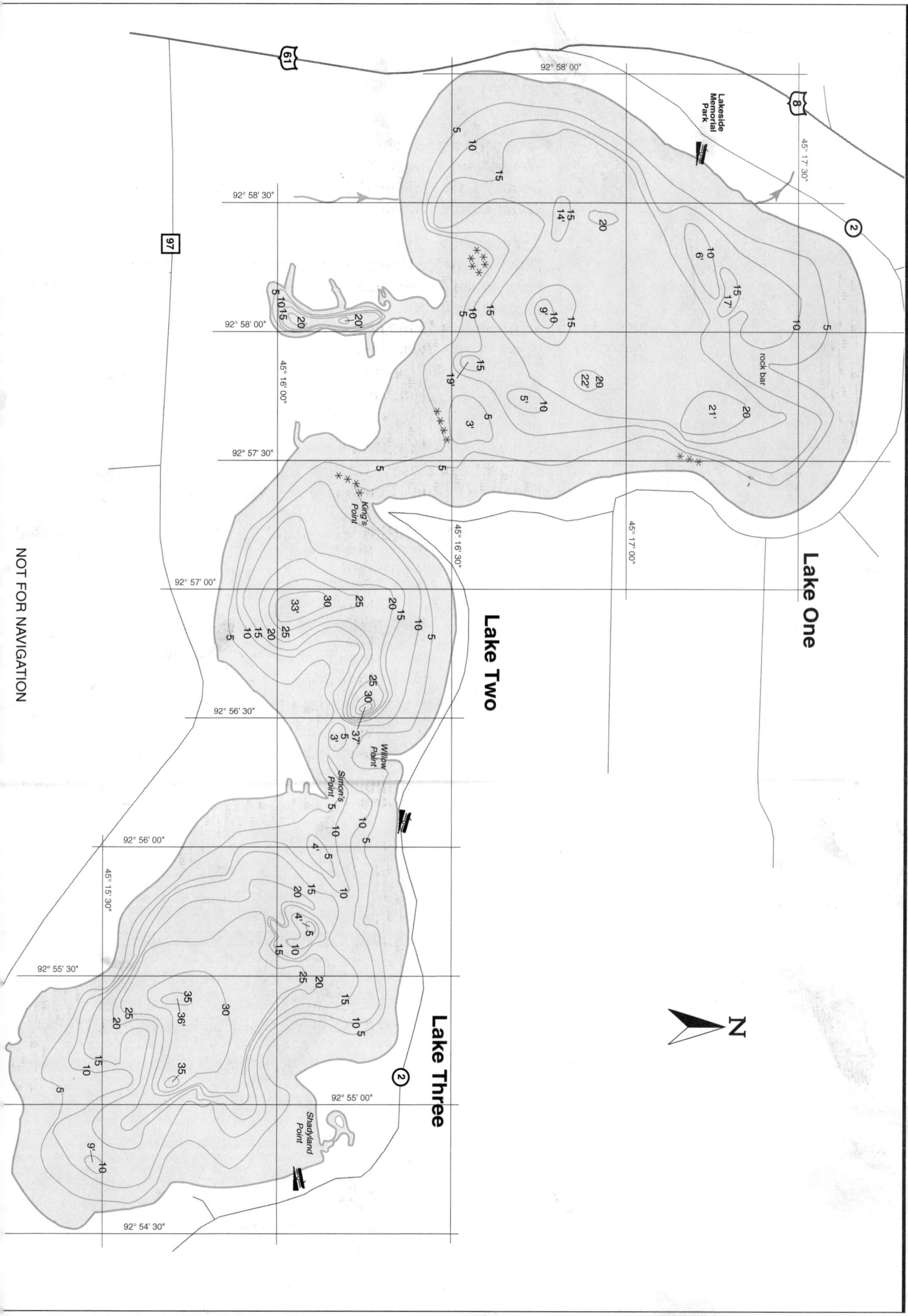

Lake One

Lake Two

Lake Three

Lakeside
Memorial
Park

rock bar

King's Point

Willow Point

Simon's Point

Shadyland Point

N

61

97

8

2

2

92° 58' 00"

92° 58' 30"

92° 58' 00"

92° 57' 30"

92° 57' 00"

92° 56' 30"

92° 56' 00"

92° 55' 30"

92° 55' 00"

92° 54' 30"

45° 17' 30"

45° 17' 00"

45° 16' 30"

45° 16' 00"

45° 15' 30"

BALD EAGLE LAKE
Ramsey County

Bordered by Bald Eagle Lake Regional Park

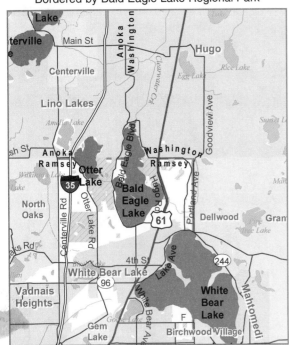

Area map pg / coord: 28 / C,D-3
Watershed: Twin Cities
Secchi disk: 2.4 feet (2008)
Water color: Green

Surface area: 1,047 acres
Shorelength: 8.0 miles
Maximum depth: 36 feet
Mean depth: 8 feet

Accessibility: County-owned public access on east shore in park
Boat ramp: Concrete
Parking: Twenty-four trailer spaces
Accommodations: Park, shore fishing, boat rental, resort, restrooms

Shoreland zoning classification: General development
Management class: Centrarchid
Ecological type: Centrarchid

FISH STOCKING DATA			
year	species	size	# released
08	Walleye	Fingerling	88,025
08	Walleye	Yearling	1
08	Walleye	Adult	2
10	Muskellunge	Fingerling	630
10	Muskellunge	Yearling	212
10	Walleye	Fingerling	50,848
10	Walleye	Yearling	8
10	Walleye	Adult	90
12	Walleye	Fingerling	46,061
12	Walleye	Yearling	1,120
12	Walleye	Adult	164
12	Muskellunge	Fingerling	873

NET CATCH DATA				
Date: 07/14/2008	Gill Nets		Trap Nets	
species	# per net	avg. fish weight (lbs.)	# per net	avg. fish weight (lbs.)
Black Crappie	39.3	0.13	13.1	0.23
Bluegill	4.0	0.15	44.2	0.15
Bowfin (Dogfish)	-	-	0.7	6.21
Common Carp	-	-	0.1	5.73
Golden Shiner	1.8	0.10	-	-
Hybrid Sunfish	-	-	0.3	0.23
Largemouth Bass	0.3	0.34	0.3	0.07
Northern Pike	3.7	2.90	-	-
Pumpkin. Sunfish	-	-	3.7	0.20
Walleye	4.7	2.94	-	-
Yellow Perch	8.2	0.15	-	-

LENGTH OF SELECTED SPECIES SAMPLED FROM ALL GEAR									
Number of fish caught for the following length categories (inches):									
species	0-5	6-8	9-11	12-14	15-19	20-24	25-29	>30	Total
Black Crappie	97	274	9	-	-	-	-	-	380
Bluegill	228	275	-	-	-	-	-	-	510
Bowfin (Dogfish)	-	-	-	-	1	1	6	-	8
Common Carp	-	-	-	-	-	1	-	-	1
Golden Shiner	5	6	-	-	-	-	-	-	11
Hybrid Sunfish	-	3	-	-	-	-	-	-	3
Largemouth Bass	3	1	1	-	-	-	-	-	5
Northern Pike	-	-	-	-	7	8	5	2	22
Pumpkin. Sunfish	13	28	-	-	-	-	-	-	41
Walleye	-	1	3	-	14	6	4	-	28
Yellow Perch	15	32	2	-	-	-	-	-	49

FISHING INFORMATION: Bald Eagle is one of the Twin Cities' better fishing lakes. Unfortunately for anglers, it's also a favorite of water-skiers. Try to fish early and late or during the work week to avoid the rush. It's worth the effort. You can get a stringer full of panfish, plus northerns, largemouth bass and walleyes and have a fair chance of taking a good-sized muskie. The lake is primarily managed for walleyes and muskies.

You'll find emergent vegetation at a number of places on the lake, and many of these weedy areas hold good numbers of bass. The south shore, the west side, near the dam on Otter Creek, and the north end, near the resort, are all worth your time. The lake is fairly clear, and you should do well with soft plastics at the weed edges. Also try a floating worm or a Senko in subtle colors like green pumpkin, watermelon seed or pumpkinseed. Topwater lures are productive early and late in the day during the summer months.

Shoreline weeds are generally good for panfish, and the small bays around the lake seem to be favorite hangouts for black crappies. Try for crappies at the weeds early with a minnow on a bare hook with or without a slip bobber. If you don't get action, try the same bait with a small marabou or tube jig. When the water warms, crappies go deeper. Try the rocks off the point near the public access on the east side. Cigar Island, at the center of the south bay, is also a good spot.

Northern pike in Bald Eagle are most frequently caught off points. The point north of the dam or the one off the beach on the east side are both good spots to try. Don't overlook Cigar Island and the deep spot just south of it. The flats from the outer edges of bulrushes to the drop-offs are good trolling areas. Use brightly colored spoons and spinnerbaits.

Muskies live in the same areas as pike, so while you're slinging a spinnerbait for a pike, don't be surprised if you latch onto a muskie.

Some of the best walleye action is along the 10- to 15-foot drop from the access over to Rocky Ridge and in similar depths around Cigar Island. The average walleye captured in the most recent DNR survey (June 2008) measured 16.95 inches and weighed 2.94 pounds. About 33% of the walleyes sampled measured over 20 inches long.

NOT FOR NAVIGATION

WHITE BEAR LAKE
Washington County

Bordered by Ramsey County Park, Matoska Park, Lions Park & Bellaire Park

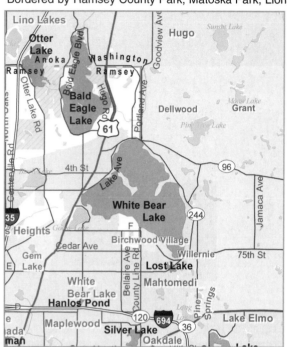

Area map pg / coord: 28 / D-3
Watershed: Twin Cities
Secchi disk: 12.9 feet (2008)
Water color: Green

Surface area: 2,428 acres
Shorelength: 11.1 miles
Maximum depth: 83 feet
Mean depth: 20 feet

Accessibility: 1) County-owned public access on north shore; 2) City-owned public access on west shore near bridge to island
Boat ramp: 1) Concrete, shallow ramp; 2) Concrete
Parking: 1) Thirty-seven trailer spaces; 2) Fifteen trailer spaces
Accommodations: Parks, fishing pier, marina, picnicking, restrooms

Shoreland zoning classification: General development
Management class: Walleye-centrarchid
Ecological type: Centrarchid

FISH STOCKING DATA

year	species	size	# released
08	Muskellunge	Fingerling	290
08	Muskellunge	Adult	117
09	Muskellunge	Fingerling	900
09	Muskellunge	Yearling	300
09	Muskellunge	Adult	2
09	Walleye	Fingerling	21,811
09	Walleye	Yearling	2,591
09	Walleye	Adult	36
10	Walleye	Fingerling	26,415
10	Walleye	Yearling	268
10	Walleye	Adult	33
11	Muskellunge	Fingerling	900
11	Muskellunge	Yearling	300
11	Walleye	Fingerling	37,727
11	Walleye	Yearling	226
11	Walleye	Adult	3
12	Walleye	Fingerling	2,014
12	Walleye	Yearling	2,009
12	Walleye	Adult	203

FISHING INFORMATION: White Bear Lake is huge. It is 2,428 acres, has a maximum depth of 83 feet and water clarity to 12.9 feet. All that space provides plenty of room for a wide variety of fish species and lots of structure for them in which to play and forage. It's like Las Vegas for fish.

White Bear is noted mostly for its largemouth bass, walleyes and, most recently, nice muskies. The DNR primarily manages the lake for walleyes and muskies. It should also garner some respect for its panfish, too. Black crappies averaged 7.6 inches and 0.24 pounds, while yellow perch measured 7.15 inches and 0.17 pounds, according to the latest DNR survey. They're both taken in good numbers at early and late ice, and, of course, during spring and summer. Small tube jigs work great for spring crappies and glow jigs tipped with a minnow or leech are dynamite during summer. Panfish move from year to year, so you'd do well to check locally on hot spots before setting out.

Walleyes are White Bear's bread and butter. They are heavily stocked and surviving well. While they are below average for abundance, they size averages are up. They run about 17.5 inches and 2.2 pounds. Walleyes congregate around bars and sandy slopes, as you would expect. Slide down slopes with leeches and crawlers, or with deep-diving crankbaits. Don't be afraid to go deep; the eyes have been known to hang out in 30 to 35 feet of water.

For bass, start with the bulrushes at the northwest corner of the lake, near White Bear or along the western bay's shoreline. The weeds, including Eurasian milfoil, get thick at those spots when the water warms, so you will have to fish the edges in deeper water. In summer, fish the docks when the sun is low. In fact, most successful anglers on White Bear will tell you that night fishing is the only way to go, especially if you want to fish deeper areas at the lake's center.

For muskies, fish the southern end of Manitou Island in spring, major points in summer and deep weedlines in about 20 feet of water in fall. The average muskie grows to 40 inches by the age of 7, but the overall average in the lake is about 27 inches and 4 pounds.

NET CATCH DATA

Date: 07/28/2008	Gill Nets		Trap Nets	
species	# per net	avg. fish weight (lbs.)	# per net	avg. fish weight (lbs.)
Black Bullhead	-	-	0.3	0.77
Black Crappie	1.4	0.26	1.3	0.22
Bluegill	17.3	0.12	48.6	0.14
Bowfin (Dogfish)	-	-	0.5	7.52
Hybrid Sunfish	-	-	10.2	0.19
Largemouth Bass	-	-	0.8	0.47
Northern Pike	6.6	1.55	0.4	1.00
Pumpkin. Sunfsih	1.0	0.18	2.5	0.22
Rock Bass	0.1	0.11	0.3	0.16
Smallmouth Bass	0.4	1.52	-	-
Walleye	2.5	2.20	0.8	1.14
Yellow Bullhead	0.4	1.16	0.3	0.85
Yellow Perch	13.0	0.17	0.3	0.08

LENGTH OF SELECTED SPECIES SAMPLED FROM ALL GEAR

Number of fish caught for the following length categories (inches):

species	0-5	6-8	9-11	12-14	15-19	20-24	25-29	>30	Total
Black Bullhead	-	-	2	1	-	-	-	-	3
Black Crappie	5	16	6	-	-	-	-	-	27
Bluegill	375	342	-	-	-	-	-	-	721
Bowfin (Dogfish)	-	-	-	-	-	-	6	-	6
Hybrid Sunfish	51	71	-	-	-	-	-	-	122
Largemouth Bass	5	2	1	1	1	-	-	-	10
Northern Pike	-	-	2	2	34	17	3	-	58
Pumpkin. Sunfish	10	28	-	-	-	-	-	-	38
Rock Bass	3	2	-	-	-	-	-	-	5
Smallmouth Bass	-	-	1	1	1	-	-	-	3
Walleye	-	1	3	8	10	6	1	-	29
Yellow Bullhead	-	-	2	4	-	-	-	-	6
Yellow Perch	11	94	2	-	-	-	-	-	107

NOT FOR NAVIGATION

LAKE DEMONTREVILLE
Washington County

Area map page/coord: 28 / E-3
Watershed: Twin Cities
Surface area: 143 acres
Maximum depth: 24 feet
Mean depth: 8 feet
Water clarity: 17.8 feet (2005)
Accessibility: State-owned public access with concrete ramp on northwest shore; twelve trailer spaces
Accommodations: Shore fishing, restrooms
Management class: Centrarchid

OLSON LAKE
Washington County

Area map page/coord: 28 / E-3
Watershed: Twin Cities
Surface area: 79 acres
Maximum depth: 15 feet
Mean depth: NA
Water clarity: 13.3 feet (2011)
Accessibility: Via navigable channel from Lake DeMontreville, state-owned concrete ramp on northwest shore
Accommodations: On DeMontreville
Management class: Centrarchid

LAKE JANE
Washington County

Area map page/coord: 28 / E-3
Watershed: Twin Cities
Surface area: 153 acres
Maximum depth: 39 feet
Mean depth: NA
Water clarity: 14.0 feet (2007)
Accessibility: State-owned public access with concrete ramp on southeast shore; parking for ten trailers
Accommodations: Shore fishing, restrooms
Management class: Centrarchid

Lake DeMontreville
FISH STOCKING DATA

year	species	size	# released
05	Walleye	Fry	416,000
05	Walleye	Fingerling	46,127
05	Walleye	Yearling	12

NET CATCH DATA
Date: 05/10/2011

	Gill Nets		Trap Nets	
		avg. fish		avg. fish
species	# per net	weight (lbs.)	# per net	weight (lbs.)
Black Bullhead	0.6	1.03	3.5	0.94
Black Crappie	1.0	0.20	7.9	0.94
Bluegill	2.6	0.07	14.5	0.07
Hybrid Sunfish	0.8	0.09	2.8	0.15
Northern Pike	12.4	2.51	0.1	0.17
Pumpkin. Sunfish	0.4	0.05	3.1	0.17
Walleye	0.4	3.69	0.1	3.18
Yellow Bullhead	0.2	0.62	3.3	0.81
Yellow Perch	10.8	0.13	-	-

LENGTH OF SELECTED SPECIES SAMPLED FROM ALL GEAR
Number of fish caught for the following length categories (inches):

species	0-5	6-8	9-11	12-14	15-19	20-24	25-29	>30	Total
Black Bullhead	-	-	6	25	-	-	-	-	31
Black Crappie	2	38	25	3	-	-	-	-	68
Bluegill	116	9	-	-	-	-	-	-	129
Hybrid Sunfish	17	-	-	-	-	-	-	-	17
Northern Pike	-	-	1	1	19	32	9	1	63
Pumpkin. Sunfish	19	8	-	-	-	-	-	-	27
Walleye	-	-	-	-	3	-	-	-	3
Yellow Bullhead	-	-	18	9	-	-	-	-	27
Yellow Perch	8	46	-	-	-	-	-	-	54

Olson Lake
FISH STOCKING DATA

year	species	size	# released
03	Walleye	Fingerling	2,340

NET CATCH DATA
Date: 06/20/2011

	Gill Nets		Trap Nets	
		avg. fish		avg. fish
species	# per net	weight (lbs.)	# per net	weight (lbs.)
Black Bullhead	-	-	0.9	1.01
Black Crappie	0.5	0.08	14.4	0.18
Bluegill	8.5	0.10	149.7	0.08
Green Sunfish	-	-	0.2	0.07
Hybrid Sunfish	-	-	17.6	0.15
Largemouth Bass	0.5	1.25	0.3	0.11
Northern Pike	8.0	2.41	0.3	2.65
Pumpkin. Sunfish	4.5	0.13	6.4	0.16
Walleye	1.0	3.81	-	-
Yellow Bullhead	1.5	0.78	1.8	0.74
Yellow Perch	19.0	0.15	0.2	0.05

LENGTH OF SELECTED SPECIES SAMPLED FROM ALL GEAR
Number of fish caught for the following length categories (inches):

species	0-5	6-8	9-11	12-14	15-19	20-24	25-29	>30	Total
Black Bullhead	-	-	-	8	-	-	-	-	8
Black Crappie	14	109	4	-	-	-	-	-	131
Bluegill	1227	132	-	-	-	-	-	-	1364
Green Sunfish	2	-	-	-	-	-	-	-	2
Hybrid Sunfish	107	51	-	-	-	-	-	-	158
Largemouth Bass	2	1	-	1	-	-	-	-	4
Northern Pike	-	-	-	-	4	13	2	-	19
Pumpkin. Sunfish	40	27	-	-	-	-	-	-	67
Walleye	-	-	-	-	1	1	-	-	2
Yellow Bullhead	-	2	17	-	-	-	-	-	19
Yellow Perch	7	33	-	-	-	-	-	-	40

Lake Jane
NO RECORD OF STOCKING

LENGTH OF SELECTED SPECIES SAMPLED FROM ALL GEAR
Survey Date: 06/25/2007   **Survey method:** gill net, trap net
Number of fish caught for the following length categories (inches):

species	0-5	6-8	9-11	12-14	15-19	20-24	25-29	>30	Total
Black Bullhead	-	2	5	1	-	-	-	-	8
Black Crappie	9	14	2	-	-	-	-	-	25
Bluegill	260	132	-	-	-	-	-	-	399
Green Sunfish	9	2	-	-	-	-	-	-	11
Hybrid Sunfish	18	30	-	-	-	-	-	-	48
Largemouth Bass	-	3	-	4	5	-	-	-	12
Northern Pike	-	-	2	24	53	11	1	2	93
Pumpkin. Sunfish	17	24	-	-	-	-	-	-	41
Walleye	-	-	-	-	1	-	-	-	1
Yellow Bullhead	1	9	28	6	-	-	-	-	44

FISHING INFORMATION: DeMontreville Lake is full of panfish. Weedlines are loaded with bluegills, as well as a good population of largemouth bass. Weeds in the northwest bay hold bass in spring, as do two points: one on the west side, the other on the southeast side. Water is clear, but your bait will have to compete with all the small bluegills for the attention of bass. Public access is on the northwest shore. Little **Olson Lake**, located to the southwest of DeMontreville, is noted for its panfish and bass populations. The hook at the south end and the small bay along the north shore are good spots. You can access the lake on the northwest shore. **Lake Jane** is loaded with bluegills, largemouth bass and, to a lesser extent, northern pike. Weedlines hold spring bass. Spinnerbaits, jigs and topwater lures flipped into openings get attention in spring. Northerns cruise the outside edges of weeds in 5 feet or more of water. Panfish are everywhere in the weeds and will take worms and small minnows on a bare hook. Public access is located along the southern shore. Lake Jane has public access with a concrete ramp and 10 parking spaces at its southeast corner. DeMontreville has public access with concrete ramp and 18 spaces off DeMontreville Trail.

DeMontreville, Olson & Jane Lakes

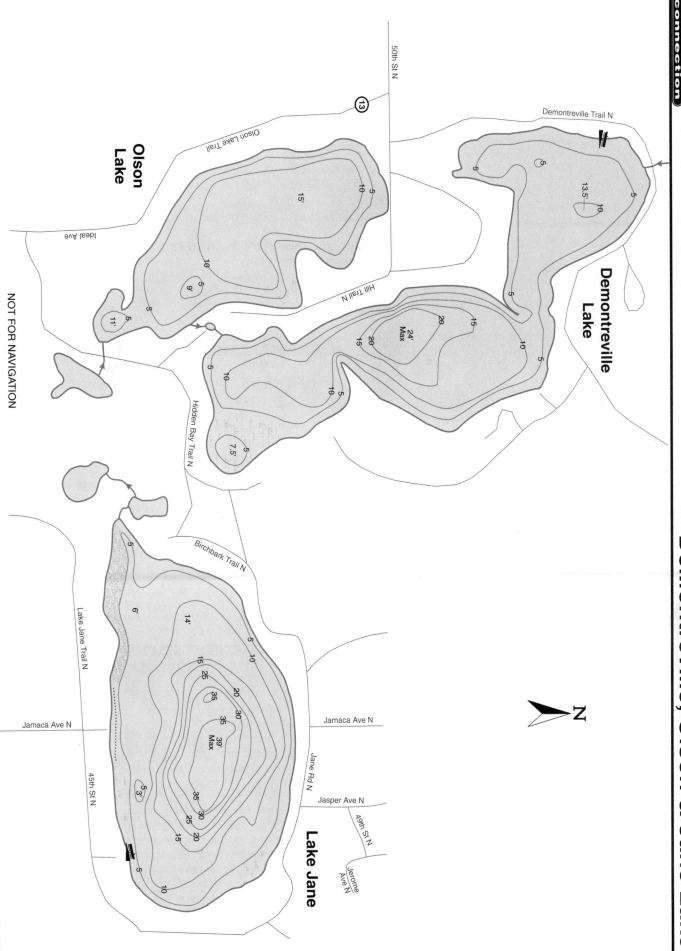

NOT FOR NAVIGATION

50th St N

(13)

Olson Lake Trail

Olson Lake

Ideal Ave

15'

10
5

10

9'
5

11'
5
5

Demontreville Trail N

Demontreville Lake

5
5
5
13.5'
10
5
5
10

Hill Trail N

24' Max
20
15
20
15
10
5

Hidden Bay Trail N

10
5
10
5
7.5'
5

Birchbark Trail N

5

Lake Jane Trail N

6'

14'
5
10
15
25
35
20
30
35
39' Max
35
30
25
20
15
10
5
5'
3'

Jamaca Ave N

Jamaca Ave N

Jane Rd N

Jasper Ave N

49th St N

Jerome Ave N

45th St N

Lake Jane

N

BONE LAKE
Washington County

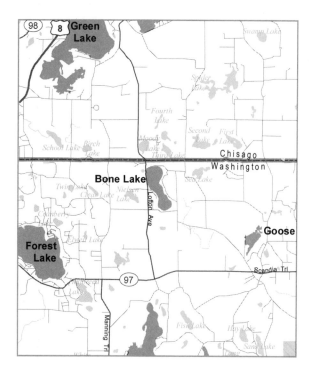

Area map pg / coord: 29 / A-4
Watershed: Lower St. Croix
Secchi disk: 3.9 feet (2012)
Water color: Green

Surface area: 221 acres
Shorelength: 2.9 miles
Maximum depth: 30 feet
Mean depth: 14 feet

Accessibility: State-owned public access on north shore
Boat ramp: Concrete
Parking: Twelve trailer spaces
Accommodations: Shore fishing

Shoreland zoning classification: Recreational development
Management class: Centrarchid
Ecological type: Centrarchid

FISH STOCKING DATA			
year	species	size	# released
08	Walleye	Fingerling	1,413
09	Walleye	Fingerling	8,764
09	Walleye	Yearling	22
10	Walleye	Fingerling	3,312
11	Walleye	Fingerling	4,874
12	Black Crappie	Adult	75
12	Walleye	Fingerling	7,580

FISHING INFORMATION: At 221 acres, Bone Lake is a nice-sized impoundment with good offerings. It has a maximum depth of 30 feet, which makes for less vertical space for walleyes to suspend. The water clarity is 3.5 feet.

Bone Lake's reputation is for bluegills, and for good reason. The 2006 DNR survey shows they are above average in abundance and size. Of the bluegills caught, the average fish was 6.7 inches and weighed 0.31 pounds. Take the kids here for a fun time bobber fishing with nightcrawlers, wax worms or red worms. The west bank is best for crappies. Start with a small minnow on a hook, getting as close into the weeds as you can. Use a bobber to keep your minnow from burying into the weeds. In summer, drift with the wind along the middle of the lake where deeper holes are found. In addition to using minnows, try a small leech to fool a few crappies. Bone Lake crappies are abundant, with an average size of 7.1 inches and a weight of 0.20 pounds. Early in the year, when bluegills are in the shallows, try your luck with a fly rod. Small ant or grasshoppers patterns can draw strikes from a bluegill or two. You can also aggravate them into striking when they're on their spawning beds by dropping a small popper directly over them. The strikes can be vicious.

The DNR has been stocking Bone Lake with walleye fingerlings on a regular basis since 1982, and this effort is paying off. The average walleye sampled in 2006 was 14.45 inches and weighed 1.35 pounds. A small sand bar on the east shore at mid-lake is a good place to find walleyes in spring. Retrieve a jig with a minnow to attract them. You can also try vertical jigging with a minnow along the drop-offs at the southeast and northwest corners of the lake. In the summer months, switch to leeches and crawlers to attract the most walleyes. Trolling with a spinner rig tipped with a leech or crawler can produce, as will a stickbait or crankbait trolled along weed edges. If you want a more relaxed approach, try a slip bobber and bait fished along the inside and outside turns of the deep weedline. A jumbo leech will be your best offering.

There's a Washington County-owned public access site with a

NET CATCH DATA				
Date: 05/07/2012	Gill Nets		Trap Nets	
species	# per net	avg. fish weight (lbs.)	# per net	avg. fish weight (lbs.)
Black Bullhead	-	-	0.8	trace
Black Crappie	1.5	0.17	31.4	0.27
Bluegill	2.8	0.16	7.2	0.21
Hybrid Sunfish	0.2	0.13	0.2	0.24
Northern Pike	4.3	6.3	0.3	11.01
Pumpkin. Sunfish	-	-	0.1	0.04
Walleye	1.3	0.77	0.2	trace
Yellow Bullhead	0.2	1.45	3.2	trace
Yellow Perch	51.5	0.11	0.3	trace

LENGTH OF SELECTED SPECIES SAMPLED FROM ALL GEAR								
Number of fish caught for the following length categories (inches):								
species	0-5	6-8	9-11	12-14	15-19	20-24	25-29	>30	Total
Black Bullhead	-	-	-	-	-	-	-	-	8
Black Crappie	2	269	47	-	-	-	-	-	323
Bluegill	26	63	-	-	-	-	-	-	89
Hybrid Sunfish	1	2	-	-	-	-	-	-	3
Northern Pike	-	-	-	-	-	7	10	12	29
Walleye	-	1	5	1	-	1	-	-	10
Yellow Bullhead	-	-	-	1	-	-	-	-	1
Yellow Perch	7	231	1	-	-	-	-	-	312

concrete ramp on the north shore, off 238th Street.

The lake is not deep, but the bottom drops away quickly beyond the vegetation, providing good structure. For northerns, try trolling those outside weed edges in spring around 10 feet down or offer a sucker minnow under a bobber. Casting a flashy lure will also draw strikes. A chrome Rat-L-Trap is a good crankbait to try. Spinnerbaits and spoons will also catch their fair share of pike. Later in the summer, fishing along the outside edges of submerged weeds with a buzzbait both early and late in the day can produce some explosive strikes. Make sure you place a steel leader on your line to prevent pike from slicing through it.

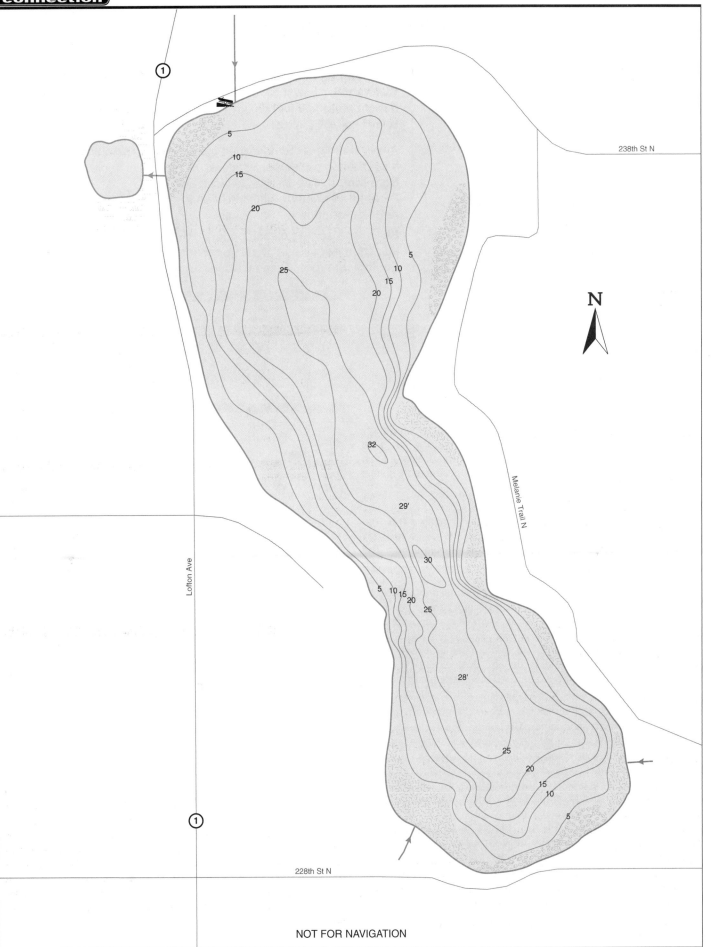

238th St N

N

Melanie Trail N

Lofton Ave

228th St N

NOT FOR NAVIGATION

Source: Minnesota Department of Natural Resources, USGS

171

© Copyright Sportsman's Connection. All Rights Reserved.

BIG MARINE LAKE
Washington County

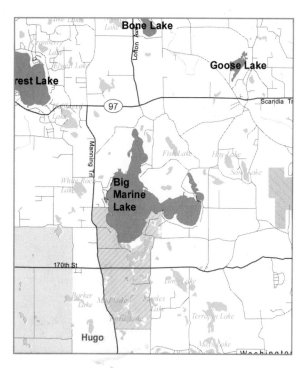

Area map pg / coord: 29 / B-4
Watershed: Lower St. Croix
Secchi disk: 8.5 feet (2008)
Water color: Light green

Surface area: 1,799 acres
Shorelength: 13.0 miles
Maximum depth: 60 feet
Mean depth: NA

Accessibility: 1) State-owned public access on north shore of north bay; 2) State-owned public access on southeast shore of south bay
Boat ramp: 1) Concrete; 2) Concrete
Parking: 1) Twenty-eight trailer spaces; 2) Eight trailer spaces
Accommodations: Shore fishing

Shoreland zoning classification: Recreational development
Management class: Walleye-centrarchid
Ecological type: Centrarchid-walleye

FISH STOCKING DATA

year	species	size	# released
10	Walleye	Fry	3,600,000
10	Walleye	Fingerling	22,630
10	Walleye	Yearling	380
11	Walleye	Yearling	240
12	Walleye	Fingerling	45,720
12	Walleye	Adult	10

NET CATCH DATA

Date: 08/04/2008

species	Gill Nets # per net	Gill Nets avg. fish weight (lbs.)	Trap Nets # per net	Trap Nets avg. fish weight (lbs.)
Black Crappie	7.4	0.13	4.9	0.46
Bluegill	5.0	0.13	48.4	0.15
Hybrid Sunfish	-	-	2.2	-
Largemouth Bass	2.8	1.02	0.7	-
Northern Pike	16.4	1.72	0.9	-
Pumpkin. Sunfish	0.8	0.07	1.7	-
Walleye	2.4	2.55	0.1	-
Yellow Perch	-	-	0.2	-

LENGTH OF SELECTED SPECIES SAMPLED FROM ALL GEAR
Number of fish caught for the following length categories (inches):

species	0-5	6-8	9-11	12-14	15-19	20-24	25-29	>30	Total
Black Crappie	39	49	42	3	-	-	-	-	133
Bluegill	342	417	-	-	-	-	-	-	766
Hybrid Sunfish	-	-	-	-	-	-	-	-	33
Largemouth Bass	1	6	3	8	4	-	-	-	32
Northern Pike	-	-	-	3	69	52	5	2	144
Pumpkin. Sunfish	5	1	-	-	-	-	-	-	32
Walleye	-	-	2	5	3	8	1	-	20
Yellow Bullhead	-	1	12	17	1	-	-	-	67
Yellow Perch	-	-	-	-	-	-	-	-	3

FISHING INFORMATION: This is another of the Washington County lakes with a great reputation for largemouth bass. It also has good numbers of walleyes, northern pike and panfish. In addition, it is an interesting lake to fish, full of small bays, points, good weeds, humps and holes.

Brad Dusenka of Frankie's Live Bait & Tackle, 10680 South Ave., Chisago City, MN, (651) 257-6334, says this is primarily a weedline lake, and "what looks good is good." He says the lake's east bay is a good area to start looking for largemouth bass in spring. The south shore of the bay is loaded with bulrushes that are loaded with largemouths. Flip soft plastics like tubes, lizards, worms or creature baits into rushes, or cast crankbaits or spinnerbaits into pockets. You'll also find crappies, walleyes and nice numbers of good-size bluegills in these areas, says Dusenka. There is a nice, reedy point at the top of the main bay where you can do well, and the far north end can be productive. Try a jig and creature bait or tube in reeds. Largemouth bass were found to be abundant, according to the DNR. Local anglers report good catches of largemouth bass here. The DNR plans more intensive sampling to better understand the population.

There are a lot of little northerns in Big Marine, and the east bay is a good place to start searching for them. Fish weeds at the east shore and in the narrows connecting the bays. Don't overlook the stump areas on the northwest corner of the main bay. Fire out spinnerbaits, jerkbaits, both hard and soft, or fish a large minnow with or without a bobber. Later in the season, troll outside of these weedlines with colorful spoons and crankbaits. Northern pike abundance is high, according to DNR statistics. The numbers are above average for this type of lake. Lake conditions are good for high pike reproduction. The average pike in the lake measure just under 20 inches long and weigh 1.72 pounds. During the 2008 DNR survey, two pike exceeding 30 inches were netted.

The walleyes here are in predictable areas, such as around the island in the main bay, the point on the north side of the channel into the east bay and the bar on the west shore of the main lake at the entrance into the small north arm. Troll crankbaits or spinner rigs or try pitching jigs tipped with bait. Fish the sandy bottoms with a Lindy rig and a shiner minnow in spring or at the nice breaks off the east-shore access site in fall. During the most recent DNR survey, walleyes were sampled in numbers within the average for this lake type. Walleyes average 18.24 inches in length and weigh 2.55 pounds.

Panfish are also available in Big Marine. Bluegills are the most abundant species in the lake. The DNR survey showed their numbers in the normal range for this type of lake. Black crappie numbers are variable. Crappies frequently have boom-and-bust cycles in this lake. The latest DNR assessment found crappies in good abundance and size. The average length was 9.28 inches, but some crappies longer than 12 inches were sampled. Basics are best for bluegills. Fish shallow weedlines and other available cover. Float a small leech, chunk of crawler or a wax worm under a bobber to take these abundant and tasty fish. Crappie anglers can try their luck on deeper weedlines with a slip float and a minnow or small leech.

Big Marine Lake

Fish Lake

N

NOT FOR NAVIGATION

173

SQUARE LAKE
Washington County

Bordered by Square Lake County Park

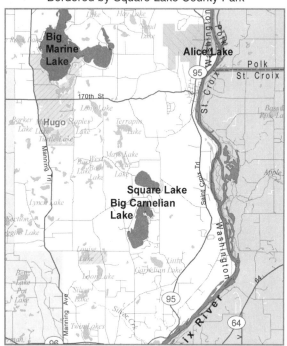

Area map pg / coord: 29 / C-4,5
Watershed: Lower St. Croix
Secchi disk: 16 feet (2008)
Water color: Clear

Surface area: 203 acres
Shorelength: NA
Maximum depth: 68 feet
Mean depth: NA

Accessibility: County-owned public access on east shore in park
Boat ramp: Concrete
Parking: Ten trailer spaces
Accommodations: Park, fishing pier, boat/motor rental, canoe rental, camping, picnicking, restrooms

Shoreland zoning classification: Recreational development
Management class: Trout
Ecological type: Centrarchid

FISH STOCKING DATA

year	species	size	# released
07	Rainbow Trout	Yearling	4,800
08	Rainbow Trout	Yearling	5,000
09	Rainbow Trout	Yearling	4,890
10	Rainbow Trout	Yearling	5,110
11	Rainbow Trout	Yearling	4,997
12	Rainbow Trout	Yearling	2,450

NET CATCH DATA

Date: 08/11/2008

species	Gill Nets # per net	Gill Nets avg. fish weight (lbs.)	Trap Nets # per net	Trap Nets avg. fish weight (lbs.)
Black Bullhead	0.2	0.37	-	-
Black Crappie	0.5	0.35	0.8	0.24
Bluegill	6.7	0.31	9.2	0.17
Green Sunfish	-	-	0.1	0.25
Hybrid Sunfish	-	-	2.7	0.28
Largemouth Bass	0.5	0.42	-	-
Northern Pike	3.8	1.84	1.3	0.55
Pumpkin. Sunfish	0.5	0.34	1.2	0.22
Yellow Bullhead	8.5	0.73	1.3	0.64
Yellow Perch	2.0	0.43		

LENGTH OF SELECTED SPECIES SAMPLED FROM ALL GEAR

Number of fish caught for the following length categories (inches):

species	0-5	6-8	9-11	12-14	15-19	20-24	25-29	>30	Total
Black Bullhead	-	-	1	-	-	-	-	-	1
Black Crappie	-	9	1	-	-	-	-	-	10
Bluegill	33	90	-	-	-	-	-	-	123
Green Sunfish	-	1	-	-	-	-	-	-	1
Hybrid Sunfish	5	18	1	-	-	-	-	-	24
Largemouth Bass	-	-	3	-	-	-	-	-	3
Northern Pike	-	-	2	20	10	-	1	2	35
Pumpkin. Sunfish	3	11	-	-	-	-	-	-	14
Yellow Bullhead	-	7	33	22	1	-	-	-	63
Yellow Perch	-	1	11	-	-	-	-	-	12

FISHING INFORMATION: This clear lake is home to, among other species, rainbow trout. This exotic is here courtesy of the DNR, which stocks 5,000 rainbows each year. The DNR stocks 3,000 rainbow trout in spring and 2,000 in fall. Square Lake is a fairly deep, spring-fed, cold body of water without too many predators to take out young trout. Trout inhabit deep waters. In shallower water, there is also a solid fishery, consisting of largemouth bass, some fair-size bluegills, crappies and northern pike. According to the latest DNR survey, Square Lake had the best water quality of any lake in the Twin Cities metro area.

The north part of the lake is considered best for trout early in the season, before the water warms. You can troll there, but be mindful that trout are easily spooked. Small spinners and spoons are excellent choices for trolling. Also try small crankbaits like Flatfish or some crappie-sized crankbaits. Stick with natural colors, though a little orange or chartreuse seems to trigger a few bites during cloudy weather. If you prefer to still-fish in the shallows, try a plain hook baited with a small crawler, salmon eggs, corn or Power Bait. As water warms over 50 degrees, trout will go deeper and you will have to change techniques. That's the time of year to fish over 30- or 40-foot bottoms, with deep-diving lures or weighted trolling rigs like cowbells or dodgers. Use your electronics to locate the thermocline and add enough weight to keep your offering above it to attract trout.

Don't forget bass; they can get fairly big here. According to the latest DNR survey, the largemouth bass population is average for this type of lake. You'll find them at limited weedy areas along the northeast shoreline. Be aware of special regulations before fishing. Since the water is clear, consider using finesse tactics or fish for bass strictly in the early morning or at dusk. Using live bait is also a good idea when fishing for bass in clear water.

Bluegills were the most abundant species in the lake, according to the DNR. Although not as abundant as some other lakes, the quality of bluegills in Square Lake is good. When the DNR last surveyed the lake, more than 60% of the bluegills sampled exceeded

6 inches in length.

There are speed limits on Square Lake. There is a restricted speed zone from the 40-foot depth contour toward the shoreline and an open speed zone from the 40-foot depth contour toward the center of the lake. The 40-foot depth contour is marked with buoys. In the restricted zone, the speed limit is 5 mph at all times. The open speed zone has no speed limit from noon to 6 p.m. on weekdays, and noon to 4 p.m. on weekends and holidays. At all other times, a 5 mph speed limit is enforced. During open speed hours, watercraft must travel in a counterclockwise direction.

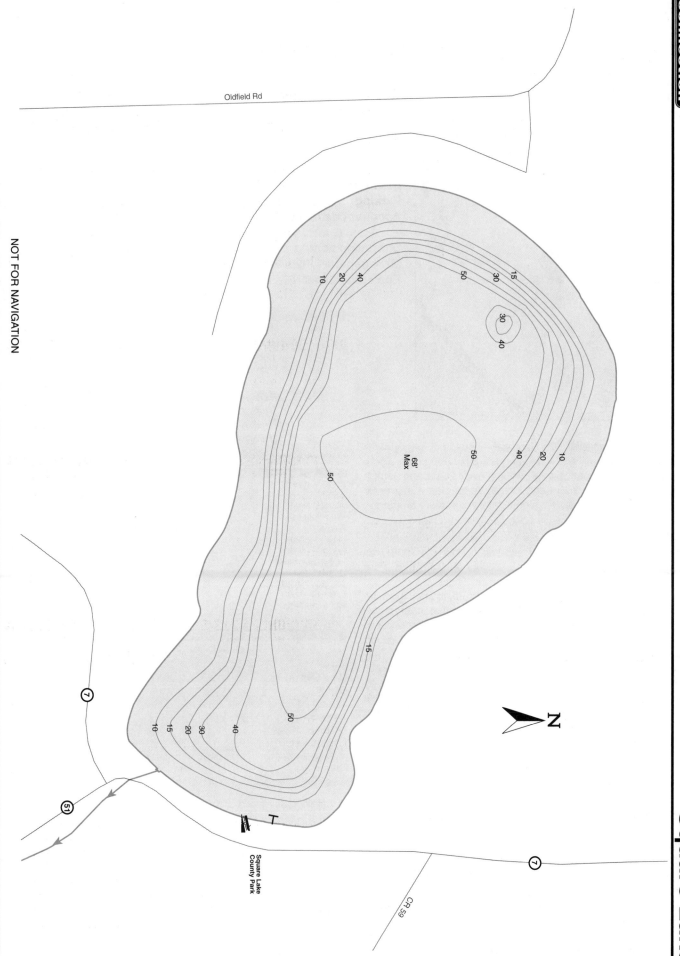

Oldfield Rd

NOT FOR NAVIGATION

N

Square Lake
County Park

Square Lake

BIG CARNELIAN LAKE
Washington County

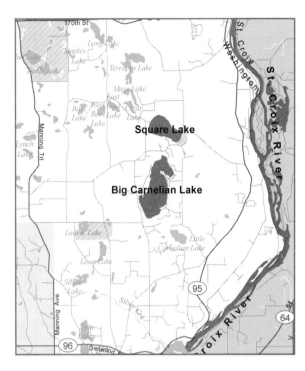

Area map pg / coord: 29 / C-5
Watershed: Lower St. Croix
Secchi disk: 24.5 feet (2009)
Water color: Green tint

Surface area: 457 acres
Shorelength: NA
Maximum depth: 66 feet
Mean depth: NA

Accessibility: State-owned public access on southwest shore
Boat ramp: Concrete
Parking: Fourteen trailer spaces
Accommodations: Shore fishing

Shoreland zoning classification: Recreational development
Management class: Centrarchid
Ecological type: Centrarchid

FISH STOCKING DATA

year	species	size	# released
09	Walleye	Fingerling	10,228
09	Walleye	Yearling	8
10	Walleye	Fingerling	5,096
10	Walleye	Yearling	145
10	Walleye	Adult	6
11	Walleye	Fingerling	8,662
11	Walleye	Yearling	12
12	Walleye	Fingerling	8,262
12	Walleye	Adult	18

NET CATCH DATA

Date: 07/27/2009

	Gill Nets		Trap Nets	
species	# per net	avg. fish weight (lbs.)	# per net	avg. fish weight (lbs.)
Black Crappie	0.7	0.33	1.7	0.32
Bluegill	10.7	0.19	19.9	0.11
Green Sunfish	-	-	0.3	0.03
Hybrid Sunfish	-	-	4.2	0.22
Largemouth Bass	0.9	1.38	0.4	0.12
Northern Pike	11.4	1.65	1.1	0.98
Pumpkin. Sunfish	1.0	0.2	1.1	0.21
Walleye	1.4	2.36	0.1	0.14
Yellow Bullhead	0.4	0.75	0.7	0.40
Yellow Perch	0.3	0.09	1.4	0.13

LENGTH OF SELECTED SPECIES SAMPLED FROM ALL GEAR

Number of fish caught for the following length categories (inches):

species	0-5	6-8	9-11	12-14	15-19	20-24	25-29	>30	Total
Black Crappie	1	14	5	-	-	-	-	-	20
Bluegill	175	75	4	-	-	-	-	-	254
Green Sunfish	3	-	-	-	-	-	-	-	3
Hybrid Sunfish	19	19	-	-	-	-	-	-	38
Largemouth Bass	2	2	1	5	-	-	-	-	10
Northern Pike	-	-	3	9	57	10	9	2	90
Pumpkin. Sunfish	8	9	-	-	-	-	-	-	17
Walleye	-	1	-	2	4	4	-	-	11
Yellow Perch	5	9	1	-	-	-	-	-	15

FISHING INFORMATION: Big Carnelian Lake is not as big as its name might elude, having a surface area around 450 acres. There is an abundance of aquatic plants, which provides bass and panfish with plenty of places to roam and forage. Water clarity is over 20 feet, which can make for some good sight fishing closer to shore.

Big Carnelian is almost synonymous with big northern pike. The 2003 DNR survey showed the highest gill net catch rate ever observed for this lake, and the latest sampling, done in 2009, was only down slightly from those numbers. Northerns are by far the most abundant predator species in this lake. There is a protected slot limit on northerns, and fish from 24 to 36 inches must be released. The good news is that the average northern caught during the 2009 survey was 18.65 inches and 1.65 pounds, making all of those fish keepers. You can keep one pike measuring over 36 inches. Northerns can be found early in the season in Stump Bay. Work the weeds there for some fast action. Northerns are in plenty of other places around the lake, too, including the small bay on the west shore near the access point, off the point at the northeast corner and around the sunken island in the south bay. Use suckers and spinnerbaits. In summer, troll the outside edges of weedlines around the east and south shores.

Catch largemouth bass in spring with a variety of techniques. Cast into pockets along weedlines with a jig and soft plastic bait or hang live bait under a bobber over submerged weeds. The sunken island at the south end of the lake can also be productive. During summer, use a topwater in the weedlines for your chance at a monster bass. Don't set the hook until you feel the bass tug your line; yanking it too soon will mean you only get to watch the water boil and don't get to enjoy a fight.

You might encounter decent-sized walleyes off the points. Fingerlings have been stocked here every year since 2001. Despite the stocking efforts, the 2009 DNR survey showed walleye to remain in the normal range for abundance. The average size sampled was 18 inches and 2.4 pounds. Think light line and live bait when attempting to boat a few walleyes. Use a split shot and

a small hook tipped with a nightcrawler or leech and drift along deeper weed edges or fish that same rig under a slip bobber.

Crappies, perch and bluegills were listed as average in abundance and small to average in size. Panfish are usually in the weeds early. Good places to find them are up in Stump Bay and around the point off the southeast shore. After they have spawned, you can find crappies in most of the lake's weedy areas. Live bait and bobbers are a good mix for catching panfish. Small worms and leeches will catch all species and minnows will lure strikes from crappies and perch. There is public access with a concrete ramp, a boat dock and 14 parking spaces in the southwest corner of the lake.

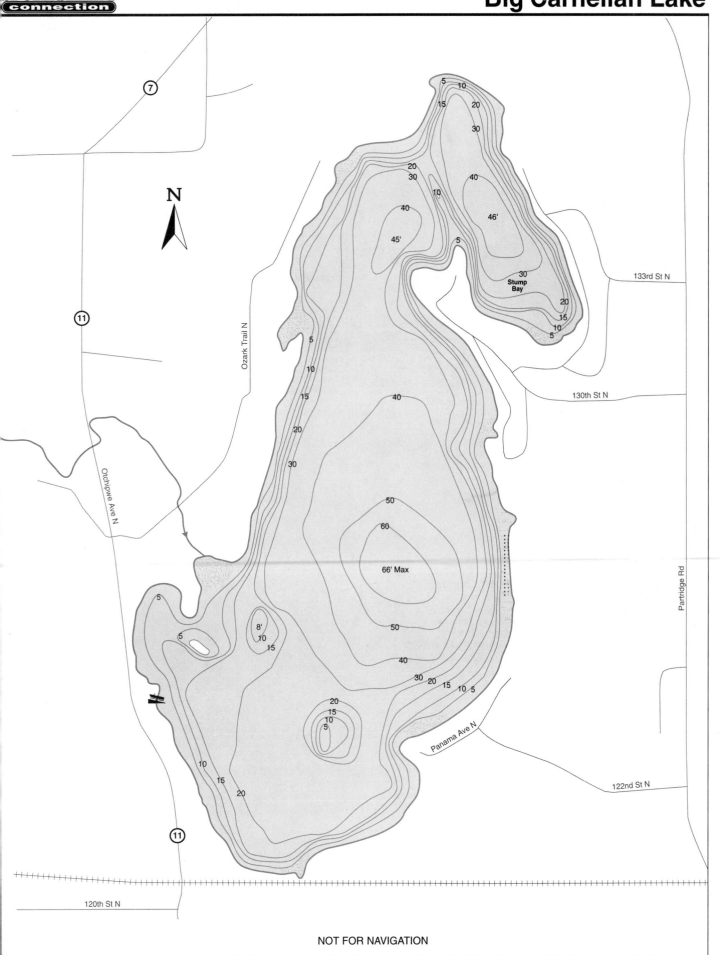

NOT FOR NAVIGATION

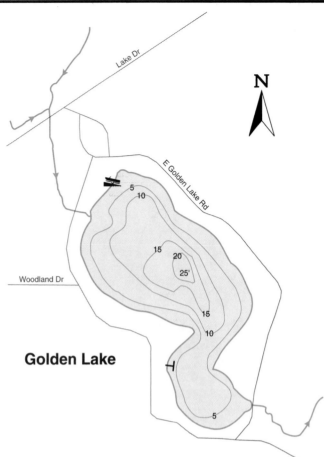

Golden Lake

N

5
10
15
20
25'
15
10
15
5

Lake Dr
E Golden Lake Rd
Woodland Dr

Golden Lake, Anoka County
Bordered by Golden Lake Park

Map pg/coord: 28 / C-1	**Surface area:** 58 acres
Watershed: Twin Cities	**Shorelength:** NA
Mgmt. classification:	**Max depth:** 25 feet
Centrarchid	**Water clarity:** 6.0 (2007)

Accessibility: City-owned public access (fee) with concrete ramp on west shore (electric motors only); parking for ten trailers
Accommodations: Park, fishing pier

FISH STOCKING DATA

year	species	size	# released
06	Channel Catfish	Yearling	2,062
07	Walleye	Fry	102,000
07	Channel Catfish	Yearling	3,004
08	Channel Catfish	Yearling	1,532
09	Walleye	Fry	110,000
09	Channel Catfish	Yearling	1,538
11	Walleye	Fry	102,000
12	Walleye	Fry	102,000

LENGTH OF SELECTED SPECIES SAMPLED FROM ALL GEAR
Survey Date: 6/18/07
Number of fish caught for the following length categories (inches):

species	0-5	6-8	9-11	12-14	15-19	20-24	25-29	>30	Total
Black Bullhead	2	1	19	-	-	-	-	-	22
Black Crappie	6	203	1	-	-	-	-	-	210
Bluegill	344	354	-	-	-	-	-	-	704
Channel Catfish	-	-	-	-	-	4	2	-	6
Hybrid Sunfish	2	1	-	-	-	-	-	-	3
Largemouth Bass	1	1	1	-	-	-	-	-	3
Northern Pike	-	-	-	-	3	6	11	-	20
Pumpkin. Sunfish	1	3	-	-	-	-	-	-	4
Walleye	-	-	-	-	-	2	-	-	2

Otter Lake, Ramsey & Anoka Counties
Bordered by Otter Lake County Park

Map pg/coord: 28 / C,D-2,3	**Surface area:** 302 acres
Watershed: Twin Cities	**Shorelength:** 4.2 miles
Mgmt. classification:	**Max depth:** 21 feet
Centrarchid	**Water clarity:** 15.5 feet (2007)

Accessibility: County-owned public access with concrete ramp on southwest shore in park; parking for ten trailers (small boats)
Accommodations: Park

FISH STOCKING DATA

year	species	size	# released
11	Largemouth Bass	Adult	60
11	Walleye	Fry	450,000

LENGTH OF SELECTED SPECIES SAMPLED FROM ALL GEAR
Survey Date: 6/11/07
Number of fish caught for the following length categories (inches):

species	0-5	6-8	9-11	12-14	15-19	20-24	25-29	>30	Total
Black Bullhead	-	61	6	-	-	-	-	-	67
Black Crappie	3	6	1	-	-	-	-	-	10
Bluegill	716	138	-	-	-	-	-	-	859
Green Sunfish	4	-	-	-	-	-	-	-	4
Hybrid Sunfish	7	3	-	-	-	-	-	-	10
Northern Pike	-	-	-	3	8	16	7	1	35
Pumpkin. Sunfish	16	12	-	-	-	-	-	-	28

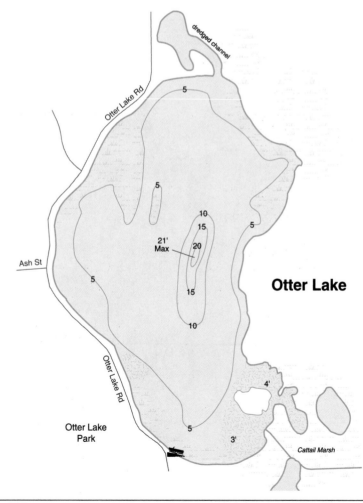

Otter Lake

dredged channel
5
5
10
15
5
21' Max
20
15
10
4'
5
3'
5
Otter Lake Rd
Ash St
Otter Lake Rd
Otter Lake Park
Cattail Marsh

NOT FOR NAVIGATION

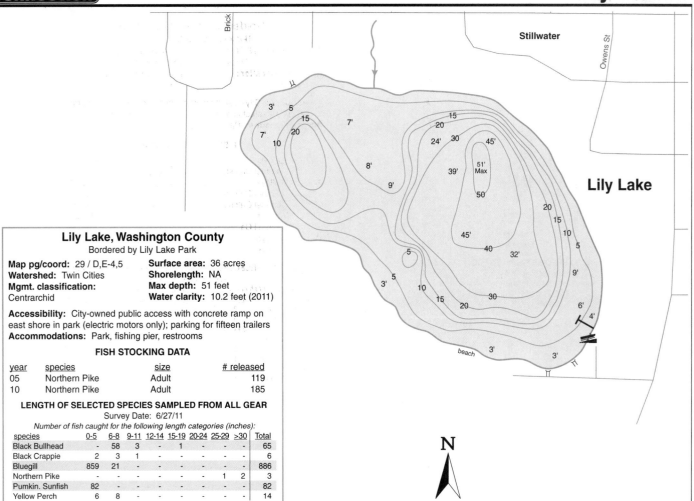

Lily Lake, Washington County
Bordered by Lily Lake Park

Map pg/coord: 29 / D,E-4,5	**Surface area:** 36 acres
Watershed: Twin Cities	**Shorelength:** NA
Mgmt. classification:	**Max depth:** 51 feet
Centrarchid	**Water clarity:** 10.2 feet (2011)

Accessibility: City-owned public access with concrete ramp on east shore in park (electric motors only); parking for fifteen trailers
Accommodations: Park, fishing pier, restrooms

FISH STOCKING DATA

year	species	size	# released
05	Northern Pike	Adult	119
10	Northern Pike	Adult	185

LENGTH OF SELECTED SPECIES SAMPLED FROM ALL GEAR
Survey Date: 6/27/11
Number of fish caught for the following length categories (inches):

species	0-5	6-8	9-11	12-14	15-19	20-24	25-29	>30	Total
Black Bullhead	-	58	3	-	1	-	-	-	65
Black Crappie	2	3	1	-	-	-	-	-	6
Bluegill	859	21	-	-	-	-	-	-	886
Northern Pike	-	-	-	-	-	-	1	2	3
Pumkin. Sunfish	82	-	-	-	-	-	-	-	82
Yellow Perch	6	8	-	-	-	-	-	-	14

Silver Lake, Anoka & Ramsey Counties

Map pg/coord: 28 / E-1	**Surface area:** 71 acres
Mgmt. classification:	**Max depth:** 47 feet
NA	**Water clarity:** 3.75 feet (2006)

Accessibility: City-owned public access with earthen ramp on southwest shore / **Accommodations:** Shore fishing

FISH STOCKING DATA

year	species	size	# released
08	Channel Catfish	Yearling	1,937
08	Walleye	Fry	126,000
09	Yellow Perch	Adult	1,618
09	Walleye	Fry	150,000
10	Walleye	Fry	490,000
12	Walleye	Fry	140,000

LENGTH OF SELECTED SPECIES SAMPLED FROM ALL GEAR
Survey Date: 7/10/06
Number of fish caught for the following length categories (inches):

species	0-5	6-8	9-11	12-14	15-19	20-24	25-29	>30	Total
Black Crappie	322	172	-	-	-	-	-	-	499
Bluegill	1280	150	-	-	-	-	-	-	1434
Channel Catfish	-	-	-	3	1	-	-	-	4
Hybrid Sunfish	12	6	-	-	-	-	-	-	18
Northern Pike	-	-	-	-	-	-	1	-	1
Pumkin. Sunfish	40	-	-	-	-	-	-	-	40
Walleye	-	-	-	-	2	6	1	-	9
Yellow Perch	7	-	-	-	-	-	-	-	7

NOT FOR NAVIGATION

Bennett Lake, Ramsey County

Map pg/coord: 28 / E-1,2   **Max depth:** 9 feet
Surface area: 28 acres   **Water clarity:** 3.0 feet (2006)

Accessibility: Fishing pier
Accommodations: Fishing pier

FISH STOCKING DATA

year	species	size	# released
07	Channel Catfish	Yearling	2,076
07	Largemouth Bass	Yearling	675
07	Bluegill	Adult	151
07	Black Crappie	Adult	92
08	Channel Catfish	Yearling	1,140
08	Bluegill	Adult	357
09	Bluegill	Adult	343
10	Bluegill	Adult	178
10	Channel Catfish	Yearling	1,110
10	Walleye	Fingerling	240
10	Walleye	Yearling	16
11	Walleye	Fingerling	1,098

LENGTH OF SELECTED SPECIES SAMPLED FROM ALL GEAR
Survey Date: 6/7/06
Number of fish caught for the following length categories (inches):

species	0-5	6-8	9-11	12-14	15-19	20-24	25-29	>30	Total
Black Bullhead	2	-	4	-	-	-	-	-	6
Black Crappie	22	2	-	-	-	-	-	-	24
Bluegill	686	27	-	-	-	-	-	-	719
Golden Shiner	-	19	-	-	-	-	-	-	19
Green Sunfish	6	-	-	-	-	-	-	-	6
Hybrid Sunfish	42	-	-	-	-	-	-	-	42
Northern Pike	-	-	-	1	6	3	2	-	12
Pumpkin. Sunfish	55	-	-	-	-	-	-	-	55
Walleye	-	1	2	-	-	-	-	-	3

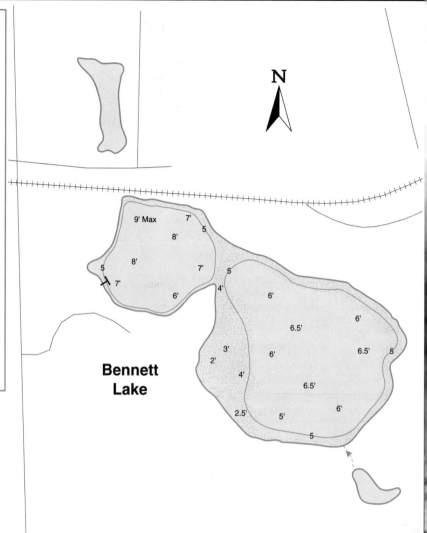

Bennett Lake

Langton Lake

Langton Lake, Ramsey County
Located in Roseville City Park

Map pg/coord: 28 / E-1   **Max depth:** 5 feet
Surface area: 30 acres   **Water clarity:** 4.5 feet (2000)

Accessibility: Shore fishing in park surrounding lake
Accommodations: Park, fishing pier

FISH STOCKING DATA

year	species	size	# released
06	Bluegill	Adult	1,005
06	Black Crappie	Adult	1,747
07	Bluegill	Adult	1,191
07	Black Crappie	Adult	1,692
08	Bluegill	Adult	1,240
09	Bluegill	Adult	827
10	Bluegill	Adult	1,110
11	Black Crappie	Adult	270
11	Bluegill	Adult	584
12	Black Crappie	Adult	20
12	Bluegill	Adult	219

LENGTH OF SELECTED SPECIES SAMPLED FROM ALL GEAR
Survey Date: 6/14/00
Number of fish caught for the following length categories (inches):

species	0-5	6-8	9-11	12-14	15-19	20-24	25-29	>30	Total
Black Bullhead	53	18	-	-	-	-	-	-	71
Bluegill	14	81	-	-	-	-	-	-	95
Hybrid Sunfish	8	3	-	-	-	-	-	-	11
Pumpkin. Sunfish	-	2	-	-	-	-	-	-	2

NOT FOR NAVIGATION

Loeb (Marydale) Lake, Ramsey County
Located in Marydale Park

Map pg/coord: 30 / A-1,2 **Max depth:** 28 feet
Surface area: 8 acres **Water clarity:** 6.5 feet (2006)

Accessibility: Shore fishing and fishing pier access in park
Accommodations: Park, fishing pier, shore fishing

FISH STOCKING DATA

year	species	size	# released
08	Black Crappie	Adult	244
08	Bluegill	Adult	380
08	Channel Catfish	Yearling	1,290
09	Channel Catfish	Yearling	622
09	Channel Catfish	Adult	47
09	Bluegill	Adult	106
09	Black Crappie	Adult	207
10	Bluegill	Adult	74
10	Channel Catfish	Yearling	1,211
10	Channel Catfish	Adult	50
11	Channel Catfish	Yearling	3,900
11	Channel Catfish	Adult	124
11	Walleye	Fingerling	3,593

LENGTH OF SELECTED SPECIES SAMPLED FROM ALL GEAR
Survey Date: 7/20/06
Number of fish caught for the following length categories (inches):

species	0-5	6-8	9-11	12-14	15-19	20-24	25-29	>30	Total
Black Bullhead	-	1	8	-	-	-	-	-	9
Black Crappie	1	6	-	-	-	-	-	-	7
Bluegill	32	16	-	-	-	-	-	-	48
Hybrid Sunfish	23	3	-	-	-	-	-	-	26
Largemouth Bass	-	1	-	-	-	-	-	-	1
Pumpkin. Sunfish	4	2	-	-	-	-	-	-	6
White Sucker	-	-	-	-	1	-	-	-	1

Loeb Lake

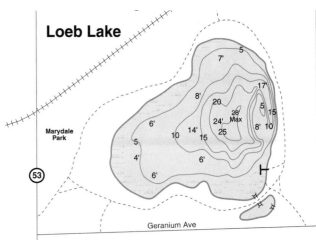

Marydale Park

Como Lake

Como Lake, Ramsey County
Located in Como Park

Map pg/coord: 30 / A-1,2 **Max depth:** 15.5 feet
Surface area: 68 acres **Water clarity:** 2.2 feet (2011)

Accessibility: Carry-down access in park
Accommodations: Park, fishing pier

FISH STOCKING DATA

year	species	size	# released
10	Bluegill	Adult	24
10	Channel Catfish	Yearling	3,900
10	Channel Catfish	Adult	91
10	Walleye	Yearling	4
11	Channel Catfish	Yearling	3,900
11	Channel Catfish	Adult	124
11	Walleye	Fingerling	3,593

LENGTH OF SELECTED SPECIES SAMPLED FROM ALL GEAR
Survey Date: 8/01/11
Number of fish caught for the following length categories (inches):

species	0-5	6-8	9-11	12-14	15-19	20-24	25-29	>30	Total
Black Bullhead	-	50	20	1	-	-	-	-	71
Black Crappie	103	160	2	-	-	-	-	-	272
Bluegill	201	31	-	-	-	-	-	-	237
Northern Pike	-	-	-	-	3	35	10	1	49
Pumpkin. Sunfish	29	-	-	-	-	-	-	-	29
Walleye	-	-	-	-	3	2	-	-	5
Yellow Bullhead	-	23	9	1	-	-	-	-	33
Yellow Perch	10	5	-	-	-	-	-	-	15

Crosby Lake, Ramsey County

Map pg/coord: 30 / B-1,2 **Max depth:** 19 feet
Surface area: 48 acres **Water clarity:** 10.5 feet (2004)

Accessibility: Carry-down access and shore fishing in city park
Accommodations: Park, shore fishing

LENGTH OF SELECTED SPECIES SAMPLED FROM ALL GEAR
Survey Date: 6/21/04
Number of fish caught for the following length categories (inches):

species	0-5	6-8	9-11	12-14	15-19	20-24	25-29	>30	Total
Black Bullhead	-	1	4	-	-	-	-	-	5
Black Crappie	15	4	-	-	-	-	-	-	19
Bluegill	108	20	-	-	-	-	-	-	128
Hybrid Sunfish	8	2	-	-	-	-	-	-	10
Northern Pike	-	-	-	-	11	12	4	1	28
Pumpkin. Sunfish	59	1	-	-	-	-	-	-	60
Yellow Bullhead	-	3	-	-	-	-	-	-	3
Yellow Perch	-	2	-	-	-	-	-	-	2

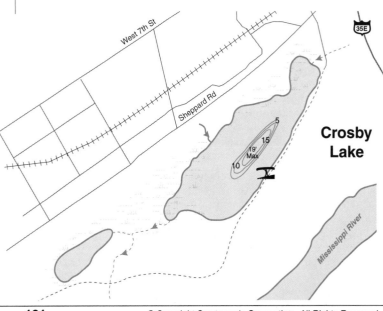

Crosby Lake

NOT FOR NAVIGATION

LAKE PHALEN
Ramsey County

Located in City of St. Paul Regional Park

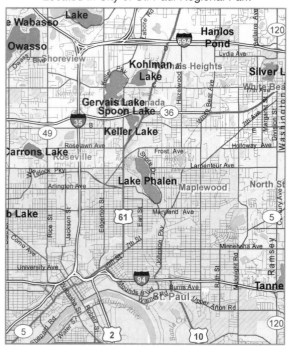

Area map pg / coord: 30 / A-2
Watershed: Twin Cities
Secchi disk: 17.2 feet (2009)
Water color: Light green

Surface area: 198 acres
Shorelength: 2.9 miles
Maximum depth: 91 feet
Mean depth: 20 feet

Accessibility: City-owned public access in park on northwest shore, south of inlet from Round Lake; water use regulations in effect
Boat ramp: Concrete
Parking: Twenty trailer spaces
Accommodations: Park, fishing pier, fishing platform, boat/motor rental, canoe rental, picnicking, restrooms

Shoreland zoning classification: Recreational development
Management class: Walleye-centrarchid
Ecological type: Centrarchid

FISH STOCKING DATA			
year	species	size	# released
07	Tiger Muskellunge	Fingerling	297
08	Walleye	Fingerling	17,153
08	Walleye	Yearling	9
09	Tiger Muskellunge	Fingerling	155
09	Tiger Muskellunge	Yearling	142
10	Walleye	Fingerling	12,640
11	Tiger Muskellunge	Fingerling	120
12	Walleye	Fingerling	12,130
12	Walleye	Adult	1

NET CATCH DATA				
Date: 06/15/2009	Gill Nets		Trap Nets	
species	# per net	avg. fish weight (lbs.)	# per net	avg. fish weight (lbs.)
Black Crappie	-	-	0.6	0.18
Bluegill	1.0	0.09	70.9	0.14
Common Carp	-	-	0.6	11.25
Green Sunfish	-	-	0.2	0.05
Hybrid Sunfish	-	-	0.7	0.10
Northern Pike	2.2	3.55	0.3	1.63
Pumpkin. Sunfish	-	-	1.6	0.10
Walleye	0.5	2.77	0.1	6.28
Yellow Bullhead	-	-	0.7	0.76
Yellow Perch	5.2	0.11	0.8	0.15

LENGTH OF SELECTED SPECIES SAMPLED FROM ALL GEAR								
Number of fish caught for the following length categories (inches):								
species	0-5	6-8	9-11	12-14	15-19	20-24	25-29	>30	Total
Black Crappie	-	5	-	-	-	-	-	-	5
Bluegill	392	248	-	-	-	-	-	-	644
Common Carp	-	-	-	-	-	1	2	2	5
Green Sunfish	2	-	-	-	-	-	-	-	2
Hybrid Sunfish	6	-	-	-	-	-	-	-	6
Northern Pike	6	-	-	-	-	-	-	-	6
Pumpkin. Sunfish	13	1	-	-	-	-	-	-	14
Walleye	-	-	-	-	1	2	1	-	4
Yellow Bullhead	-	-	6	-	-	-	-	-	6
Yellow Perch	12	25	1	-	-	-	-	-	38

FISHING INFORMATION: Phalen is a small, inner-city lake that offers good fishing for walleyes, largemouth bass and bluegills. There are northern pike, too, in moderate numbers, and the population includes some fish over 30 inches. This 198-acre lake is fairly deep, measuring 91 feet in spots. It has an abundance of aquatic plants. One of the bright aspects of Phalen is good shore fishing; so good, in fact, that the DNR estimates it accounts for approximately 90% of angling pressure.

Look for walleyes off Sandy Point on the east side. Another good area is the narrows just north of Sandy Point. You can find walleyes throughout the lake at various drop-offs and deep holes. Bump minnows or leeches along the bottom with a Lindy rig or drop a line under a slip bobber. The water in Phalen is very clear, so you don't have to show a lot of color to get attention. You might also work the channels to little Round Lake at the northwest corner. Later in the season when water is warm, walleyes will be suspended at deep holes in the north and south bays. Walleye numbers may be dwindling a bit, as the last two DNR surveys found low abundance of the species. Average size of walleyes caught were 19.9 inches and 2.8 pounds.

Crappies were sampled in low numbers, according to the survey. If you really want to fish for them, try the lagoon at the lake's northwest end; it's considered a hot spot in spring. Later, switch to the east and west shores of the south bay. Bluegills are far more abundant, although only 4% of fish captured were 7 inches or bigger. But if action is more important than size, then this is your bluegill lake.

Northerns and tiger muskies are found off the lake's points, particularly near the fishing pier in the north bay. Fishing the flats in the south bay between the deep hole and the shoreline can also be productive. No hybrid muskies were caught during the 2009 DNR survey, although they are stocked frequently. The average size of northerns was 18.7 inches and 1.7 pounds. They were sampled above a median level for abundance and have an average growth rate. Try casting white, black or chartreuse spinnerbaits or bucktails on flats for pike and muskies. Another option is to drift a bottom

bouncer with a large minnow on points to entice a strike from either species. This is particularly effective during fall when the weather starts to cool down.

There is public access with a concrete ramp on the northwest shore. You'll find handicapped-accessible fishing piers on the north and west sides. There are boat and canoe rentals at the Lakeside Activity Center on the west side. Use electric motors only.

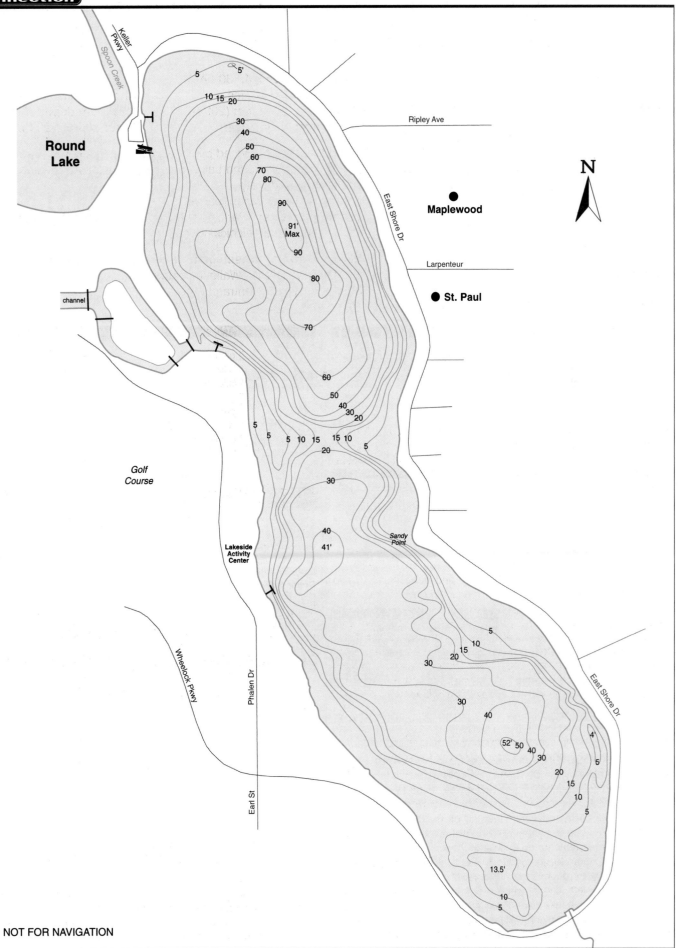

NOT FOR NAVIGATION

Source: Minnesota Department of Natural Resources, USGS

TANNERS LAKE

Bordered by Tanners Lake City Park

Area map page/coord: 30 / A,B-3
Watershed: Twin Cities
Surface area: 70 acres
Shorelength: NA
Maximum depth: 46 feet
Mean depth: NA
Secchi disk: 8.0 feet (2011)
Water color: NA
Accessibility: City-owned public access with concrete ramp on east shore in park; parking for ten trailers; 10 mph speed limit enforced on entire lake
Accommodations: Park, fishing pier, restrooms
Shoreland zoning: General dev.
Management class: Centrarchid
Ecological type: Centrarchid

Washington County

BATTLE CREEK LAKE

Bordered by Shawnee Park & Menomini Park

Area map page/coord: 30 / A,B-3
Watershed: Twin Cities
Surface area: 103 acres
Shorelength: NA
Maximum depth: 14 feet
Mean depth: NA
Secchi disk: 4.0 feet (2009)
Water color: NA
Accessibility: City-owned public access with concrete ramp on west shore; parking for two trailers
Accommodations: Park, fishing pier
Shoreland zoning: General dev.
Management class: Centrarchid
Ecological type: Centrarchid

FISH STOCKING DATA

year	species	size	# released
09	Channel Catfish	Yearling	1,685
09	Yellow Perch	Adult	1,224
10	Channel Catfish	Fingerling	6,604
10	Walleye	Fry	1,100,000
10	Walleye	Fingerling	4,908
10	Walleye	Yearling	130
12	Walleye	Fingerling	4,908
12	Walleye	Adult	4,908

NET CATCH DATA

Date: 08/01/2011

	Gill Nets		Trap Nets	
species	# per net	avg. fish weight (lbs.)	# per net	avg. fish weight (lbs.)
Black Crappie	-		3.0	0.14
Bluegill	2.0	0.20	13.8	0.12
Hybrid Sunfish	0.5	0.15	1.6	0.08
Northern Pike	5.5	2.92	0.5	2.11
Pumpkin. Sunfish	-	-	4.3	0.05
Walleye	-	-	0.3	0.27
Yellow Bullhead	-	-	2.4	0.73
Yellow Perch	5.5	0.11	0.1	0.10

LENGTH OF SELECTED SPECIES SAMPLED FROM ALL GEAR

Number of fish caught for the following length categories (inches):

species	0-5	6-8	9-11	12-14	15-19	20-24	25-29	>30	Total
Black Crappie	13	11	-	-	-	-	-	-	24
Bluegill	81	29	-	-	-	-	-	-	114
Hybrid Sunfish	13	1	-	-	-	-	-	-	14
Northern Pike	-	-	-	-	6	5	4	-	15
Pumpkin. Sunfish	34	-	-	-	-	-	-	-	34
Walleye	-	1	1	-	-	-	-	-	2
Yellow Bullhead	-	2	13	4	-	-	-	-	19
Yellow Perch	3	9	-	-	-	-	-	-	12

FISH STOCKING DATA

year	species	size	# released
07	Black Crappie	Fingerling	45,234

NET CATCH DATA

Date: 08/24/2009

	Gill Nets		Trap Nets	
species	# per net	avg. fish weight (lbs.)	# per net	avg. fish weight (lbs.)
Black Crappie	1.0	0.07	2.6	0.16
Bluegill	6.0	0.13	15.4	0.19
Largemouth Bass	-	-	1.0	1.16
Northern Pike	20.0	4.0	1.2	3.00
Pumpkin. Sunfish	1.0	0.17	2.6	0.10
Yellow Bullhead	9.0	0.57	2.8	0.52
Yellow Perch	2.0	0.14	0.6	0.14

LENGTH OF SELECTED SPECIES SAMPLED FROM ALL GEAR

Number of fish caught for the following length categories (inches):

species	0-5	6-8	9-11	12-14	15-19	20-24	25-29	>30	Total
Black Crappie	3	11	-	-	-	-	-	-	14
Bluegill	30	50	-	-	-	-	-	-	83
Largemouth Bass	1	1	-	2	1	-	-	-	5
Northern Pike	-	-	-	-	12	13	-	-	26
Pumpkin. Sunfish	14	-	-	-	-	-	-	-	14
Yellow Bullhead	-	2	20	1	-	-	-	-	23
Yellow Perch	2	3	-	-	-	-	-	-	5

in the year and in fall. Tanners Lake is connected with Battle Creek Lake by a large culvert under I-94. The lake is limited to a 10-mph speed limit.

Battle Creek is a shallow basin that's viable as a fishery only because of an aeration system that staves off winterkill. It has a decent population of northern pike, with a good size range of 20 to nearly 34 inches. You can find bluegills and crappies in heavy weedlines early in spring, but you will have to move toward mid-lake as water warms and weeds expand. Small leeches are an excellent bait to try during summer for both bluegills and crappies. Fish bass and northerns between the center of the lake and outside weed edges. Spinnerbaits are a good lure to use for catching bass and pike. Floating a large minnow under a bobber will also get a fair amount of attention from both species.

There is a 10 mph-restriction on outboard motors, making this an angler's heaven by keeping water-skiers and jet-skiers off the lake. There's public access with a concrete ramp, operated by the City of Oakdale, at the park on the east shore of Tanners. Battle Creek Lake has a concrete ramp operated by the City of Woodbury on Edgewood Avenue.

FISHING INFORMATION: Tanners Lake has been stocked periodically with walleyes by the DNR, but it is really a panfish lake, full of small bluegills and crappies. There isn't a well-defined weedline, but you can find crappies close to most of the shorelines in spring. In summer, try the south end, where they will be suspended at 10 to 15 feet. Use a slip bobber, changing depth until you find them. Spring bass fishing is good along the east side of the lake. Fish the weeds from the public access spot north to the shallow end. Flip tubes or jigs to the weed pockets, or try a small spinnerbait. Walleyes, although not plentiful, can be found at the edges of drop-offs and at the small point on the lake's west side. Live-bait techniques will draw strikes from the available walleye population. Leeches and crawlers are best in late spring and summer, while minnows work best earlier

Tanners & Battle Creek Lakes

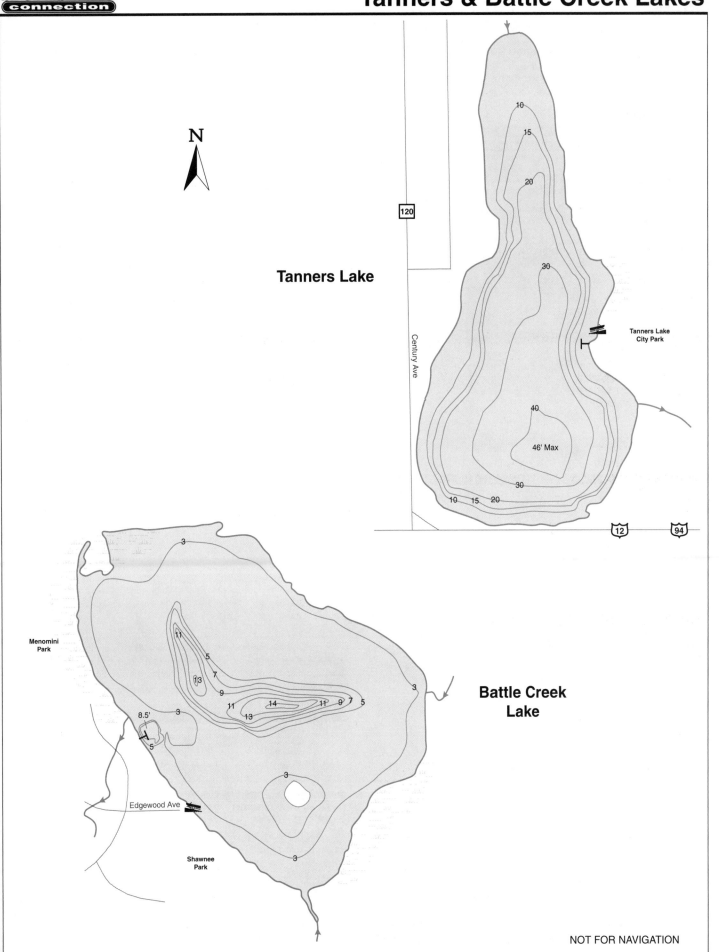

N

Tanners Lake

120

Century Ave

10

15

20

30

Tanners Lake
City Park

40

46' Max

30

10 15 20

12   94

3

Menomini
Park

11

5

7

13

9

3

11

13

14

11 9 7 5

3

**Battle Creek
Lake**

8.5'

5

Edgewood Ave

3

Shawnee
Park

3

3

NOT FOR NAVIGATION

Goose Lake, Washington County

Map pg/coord: 29 / A-5 **Max depth:** 25 feet
Surface area: 74 acres **Water clarity:** 7.9 feet (2010)

Accessibility: Township-owned public access with concrete ramp on west shore
Accommodations: Shore fishing

NO RECORD OF STOCKING SINCE 2000

LENGTH OF SELECTED SPECIES SAMPLED FROM ALL GEAR
Survey Date: 06/28/2010 **Survey method:** gill net, trap net
Number of fish caught for the following length categories (inches):

species	0-5	6-8	9-11	12-14	15-19	20-24	25-29	>30	Total
Black Bullhead	-	-	-	2	-	-	-	-	2
Black Crappie	2	4	7	-	-	-	-	-	13
Bluegill	50	245	4	-	-	-	-	-	307
Golden Shiner	3	15	-	-	-	-	-	-	18
Largemouth Bass	3	-	4	1	-	-	-	-	8
Northern Pike	-	-	-	-	2	1	4	2	9
Pumpkin. Sunfish	-	16	1	-	-	-	-	-	17
Yellow Perch	-	1	-	-	-	-	-	-	1

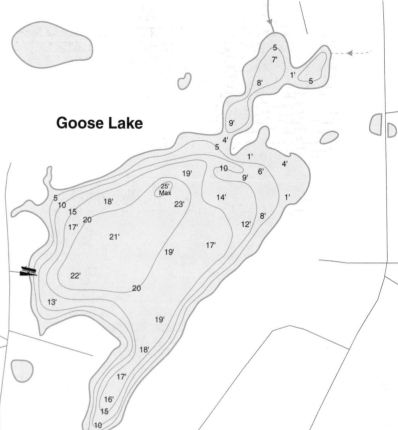

Goose Lake

N

Alice Lake

Alice Lake, Washington County

Map pg/coord: 29 / B-5 **Max depth:** 9 feet
Surface area: 26 acres **Water clarity:** 6.8 feet (2011)

Accessibility: Carry-down access and fishing pier on south shore
Accommodations: Fishing pier

FISH STOCKING DATA

year	species	size	# released
07	Black Crappie	Adult	721
07	White Bass	Adult	208
08	Bluegill	Adult	231
09	Bluegill	Adult	86

LENGTH OF SELECTED SPECIES SAMPLED FROM ALL GEAR
Survey Date: 06/13/2011 **Survey method:** gill net, trap net
Number of fish caught for the following length categories (inches):

species	0-5	6-8	9-11	12-14	15-19	20-24	25-29	>30	Total
Black Crappie	-	3	-	-	-	-	-	-	3
Bluegill	366	7	-	-	-	-	-	-	376
Hybrid Sunfish	29	3	-	-	-	-	-	-	32
Northern Pike	-	-	-	-	-	4	2	-	6
Pumpkin. Sunfish	13	-	-	-	-	-	-	-	13
Yellow Bullhead	1	3	1	-	-	-	-	-	5

NOT FOR NAVIGATION

Carver Lake, Washington County
Bordered by Carver Lake Park

Map pg/coord: 30 / B-3 **Max depth:** 36 feet
Surface area: 49 acres **Water clarity:** 6.5 feet (2009)

Accessibility: City-owned public access with earthen ramp in park
Accommodations: Park, platform fishing

NO RECORD OF STOCKING

LENGTH OF SELECTED SPECIES SAMPLED FROM ALL GEAR
Survey Date: 08/04/2009 **Survey method:** gill net, trap net
Number of fish caught for the following length categories (inches):

species	0-5	6-8	9-11	12-14	15-19	20-24	25-29	>30	Total
Black Crappie	15	7	-	-	-	-	-	-	22
Bluegill	418	34	-	-	-	-	-	-	457
Hybrid Sunfish	4	-	-	-	-	-	-	-	4
Northern Pike	-	-	-	-	2	1	4	-	7
Pumpkin. Sunfish	6	-	-	-	-	-	-	-	6
Yellow Perch	6	-	-	-	-	-	-	-	6

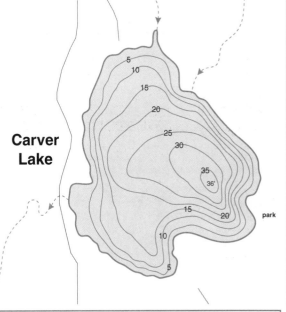

Carver Lake

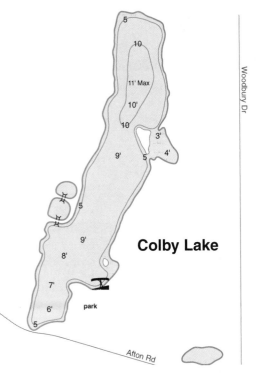

Colby Lake

N

Colby Lake, Washington County
Map pg/coord: 31 / B-4 **Max depth:** 11 feet
Surface area: 69 acres **Water clarity:** 1.5 feet (2007)

Accessibility: Carry-down access in city park on south shore
Accommodations: Park, shore fishing

FISH STOCKING DATA

year	species	size	# released
11	Black Crappie	Adult	256
11	Bluegill	Adult	244
12	Bluegill	Adult	815
12	Channel Catfish	Yearling	2,744

LENGTH OF SELECTED SPECIES SAMPLED FROM ALL GEAR
Survey Date: **Survey method:** gill net, trap net
Number of fish caught for the following length categories (inches):

species	0-5	6-8	9-11	12-14	15-19	20-24	25-29	>30	Total
Black Bullhead	89	1697	66	-	-	-	-	-	1859
Black Crappie	39	177	-	-	-	-	-	-	220
Bluegill	518	39	-	-	-	-	-	-	559
Hybrid Sunfish	9	3	-	-	-	-	-	-	12
Northern Pike	-	-	-	-	-	1	2	2	5
Pumpkin. Sunfish	7	1	-	-	-	-	-	-	8
White Sucker	-	-	1	10	13	-	-	-	24

Lost Lake, Washington County
Map pg/coord: 28 / D,E-3 **Max depth:** 26 feet
Surface area: 9 acres **Water clarity:** 7.0 feet (2012)

Accessibility: Fishing pier in park, no boat ramp
Accommodations: Fishing pier

FISH STOCKING DATA

year	species	size	# released
10	Bluegill	Adult	612
11	Black Crappie	Adult	194
11	Bluegill	Adult	428

LENGTH OF SELECTED SPECIES SAMPLED FROM ALL GEAR
Survey Date: 05/29/2012 **Survey method:** gill net, trap net
Number of fish caught for the following length categories (inches):

species	0-5	6-8	9-11	12-14	15-19	20-24	25-29	>30	Total
Black Bullhead	9	28	-	-	-	-	-	-	37
Bluegill	5	28	-	-	-	-	-	-	33
Hybrid Sunfish	3	11	-	-	-	-	-	-	14
Northern Pike	-	-	10	10	7	8	-	-	35
Pumpkin. Sunfish	25	-	-	-	-	-	-	-	25

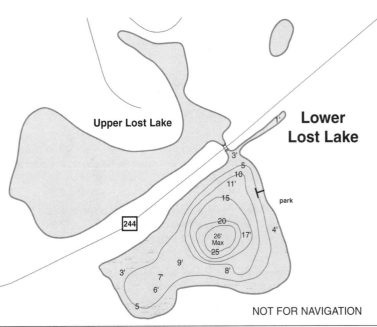

Upper Lost Lake

Lower Lost Lake

NOT FOR NAVIGATION

LAKE ELMO
Washington County

Bordered by Lake Elmo Regional Park

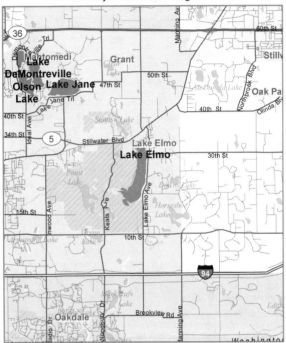

Area map pg / coord: 31 / A-4
Watershed: Lower St. Croix
Secchi disk: 16.5 feet (2008)
Water color: Clear

Surface area: 281 acres
Shorelength: 3.8 miles
Maximum depth: 140 feet
Mean depth: 31 feet

Accessibility: County-owned public access on west shore in park
Boat ramp: Concrete
Parking: Twenty trailer spaces
Accommodations: Park, fishing pier, camping, picnicking, restrooms

Shoreland zoning classification: Recreational development
Management class: Centrarchid
Ecological type: Centrarchid

FISHING INFORMATION: There is good news and bad news for anglers heading for Lake Elmo. The good news is there are a lot of northern pike in the lake. The bad news is Elmo is a very tough lake to fish. Elmo is the deepest lake in the metropolitan area, with a maximum depth of 140 feet. It also has clear water and not too much vegetation. There are weeds and trees at the north end of the lake and in the bay at the southwest corner. You'll want to target the weedy areas when you're chasing pike earlier in the year.

Basic methods tend to work best here. In spring, try a jig-and-minnow combo or a bobber with a large minnow. Pike will usually be in the shallows earlier in the year. Other favorite approaches include casting a large bass-style spinnerbait or a jerkbait. Of course, if still-fishing with bait or endless casting isn't your style, break out trolling gear and work deeper weed edges. You can use crankbaits or stickbaits to trigger a strike.

Once the deeper water warms, you'll have to move there. This can be a problem, because there is oxygen all the way down to 50 feet at the deeper spots and it's tough to tell just where northern pike will be. A good way to eliminate unproductive water is to use your depth finder and search for clouds of baitfish, such as tullibees. Don't fish areas where you don't see any activity. Once you've located a likely area, try trolling with spoons or vertically jigging.

Black crappies are available in decent numbers, according to the most recent DNR survey. There are some decent specimens in excess of 10 inches long. Fish weedlines with a slip bobber and a small minnow or try a small tube jig with or without a minnow.

The DNR has stocked walleye fingerlings in Elmo for more than a decade. Elmo is primarily managed for walleyes. In the latest DNR survey, the average walleye was 19.27 inches long, weighing 2.7 pounds.

Bluegills are abundant, although their size is smaller than most anglers prefer to catch, but larger fish do exist.

Rainbow trout have been planted in Lake Elmo, with stockings of

both yearlings and adults.

Public access requires a county park permit. The site offers a concrete ramp and 20 parking spaces, and there is also a handicapped-accessible pier south of the launch site.

FISH STOCKING DATA

year	species	size	# released
07	Tiger Muskellunge	Fry	17,900
07	Tiger Muskellunge	Fingerling	206
09	Tiger Muskellunge	Fingerling	546
09	Walleye	Fry	1,600,000
10	Walleye	Fingerling	15,508
11	Tiger Muskellunge	Fingerling	202
11	Walleye	Fry	206,000
12	Rainbow Trout	Yearling	1,004
12	Rainbow Trout	Adult	150

NET CATCH DATA

Date: 06/16/2008	Gill Nets		Trap Nets	
species	# per net	avg. fish weight (lbs.)	# per net	avg. fish weight (lbs.)
Black Crappie	0.3	0.34	0.2	0.24
Bluegill	1.3	0.09	72.8	0.12
Common Carp	0.3	8.02	0.1	3.91
Green Sunfish	-	-	0.1	0.08
Hybrid Sunfish	0.2	0.02	0.2	0.23
Largemouth Bass	0.3	0.95	-	-
Northern Pike	5.0	4.17	0.2	2.78
Pumpkin. Sunfish	0.2	0.12	-	-
Tiger Muskellunge	0.5	3.23	-	-
Tullibee (Cisco)	8.7	0.46	-	-
Walleye	2.5	2.70	-	-
White Sucker	0.7	1.81	-	-
Yellow Perch	0.2	0.08	-	-

LENGTH OF SELECTED SPECIES SAMPLED FROM ALL GEAR

Number of fish caught for the following length categories (inches):

species	0-5	6-8	9-11	12-14	15-19	20-24	25-29	>30	Total
Black Crappie	2	0	2	-	-	-	-	-	4
Bluegill	439	217	-	-	-	-	-	-	663
Common Carp	-	-	-	-	-	2	1	-	3
Hybrid Sunfish	2	1	-	-	-	-	-	-	3
Largemouth Bass	-	-	1	1	-	-	-	-	2
Northern Pike	-	-	-	-	1	18	9	4	32
Pumpkin. Sunfish	1	-	-	-	-	-	-	-	1
Tiger Muskellunge	-	-	-	-	-	2	1	-	3
Tullibee (Cisco)	-	6	27	19	-	-	-	-	52
Walleye	-	-	-	1	8	5	1	-	15
Yellow Perch	-	1	-	-	-	-	-	-	1

Lake Elmo

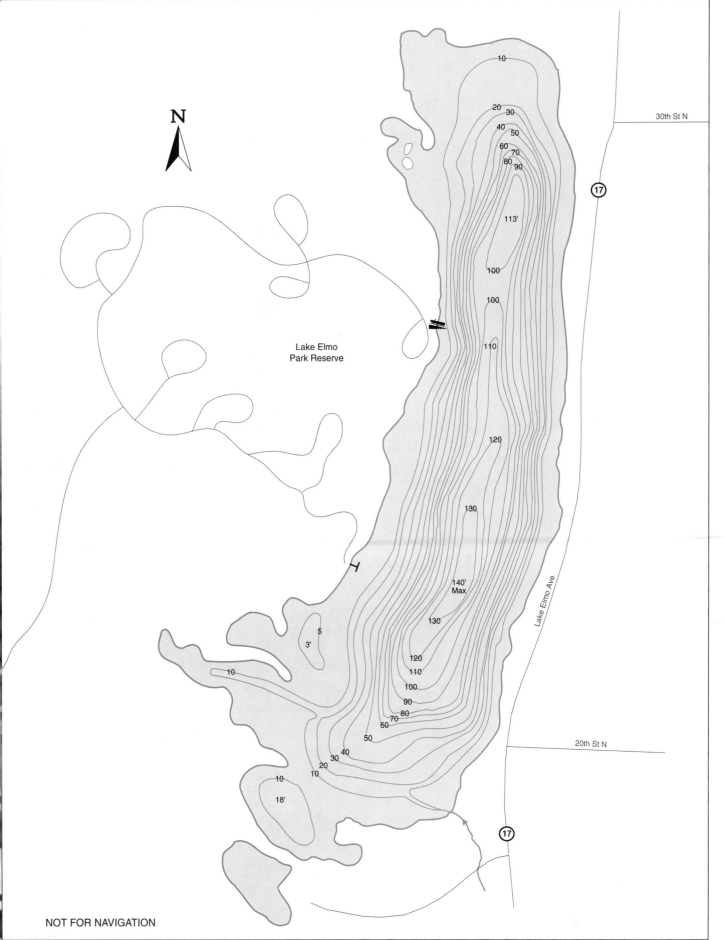

17

Lake Elmo
Park Reserve

10

20
30
40
50
60
70
80 90

113'

100

100

110

120

130

140'
Max

130

5

3'

10

120
110
100
90
80
70
60
50

40
30
20
10

10

18'

Lake Elmo Ave

20th St N

17

N

NOT FOR NAVIGATION

Source: Minnesota Department of Natural Resources, USGS

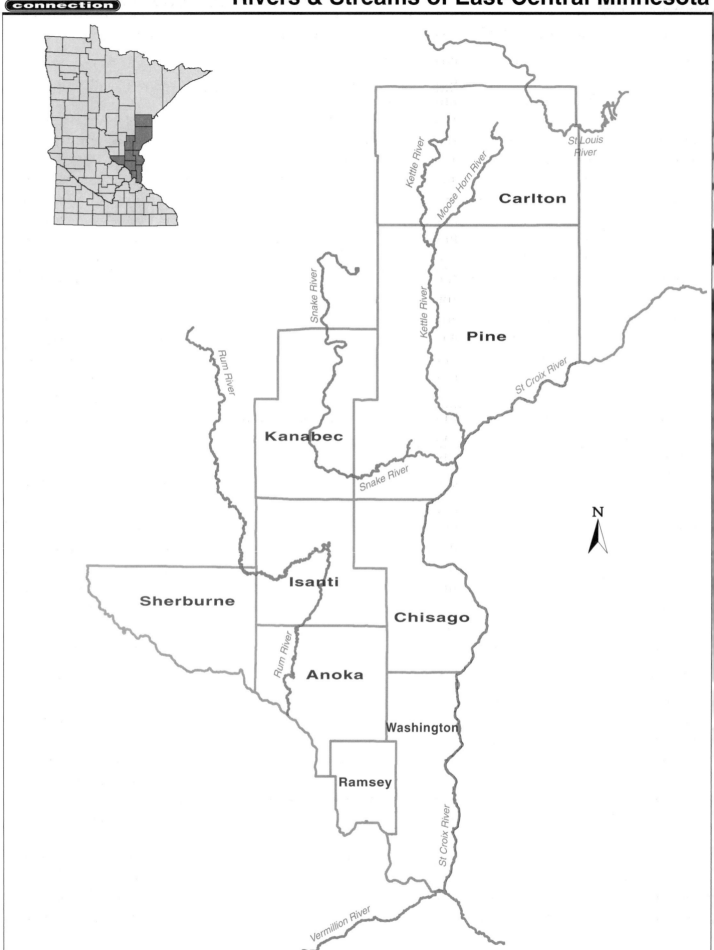

SPORTSMAN'S
connection

Carlton

Pine

Snake River

Kettle River

Moose Horn River

St Louis River

St Croix River

Rum River

Kanabec

Snake River

Sherburne

Isanti

Chisago

Rum River

Anoka

Washington

Ramsey

St Croix River

Vermillion River

N

River	Access	Page	Launch, Type	County	Administrator	Latitude	Longitude
St. Louis River	1	193	Carry-in	Carlton	Scanlon	46° 42' 18.00" N	92° 25' 16.00" W
St. Louis River	2	193	Carry-in	Carlton	Thomson Reservoir access	46° 39' 59.00" N	92° 24' 90.00" W
Snake River	S-1	194	Carry-in	Aitkin	DNR T&W, McGrath	46° 14' 51.70" N	93° 15' 45.44" W
Snake River	S-2	194	Ramp, rock	Aitkin	Aitkin Co Parks	46° 11' 42.05" N	93° 15' 04.45" W
Snake River	S-3	194	Carry-in	Aitkin	Aitkin Co Parks	46° 09' 42.82" N	93° 14' 42.12" W
Snake River	S-4	194	Carry-in	Kanabec	DNR T&W, Co. Rd. 3	46° 01' 27.60" N	93° 13' 51.97" W
Snake River	S-5	194	Carry-in	Kanabec	City Parks Department, Mora	45° 52' 56.40" N	93° 18' 37.56" W
Snake River	S-6	194	Ramp, plank	Kanabec	DNR T&W, Twin	45° 48' 41.26" N	93° 15' 53.50" W
Snake River	S-7	194	Carry-in	Pine	DNR T&W	45° 47' 44.25" N	93° 04' 47.43" W
Snake River	S-8	194	Ramp, plank	Pine	DNR T&W, Cross Lake	45° 50' 24.44" N	92° 56' 25.45" W
Snake River	S-9	194	Carry-in	Pine	DNR T&W	45° 50' 24.08" N	92° 56' 09.63" W
Kettle River	K-1	194	Ramp, gravel	Pine	DNR T&W	46° 10' 48.32" N	92° 49' 55.92" W
Kettle River	K-2	194	Ramp, plank	Pine	DNR Parks & Recreation	46° 09' 46.73" N	92° 50' 00.69" W
Kettle River	K-3	194	Ramp, plank	Pine	City Parks Department	46° 07' 45.57" N	92° 51' 23.74" W
Kettle River	K-4	194	Carry-in	Pine	DNR Parks & Recreation	46° 06' 26.48" N	92° 51' 48.52" W
Kettle River	K-5	194	Ramp, plank	Pine	DNR T&W	46° 00' 38.94" N	92° 50' 23.21" W
Kettle River	K-6	194	Carry-in	Pine	DNR Parks & Recreation	45° 56' 41.44" N	92° 46' 29.47" W
Kettle River	K-7	194	Ramp, gravel	Pine	DNR Parks & Recreation	45° 54' 17.72" N	92° 43' 57.62" W
Moose Horn River	M-1	195	Carry-in	Carlton	City Parks Dept., Moose Horn River Bar	46° 30' 10.91" N	92° 41' 25.73" W
Moose Horn River	M-2	195	Ramp, gravel	Carlton	DNR T&W, Moose Horn Lake	46° 26' 41.54" N	92° 46' 25.32" W
Rum River	1	196	Ramp, plank	Mille Lacs	DNR Parks & Recreation	46° 07' 20.63" N	93° 45' 35.72" W
Rum River/ Shakopee Lake	2	196	Ramp, plank	Mille Lacs	DNR Parks & Recreation, Shakopee Lake	46° 06' 12.85" N	93° 43' 26.44" W
Rum River	3	196	Carry-in	Mille Lacs	DNR T&W	46° 04' 08.95" N	93° 40' 49.29" W
Rum River	4	196	Carry-in	Mille Lacs	DNR T&W	45° 55' 33.36" N	93° 39' 50.74" W
Rum River	5	196	Carry-in	Mille Lacs	City Parks Department, Milaca Dam Site	45° 45' 16.90" N	93° 39' 36.88" W
Rum River	6	196	Carry-in	Mille Lacs	City Parks Department, Riverview Park	45° 44' 39.37" N	93° 38' 55.06" W
Rum River	7	196	Carry-in	Mille Lacs	Bogus Brook Twp, Mille Lacs Co Rd 4	45° 42' 11.71" N	93° 35' 08.05" W
Rum River	8	196	Carry-in	Mille Lacs	City Parks Department, Princeton	45° 34' 16.53" N	93° 34' 40.35" W
Rum River	9	196	Carry-in	Isanti	DNR T&W, Hwy. 7	45° 31' 44.52" N	93° 26' 23.10" W
Rum River	10	196	Ramp, wood	Isanti	DNR T&W, Walbo	45° 34' 44.84" N	93° 19' 22.27" W
Rum River	11	196	Ramp, earthen	Isanti	DNR T&W, Hwy. 14	45° 36' 32.37" N	93° 15' 25.19" W
Rum River	12	196	Carry-in	Isanti	City Parks Department, Cambridge	45° 34' 17.56" N	93° 14' 07.02" W
Rum River	13	196	Ramp, plank	Isanti	DNR T&W, Martins	45° 29' 19.68" N	93° 16' 00.95" W
Rum River	14	196	Carry-in	Anoka	Anoka Co Parks	45° 23' 20.15" N	93° 21' 28.82" W
Rum River	15	196	Carry-in	Anoka	Anoka Co Parks	45° 17' 47.10" N	93° 22' 37.58" W
Rum River	16	196	Carry-in	Anoka		45° 17' 22.56" N	93° 22' 53.90" W
Rum River	17	196	Carry-in	Anoka	DNR T&W Region Office 6B	45° 15' 01.94" N	93° 22' 55.72" W
Rum River	18	196	Carry-in	Anoka		45° 13' 23.61" N	93° 23' 25.69" W
Rum River	19	196	Ramp, plank	Anoka	Anoka Co Parks, Co. Rd. 288	45° 12' 50.09" N	93° 23' 21.75" W
Rum River	20	196	Ramp, plank	Anoka	Anoka City Parks	45° 11' 32.73" N	93° 23' 24.20" W
Vermillion River	1	197	Ramp, slab	Dakota	DNR T&W, Upper Vermillion	44° 42' 09.40" N	92° 45' 30.15" W
Vermillion River	2	197	Ramp, plank	Dakota	DNR T&W, Lower Vermillion	44° 39' 57.84" N	92° 44' 08.28" W
Vermillion River	3	197	Ramp, plank	Goodhue	DNR T&W	44° 36' 10.76" N	92° 37' 09.20" W

Other Significant East-Central Minnesota Streams

Place	County	*Lat	*Long
Albrechts Creek	Pine	46.078°N	92.379°W
Anderson Creek	Carlton	46.481°N	92.451°W
Ann River	Kanabec	45.915°N	93.420°W
Ann River	Kanabec	45.831°N	93.334°W
Annamahasung Creek	Carlton	46.696°N	92.703°W
Bangs Brook	Pine	46.012°N	92.529°W
Bass Creek	Pine	45.835°N	92.834°W
Battle Brook	Sherburne	45.469°N	93.641°W
Battle Creek	Ramsey	44.927°N	93.029°W
Bean Brook	Kanabec	45.994°N	93.334°W
Bear Creek	Pine	45.841°N	92.877°W
Bear Creek	Pine	45.916°N	92.673°W
Bear Creek, Little	Pine	46.048°N	92.746°W
Bear Paw Creek	Pine	45.904°N	92.695°W
Beckins Creek	Isanti	45.593°N	93.233°W
Bergman Brook	Kanabec	46.156°N	93.246°W
Birch Creek	Pine	46.369°N	92.869°W
Bjorks Creek	Pine	46.130°N	92.369°W
Blackhoof River	Carlton	46.519°N	92.398°W
Bremen Creek	Pine	46.284°N	92.972°W
Bremen Creek, Little	Pine	46.278°N	93.019°W
Briggs Creek	Sherburne	45.506°N	93.930°W
Browns Creek	Washington	45.076°N	92.804°W
Camp Creek	Kanabec	45.912°N	93.429°W
Cane Creek	Pine	46.225°N	92.835°W
Cedar Creek	Anoka	45.292°N	93.369°W
Cedar Creek	Pine	45.953°N	92.812°W
Chelsey Brook	Kanabec	46.127°N	93.186°W
Clear Creek	Carlton	46.554°N	92.240°W
Clear Creek	Carlton	46.488°N	92.439°W
Clearwater Creek	Washington	45.174°N	93.054°W
Coon Creek	Anoka	45.133°N	93.300°W
Crooked Brook	Anoka	45.336°N	93.261°W
Crooked Creek	Pine	45.983°N	92.515°W
Crooked Creek, West Fork	Pine	46.044°N	92.563°W
Crystal Creek	Carlton	46.691°N	92.413°W
Crystal Creek	Pine	46.041°N	92.344°W
Dead Moose River	Carlton	46.498°N	92.896°W
Deer Creek	Carlton	46.524°N	92.373°W
Deer Creek	Chisago	45.513°N	92.726°W
Deer Creek	Pine	45.905°N	92.733°W
Deer Creek	Pine	46.051°N	92.868°W
Dry Creek	Chisago	45.468°N	92.683°W
Dry Creek	Chisago	45.518°N	92.729°W
Dry Creek	Chisago	45.497°N	92.757°W
East Branch Hay Creek	Pine	46.281°N	92.296°W
East Fork Crooked Creek	Pine	46.044°N	92.563°W
East Pokegama Creek	Pine	45.920°N	93.067°W
Elk River	Sherburne	45.298°N	93.572°W
Fish Creek	Ramsey	44.898°N	93.013°W
Fond du Lac Creek	Carlton	46.752°N	92.492°W
Ford Brook	Anoka	45.288°N	93.420°W
Fox Creek	Pine	46.044°N	92.869°W
Gill Creek	Carlton	46.663°N	92.325°W
Gillespie Brook	Carlton	46.448°N	92.877°W
Goose Creek	Chisago	45.583°N	92.884°W
Green Lake Brook	Isanti	45.564°N	93.387°W
Grindstone River	Pine	46.028°N	92.863°W
Grindstone River, North Branch	Pine	46.022°N	92.945°W
Grindstone River, South Branch	Pine	46.022°N	92.945°W
Groundhouse River	Kanabec	45.811°N	93.262°W

Place	County	*Lat	*Long
Groundhouse River, South Fork	Kanabec	45.789°N	93.385°W
Hanson Creek	Pine	46.114°N	92.385°W
Hardwood Creek	Anoka	45.202°N	93.046°W
Hay Creek	Carlton	46.728°N	92.348°W
Hay Creek	Chisago	45.528°N	92.868°W
Hay Creek	Kanabec	46.129°N	93.252°W
Hay Creek	Pine	45.936°N	92.640°W
Hay Creek	Pine	46.084°N	92.410°W
Hay Creek	Pine	46.084°N	92.674°W
Hay Creek	Pine	46.353°N	92.686°W
Hay Creek, Little	Pine	45.964°N	92.624°W
Hay Creek, West Branch	Pine	46.281°N	92.296°W
Heikkila Creek	Carlton	46.569°N	92.881°W
Hunters Creek	Carlton	46.474°N	92.557°W
Isanti Brook	Isanti	45.503°N	93.265°W
Johnson Creek	Pine	46.187°N	92.505°W
Keene Creek	Pine	46.124°N	92.500°W
Kennedy Brook	Pine	45.904°N	92.730°W
Kenney Brook	Pine	46.015°N	92.532°W
Kettle River	Pine	45.858°N	92.736°W
Kettle River, West Branch	Carlton	46.539°N	92.889°W
King Creek	Carlton	46.547°N	92.674°W
Knife River	Kanabec	45.908°N	93.298°W
Larsons Creek	Pine	46.355°N	92.523°W
Lawrence Creek	Chisago	45.361°N	92.701°W
Lilly Creek	Sherburne	45.478°N	93.941°W
Little River	Carlton	46.669°N	92.309°W
Log Drive Creek	Pine	46.206°N	92.830°W
Longstrem Brook	Pine	46.103°N	92.398°W
Lost Creek	Pine	45.938°N	92.698°W
Mackey Brook	Kanabec	45.949°N	93.413°W
Mahoney Brook	Anoka	45.311°N	93.319°W
McDermott Creek	Pine	46.091°N	92.473°W
McDermott Creek, Little	Pine	46.199°N	92.405°W
Medicine Creek	Pine	46.249°N	92.883°W
Meekers Creek	Pine	46.093°N	92.366°W
Midway River	Carlton	46.672°N	92.397°W
Mission Creek	Pine	45.817°N	93.031°W
Moose Creek	Pine	46.044°N	92.519°W
Moose Horn River	Carlton	46.364°N	92.844°W
Moose Horn River, West Fork	Carlton	46.516°N	92.698°W
Mud Creek	Carlton	46.550°N	92.248°W
Mud Creek	Kanabec	45.794°N	93.190°W
Nemadji Creek	Carlton	46.484°N	92.499°W
Nemadji River, South Fork	Carlton	46.532°N	92.281°W
Net River	Carlton	46.512°N	92.347°W
Net River, Little	Carlton	46.502°N	92.359°W
North Brook	Isanti	45.583°N	93.435°W
Otter Creek	Carlton	46.663°N	92.404°W
Otter Creek, Little	Carlton	46.650°N	92.484°W
Ox Creek	Pine	46.157°N	92.474°W
Ox Creek, Little	Pine	46.130°N	92.490°W
Park Lake Creek	Carlton	46.577°N	92.640°W
Partridge Creek	Pine	46.097°N	92.725°W
Pelkey Creek	Pine	45.981°N	92.839°W
Pickle Creek	Pine	46.194°N	92.681°W
Pine Brook	Isanti	45.571°N	93.378°W
Pine Creek, Little	Pine	46.236°N	92.987°W
Pine River	Pine	46.260°N	92.862°W
Pokegama Creek	Pine	45.867°N	93.042°W
Portage River	Carlton	46.452°N	92.744°W
Redhorse Creek	Pine	45.834°N	92.762°W
Redhorse Creek, West Fork	Pine	45.857°N	92.767°W

Place	County	*Lat	*Long
Rhine Creek	Pine	46.248°N	92.986°W
Rice Creek	Anoka	45.089°N	93.279°W
Rice Creek	Kanabec	45.795°N	93.195°W
Rice Creek	Sherburne	45.483°N	93.975°W
Rock Creek	Carlton	46.536°N	92.308°W
Rock Creek	Chisago	45.713°N	92.868°W
Rum River	Anoka	45.190°N	93.390°W
Rush Creek	Chisago	45.653°N	92.884°W
Saint Croix River	Washington	44.746°N	92.803°W
Saint Francis River	Sherburne	45.359°N	93.737°W
Sand Creek	Anoka	45.183°N	93.305°W
Sand Creek	Pine	45.934°N	92.640°W
Sand Creek, Little	Pine	45.968°N	92.669°W
Sangeta Creek	Pine	46.027°N	92.405°W
Section Thirty-six Creek	Carlton	46.518°N	92.306°W
Seelye Brook	Anoka	45.360°N	93.364°W
Silver Creek	Washington	45.079°N	92.802°W
Silver Creek	Carlton	46.474°N	92.459°W
Silver Creek	Carlton	46.473°N	92.883°W
Silver Creek	Carlton	46.645°N	92.351°W
Skunk Creek	Pine	46.107°N	92.864°W
Snake River	Pine	45.824°N	92.764°W
Snake River	Sherburne	45.380°N	93.761°W
Snowshoe Brook	Kanabec	46.023°N	93.236°W
Spencer Brook	Isanti	45.529°N	93.439°W
Split Rock River	Carlton	46.429°N	92.894°W
Spring Brook	Kanabec	45.909°N	93.412°W
Spring Brook	Kanabec	45.852°N	93.284°W
Spring Creek	Pine	46.021°N	92.871°W
Squib Creek	Pine	46.133°N	92.436°W
Stanchfield Branch, Lower	Isanti	45.637°N	93.231°W
Stanchfield Creek	Isanti	45.603°N	93.289°W
State Line Creek	Carlton	46.521°N	92.293°W
Stevens Creek	Pine	45.729°N	92.845°W
Stony Brook	Carlton	46.488°N	92.439°W
Stony Brook	Sherburne	45.544°N	93.932°W
Strawberry Creek	Pine	46.148°N	92.613°W
Sunrise River	Chisago	45.567°N	92.863°W
Sunrise River, North Branch	Chisago	45.527°N	92.867°W
Sunrise River, South Branch	Chisago	45.358°N	92.971°W
Sunrise River, West Branch	Chisago	45.390°N	92.964°W
Tamarack River, Lower	Pine	46.028°N	92.419°W
Tamarack River, Upper	Pine	46.070°N	92.319°W
Thunder Creek	Pine	46.064°N	92.589°W
Tibbits Brook	Sherburne	45.335°N	93.658°W
Ties Creek	Isanti	45.680°N	93.334°W
Trout Brook	Anoka	45.287°N	93.404°W
Trout Brook	Ramsey	44.985°N	93.097°W
Trout Brook	Washington	44.859°N	92.773°W
Trout Brook	Pine	46.066°N	92.330°W
Valley Branch	Washington	44.906°N	92.775°W
Wilbur Brook	Pine	46.003°N	92.529°W
Wilburn Creek	Pine	46.021°N	92.851°W
Willow River	Pine	46.320°N	92.846°W
Willow River, Little	Pine	46.342°N	92.719°W
Wolf Creek	Pine	46.145°N	92.861°W
Wolf Creek	Pine	46.126°N	92.620°W
Wyanett Creek	Isanti	45.569°N	93.451°W
Zimbrick Brook	Pine	46.046°N	92.662°W

Latitude and Longitude coordinates mark the mouth of the stream

Source: Minnesota Department of Natural Resources, USGS   **192**

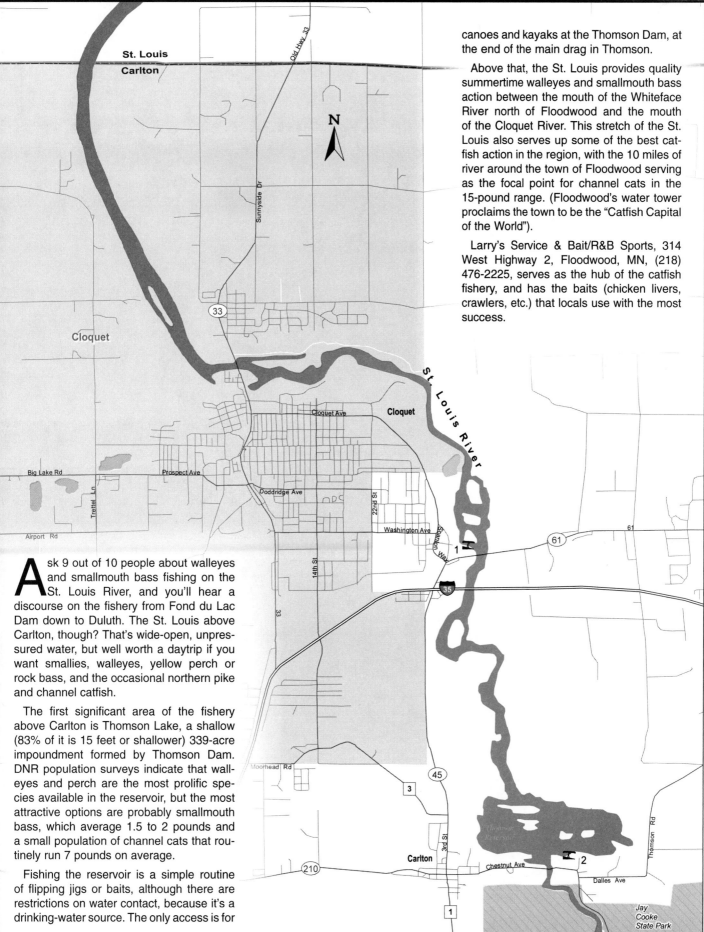

canoes and kayaks at the Thomson Dam, at the end of the main drag in Thomson.

Above that, the St. Louis provides quality summertime walleyes and smallmouth bass action between the mouth of the Whiteface River north of Floodwood and the mouth of the Cloquet River. This stretch of the St. Louis also serves up some of the best catfish action in the region, with the 10 miles of river around the town of Floodwood serving as the focal point for channel cats in the 15-pound range. (Floodwood's water tower proclaims the town to be the "Catfish Capital of the World").

Larry's Service & Bait/R&B Sports, 314 West Highway 2, Floodwood, MN, (218) 476-2225, serves as the hub of the catfish fishery, and has the baits (chicken livers, crawlers, etc.) that locals use with the most success.

Ask 9 out of 10 people about walleyes and smallmouth bass fishing on the St. Louis River, and you'll hear a discourse on the fishery from Fond du Lac Dam down to Duluth. The St. Louis above Carlton, though? That's wide-open, unpressured water, but well worth a daytrip if you want smallies, walleyes, yellow perch or rock bass, and the occasional northern pike and channel catfish.

The first significant area of the fishery above Carlton is Thomson Lake, a shallow (83% of it is 15 feet or shallower) 339-acre impoundment formed by Thomson Dam. DNR population surveys indicate that walleyes and perch are the most prolific species available in the reservoir, but the most attractive options are probably smallmouth bass, which average 1.5 to 2 pounds and a small population of channel cats that routinely run 7 pounds on average.

Fishing the reservoir is a simple routine of flipping jigs or baits, although there are restrictions on water contact, because it's a drinking-water source. The only access is for

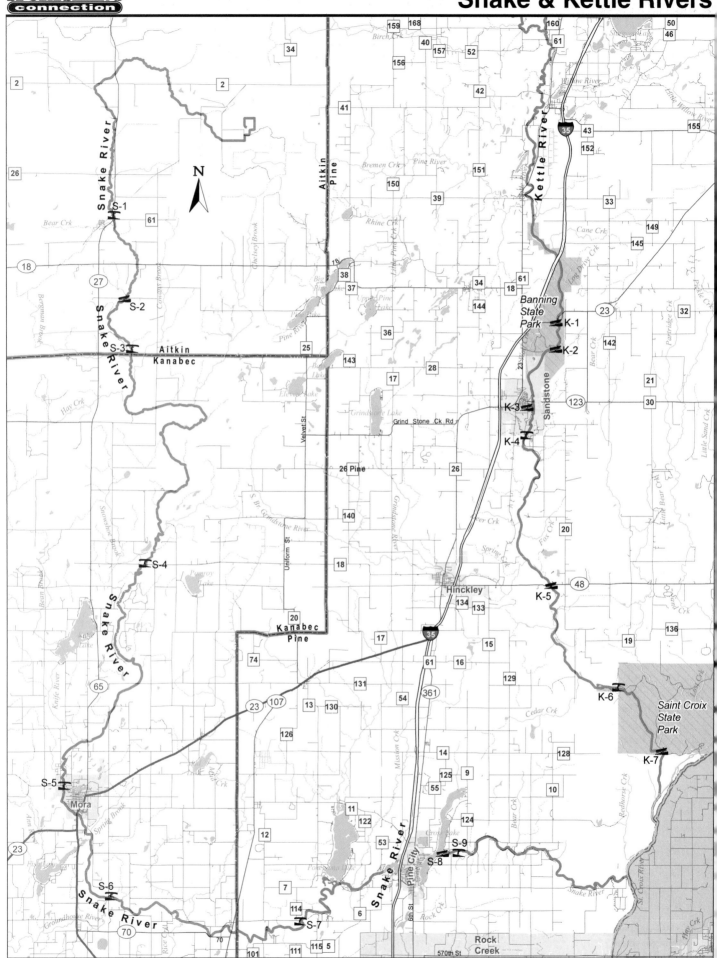

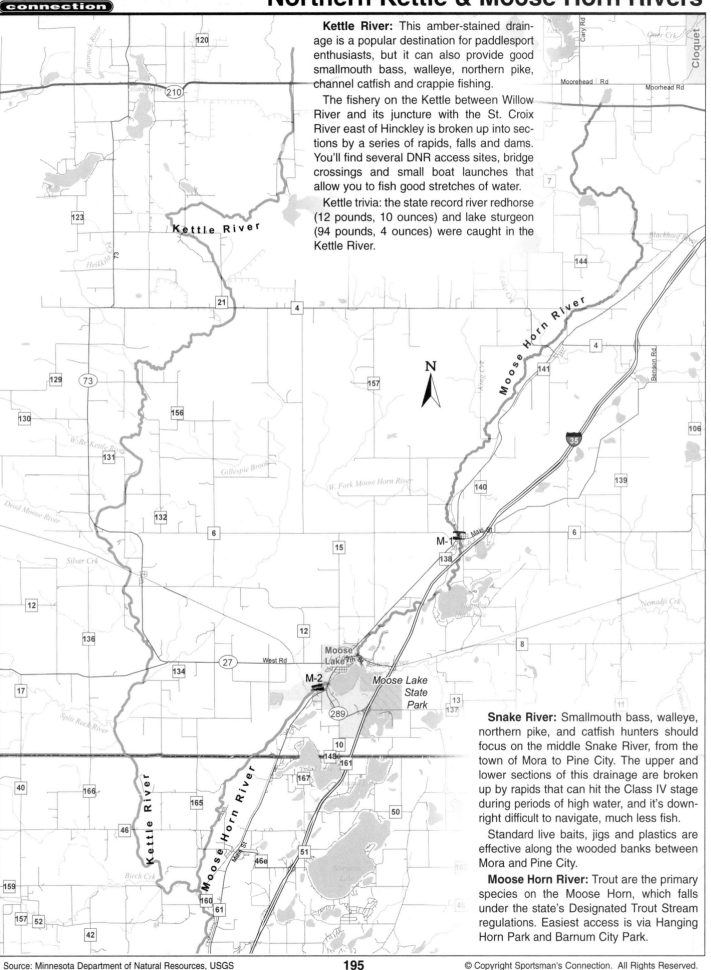

Kettle River: This amber-stained drainage is a popular destination for paddlesport enthusiasts, but it can also provide good smallmouth bass, walleye, northern pike, channel catfish and crappie fishing.

The fishery on the Kettle between Willow River and its juncture with the St. Croix River east of Hinckley is broken up into sections by a series of rapids, falls and dams. You'll find several DNR access sites, bridge crossings and small boat launches that allow you to fish good stretches of water.

Kettle trivia: the state record river redhorse (12 pounds, 10 ounces) and lake sturgeon (94 pounds, 4 ounces) were caught in the Kettle River.

Snake River: Smallmouth bass, walleye, northern pike, and catfish hunters should focus on the middle Snake River, from the town of Mora to Pine City. The upper and lower sections of this drainage are broken up by rapids that can hit the Class IV stage during periods of high water, and it's downright difficult to navigate, much less fish.

Standard live baits, jigs and plastics are effective along the wooded banks between Mora and Pine City.

Moose Horn River: Trout are the primary species on the Moose Horn, which falls under the state's Designated Trout Stream regulations. Easiest access is via Hanging Horn Park and Barnum City Park.

The Rum River is a solid bet for smallmouth bass, walleyes and northern pike, all of which are available in average to above-average abundance in this tributary of the Mississippi River. You'll also find largemouths, rock bass, yellow perch, crappies, bluegills and bullheads in the lower end of the river, but DNR population samplings indicate that smallies, pike and walleyes make up nearly 30 percent of the Rum's biomass, and an easy majority of its gamefish species.

The Rum spills out of Lake Mille Lacs and runs a 145-mile course through Isanti and Anoka Counties before pooling up at the Anoka Dam and pouring into the Mississippi. It's a popular destination for canoeists, offering dozens of carry-in, small-boat access points from river mile 123 down. Access for trailerable boats in the most fishable sections of the Rum lie at river miles 83.1 in Princeton (Highway 95 bridge), 55.3 in Walbo (Walbo Ferry), 32.1 in Isanti (Martin's Landing), and river miles 13.1 and 2.0 (Rum River Central and South county parks). The lowest access point above Anoka Dam is at river mile 0.9 (Akin Riverside City Park).

Several of the county and city parks on the lower 13 miles have small fishing piers that provide access to the Rum's largest populations of core species, all of which will readily bite traditional live baits. The crappie fishery is especially strong. Fish micro jigs tipped with a piece of minnow or crawler.

The 36 miles of water between Princeton and Cambridge absorb the bulk of the smallmouth and pike fishing pressure on the Rum, and it's safe to say that 8 out of 10 anglers fish nothing more than nightcrawlers (and occasionally minnows), but you'll also do well for smallies on 1/8- to 1/4-ounce jigs and crayfish-colored Yamamoto and Gitzit tubes. It's a similar bait-driven smallie fishery (crawlers, minnows and leeches) in the lower river around Anoka, but you'll also see a topwater bite on Pop Rs and Chug Bugs.

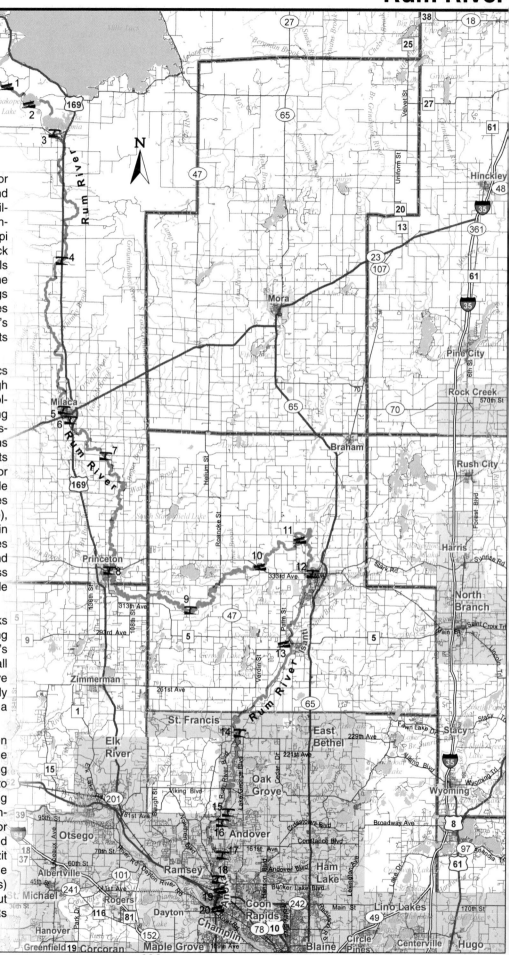

Source: Minnesota Department of Natural Resources, USGS

This Dakota County trout fishery offers very little easy public fishing access, which translates into relatively light pressure. Anglers who take the time to familiarize themselves with the Vermillion, though, could encounter some of the highest quality German brown trout fishing available in any metropolitan area in the country.

The Vermillion meanders from its headwaters near the town of Elko in Scott County through 38 miles of flat prairie/farmland before tumbling over 90-foot falls, splitting into two branches and joining the Mississippi River Flood Plain below Hastings. The river was well-known throughout the first half of the 20th Century as a trophy brook trout stream, but water quality dropped so drastically that the fishery was declared unfit for gamefish by the early 1960s. The watershed has since become a "favorite son" of the DNR and enhancement/conservation groups, who have brought the brown trout fishery back and imposed strict harvest regulations to help maintain the population.

The bulk of the fishery is Designated Trout Stream under catch-and-release guidelines, with the exception of a 2-mile easement that allows the typical statewide 5-fish limit between Denmark Avenue and the Highway 52 bridge in Farmington (where the DNR stocks 500 yearling rainbows annually in Rambling River Park to provide a catch-and-keep option).

Browns in excess of 5 pounds are scattered throughout the watershed's 45.5 miles of DT waters, but there are only a handful of established streamside access points to choose from: the city of Lakeview; the above-mentioned access in the city of Farmington in Rambling River Park; Empire Township; the Miles AMA on the north side of Highway 66 just east of Empire.

Because of its long-standing reputation as a producer of trophy-class browns and its catch-and-release management, the Vermillion hosts its share of flyrodders. The hatch schedule runs the gamut from caddis to terrestrials, so a flybox stocked with Elk Hair Caddis, Prince Nymphs, Brassies, assorted terrestrials (ants, beetles, some hoppers) and other basic patterns will produce fish.

LAKE ST. CROIX

Washington County

Area map pg / coord: 29, 31
Surface area: 7,800 acres
Maximum depth: 78 feet
Secchi disk (water clarity): 8.4 feet (2009)

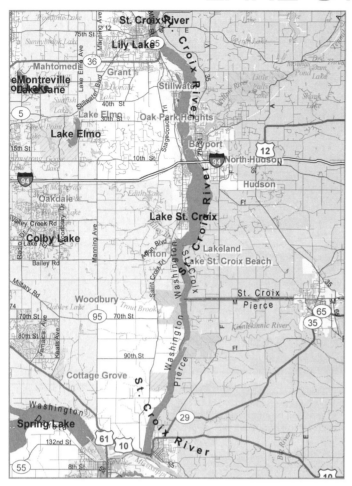

FISH STOCKING DATA

year	species	size	# released
07	Muskellunge	Fingerling	1,077
08	Muskellunge	Fingerling	9,069
09	Muskellunge	Fry	178,750
09	Muskellunge	Fingerling	3,998
10	Muskellunge	Fry	110,134
10	Muskellunge	Fingerling	314
11	Muskellunge	Fry	20,911
11	Muskellunge	Fingerling	3,952

NET CATCH DATA

Date: 07/07/2009

	Gill Nets		Trap Nets	
species	# per net	avg. fish weight (lbs.)	# per net	avg. fish weight (lbs.)
Black Crappie	0.3	0.29	1.1	0.2`
Bluegill	-	-	1.7	0.22
Channel Catfish	1.8	2.21	0.1	1.20
Common Carp	0.1	4.02	0.6	7.05
Flathead Catfish	0.1	4.74	0.1	2.72
Gizzard Shad	0.3	1.81	-	-
Lake Sturgeon	0.3	3.78	-	-
Northern Pike	0.3	4.55	0.1	7.39
Rock Bass	0.1	0.15	0.7	0.11
Sauger	1.1	0.69	-	-
Smallmouth Bass	0.8	0.79	0.1	0.39
Walleye	1.1	1.59	-	-
White Bass	2.8	1.15	0.1	0.16
White Crappie	0.4	0.09	-	-
Yellow Perch	2.8	0.16	0.3	0.25

LENGTH OF SELECTED SPECIES SAMPLED FROM ALL GEAR

Number of fish caught for the following length categories (inches):

species	0-5	6-8	9-11	12-14	15-19	20-24	25-29	>30	Total
Black Crappie	12	15	3	-	-	-	-	-	30
Bluegill	11	29	-	-	-	-	-	-	40
Channel Catfish	-	-	2	8	11	7	1	-	29
Common Carp	-	-	-	1	1	6	6	-	14
Flathead Catfish	-	-	-	-	1	3	-	-	4
Freshwater Drum	1	13	30	9	3	2	-	-	58
Gizzard Shad	-	-	-	-	4	-	-	-	4
Golden Redhorse	-	-	1	8	4	-	-	-	13
Lake Sturgeon	-	-	-	1	-	-	1	2	4
Longnose Gar	-	-	-	-	-	1	1	3	5
Mooneye	-	-	-	1	-	-	-	-	1
Northern Pike	-	-	-	-	-	-	5	1	6
Quillback	-	-	-	5	4	-	-	-	9
River Redhorse	-	-	-	-	-	-	1	-	1
Rock Bass	15	3	-	-	-	-	-	-	18
Sauger	-	3	3	8	4	-	-	-	18
Shorthead Redhorse	-	-	3	15	2	-	-	-	20
Shortnose Gar	-	-	-	-	-	4	3	-	7
Silver Redhorse	-	-	10	7	69	4	-	-	91
Smallmouth Bass	-	3	5	3	-	-	-	-	13
Smallmouth Buffalo	-	-	-	-	4	11	-	-	16
Spotted Sucker	-	-	-	-	1	-	-	-	1
Walleye	-	-	2	5	8	2	1	-	18
White Bass	-	4	3	32	6	-	-	-	45
White Crappie	5	1	-	-	-	-	-	-	6
Yellow Perch	8	37	6	-	-	-	-	-	51

FISHING INFORMATION: If a varied fishing experience is what you crave, haul your rig to the lower St. Croix River/Lake St. Croix. This water has variety in spades – and in hearts, diamonds and clubs. No matter what you're after, you'll likely find the St. Croix offers a winning hand.

If that seems like extravagant praise, consider that the lower St. Croix/Lake St. Croix encompasses about 22 miles of light iced tea-colored water in channels which vary from a couple of hundred yards to over a mile wide. There are depths varying from just a foot or two in some of the backwaters on up to over 70 feet in the main channel. There is structure, too; lots and lots of structure. You'll find bars, current cuts, deep holes, railroad trestles, bridge pilings, riprap shoreline, sandy bottom, mucky bottom, broken rocks: just about everything you can imagine for aquatic life to hide in, feed near or reproduce around. Anglers can simply head to the right spot and use their favorite methods to catch fish.

It's small wonder, then, that there's plenty of life in this stretch of the river. According to the Minnesota Pollution Control Agency (MPCA), the number of species, both land and aquatic, which inhabit these waters runs into the hundreds. There are 41 species of freshwater mussels alone in the St. Croix.

According to the MPCA, you'll find 95 different fish species in the St. Croix. True, not all of these appeal to anglers. After all, there are lots of fish there that make their living either rooting around on the bottom or "sucking up" to those species that do. Never fear though; there are also plenty of fish that are a little higher on the food chain. They range from perch and bluegills on up to monster northern pike and the mighty muskellunge. One threat to this extensive fishery is exotic Asian carp. As of this writing, a few bighead carp had been

Access	Page	Launch	Latitude	Longitude
1	201	Ramp, slab	44° 47' 55.72" N	92° 47' 14.29" W
2	204	Ramp	44° 54' 07.87" N	92° 46' 48.12" W
3	205	Ramp	44° 56' 07.17" N	92° 44' 20.26" W
4	205	Ramp	44° 57' 41.12" N	92° 45' 58.21" W
5	205	Ramp	44° 57' 55.98" N	92° 45' 20.92" W
6	206	Ramp	44° 58' 17.74" N	92° 45' 32.91" W
7	206	Carry-in	44° 58' 45.09" N	92° 45' 35.70" W
8	207	Ramp	45° 00' 15.03" N	92° 45' 47.15" W
9	207	Ramp	45° 00' 22.53" N	92° 46' 38.74" W
10	207	Ramp	45° 01' 03.61" N	92° 46' 24.54" W
11	207	Ramp	45° 01' 18.08" N	92° 46' 28.44" W
12	108	Marina	45° 02' 09.03" N	92° 47' 03.31" W
13	208	Marina	45° 03' 32.45" N	92° 48' 16.59" W

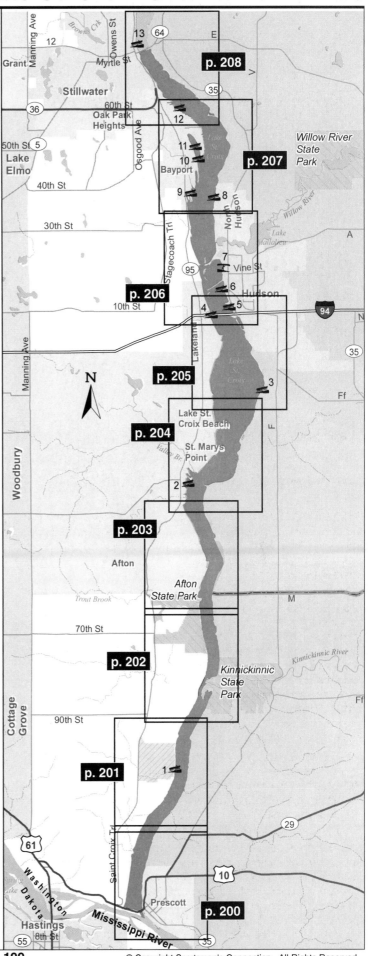

reported on the St. Croix. DNA from silver carp - the fish that commonly jump out of the water when they feel vibration from motorboats - was detected in 2011, although a subsequent test in 2012 failed to find silver carp DNA from the same stretch of river. These exotics could wreak havoc on the fishery because they eat a tremendous amount of plankton and would compete other native species.

Mike Wren, manager of Jimmy's Bait & Tackle, 806 Main Street South, Stillwater, MN, (651) 430-2554, says the lower St. Croix/Lake St. Croix offers a fishery second to none, although not all that many people know it. "The fishing is definitely very good here," he said. "There are some real big walleyes taken out of this system, along with smallmouth bass and other gamefish."

The lower St. Croix is one of the better spots in the area for muskie fishing. There are reports of 50-inch-plus fish being taken every year, and locals see 43- to 47-inch- muskies several times a season. That's not bad for water just outside the Twin Cities.

Both black and white crappies inhabit the river, and they're typically about 10 inches and .75 pounds; although some 14- and 15-inchers are taken every year, particularly through the ice. Bluegills aren't overly numerous, but they are pretty nice and can be taken in fair quantities in the backwaters. A 9-inch bluegill is, if not typical, at least a daily experience, and there are lots of 6-, 7-, and 8-inchers. White bass, typically a mainstay of the fishery in the lower St. Croix, have been less numerous lately, for some reason. The Prescott Narrows is one of the more reliable spots on the lower St. Croix. It can turn on anytime, although it's probably chiefly known as a spring and fall producer of nice walleyes and sauger. Some anglers catch muskies there, as well. The 'eyes you'll find in this spot typically run around 16 or 17 inches, although 22- to 24-inch fish are not uncommon, and a few 26- or 27-inch fish are taken every year. Saugers run smaller; about 13 inches on average. Jig-and-minnow combos work nicely early. Switch to Lindy rigs with crawlers by June. In July, a Lindy rig and a leech will do nicely, as will a spinner. If that doesn't produce, move, because the fish just aren't there or aren't interested.

If you decide to move, work your way upstream, fishing the "billion little points," particularly those along the east shoreline. The prominent point off the west shore, about a mile upstream from the narrows, can be really hot during summer, depending on water levels. Vertically jig the upper side of this, along with the drop, for walleyes and saugers. In the backwater formed on the point's downstream side, you'll find a weedbed that's worth a good look for monster pike and muskies. A few casts into these

Continued on page 202

Source: Minnesota Department of Natural Resources, USGS

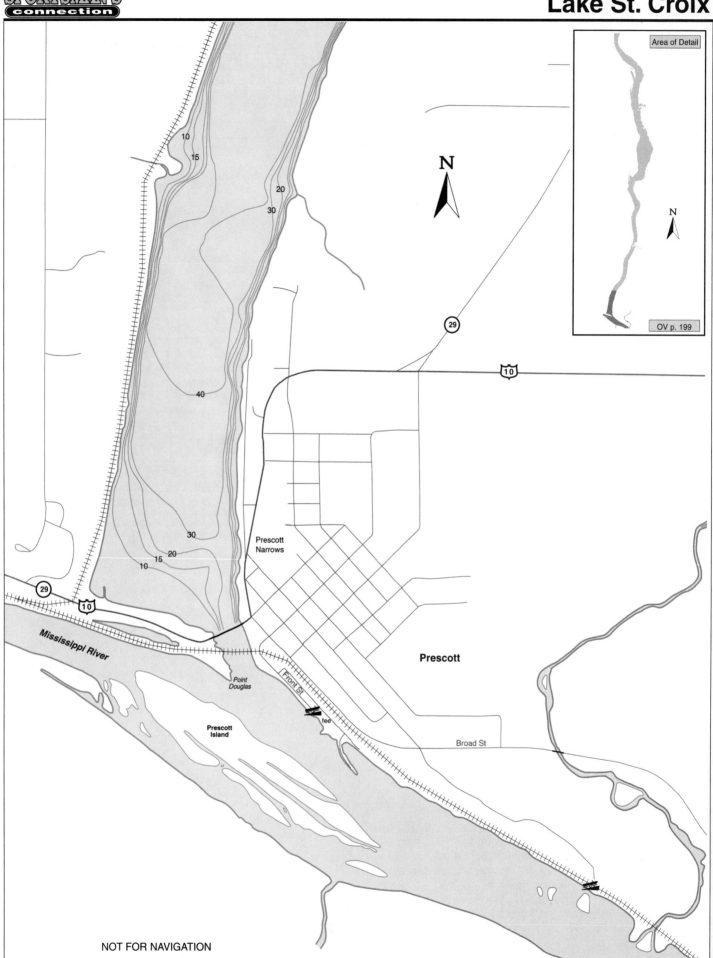

Area of Detail

N

N

OV p. 199

29

10

29

10

Prescott
Narrows

Prescott

Mississippi River

Front St

Point
Douglas

fee

Prescott
Island

Broad St

NOT FOR NAVIGATION

Source: Minnesota Department of Natural Resources, USGS   © Copyright Sportsman's Connection. All Rights Reserved.

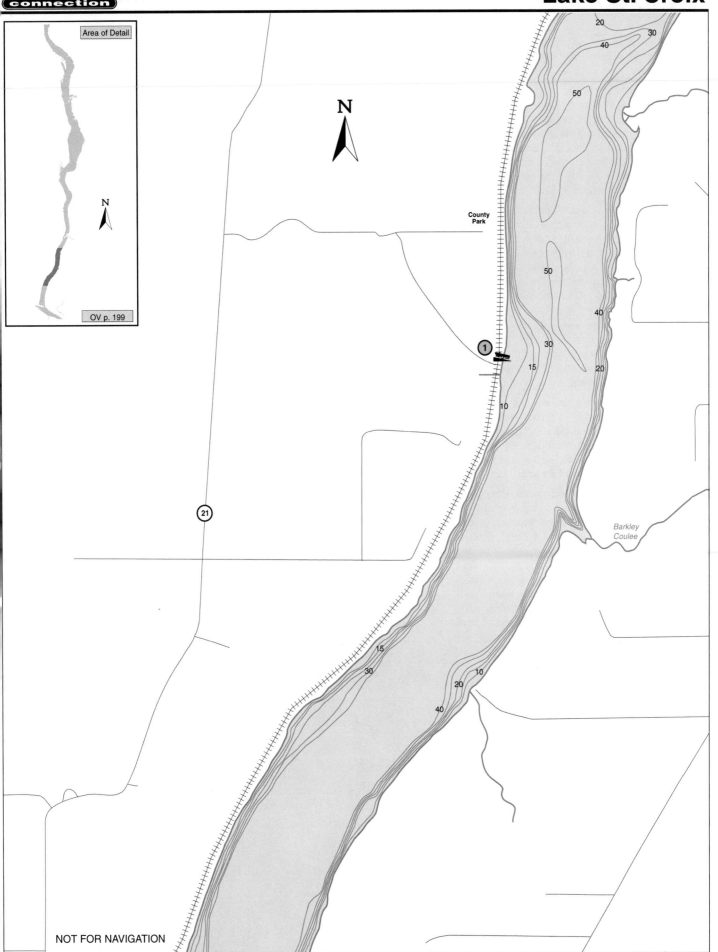

Source: Minnesota Department of Natural Resources, USGS

201

NOT FOR NAVIGATION

Lake St. Croix

Continued from page 199

weeds will sometimes produce a trophy, as northern pike over 40 inches have been caught here, along with 45-inch muskies.

Heading upstream, the tight inside turn off the east shore at Barkley Cooley can be hard to fish because of its small size, but it frequently yields nice catches of white bass and smallies. A small spinner or crank will get lots of attention. You'll need electronics to stay on this structure; so if your boat doesn't have a depth finder, find another spot.

That isn't a huge loss, though, as there's a broad bar off the west shore, about a quarter-mile farther upstream. This is at a county park, and the bar's upstream face offers good shore-fishing for 'eyes and pike. The area's broken rock, usually marked by a buoy, is a hotspot for smallies. The whole area can be worked for catfish as well. Be careful about fishing this structure from a boat, though, as recreational traffic can be heavy. In fact, if there's one drawback to fishing the lower St. Croix, it's all the competition from power boats and tournament anglers.

About a quarter-mile farther upstream is a bar off a broad point on the east shore. This frequently holds 'eyes and sauger during summer, along with a few smallies. Troll the drop-off, down as deep as 40 feet, with Rapalas. This area can be worked for catfish, too.

Farther north, the Kinnickinnic Narrows offers great fishing for just about everything. It's super for early 'eyes and saugers. Look for crappies in the fall-downs along shorelines. The Kinnickinnic River itself attracts nice northerns in summer and early fall. Try trolling a big crank or spinnerbait near the river mouth, as well as just downstream from it, where the river's cooler water holds fish. While you're in this area, don't neglect the

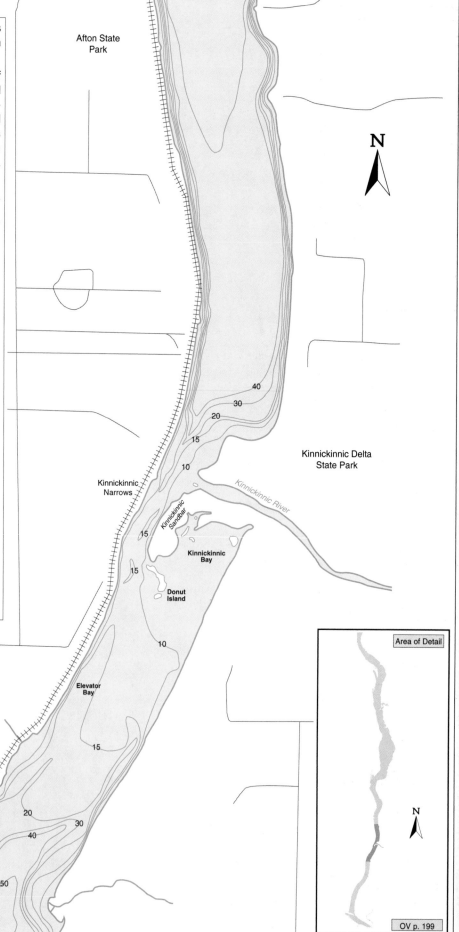

NOT FOR NAVIGATION

Source: Minnesota Department of Natural Resources, USGS   **202**   © Copyright Sportsman's Connection. All Rights Reserved.

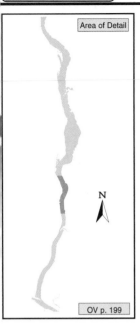

Area of Detail

N

OV p. 199

N

Black Bass Bar

50 40
35'
10
15
20
30
40
50

60
Ilwaco Springs

10
15
20
30
40
70
71'
50

Trout Brook

Afton State Park

structure just north of the narrows. You can find just about everything there, particularly walleyes and smallies, as well as channel cats in sand. Jigging works best there for 'eyes and sauger, especially in fall. You can sometimes find bass in as little as a foot or two of water near the east shore.

Afton State Park, upstream along the western shore, offers excellent shore fishing for walleyes and smallies along its shoreline of broken rock and attendant quick drop. The park's point, just above the Trout Brook inlet, presents a great place to troll deep-diving crankbaits or Lindy rigs parallel to the drop-off at 20 feet or so. On the point's downstream side is another of those backwaters, which often produce nice pike and muskies. Cast the area with cranks or bucktails.

Farther upstream off the eastern shore, you'll find Black Bass Bar. A buoy marks the rocks there, and these are a hotbed of smallmouth action. They're worth working in anything from 2 to 30 feet of water. Catfish Bar, opposite Afton and south of St. Mary's Point, is another great spot. Fish the whole area, both south and north of the point. You'll find 'eyes, sauger, pike, crappies and white bass there, and the catfish action is especially good. For these whiskered guys, try using cut bait or stink baits in 14 to 16 feet of water.

The shorelines on both sides heading up toward Lakeland Shores and Hudson often are good producers of walleyes and sauger. The bottom and sides there are sand, and they offer a great long trolling run. Drag Thundersticks or Shad Raps in blues, char-

Continued on page 207

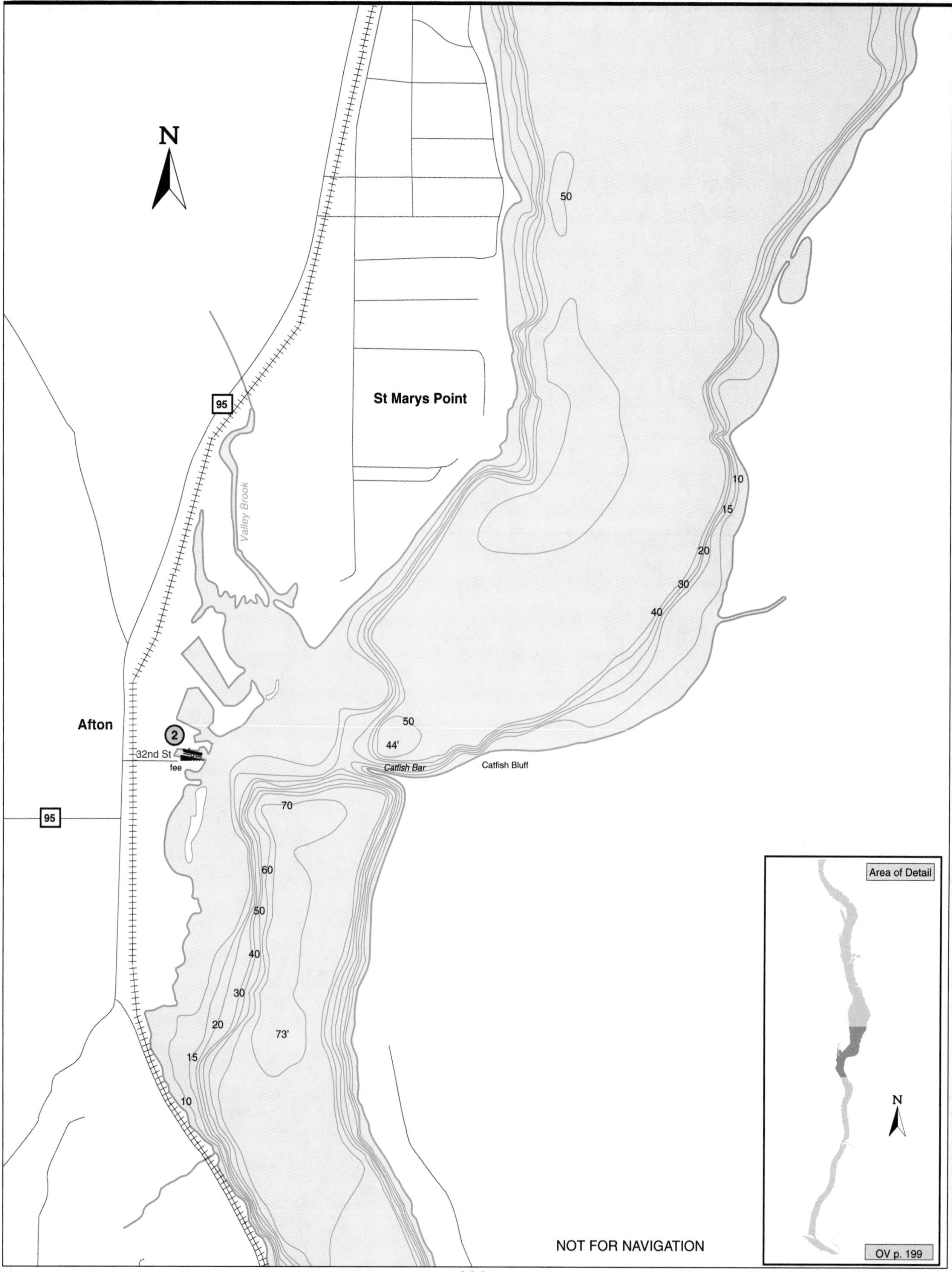

OV p. 199

N

St Marys Point

50

Valley Brook

95

10

15

20

30

40

Afton

(2)

32nd St
fee

50

44'

Catfish Bar

Catfish Bluff

70

60

50

40

30

20

73'

15

10

95

Area of Detail

N

NOT FOR NAVIGATION

OV p. 199

Lake St. Croix

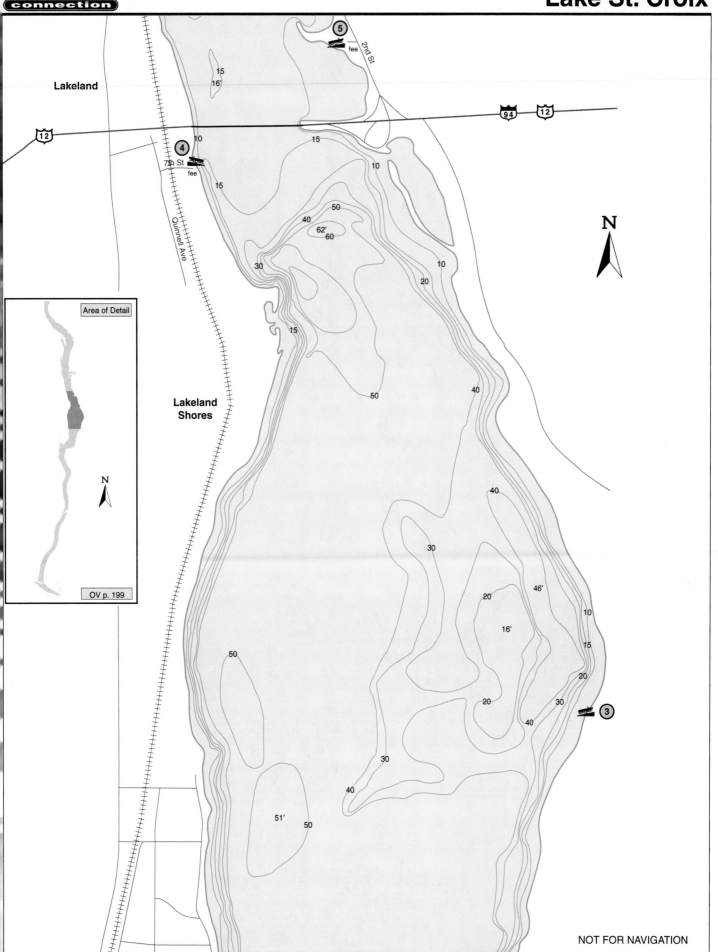

Lakeland

Lakeland
Shores

Quinnell Ave

7th St

2nd St

N

Area of Detail

N

OV p. 199

15
16'

10

15

50

15

30

15

50

15

10

10

20

40

62'
60
40

50

40

40

30

20

46'
16'
10
15
20
30
40

50

20

20

30

51'
50

40

Source: Minnesota Department of Natural Resources, USGS   **205**

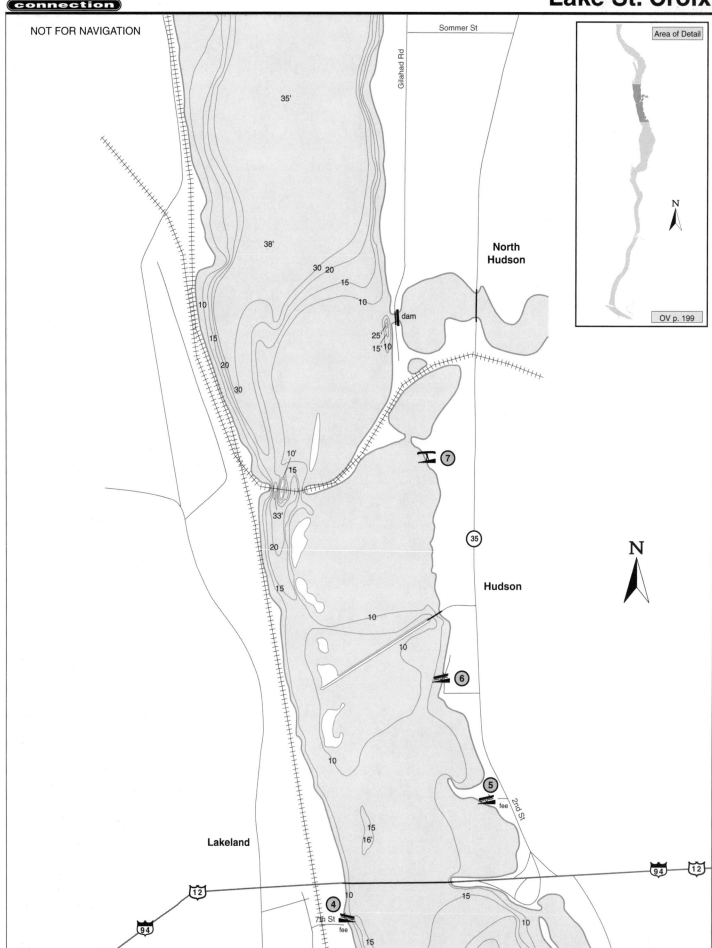

SPORTSMAN'S connection

NOT FOR NAVIGATION

Area of Detail

N

OV p. 199

Sommer St

Gilahad Rd

35'

38'

30 20

15

10

10

dam

25'

15' 10

North
Hudson

10'

15

33'

20

15

7

35

Hudson

10

10

6

10

5

fee

2nd St

15

16'

Lakeland

N

94   12

12

10

15

10

4

7th St

fee

15

94

Lake St. Croix

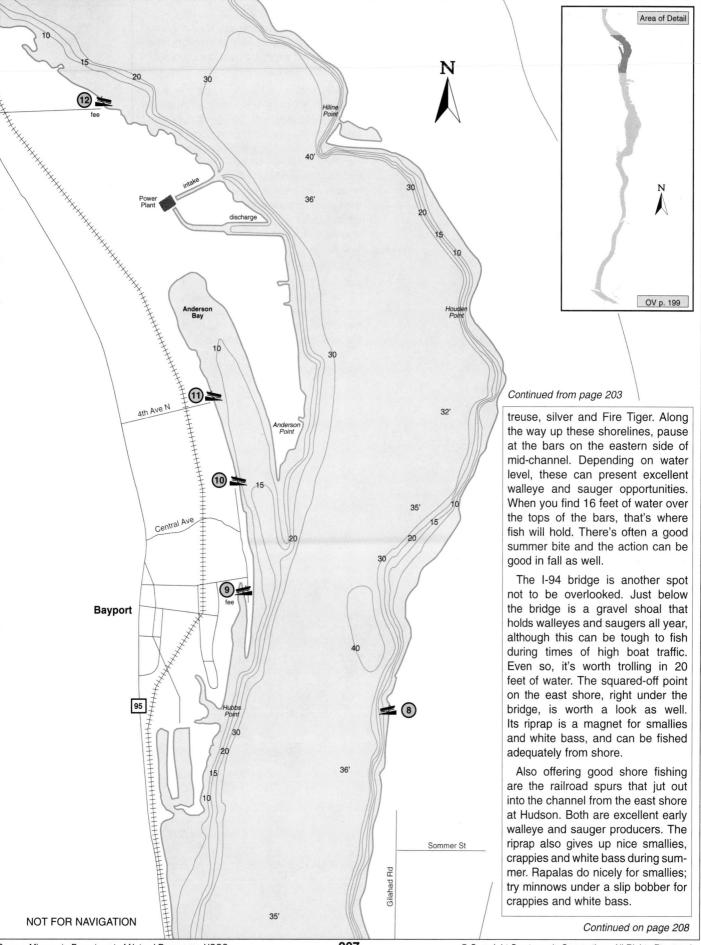

Area of Detail

N

OV p. 199

Hiline
Point

40'

Power
Plant

intake

discharge

36'

30

20

15

10

Houden
Point

Anderson
Bay

10

30

32'

Anderson
Point

4th Ave N

15

Central Ave

35'

10

20

15

20

30

Bayport

9

fee

40

95

Hubbs
Point

30

20

15

10

35'

36'

Sommer St

Gilahad Rd

Continued from page 203

treuse, silver and Fire Tiger. Along the way up these shorelines, pause at the bars on the eastern side of mid-channel. Depending on water level, these can present excellent walleye and sauger opportunities. When you find 16 feet of water over the tops of the bars, that's where fish will hold. There's often a good summer bite and the action can be good in fall as well.

The I-94 bridge is another spot not to be overlooked. Just below the bridge is a gravel shoal that holds walleyes and saugers all year, although this can be tough to fish during times of high boat traffic. Even so, it's worth trolling in 20 feet of water. The squared-off point on the east shore, right under the bridge, is worth a look as well. Its riprap is a magnet for smallies and white bass, and can be fished adequately from shore.

Also offering good shore fishing are the railroad spurs that jut out into the channel from the east shore at Hudson. Both are excellent early walleye and sauger producers. The riprap also gives up nice smallies, crappies and white bass during summer. Rapalas do nicely for smallies; try minnows under a slip bobber for crappies and white bass.

NOT FOR NAVIGATION

Continued on page 208

Source: Minnesota Department of Natural Resources, USGS

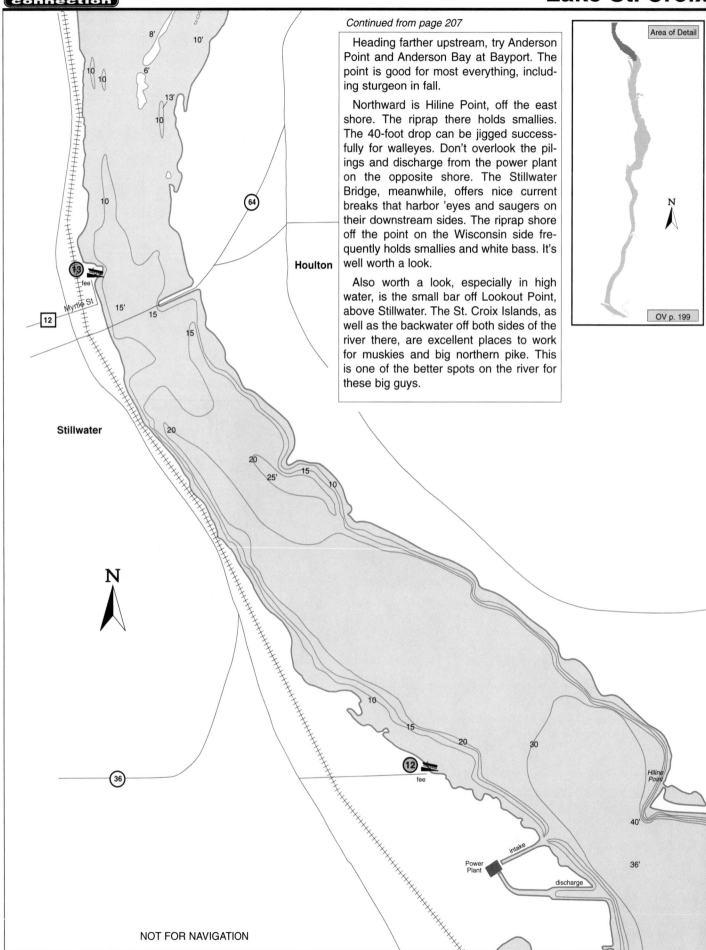

Continued from page 207

Heading farther upstream, try Anderson Point and Anderson Bay at Bayport. The point is good for most everything, including sturgeon in fall.

Northward is Hiline Point, off the east shore. The riprap there holds smallies. The 40-foot drop can be jigged successfully for walleyes. Don't overlook the pilings and discharge from the power plant on the opposite shore. The Stillwater Bridge, meanwhile, offers nice current breaks that harbor 'eyes and saugers on their downstream sides. The riprap shore off the point on the Wisconsin side frequently holds smallies and white bass. It's well worth a look.

Also worth a look, especially in high water, is the small bar off Lookout Point, above Stillwater. The St. Croix Islands, as well as the backwater off both sides of the river there, are excellent places to work for muskies and big northern pike. This is one of the better spots on the river for these big guys.

Area of Detail

N

OV p. 199

NOT FOR NAVIGATION

St. Croix River Overview

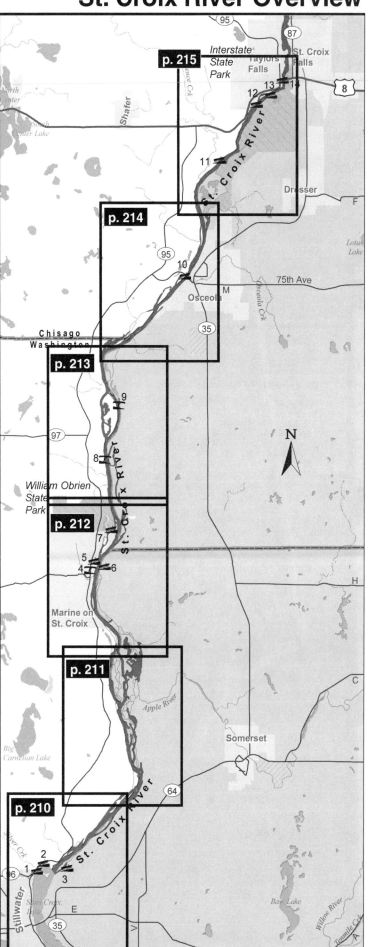

Access	Page	Launch	Latitude	Longitude
1	210	Ramp	45° 04' 42.03" N	92° 48' 10.68" W
2	210	Ramp, plank	45° 04' 51.76" N	92° 47' 59.83" W
3	210	Ramp	45° 04' 45.93" N	92° 47' 08.94" W
4	212	Carry-in	45° 12' 01.65" N	92° 46' 01.58" W
5	212	Ramp	45° 12' 11.07" N	92° 45' 55.53" W
6	212	Ramp	45° 12' 12.12" N	92° 45' 49.36" W
7	212	Ramp, slab	45° 13' 02.39" N	92° 45' 32.11" W
8	213	Carry-in	45° 14' 47.80" N	92° 45' 38.90" W
9	213	Carry-in	45° 16' 05.44" N	92° 45' 08.17" W
10	214	Ramp, slab	45° 19' 18.59" N	92° 42' 41.30" W
11	215	Ramp	45° 22' 07.47" N	92° 41' 24.02" W
12	215	Ramp, plank	45° 23' 32.11" N	92° 40' 02.53" W
13	215	Ramp	45° 23' 43.51" N	92° 39' 29.11" W
14	215	Ramp	45° 24' 03.85" N	92° 39' 03.12" W

FISHING INFORMATION: If you're looking to slow the pace a little, sometimes going fishing will do the trick; just you, your boat and the fish, right? Sometimes you end up communing with pleasure boaters, jet-skiers and what seems like every human being in the world, though. That ends up raising your blood pressure, rather than lowering it. So, you start to wonder, where can I find a peaceful place with the major excitement being a good bite, rather than watching water-skiers do cartwheels across the water?

The idyllic world exists at the St. Croix River. At least on a good share of the St. Croix River above Stillwater. According to Mike Wren of Jimmy's Bait and Tackle, 806 South Main, Stillwater, MN, (651) 430-2554, this stretch of the river is home to some pretty nice walleyes, saugers, smallmouth bass, crappies, white bass, and even the occasional muskellunge. Moreover, this stretch of the river is actually underfished, enough so that it's a reliable fishery; one which can stand a lot more pressure than it's now getting.

OK, so there's a catch. It's time to note that the upper St. Croix can be divided into two segments. One is between Stillwater and the Apple River inlet, and the other is above. The lower segment gets heavy recreational boat traffic and is heavily fished, as well. That is, when anglers can dodge the jet-skis long enough to get their line in the water.

All that changes, though, when you reach the Arcola Sandbar, opposite the mouth of the Apple River. There, the water shoals considerably, effectively keeping larger boats from accessing the upper reaches. The DNR maintains a checkpoint at this bar. Boaters are required to haul their rigs out to prevent transmission of zebra mussels to the upper stretches of the river. There are spots above where you can launch again, once you've made sure your boat is free of bivalve hitchhikers. This upper stretch of the river is part of the St. Croix National Scenic Riverway and is subject to speed restrictions. In fact, the entire stretch is a "slow speed zone" in which one must proceed at a leisurely pace below planing speed. Even this speed is too fast in several areas, which are designated as no-wake zones. These are posted, and boaters are required to slow to the point where they can do little more than maintain boat control.

The speed restrictions keep boat traffic down. Because the river shoals in many places above Arcola, one wouldn't want to roar around with a big powerboat, anyway. Locals learn to navigate the upper river quite handily, but the educational process takes years and can chew up a bunch of props in the process.

Continued on page 210

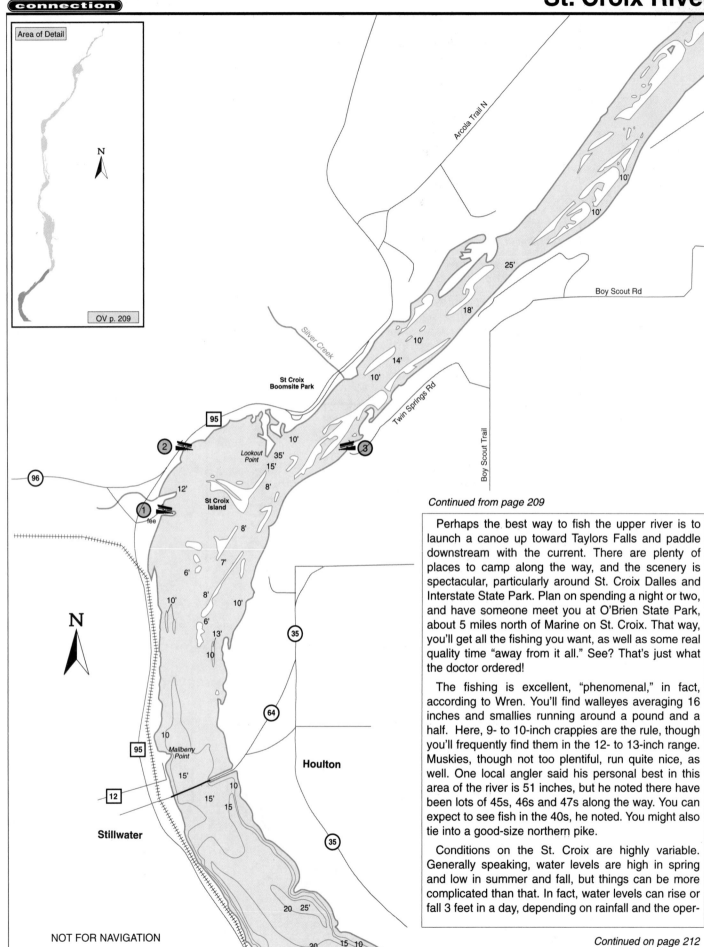

Area of Detail

N

OV p. 209

Arcola Trail N

Boy Scout Rd

Silver Creek

St Croix
Boomsite Park

Twin Springs Rd

Boy Scout Trail

95

96

Lookout
Point

St Croix
Island

fee

N

35

64

Houlton

95

Mallberry
Point

12

Stillwater

35

Continued from page 209

Perhaps the best way to fish the upper river is to launch a canoe up toward Taylors Falls and paddle downstream with the current. There are plenty of places to camp along the way, and the scenery is spectacular, particularly around St. Croix Dalles and Interstate State Park. Plan on spending a night or two, and have someone meet you at O'Brien State Park, about 5 miles north of Marine on St. Croix. That way, you'll get all the fishing you want, as well as some real quality time "away from it all." See? That's just what the doctor ordered!

The fishing is excellent, "phenomenal," in fact, according to Wren. You'll find walleyes averaging 16 inches and smallies running around a pound and a half. Here, 9- to 10-inch crappies are the rule, though you'll frequently find them in the 12- to 13-inch range. Muskies, though not too plentiful, run quite nice, as well. One local angler said his personal best in this area of the river is 51 inches, but he noted there have been lots of 45s, 46s and 47s along the way. You can expect to see fish in the 40s, he noted. You might also tie into a good-size northern pike.

Conditions on the St. Croix are highly variable. Generally speaking, water levels are high in spring and low in summer and fall, but things can be more complicated than that. In fact, water levels can rise or fall 3 feet in a day, depending on rainfall and the oper-

NOT FOR NAVIGATION

Continued on page 212

Source: Minnesota Department of Natural Resources, USGS   **210**

Area of Detail

N

OV p. 209

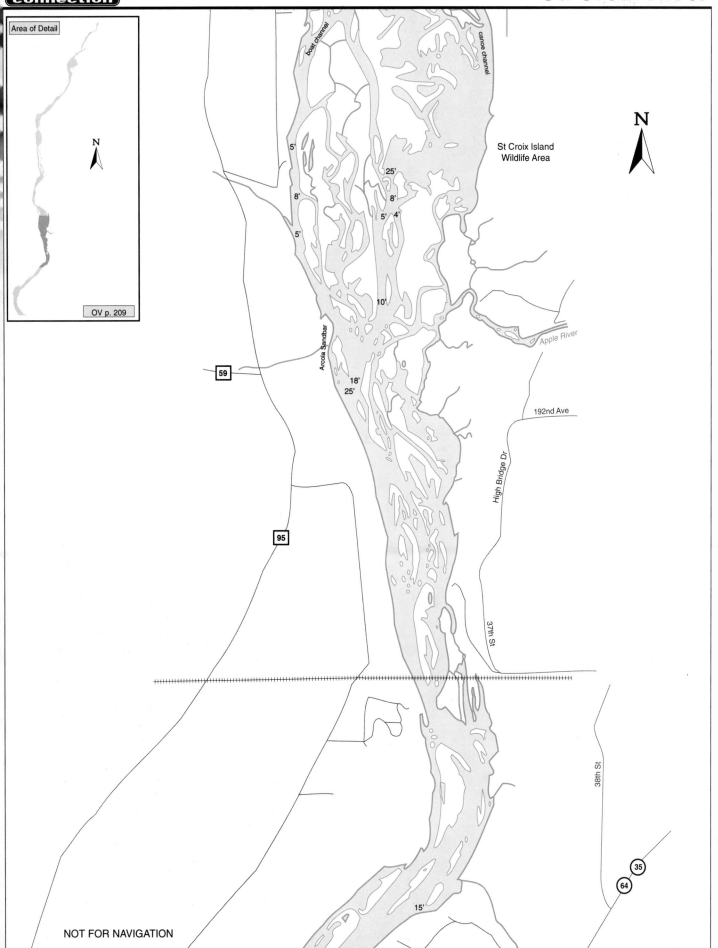

boat channel

canoe channel

5'

25'

St Croix Island
Wildlife Area

N

8'

8'

5' 4'

5'

10'

Arcola Sandbar

Apple River

192nd Ave

59

18'
25'

High Bridge Dr

95

37th St

38th St

35

64

15'

NOT FOR NAVIGATION

NOT FOR NAVIGATION

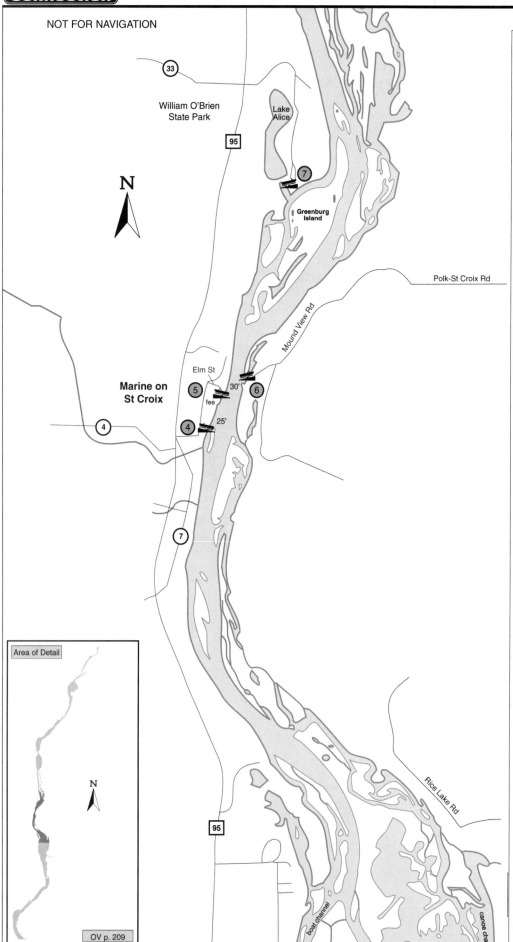

33

William O'Brien
State Park

Lake
Alice

95

N

7

Greenburg
Island

Polk-St Croix Rd

Mound View Rd

Elm St

Marine on
St Croix

5   30'   6

fee

4   25'

4

7

95

Rice Lake Rd

Area of Detail

N

boat channel

canoe chann

OV p. 209

Continued from page 210

ations of the power dam at St. Croix Falls. At the dam, flow-through for power generation typically begins between 8 and 9 a.m. each day and shuts down late in the afternoon. You can practically watch the river rise and fall with the power-generation cycle.

All of this means, of course, that no particular spots will reliably produce fish at all times; you'll just have to see which places hold fish on any given day, or hour, for that matter.

Some generalities can be offered about location, however. Walleyes and sauger head upstream to spawn in spring. You'll find larger fish upriver through the second week in May. Look for eddies and current breaks in 2 to 10 feet of water, and toss jig-and-minnow combinations for 'eyes and saugers. Or, troll Thundersticks slowly upstream along shelving shorelines. As the season advances, larger fish head back downstream toward Lake St. Croix and the lower reaches of the river. So, if you're fishing the upper section of the river from June on, plan to catch smaller fish in the 12- to 16-inch range. Look for them in deeper holes, where you might also turn up a channel cat.

The river's rocky shorelines will typically produce most of the smallies. Backwaters are the places to try for crappies, northerns and muskies. A small minnow under a slip bobber will do nicely anytime for crappies. Pike and muskies will hit on large stickbaits, like #13 to #18 Rapalas in chartreuse or orange in spring or bucktails in black and silver. Cast into 3 to 5 feet of water where there's a bottleneck or a little bit of current, and be prepared for a thrill.

In addition to the general guidelines, the folks at Jimmy's Bait and Tackle offer several spots to give you a start on St. Croix fishing.

The main channel above Lookout Point, near Stillwater can be trolled, primarily in late spring and early summer, for walleyes and sauger. Crankbaits in natural colors work best at this time of year.

Moving upstream, pay attention to your depth-finder and locate the 25-foot-deep holes in mid-channel. These can be tough to fish on week-

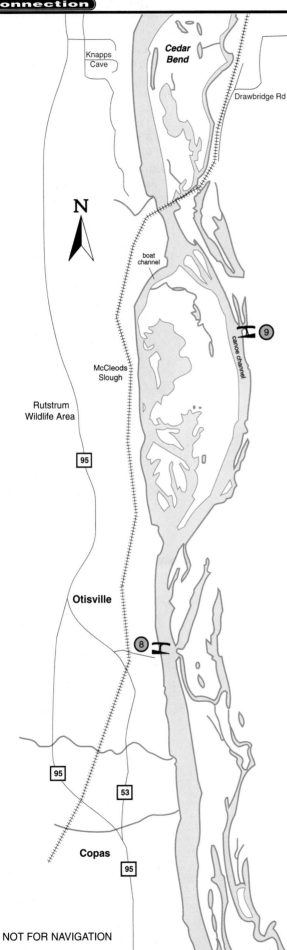

Knapps Cave

Cedar Bend

Drawbridge Rd

N

boat channel

canoe channel ⑨

McCleods Slough

Rutstrum Wildlife Area

95

Otisville

⑧

95

53

Copas

95

NOT FOR NAVIGATION

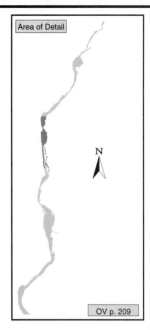

Area of Detail

N

OV p. 209

ends because of boat traffic, but they can be worked successfully for walleyes and saugers with jig-and-minnow combos. Shoreline stumps and timber in the same area often yield smallmouth bass.

Just below the railroad bridge at Arcola, the downstream ends of the islands deserve a look in May and June for walleyes and saugers. The islands have sand points on their downstream ends that usually hold fish, and submerged timber in these areas often produce smallies. You'll also find channel cats in 25 feet of water in the main channel around these islands.

Below the Apple River inlets on the Wisconsin shore, you'll find a weedy backwater that yields nice muskies and trophy pike. Fish this area during high-water periods in summer. Work the same area in spring for spawning white bass.

Above the Arcola Sandbar and the DNR checkpoint, troll the west channel in spring for walleyes and saugers, as well as smallies. Crankbaits will do nicely here; make sure they get down 5 to 8 feet, depending on water level. Across the river, you'll find another weedy backwater off the Wisconsin shore. This is another excellent high-water spot for northerns and muskies. It sometimes yields a largemouth bass to anglers who toss topwater gear in summer. This same area, too, offers good winter angling for crappies and the few nice bluegills the river has to offer.

You'll find good spring walleye and sauger action both upstream and downstream from the fee access at Marine on St. Croix. Look for current breaks and scattered rock in this area, and toss prepared baits or cut bait into the 30-foot holes for channel cats. Good shore fishing for walleyes, saugers and smallies is available both above and below the bridge to Greenburg Island in William O'Brien State Park. The concrete landing there is nice, and you'll find camping, picnic facilities, washrooms and canoe rental there, as well. Farther upstream, McLeods Slough, a backwater off the west shore, offers good spring and fall action for walleyes and saugers, as well as good fishing for smallies throughout the open-water season.

The laydowns there are bass magnets, and you'll frequently find crappies there in spring, as well.

Speaking of crappies, the old swinging bridge some 3.5 miles south of Osceola offers phenomenal fishing. The bridge's base forms a big backwater and eddy that draws fish like you wouldn't believe. Not only crappies live here, but walleyes and saugers as well. You'll catch these latter species primarily in spring and summer, mainly on trolled crankbaits. This spot is excellent, too, for channel cats. There's a 30-foot-deep hole downstream from the bridge base, and cut baits do well there.

Farther upstream you'll find the best spring action for walleyes and sauger around Rock Island and the crossing for the gas pipeline, three miles or so below Taylors Falls. Troll crankbaits in this area or, when current permits, anchor and jig the rocky bottom. The boulders in this area often produce trophy smallmouth bass as well. You can frequently take smallies in the smaller shoreline rocks throughout the open-water season.

Shallow shorelines just below the Highway 8 bridge also deserve a look in spring. These produce walleyes, saugers and frequently smallies, as well.

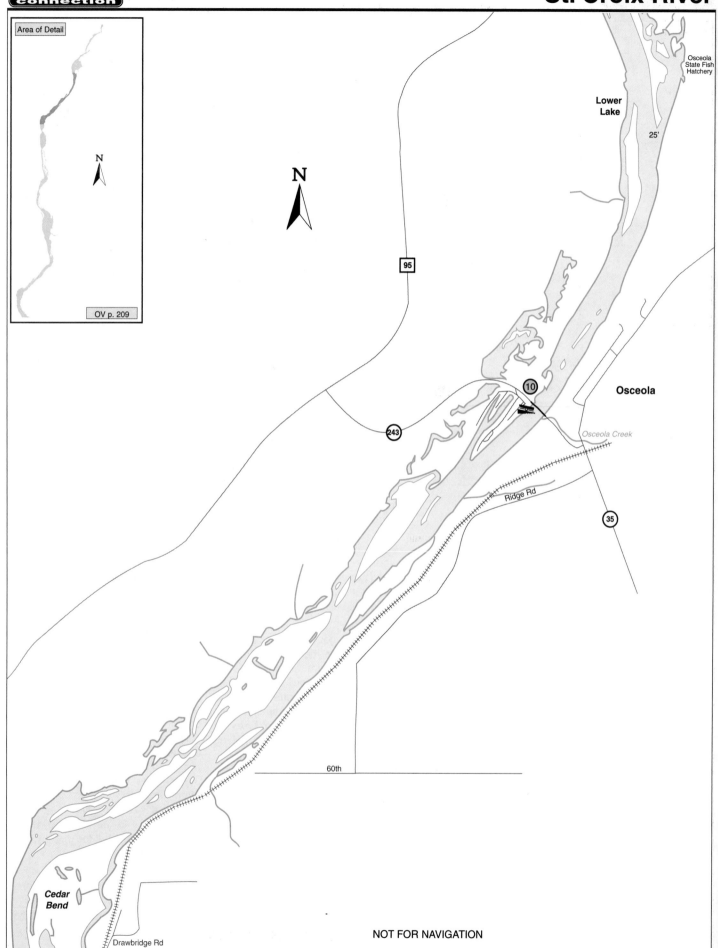

Area of Detail

N

OV p. 209

N

95

243

Lower
Lake

Osceola
State Fish
Hatchery

25'

10

Osceola

Osceola Creek

35

Ridge Rd

60th

Cedar
Bend

Drawbridge Rd

NOT FOR NAVIGATION

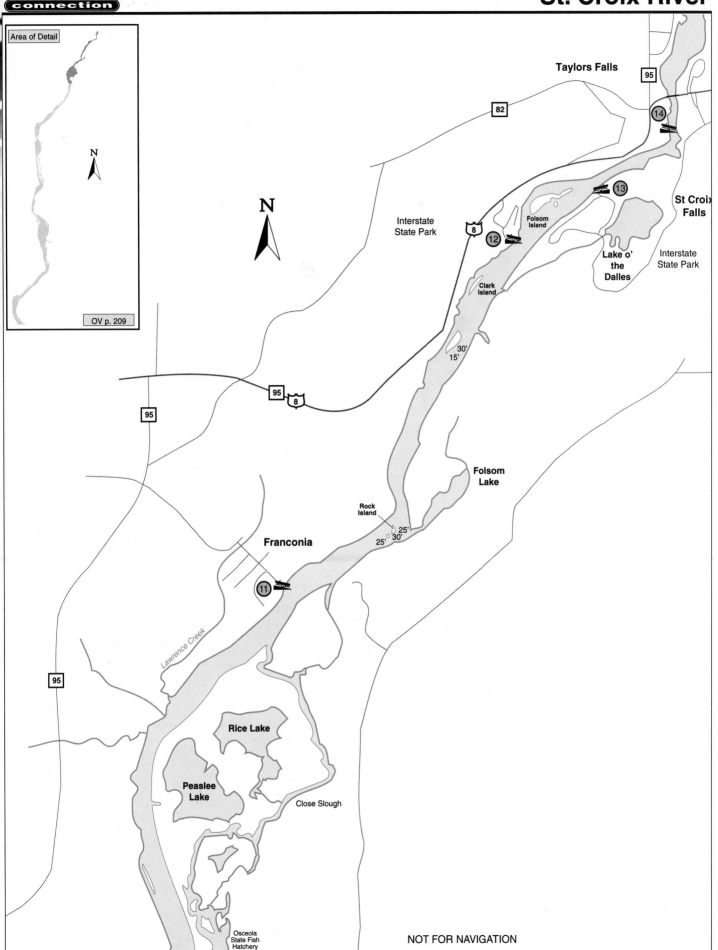

Area of Detail

N

OV p. 209

N

Taylors Falls

82

95

14

Interstate
State Park

13

Folsom
Island

St Croix
Falls

8

12

Lake o'
the
Dalles

Interstate
State Park

Clark
Island

30'
15'

95   8

95

Folsom
Lake

Rock
Island

25'
30'
25'

Franconia

11

95

Lawrence Creek

Rice Lake

Peaslee
Lake

Close Slough

Osceola
State Fish
Hatchery

NOT FOR NAVIGATION

Spring Lake of the Mississippi River
Dakota County

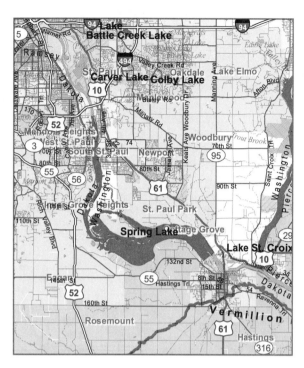

Area map pg / coord: 30 / D,E-3
Watershed: Mississippi River
Secchi disk: 1.1 feet (2001)
Water color: NA

Surface area: 1,839 acres
Shorelength: NA
Maximum depth: 17 feet
Mean depth: NA

FISH STOCKING DATA			
year	species	size	# released
04	Muskellunge	Fry	35,421
06	Muskellunge	Fry	31,344
07	Muskellunge	Fry	30,701

NET CATCH DATA				
Date: 07/30/2001	Gill Nets		Trap Nets	
species	# per net	avg. fish weight (lbs.)	# per net	avg. fish weight (lbs.)
Black Crappie	-	-	1.1	0.30
Bluegill	-	-	1.6	0.17
Channel Catfish	9.5	0.87	0.7	2.36
Flathead Catfish	-	-	trace	5.92
Northern Pike	-	-	trace	2.89
Smallmouth Buffalo	-	-	trace	3.45
Sauger	2.5	1.60	trace	1.49
Walleye	2.5	2.04	trace	1.59
White Bass	2.0	0.86	0.6	0.75
White Crappie	-	-	trace	0.74

LENGTH OF SELECTED SPECIES SAMPLED FROM ALL GEAR								
Number of fish caught for the following length categories (inches):								
species	0-5	6-8	9-11	12-14	15-19	20-24	25-29	>30	Total
Black Crappie	11	8	12	-	-	-	-	-	31
Bluegill	26	16	-	-	-	-	-	-	42
Channel Catfish	1	3	10	9	7	5	3	-	38
Flathead Catfish	-	-	-	-	-	2	-	-	2
Northern Pike	-	1	-	-	-	-	1	-	2
Sauger	-	-	-	-	7	-	-	-	7
Walleye	-	-	-	-	5	1	-	-	6
White Bass	1	6	3	10	-	-	-	-	20
White Crappie	-	-	1	1	-	-	-	-	2

FISHING INFORMATION: Spring Lake is a large, shallow, 1,839-acre, Dakota County widening of the Mississippi River. Because of its riverine nature, Spring is murky, with water clarity readings down to only a foot or so. Its waters contain a diverse collection of warm-water river species. The lake can be accessed through numerous locations on the Mississippi River, as well as a DNR-owned ramp off Dakota Co. 42 on Hilary Path. This ramp is on Spring Lake approximately three miles downstream from Baldwin Lake. Dakota County proudly trumpets the beauty and recreational opportunity of Spring Lake Park Reserve that is stretched along the southern shoreline of Spring Lake. Winter- and summer-use trails, an archery trail, a model airplane flying field and numerous picnic and park facilities can be enjoyed by visitors not inclined to fish the waters. There are limited shore fishing opportunities available in the park. Don't forget that this area is considered navigable waters and is under the authority of the U.S. Coast Guard. You'll need to follow all regulations the Coast Guard has for Spring Lake.

Other than abundant numbers of riverine species such as carp, goldeye, sucker, smallmouth buffalo, quillback, mooneye, freshwater drum and various types of redhorse, Spring Lake is home to channel and flathead catfish; saugers and walleyes; northern pike and muskellunge; bluegills; white and black crappies; and largemouth, smallmouth and white bass. White bass, of course, are not at all closely related to the cool-water bronzebacks and largemouths famous in Minnesota, but are members of the temperate bass family and are notorious for their fighting ability, considering their smaller size. Muskellunge fry are stocked on occasion, and time will tell if this mighty predator thrives in the cloudy waters of Spring Lake.

Master your catfishing techniques on Spring Lake, because these hard-fighting beasts are abundant and of good size. Or perfect your bass fishing skills by casting into the many shoreline pockets and shallow, sparse weedbeds emerging from this littoral lake. Better yet, before the statewide fishing opener or any time of the year, use Spring Lake to test your rods, reels, arms and elbows. Minnesota waters of the Mississippi are open year-round, so why

not fish them? Walleyes and pike can grow to decent size, crappies are big and white bass are plentiful. White bass can be found, at times, feeding on baitfish right at or just below the surface; small, white spinners or little, bright spoons will attract their attention when thrown right into the middle of the fray. Trolling is arguably the most effective tactic for catching fish in a lake like Spring because of its fairly constant shallow depth, lack of heavy vegetation, tremendous species diversity and underwater riverine-like structure. According to DNR information, walleyes are below average in abundance and average sized, as are northern pike. Smallmouth bass are below average in abundance and smaller than average size. Bluegills are below average in abundance, but above average size, as are crappies.

Spring Lake is posted with fish-consumption advisories, because of the DNR's detection of higher-than-normal levels of PCBs and mercury present in most of the fish; in fact, special regulations require catch-and-release of walleyes, saugers and largemouth and smallmouth bass. Anglers choosing to fish Spring Lake in fall need to be aware that it's a popular duck hunting area, so take appropriate measures to prevent any potential problems.

#	River Mile	Spring Lake Access	# ramps, structure
1	832.40 R	City of South St. Paul Access	concrete ramp, floating dock, shorefishing
2	830.50 R	Twin City Marina	private marina
3	830.40 R	River Heights Marina	fuel, ramp, repairs
4	829.60 L	Lions Levee Park	ramp, park, picnic, restrooms
5	829.30 L	Willies Hidden Harbor Marina	private marina
6	826.20 R	River Grove Marina	private marina
7	822.20 L	Grey Cloud Park	concrete ramp
8	820.00 R	Hilary Path	DNR carry-down access

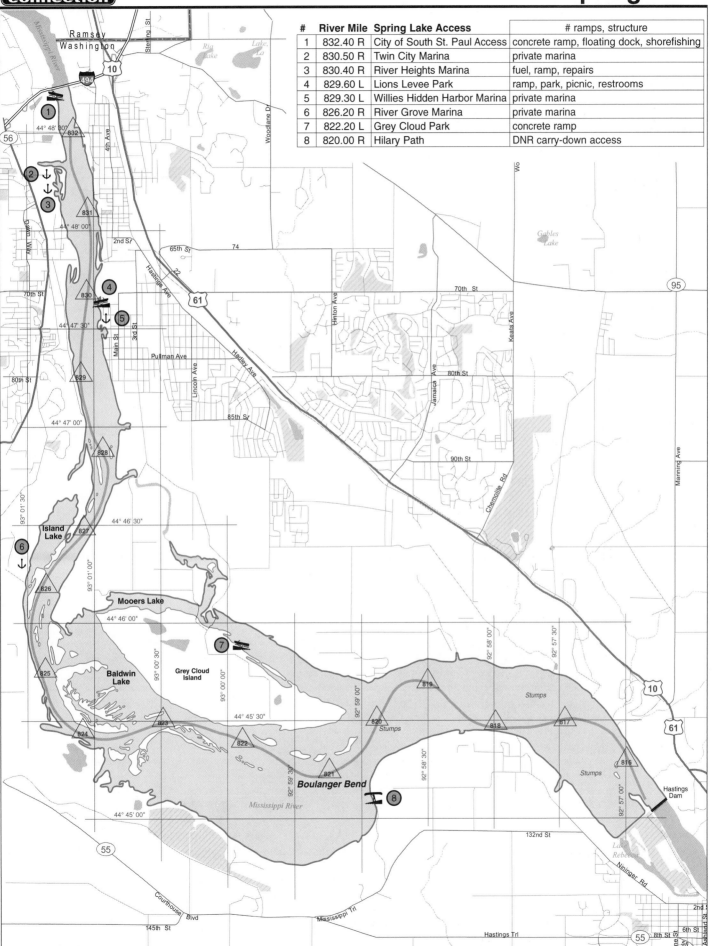

Source: Minnesota Department of Natural Resources, USGS

Mississippi River Access Information

River Mile	Page #	Boat ramp	Other fishing	Parking	Site hours	Operating agency	Phone	Directions to site
866.3L	222	concrete	shore	30	daylight	Hennepin	763-559-9000	Co. 1/Egret Blvd, S 1 mi to Coon Rapids Dam Regional Park (access upstream of dam)
863.0R	222	concrete	shore	6	8 am - 10 pm	Brooklyn Park	763-424-8000	Hwy 252/83rd Ave N, 1/2 mile E to site
860.2R	222	-	pier	10	sunrise - sunset	Three Rivers Park District	763-559-9000	Lyndale/57th St, N on Park Rd to parking lot (N. Mississippi Regional Park)
860.1L	222	concrete	shore	8	7:30 am - 9:30 pm	Anoka County	763-757-3920	At 53rd Way and E River Rd in Fridley (Riverfront Regional Park)
857.7R	222	concrete	pier	43	6 am - 10 pm	Mpls Parks	612-661-4800	Memorial Pkwy / Webber Pkwy, SE to Lyndale, L to Washington, N to site
854.5L	222	concrete	platform	30	6 am - 10 pm	Mpls Parks	612-661-4800	Washington/Plymouth Ave, E across river to site near lighthouse (Boom Island Park)
853.2R	222	carry-down	shore	40	6 am - 10 pm	Mpls Parks	612-661-4800	W River Rd near 10th St bridge
852.5L	222	carry-down	shore	40	6 am - 10 pm	Mpls Parks	612-661-4800	E River Rd on U of M campus
851.5L	222	carry-down	shore	street	6 am - 10 pm	Mpls Parks	612-661-4800	E Riv Rd at Cecil St near Shriners Hospital, W Riv Rd at Lake St.
846.6L	223	concrete	shore	50	sunrise - 9:30 pm	St. Paul Parks	651-266-6400	Miss River Blvd / Magoffin, down hill to park (Hidden Falls Regional Park)
840.2R	223	concrete	shore	30	sunrise - 11 pm	St. Paul	651-266-6400	Hwy 52/Plato Blvd, W to Water St, W 2 mi to Lilydale access (Lilydale/Harriet Island Regional Park)
832.4R	223	concrete	platform	29	5 am - 11 pm	South St. Paul	651-306-3690	I494/Hardmann Ave, N to Verderosa Ave, E and over tracks to site
829.5L	224	concrete	shore	20	5 am - 11 pm	St. Paul Park	651-459-9785	3rd St, W on 7th St to park
820.1R	224	concrete	shore	5	24 hours	DNR	651-772-7935	Hwy 55/Co 42, NE to Hilary Path, N to site (on Spring Lake)
814.1R	225	concrete	shore	40	24 hours	Hastings	651-437-5858	Hwy. 61, 1/2 mile W on road to Lock & Dam #2

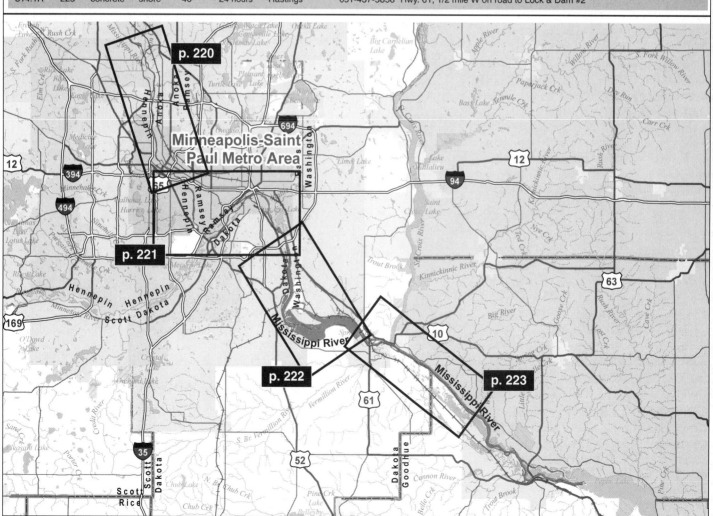

Source: U.S. Army Corps of Engineers

It's very rare that you can pull trophy-class walleye, bragging-board sauger and good numbers of smallmouth—plus the occasional largemouth, crappie, pike, muskie and catfish—from the same body of water in a city of over 2 million people. But that's exactly how abundant the fishing opportunity is in the Mississippi River between Coon Rapids Dam and Lock & Dam No. 2 in the Twin Cities.

It's almost impossible to effectively sum up the overall quality of the fisheries in the East Metro area of the Mississippi in a paragraph, but we'll take a stab at it: walleye fishing in this section of the Big River is as good as (or, in most cases, better than) any walleye fishery in the country, with 8- to 10-plus-pound 'eyes caught regularly at certain times of the year. In addition, sauger fishing is some of the best in the region, with 18- to 20-inchers representing the typical bag. The smallmouth fishing, while not as productive for hawg smallies as the water above Coon Rapids, is good for numbers of fish in the 2-pound range.

Compound that wealth of species with almost unlimited access and hundreds of square miles of good water to choose from and you have one of the state's signature fisheries.

The East Metro section of the Mississippi, basically from Coon Rapids Dam down to the mouth of the St. Croix River below Hastings, covers 54 river miles, but there are also dozens of sloughs, backwater lakes and side channels that provide acre upon fishy acre of access to all of the species mentioned above. There are no less than 15 publicly owned (DNR, St. Paul Parks, Minneapolis Parks, etc.) boat launches/access sites in those 54 miles, and several marinas on both sides of the river throughout Minneapolis and St. Paul, so John Q. Public can fish virtually every square inch of the Mississippi and be within minutes of a launch at any time.

Multi-species productivity aside, though, walleyes are by far the most popular target for sport anglers on the Mississippi, and for good reason: the potential to hook trophy 'eyes exists 365 days a year.

"That's just an awesome fishery, especially Pool 2," says Dave Lofgren of St. Croix Rods, who fishes this section of the Mississippi regularly. "It's a great wing dam fishery. You can catch bunches of walleyes over 8 pounds, if you're on the right wing dam at the right time of year. You can do well at almost any time of the year, if you understand how to fish wing dams, but there are also times when you can fish deeper in channels or fish really shallow along shorelines and catch a whole bunch of big walleyes, too."

The very best times to find concentrations of big fish are in early spring (March, April, May) and late fall/early winter (September to December), when bigger fish are most active and aggressive. Not to say that you can't locate trophy-class 'eyes in the heat of summer or dead of winter (more on these options later), but your fish per hour will almost certainly be much higher during the two prime seasons.

As veteran Mississippi guide and tournament pro Steve Dezurik points out, the aforementioned wing dam structures are walleye magnets throughout the year, and they're especially productive at certain key parts of the calendar.

"Wing dams are incredibly numerous on stretches of the Mississippi, and have produced some of my biggest river walleyes," Dezurik says.

Both Dezurik and Lofgren agree that the 32 miles of Pool 2 offer the most productive wing dam options in the Twin Cities area, but it's not as simple as pulling up to any dam on the river and fan casting like a demon. Look for dams that provide a good current break AND proximity to a deeper channel or slot, and study how the current breaks around both the upriver and downriver ends of the dam. If you can find dams that create a good eddy or seam just off the main channel, you're in business.

"Big walleyes will usually be on the first break near the wing dams in 14 feet of water or less, especially in spring," Lofgren says.

The stretch between the I-494 bridge in South St. Paul and the St. Paul Municipal Airport offers a handful of such options, starting at the South St. Paul Access at I-494, moving just upstream on the lefthand side of the river.

"From the 494 bridge, you can tool upriver for about a half-mile and you'll see the green marker buoys on the lefthand side," Lofgren says. "There's a pair of nice wing dams right there that are really good late in spring and on into summer. They actually turn on a bit more in summer, when fish relate more to the tips of those dams. The water will swing right off the upstream side on the tips and roll right around into a washout in deeper water. You can fish that a couple of different ways, but if you get out there with a jig and minnow, you'll catch some really big catfish, too."

Moving upriver about a mile and a half, look for the orange landings and the airport on the left and the waste management facility on the right. You'll find a pair of red buoys and two wing dams that lie just off the main channel. The dams create a break in 7 to 14 feet of water right where they meet the main channel (which drops off to 18 to 22 feet). Both jigs and crankbaits are effective here.

Of course, the Mississippi isn't just a wing dam fishery. Stepping through the seasons from spring to winter, you can run the gamut of techniques and depths, from casting or 3-way-rigging crankbaits and stickbaits in deep channels to slip jigging, and there are multiple places to use every walleye bait under the sun. Just before spring, runoff pushes higher volumes of water through the Mississippi, and you can pick up both walleye and sauger by shading just a few feet shallower off your usual 20- to 24-foot current line with jigs Springtime is also a good time for shore fishermen on the upper end of Pool 2, many of whom are successful pitching jigs/minnow from Hidden Falls Regional Park. The water moves faster through this part of the river up to Ford Dam, but, as Lofgren points out, "If you can find slackwater eddies in there, you're going to find fish."

Just below that, between Watergate Marina and Hidden Falls, you can catch a combination of walleyes and smallmouth bass throwing crankbaits along riprap. Just downstream from there, from the mouth of the Minnesota River up to Watergate Marina, you can troll the break on the right-hand side with a No. 5 Shad Rap on the shallow side and a No. 8 on the deep side, and pick up fish after fish (especially in wintertime).

Later in spring and through summer, when water rises to bathwater temperature, Lofgren has found success along bridge pilings, throwing No. 10 or 12 Husky Jerks in glass, clown, pink and blue.

INFORMATION

• Joe's Sporting Goods, (651) 488-5511, Little Canada, MN;

• Steve Dezurik (guide), (612) 860-9329

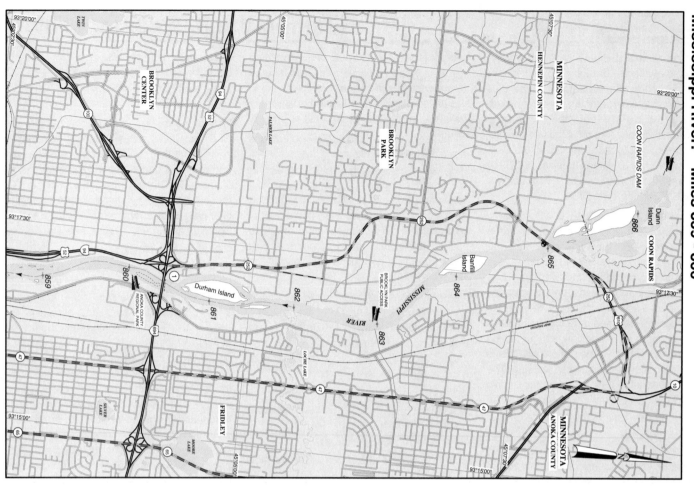

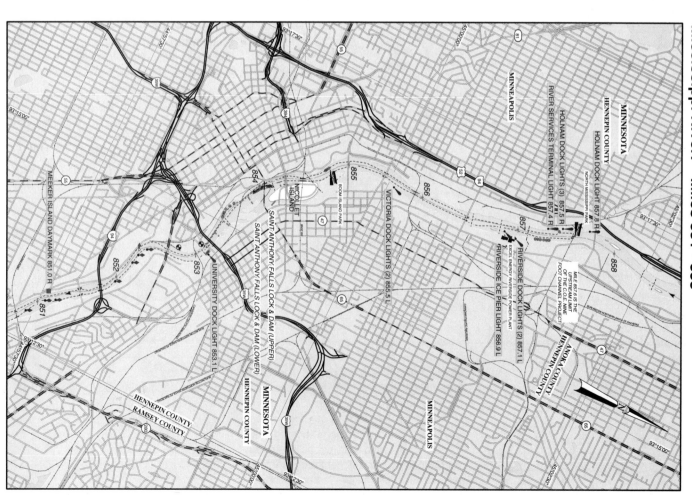

Source: U.S. Army Corps of Engineers

220

Scale: One Inch = 0.986 Miles (Not for Navigation)

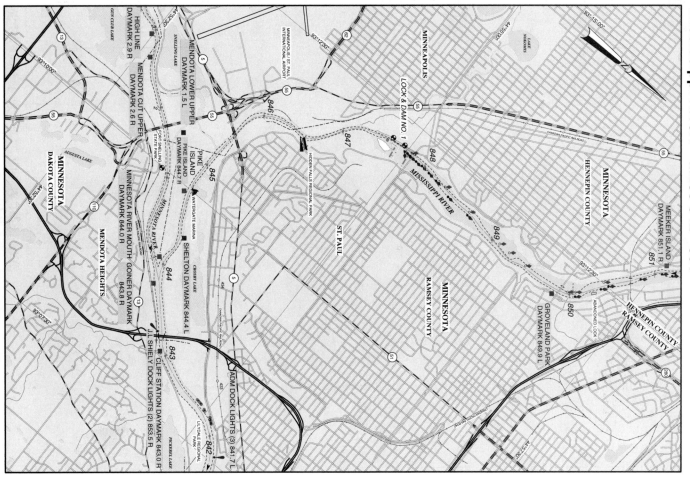

Mississippi River: Miles 842 - 851

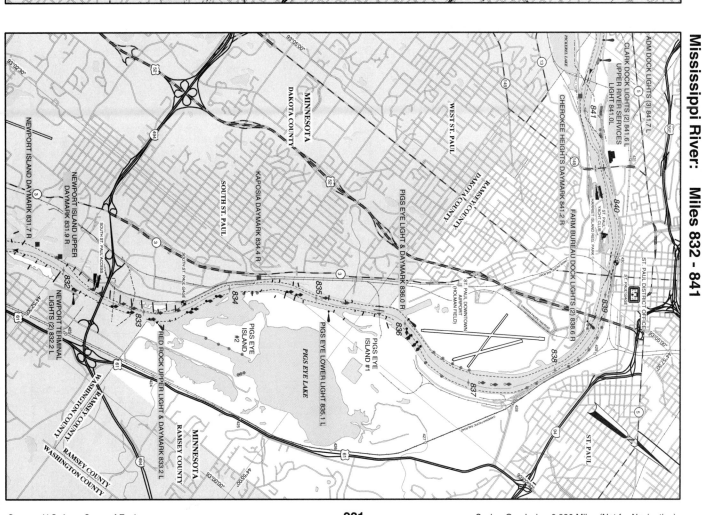

Mississippi River: Miles 832 - 841

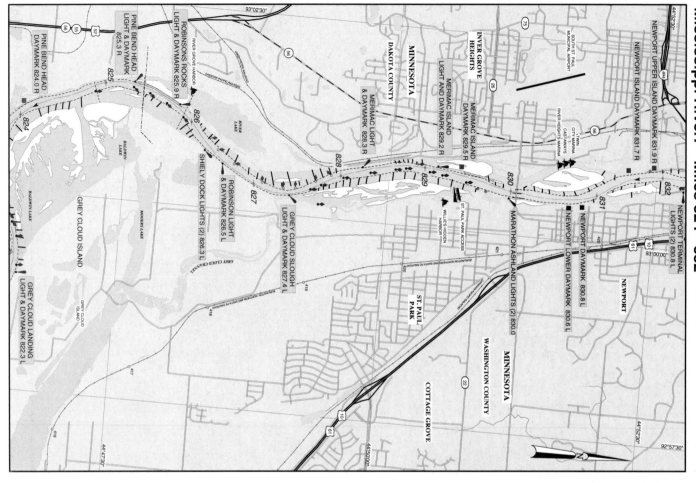

Mississippi River: Miles 824 - 832

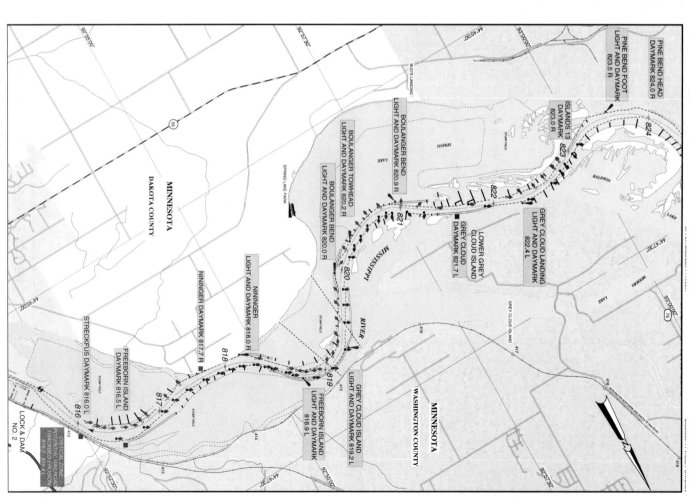

Mississippi River: Miles 816 - 824

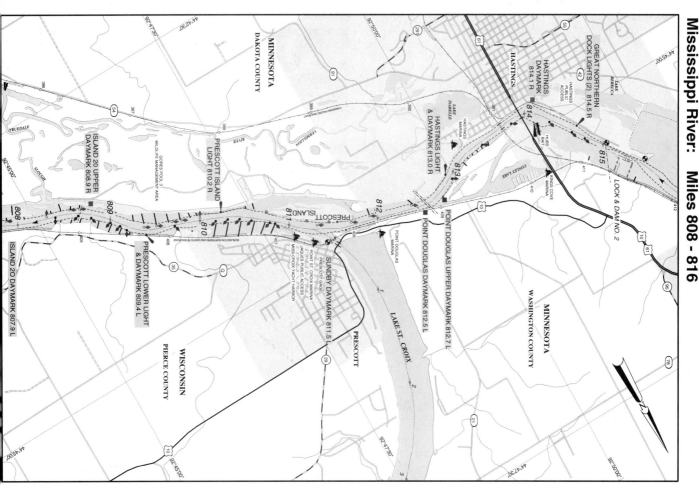

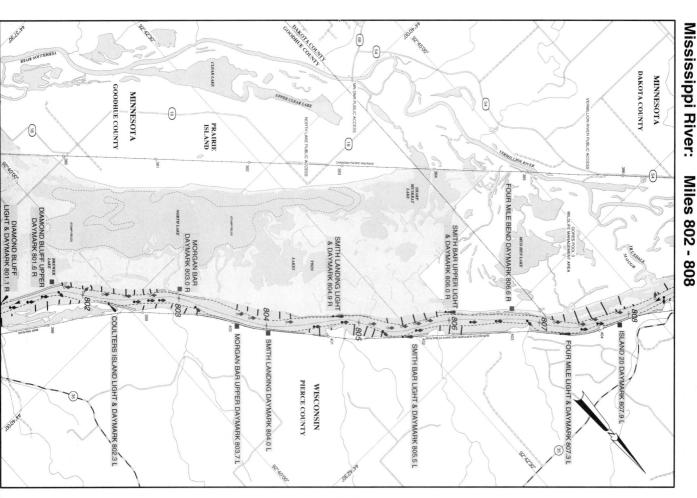

Source: U.S. Army Corps of Engineers

Scale: One Inch = 0.986 Miles (Not for Navigation)

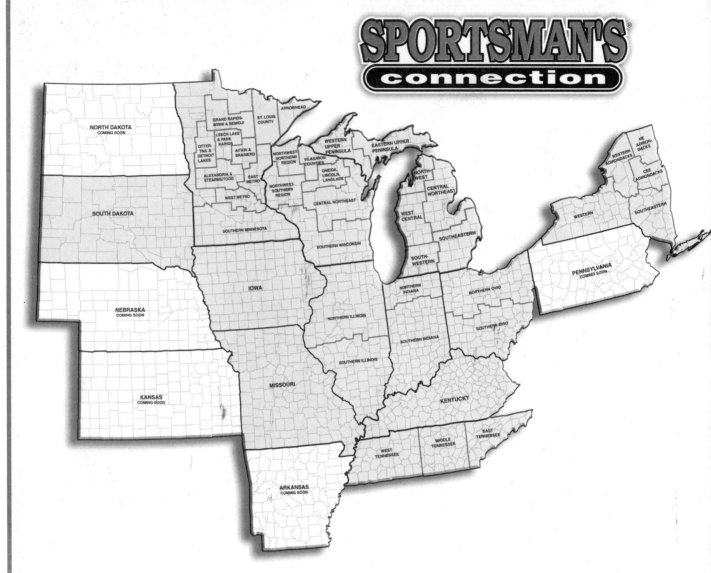

6691-05-2013